EVERYBODY KNOWS

Corruption in America

EVERYBODY KNOWS

Corruption in America

Sarah Chayes

HURST & COMPANY, LONDON

First published in the United Kingdom in 2020 by

C. Hurst & Co. (Publishers) Ltd.,
41 Great Russell Street, London, WC1B 3PL

Printed in the United Kingdom

A Cataloguing-in-Publication data record for this book is available from the British Library.

ISBN: 9781787383807

This book is printed using paper from registered sustainable and managed sources.

www.hurstpublishers.com

Printed in Great Britain by Bell and Bain Ltd, Glasgow

This book is dedicated to my sisters,
Eve Chayes Lyman and Angelica Chayes,
without whom neither it nor I would be what we are.

It used to matter where your money came from.

—*Elder, Benin City, Nigeria*

Contents

Prologue: Dismissing Corruption (June 27, 2016)   3

I. MONEY (Ca. 650 BC–AD 33)

1 Midas   21
2 Jesus   34
3 Aristotle   44

II. CRAZY MONEY (1873–1935)

1 Europe   59
2 The United States   71
3 The Late-Born Baron   82

III. THE HYDRA (1980s–)

1 "Eight Mortal Heads"   95
2 Powers Wielded: The Scales   113
3 Powers Wielded: The Pen and the Mace   124
4 Powers Wielded: The Purse   133
5 Powers Sabotaged   144
6 Bowing to the Money Changers   157
7 Tactics and Countermoves   171
8 Colluders   187

IV. IT THROVE ON WOUNDS (1870s–1945)

1 Fighting the Hydra: The Cities   201

2 Fighting the Hydra: The Countryside   217

3 "It Had Needed a War"   229

V. THE PATTERN (1980–)

1 The Turning (1980s)   247

2 The Validation (1980s–1990s)   258

3 Courting Calamity (1990s–)   269

Epilogue: Breaking the Pattern (Now)   285

Acknowledgments   307

Notes   311

Index   397

Illustration Credits   415

EVERYBODY KNOWS

Corruption in America

Dismissing Corruption

June 27, 2016

A momentous ruling was handed down that day.

Since morning they had gathered, carrying bullhorns, carrying signs cut out in the shape of Texas, signs with a uterus like the head of a longhorn steer, the photo of a fetus cradled aloft in two disembodied hands. Some chanted. Some wore black. Some covered their mouths with red duct tape, LIFE magic-markered across the gag.

They stood at the foot of the serried columns of the United States Supreme Court, which rises like a temple on Capitol Hill. They were there for the last announcements of the 2015 term. They were there for the abortion case: *Whole Woman's Health v. Hellerstedt.*

The court was short, then, by one justice. The vote might be split. When the 5–3 decision came down, voiding a Texas law that required doctors who performed abortions to have hospital admitting privileges, a roar went up. Demonstrators fell into each other's arms, ecstatic mouths wide. A woman in a pale blue sundress dubbed her disappointment "a little setback, a bump." The cascade of media coverage poured forth for days.

It was important. But it is not the momentous ruling I'm talking about.

There was another case decided that day: *McDonnell v. United States.* That's the one I mean. It concerned the conduct of those who hold public office. It went to the heart of how a democracy should be run. But it got scant attention.

Petitioner Bob McDonnell was governor of the state of Virginia when he did what he did. During his race for that office in 2009, the CEO of a Virginia tobacco company who was attempting conversion to pharmaceuticals offered him rides to campaign stops on a private jet. The CEO's name was Jonnie Williams. Williams's company had formulated a tobacco-based "dietary supplement" that was supposed to have anti-inflammatory properties and to help athletes with sore joints or injuries on the mend. Pamphlets and online comments swore that the tablets improved conditions from Alzheimer's to thyroid disease to traumatic brain injury, even rashes. But the pills had never undergone independent clinical trials.

That's what Williams wanted from the victorious McDonnell. Aboard the private jet again in the fall of 2010, Williams asked the new governor to set him up with whatever state official he "needed to talk to" to get the University of Virginia to run the trials. McDonnell directed his secretary of health and human resources to meet with his benefactor. The official, according to the Supreme Court opinion, was "skeptical of the science."

Williams kept trying. He "took Mrs. McDonnell on a shopping trip and bought her $20,000 worth of designer clothing." He listened sympathetically to her worries about rental properties the McDonnells owned in Virginia Beach, the mounting cost of their daughter's coming wedding. "The Governor says it's okay for me to help you," Williams testified she assured him. "But I need you to help me . . . with this financial situation." He came across with a total of $65,000 in loans and cash gifts. He invited the gubernatorial couple to his multimillion-dollar vacation home; had his Ferrari delivered there for the McDonnells' use; paid for the governor's golf outings; bought a Rolex just like his own for Mrs. McDonnell to box up for her husband for Christmas.

McDonnell tried too. Sometimes his phone calls to subordinates came just minutes after a conversation with Williams. McDonnell directed his health and human resources secretary to send staff to listen to Williams's pitch. He threw a luncheon party touting Williams's product, at which the CEO handed out $25,000 checks to Virginia public university researchers to cover the cost of writing grant proposals. In the midst of negotiating another $50,000 Williams loan, McDonnell called around to find out why no such application had materialized. He hosted a health-care industry reception so Williams could do more lobbying. He popped Williams's pills at a meeting with two state officials, urging them to list the product with medications covered by the state employees' insurance plan.

Williams's gifts and loans continued, totaling in the end more than $175,000 plus vacations and such luxuries.

On September 4, 2014, a jury in federal district court convicted McDonnell on four counts of honest services wire fraud, and conspiracy (18 USC 1343 and 1349), and seven counts of extorting property under color of official right, and conspiracy (18 USC 1951), all of which carry a maximum twenty-year prison term. McDonnell was sentenced to two years in prison—well below the prosecution's request, which was already at the low end of the Federal Sentencing Guidelines' recommended range. He appealed. On July 10, 2015, the U.S. Court of Appeals for the Fourth Circuit ruled he had been "duly convicted by a jury of his fellow Virginians." It affirmed the decision against him. All three judges on the panel joined the opinion.

McDonnell appealed to the Supreme Court. The ruling came down on June 27, 2016.

That evening I stood in my narrow kitchen with the radio on. It's how I love to end the day: a beer and slab bacon and a mess of vegetables in a skillet, an ear to the news. Just four days back, the people of the United Kingdom had reversed a half century of European history, voting to "Brexit" the Union. Presidential candidate Hillary Clinton had widened her lead over Donald Trump in a campaign that was careening from one dumbfounding episode to the next. And there was the end of the Supreme Court's 2015 term. Through the din, that's what I was listening for.

For a decade, I had been working to combat corruption. I'd analyzed it in countries like Nigeria and Afghanistan—where I had lived for years after the terrorist attacks of 9/11.

I had set up a small manufacturing cooperative in downtown Kandahar: Taliban country. We were women and men working together—a minor revolution. We were nine different tribes and ethnic groups, ten if you count me, in twenty people. With improvised bombs detonating sometimes every day, we bought apricot kernels in bulk and pressed wild pistachios and distilled essential oils and laughed our heads off as we mixed and kneaded and polished soaps to look like river-worn cobbles and concocted fragrant lotions, and talked politics all day long. And I discovered something I could never have imagined. Religious fanaticism, these men and women told me, was not driving their friends and cousins into the arms of the extremist Taliban. Indignation at their government's corruption was—and at Americans' role in enabling it.

It was a remarkable idea. I asked around, trying it out on other Afghans, trying to understand the structure of what I soon could see was a system. I went to work for the U.S. military leadership: serving two commanders of the international forces in Kabul, then the chairman of the Joint Chiefs of Staff in the Pentagon. I helped launch the first anticorruption efforts the United States undertook. In 2010, in response to an almost comically ambivalent plan put forth by the State Department, Joint Chiefs of Staff chairman Admiral Mike Mullen—my boss—persuaded his colleagues that it was time, in his words, "to get serious." He put me in charge of redrafting the plan. He passed the result to the deputy national security advisor for Iraq and Afghanistan, Douglas Lute.

And there it sat.

Mullen retired at the end of 2011, and I left government. During those years, I discovered that the corrupt practices I had observed—and victims' violent reactions—were not just an Afghan anomaly. I traveled through the 2011 Arab Spring for Mullen. Banners brandished in protests across the breadth of a continent showed pictures of venal government officials behind bars. Later, on a research trip in Nigeria, I discovered that people applauded the Boko Haram militant group because of corruption, especially in the police. In Uzbekistan, journalists and human rights activists said that anger at their government's abusive corruption was driving some people across the border into terrorist groups. The link between corruption and violent extremism was so compelling I wrote a book about it, called *Thieves of State: Why Corruption Threatens Global Security.*

Since then, I've watched outraged peoples around the world revolt against rigged systems they could no longer tolerate. Insurrections that upended Ukraine as well as the Arab world were about corruption. In Lebanon, a corrupt waste management contract left the streets of Beirut choked with offal. "You stink!" protesters roared at the whole political class and its intricate system of sweetheart deals for public services privatized into officials' own hands. From Brazil to Burkina Faso, South Korea to Malaysia to Iceland, citizens have been demanding an end to government in the service of governing cliques. Presidents and prime ministers have come tumbling down.

With just a little digging, in fact, it's not hard to find corruption at the root of most of the crises afflicting the globe, from mass migration out of Central America and Africa, to the rise of autocracy in Hungary or Turkey, to war in Sudan and environmental devastation in Cambodia—indeed the whole calamity of our slowly dying globe.

And yet, just as General David Petraeus ignored three separate plans a team of us developed for a "governance surge" in southern Afghanistan, and just as the national security advisor let the serious approach die its Washington death, corruption is mostly ignored by Western decision-makers. That's what I have been working to change for more than a decade. On June 27, 2016, in fact, I was getting ready for a long trip to Honduras, to test whether my findings on the structure and practices of corrupt governing systems applied to that country. And the U.S. Supreme Court was ruling on corruption right here at home.

I scrape onions into the sizzling pan. I'm listening to *The Diane Rehm Show,* a thoughtful current-events program on National Public Radio—where I was once a reporter. Suddenly, I am transfixed. The Supreme Court overturned Bob McDonnell's corruption conviction. The vote, I'm hearing, was 8–0.

Not a single one of the Supreme Court justices could find a way to follow the reasoning of that jury of Virginians, or of his or her own colleagues on the U.S. Court of Appeals? Not one could figure out why McDonnell's behavior might be criminally corrupt?

The justices saw it this way: The case fell under the statute that makes bribing public officials illegal in the United States. It says a public official may not even indirectly "demand, seek, receive, accept, or agree to receive or accept anything of value personally, or for any other person or entity in return for being influenced in the performance of any official act."

The court homed in on those two words. "The issue in this case," the justices ruled—the sole issue—"is the proper interpretation of the term 'official act.' " It is defined by law. "The term 'official act,' " reads 18 U.S. Code §201 (a) (3), "means any decision or action on any question, matter, cause, suit, proceeding, or controversy, which may at any time be pending, or which may by law be brought before any public official, in such official's official capacity, or in such official's place of trust or profit."

It is hard to imagine a broader way of describing the duties of a public servant. But that's not how the Supreme Court took it.

Explaining the justices' ruling, the opinion embarks on a seven-page discussion of such words as "decision," "action," "question," and "cause." For a couple of those pages it examines and dismisses the notion that a "typical meeting or telephone call or event arranged by an official" qualifies as a cause or suit—a logical absurdity that needlessly complicates the prose. Obviously, the "matter" or "cause" at hand was whether public institutions of the state of Virginia should conduct clinical trials of Williams's product, or officially promote it.

The justices' explanation moves on to the more relevant question of whether conducting such meetings and whatnot qualify as "actions." Again their answer is no.

Even though they agree that "using [one's] official position to exert pressure on *another* official to perform an 'official act' " would indeed qualify as an official act, what McDonnell did fails, in their view, to meet this standard. The way he leaned on his subordinates, called them on his office phone, used the governor's mansion and its staff and stationery for the events he organized on Williams's behalf, the way he pulled a pill bottle out of his own pocket and urged a subordinate to make the product reimbursable, none of that added up to pressure, none of it was official.

Thus did the unanimous Supreme Court transform a broad, commonsense definition of bribery into something narrow and technical.

I doubt its opinion in *McDonnell* turned mainly on dictionary definitions, however. The next section is pivotal. It examines how we do politics. "Conscientious public officials arrange meetings for constituents, contact other officials on their behalf, and include them in events all the time," the opinion reads. "The basic compact underlying representative government *assumes* that public officials will hear from their constituents and act appropriately on their concerns—

whether it is the union official worried about a plant closing or the homeowners who wonder why it took five days to restore power to their neighborhood after a storm." If the *McDonnell* decision stood, the justices fretted, "officials might wonder whether they could respond to even the most commonplace requests for assistance, and citizens with legitimate concerns might shrink from participating in democratic discourse."

Never mind the false equivalency. Never mind that most "citizens with legitimate concerns" do not dispose of tens of thousands of dollars or Ferraris they can loan to help focus officials' attention on those concerns. Never mind that it is hard to describe ramming an obviously questionable drug through clinical trials as a "legitimate concern." Letting the McDonnell conviction stand, opined the justices, would mean criminalizing politics—at least politics as currently practiced.

That is the consensus I got from several veteran court watchers I asked to explain the justices' thinking. I could not get any to speak on the record, so robust is this mainstream view in Washington. No one cared to stand out. "People think you shouldn't criminalize politics," one person said, echoing the chorus, noting that different expectations seem to apply to elected versus judicial officials. "If a judge were to do what McDonnell did, he would be in jail."

No justice even troubled to write a concurring opinion, perhaps regretting the way the language of the law seemed to force his or her hand. None of the eight men and women presiding over the affairs of the nation in that august building stopped to spell out the likely implications for the integrity of American politics.

Diane Rehm's quavering voice and gentle but heartfelt civility belie a talent for piercing to the heart of the matter. She's grilling her guests. Jeffrey Rosen, a Yale Law School graduate, George Washington University law professor, and CEO of the congressionally mandated National Constitution Center, declares it's "great that this is an area that unites justices of all descriptions, because it just shows a commitment not to construe vagueness against defendants."

He is actually applauding the unanimity of this decision. He means the court is right to give defendants—any defendants—the benefit of any doubt at all, such as the slightest imprecision in the language of the law. He's talking about how important it is to protect accused people against unreasonable searches of their homes or cell phones, as though that is a reasonable comparison to what happened to McDonnell. Harvard Law graduate and legal commentator Stuart Taylor worries about the "huge power that could be abused . . . in the hands of prosecutors" if McDonnell's conviction were allowed to stand.

It is another false equivalency. The panelists are lumping McDonnell and high rollers of his stripe together with the destitute or disadvantaged people arrested every day for drug offenses or assault. In street cases like those, police and prosecutorial abuse is well documented. But corruption and white-collar crime are different. Potential offenders in that category start with expert counsel at their elbows—like the Virginia governor's in-house lawyer who instructed Mrs. McDonnell to decline Williams's offer of an inaugural gown. Then, if people like her cross the lines anyway and get arrested, they can command influential firms with their phalanxes of partners and paralegals to defend them—resources that often dwarf what government prosecutors can bring to bear.

How many recent examples do we really have in the United States of overzealous enforcement against corruption and white-collar crime?

Yet Taylor continues: "If this was illegal . . . then almost all politicians are in danger of being prosecuted."

That's right, I think.

Diane breaks in, indignant: "Well they ought to be, if they're taking stuff!"

Ignoring her, the three panelists—selected to span the political spectrum—fall into line, announcing one by one that they too would have joined the unanimous Supreme Court in overturning McDonnell's conviction. It's a sweep. Not just the court; the pundits too, across the board.

Diane tries to rattle them with the obvious point: "Isn't this part of the underlying reason why people are *so furious* these days? Because politicians get away with *stuff,* and this is stuff that the ordinary human being simply would not."

She has just put her finger on what I discovered in Afghanistan, and again in Nigeria and Honduras and Tunisia and Egypt. Systemic corruption, leaving no means of redress or civic appeal, drives citizens to extremes.

I had spent a decade analyzing how such corrupt systems are organized, how they operate. I had dissected their practices on four continents. I was discovering some obvious patterns. That June evening, I realized with a jolt: it's time to start turning this analytical framework onto my own country, the United States.

That is what this book sets out to do.

There may be a reason, apart from deep reverence for defendants' rights, why the *McDonnell* decision stirred so little fuss. There was that other case grabbing all the attention: *Whole Woman's Health v. Hellerstedt.* The contrast in public and media reaction to the two rulings illustrates how angry divides over cultural and identity-group issues often mask—in fact may be deliberately used to mask—unanimity at the top of the system when it comes to condoning or participating in corruption.

That is one of the patterns I have observed overseas.

While speculation was running high as to the implications of the abortion decision for states outside Texas, *McDonnell* was changing law too. Prosecutors scrambled to amend indictments they had filed before the decision came down. The splashy convictions of two powerful politicians on both sides of New York State's notorious political machinery—for crimes including bribery, extortion, conspiracy, and money laundering—were reversed because of the *McDonnell* ruling's new precedent. And the top Democrat on the Senate Foreign Relations Committee, Robert Menendez, escaped his own conviction on multiple counts of bribery (18 USC 201), honest services fraud (18 USC 1341, 1343, 1346), and making false statements in his financial disclosure statement (18 USC 1001), among other allegations, when the jury failed to reach a verdict in a 2017 trial conducted under the shadow of *McDonnell.*

A friend of Menendez's—later sentenced to seventeen years in jail for scamming Medicare by prescribing tens of millions of dollars' worth of painful but unnecessary eye procedures to elderly patients—showered the New Jersey senator with Caribbean vacations, one of those Rolexes that figure in so many such cases, and about a million dollars in campaign contributions. A grateful Menendez argued with the secretary of health and human services in person for payment of the fraudulent reimbursements. He directed his staff to help browbeat top Medicare officials. He intervened with U.S. State Department and Customs officials to protect his doctor friend's business interests in the Dominican Republic.

But all this failed to convince even most of the jurors that the actions Menendez took on his friend's behalf met the new Supreme Court standard for bribery. The jury hung and the judge dismissed the case. In January 2018, after attempting a retrial, the U.S. Department of Justice abandoned the effort.

Writing out these details, I wince. The thought of how Democratic Party leaders congratulated Menendez when his case was dropped and locked arms to fend off any 2018 primary challenge sends a flush through my gut. Is this who we've become? Does this country—perhaps the only one founded explicitly on a set of ideals—truly defend the defenders of doctors who jab instruments into old people's eyes for the sole purpose of amassing more and more money?

In the years since *McDonnell,* I've spoken to several former and serving federal prosecutors about the ruling's effect. Those still in the Justice Department did not wish to be named. I encountered one in a social setting on Capitol Hill. We had both arrived early and, drinks in hand, introduced ourselves. Hearing his line of work, I hit him with the *McDonnell* question. What had it done? The look he shot back has stayed with me. "A sea change," he blurted.

With this curt confirmation of my foreboding, a line of poetry came to mind like a dirge: "Full fathom five thy father lies . . ." I saw a ghoulish body, seaweed for its beard, which "doth suffer a seachange." A shoal of fish comes near, then swerves as one to skirt it.

In unison, legal practitioners were swerving.

In a 2018 article aimed at state-level prosecutors on how to go after corruption in spite of *McDonnell,* Amie Ely calculated that by April of that year, federal judges in every circuit in the nation had cited the case, as had seven state courts, and that it had induced prosecutors to drop some corruption charges. Ely, a former prosecutor herself, now at the National Association of Attorneys General, was working to limit the damage. She urged me not to overdramatize.

"*McDonnell* means prosecutors' job is harder," she insisted, "not that the game is over. My job is to contain it, to tell state attorneys general, 'Don't be so scared of *McDonnell* you give it more power than it actually has.'"

She's got her work cut out for her. It's hard to mistake the pall that has fallen over what is called the "public integrity" beat. One federal prosecutor who was working corruption cases when we spoke told me he was switching divisions. "They've made it so only bad criminals can get convicted," he complained. "And I don't mean dangerous criminals. I mean people who are just really bad at being corrupt."

According to the U.S. Sentencing Commission, bribery convictions fell by nearly one-third between 2014 and 2018. During that period, prison sentences averaged a bit over twenty months, approximately half the minimum recommended in the Federal Sentencing Guidelines.

University of Pennsylvania law professor Howard Master had to watch the conviction he won against one of those powerful New York State politicians get overturned in the wake of *McDonnell*. (The defendant, Sheldon Silver, was retried and convicted a second time in May 2018 and sentenced to seven years in jail.) "An overall change in the atmosphere leaves a lot more behavior free of prosecution now than twenty years ago," he assessed.

Master is pointing to what may be the most damaging effect of decisions like *McDonnell*: the implicit blessing they bestow on a whole range of practices.

For a community to deliberately hurt one of its members—to punish him or her—is a radical step. There must be powerful reasons. Such a sanction exacts, on victims' behalf, retribution or payment for harm done, so they don't feel obliged to seek it themselves, plunging the whole group into an endless series of reprisals. Punishment may make other wrongdoers reconsider their practices as too risky. Or it can deter would-be copycats from even trying.

Another purpose of punishment is to broadcast to the entire community, by way of unmistakable deeds, where it draws the line. What does this society consider acceptable behavior—what does it deem right or OK—and what does it brand as wrong? Some core elements of these value judgments are quite universal: murder of group members is almost always severely punished, as is incest, or freeloading on others' contributions to the common welfare. Other values may differ from community to community and may change over time. No list of commandments, no ethics classes in school or on the job spell them out better than what actually gets punished.

In the United States, serious and damaging public corruption is not getting punished. That means, by default, that we deem it to be just fine.

Chief Justice John Roberts summed up his opinion in the *McDonnell* case with a ringing declaration. "There is no doubt that this case is distasteful," he admitted. "But our concern is not with tawdry tales of Ferraris, Rolexes, and ball gowns. It is instead with the broader legal implications of the Government's boundless interpretation of the federal bribery statute."

Who selects words with more care than judges? "No word is innocent," a friend reminds me. Roberts selected "distasteful." He wrote "tawdry." Such words say that polite people ought best to avert their eyes, for unpleasant behavior, showy and cheap, is on display.

This is how corruption gets overlooked in the United States. This is how the wealthier and better educated Americans downplay it. They cast it as an embarrassing aberration, a scandal beneath mention, best shrugged off with a roll of the eyes.

But to regard corruption this way is to dangerously underestimate its significance. Corruption is not an isolated scandal or even a whole stack of them. Corruption is better understood as the deliberate mode of functioning—the operating system, you might say—of sophisticated, and astonishingly successful, networks.

What makes these networks so effective is their ability to weave across what most people think of as separate, even antagonistic segments of society: job creators and regulators, law-enforcement professionals and the out-and-out criminals they are sworn to combat. These apparent foes in fact work arm in arm within the powerful webs that promote corrupt practices. That integration across boundaries is the most fundamental pattern I observed in foreign countries.

By including members from all these walks of life, corrupt networks can command a vast array of talents, tools, and resources in pursuit of their single-minded objective: making money for their members, no matter the cost to other people or things. These webs are durable and adaptive, and like everything else these days, they are transnational. To facilitate their operations, they enjoy the assistance—witting or unwitting—of legions of service providers and enablers, ranging from real estate agents and art dealers who choose to ignore the color of the money that comes their way, to prestigious universities who name centers after kleptocrat donors, to lawyers who open shell companies for them or argue their cases before the Supreme Court. It is impossible to do business with these networks, to invest in the main sources of revenue they capture in their countries, without becoming enmeshed.

Not that the networks I've studied are all configured or operate in exactly the same way. Some are more disciplined and tightly structured than others. Some are turbulent, beset by violent internal rivalries. Sometimes business oligarchs take the lead, leaving government officials few options but to do their bidding. In other countries, a strongman and his family grip the reins of economic as well as political power. Kleptocratic networks hold sway in military dictatorships and in apparent democracies, under leftist regimes and in countries whose leadership champions ultra-free-market capitalism. Like an invisible, odorless gas, the phenomenon has spread, unnoticed, throughout much of the world.

For Justice Roberts and his seven colleagues on the Supreme Court, manifestations of this phenomenon in the United States are beneath their concern. In their view, the American system is threatened not by corruption but—incredibly—by efforts to *fight* corruption. It was the Justice Department's "boundless interpretation" of bribery laws that worried conservative and liberal justices alike.

They could not have been more wrong. At the very moment they were dismissing corruption, that summer of 2016, corruption was poised to upend the U.S. presidential contest. Fervent young voters had flocked to a "political revolution" led by an improbable white-haired self-described socialist, Bernie Sanders, who denounced systemic corruption in every speech. Revelations suggesting that the Clinton Foundation served as a cover for international influence peddling, and that the Clintons were using the charity to enrich themselves, were deflating much of the presumptive next president's natural constituency. And Donald Trump was about to capitalize on her discomfiture and set his base afire with chants of "Drain the swamp!" Even with all the other factors in play, there is no question that his upset victory resulted partly from Americans' disgust at the rigged system.

Perversely, Trump's drain-the-swamp administration proceeded to crystallize and put into practice—in barefaced ways unseen in the United States for a century—exactly the type of systemic corruption Americans decry. With members of the clan ensconced in top government jobs, the Trumps began openly using their privileged positions to gain advantages for the businesses they continued to run: clientele and free advertising, hard-to-get government authorizations in foreign countries, loans and investments. Meanwhile, the big-business strand of America's emerging kleptocratic network was awarded control of the agencies whose job is to protect the public from the worst effects of those very businesses' profit-seeking practices. The executives- and lobbyists-turned-government-officials went straight to work rewriting the rules in ways designed to maximize the gush of money into their collective coffers, not ease burdens on ordinary Americans. Illegal travel perks and self-aggrandizing security details, which cost several top officials their jobs, were just the most visible frills.

Startling and outrageous though those excesses may seem, however, they are not total aberrations. The United States has seen episodes of corruption before, and the systemic version unique to this moment has been more than thirty years in the making—abetted by political leaders of all persuasions and the wealthy who have directly and indirectly benefited.

Ordinary Americans—the 90 percent—have been noticing. And they are rightly furious. Corruption to the degree and intensity we are now witnessing is an affront. It also brings down economies, ignites wars, exterminates peoples and species, and tears irrevocable scars across the face of the earth. It is an existential threat not just to the democratic principles we claim to revere, but to the very survival of our society.

In the shadow of the likely calamity, and given the resources and determination of the cabals that seem bent on bringing it on, most of us feel powerless and overwhelmed. We go limp. Throw our energy into something else. But, if the other side has the money, we have the numbers. That is a potent force. The task is to bring it fully to bear.

To do that, we need a clear picture of what it is we're dealing with.

I

MONEY

Ca. 650 BC–AD 33

1

Midas

When it comes to corruption, money is at the heart of the matter.

Money was on everyone's lips, for example, when I asked about the state of American politics during the 2018 campaign.

The United States, by then, had gone the way of so many other countries: corruption had upended our politics. But what did that word even signify to Americans? I had asked Afghans and Egyptians and Serbs to give their definitions. I often got stories, not synonyms. But the core was always the same. Corruption was when people in positions of power used their power to capture the community's sources of money—including by extorting ordinary people's meager earnings in the form of bribes. Corruption was when those ordinary people had no recourse, no means of redress.

What about us? How do Americans understand corruption? Applying the methodology I used overseas meant I had to go out and ask.

One time I did so was canvassing alongside a candidate for the West Virginia House of Delegates, Lissa Lucas. We were in St. Marys, a tiny town strung out along the Ohio River, on a rainy afternoon that very rainy August. Did residents, I wanted to know, think our system is rigged? And if so, what did they mean?

"It's all about that dollar," one young man answered. He glanced away, his face in a grimace, as he tried to find words to describe his disgust for government.

"Whoever gives them the most money, they do what they say."

That was a young woman in a tie-dyed T-shirt. Like her pained neighbor, she does not vote.

"They're all bought off. It just depends on who has more money."

"Money washes hands." Meaning: Do your dirt; if you have money, you're purified, considered upstanding.

These are the answers I keep getting.

There seems no making sense of corruption today without stopping to consider what money has come to mean to us—the hold it has gained on our hearts.

It is a substance that has bedeviled humans since they first imagined it into being, roughly 2,600 years ago. Through the ages, money has inspired aphorisms and admonitions, philosophical treatises, great works of art, hit songs and movies, and myths—or sacred stories.

Myths are a type of wisdom that has gone out of fashion among most educated Westerners. The scientific method of experimentation, three centuries old, replaced them with a different way to explore and order reality. The knowledge thus gained is immeasurable. And I would hate to live without the scientific framework for sorting ungrounded declaration from demonstrable fact. But in the process, we have grown relentlessly literal, banishing poetry. "Myth" has become a word of contempt to describe something patently false but gullibly believed in. It is an epithet flung to disparage a thought and its thinker, both.

But it is myth that has helped humans understand and deal with ourselves for tens of thousands of years. The profound, often funny, sometimes frustrating tales we have told of gods and supernatural beings provide unparalleled teachings, precious insight into what we as a species have held to be of sacred importance. "Whenever [myth] . . . has been dismissed as a mere priestly fraud or a sign of inferior intelligence," wrote Joseph Campbell, who spent his life studying such stories, "truth has slipped out the other door."

So myth is part of my methodology, too. In Honduras, about a month after the *McDonnell* decision came down, I stood in a small earthen shelter on the flank of a mountain and faced in each of the cardinal directions with a clutch of villagers, as they opened our interview with a prayer. They thanked me for returning again and again to the spiritual dimension of their struggle against the corrupt Honduran government. They talked about their *cosmovisión:* their worldview. According to that vision, the river being dammed a five-hour scramble down their steep wooded slope was sacred. Not sacred to their specific clan or tribe, like some private household god. Sacred, period. Sacred to humanity, and in the absence of humanity. And the beings it nurtures, the fish and the orchids and the turtles and salamanders and the cackling birds, have just as much right to live in communion with it as we do.

Damming a river in that context, I realized, is not just an environmental crime. It is deicide. It's nailing Christ to the cross.

In Nigeria, I watched as a priestess dressed in white drew designs in chalk on the beaten earth before her door. She was preparing for the annual ceremony in honor of Olokun, the god of the rivers and the sea. This androgynous fish-tailed being is the primary deity worshipped by those who have kept the old faiths where the Niger River and its acolytes reach out their fingers to the Atlantic. Olokun is also the god of wealth: wealth from the sea. "If you pray to Olokun for money or children," another worshipper assured me, "whatever riches you want, Olokun will give it to you."

I thought about that. Olokun had given southern Nigeria riches, all right. Olokun had given this land oil. Oil bubbled up right there in the Gulf of Guinea. And oil was destroying Nigeria. It was the crux of the country's corruption.

Before that, Olokun had bestowed a different type of riches on this people. He had turned them and their neighbors *into* wealth. For the coast nearby is where the ships set to sea with their heartbroken cargoes of living gold.

My head swam. There was a question I had to ask. I was sipping schnapps with the priestess and a holy man who had taken part in her ceremony. We were seated in his sacred grove: a silent place in the cacophonous city, vaulted by giant trees that had never been touched by a metal blade. Bouquets of medicinal plants were tufted here and there. We were discussing Nigerians' addiction to money, the damage the sickness was doing.

"But then," I finally voiced it, "if that's what you think, how can you worship Olokun, the god of wealth?"

"Don't you know?" the two elders shot back, almost together. "Olokun gives money to people he hates. It destroys them."

And there it was: the whole tortured paradox.

Now, as I set about grappling with the fraught and potent force that is money, another myth is beckoning. It comes from ancient Greece. It is the story of Midas.

Midas, goes the tale, was king in Phrygia, a land across the Aegean Sea from Greece (now a part of Turkey). A complicated god named Dionysus, who introduced the mixed blessings of wine and sacred sex to humans, was picnicking in nearby Lydia, his native land. With his band of satyrs—hairy, lustful woodland spirits—he was making merry. The Latin author Ovid tells the story best, threading his poetic tapestry with the ancient strands. One satyr, says Ovid, went missing. Lost and probably none too sober, he was discovered by locals, wobbling along beside a river. Braiding flowers into ropes, they bound him and conducted him to their king, Midas. Midas treated the old satyr with honor, keeping "joyful festival . . . twice five days." Then he escorted him back across the border to the god in Lydia. Grateful Dionysus "allowed the king to choose his own reward."

Midas piped right up: "Cause everything I shall touch to turn at once to yellow gold." Rueful, the god bestowed the Midas touch. The king rushed off to test it.

Here is where Ovid really sings:

He pulled a twig down from a holm-oak, growing on a low-hung branch. The twig was turned to gold. . . . He touched a clod and by his potent touch, the clod became a mass of shining gold. . . . He could now conceive his large hopes in his grasping mind, as he imagined everything of gold. And while he was rejoicing in great wealth, his servants set a table for his meal, with many dainties and with needful bread. But when he touched [the loaf] with his right hand, instantly [it] stiffened to gold; or if he tried to bite with hungry teeth a tender bit of meat, the dainty, as his teeth but touched it, shone at once with yellow shreds and flakes of gold. And wine . . . when he mixed it with pure water, can be seen in his astonished mouth as liquid gold.

Midas—"rich and wretched"—panics. "No food relieves his hunger; his throat is dry / With burning thirst; he is tortured, as he should be / By the hateful gold."

The king lifts up his arms, beseeching Dionysus to save him from what he now understands is no gift, but a curse. The god forgives the foolish king and sends him to a river flowing by the Lydian capital, the city of Sardis. Midas follows the river up to its source and washes. And the golden touch leaves his body and enters the river.

This tale is usually told as a simple allegory of greed. But there is more to it than that. Literal-minded science adds a perspective.

Midas, it turns out, existed. And he was king in Phrygia. According to the great Greek historian Herodotus, writing in the mid-400s BC, Midas "dedicated the royal throne upon which he sat when giving judgment" to Delphi, one of the most important ancient Greek shrines. An analysis that compares this and other Greek sources with Roman and Assyrian texts, adjusting for their differing calendars, reckons this Midas lived and reigned about two hundred years before Herodotus wrote. He probably died around 677 BC.

Science—as so often—provides some basis for the myth.

But what about money? The topic here is not gold in general, or any of the other commodities that have been used as means of exchange: sheep and goats, wampum or cowrie shells. It is coined money. That's the stuff that changed the world. So, what does science say about the origins of money?

Numismatists, including an economist at the Chicago Federal Reserve, have devoted their own meticulous work to that puzzle. A cache of fat, roundish metal globules, stamped with a rectangular mark and a paw print or the head of some noble animal, was discovered more than a century ago. They are the earliest known coins. To this day they are the subject of cutting-edge subatomic analysis and heated debate.

The ancient city of Ephesus, where they were unearthed, stood far from the centers of the great civilizations of the time—Babylon or China, for example. That's where I expected to find the first traces

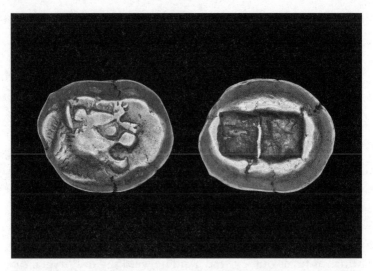

Money makes its appearance. A stater, made of the natural alloy of gold and silver known as electrum, ca. 600 BC.

of such a breakthrough. Ephesus was a backwater, on the Aegean coast of today's Turkey, facing Greece. Not far, that is, from Midas's little kingdom of Phrygia.

Scientists have assayed the metal these often tiny coins are made of. It is a natural alloy of gold and silver called electrum. That evidence, together with the names and script engraved upon them, indicate that many came from nearby Sardis. In fact, the historical rulers of Sardis were known for their wealth, because electrum was abundant in the river that flows by the city.

And that is precisely the river Dionysus told the mythical Midas to trace to its source and wash in to do away with his hated gift. According to scholarly consensus, in other words, money was born in Lydia, the land where Midas delivered the intoxicated old satyr to Dionysus and found and then lost his golden curse. By some accounts, in fact, Lydia was the successor state to Midas's Phrygia. The two realms are interchangeable.

And the date of these first coins? As near as can be determined from the archaeological layers, the late seventh century BC, probably around 630 BC.

That number glinted on the page like a flake of gold in the erudite sand. Deep in the technical details, relentlessly literal as befits our age, the classicists and numismatists were not quite putting two and two together. The best estimates are a few decades off; the overlapping kingdoms have different names. But it's close enough for poetry: Midas of the golden touch is the man who invented money.

And that gives the myth a whole new meaning.

What makes the bits of ancient metal discovered at Ephesus coins— that unprecedented novelty—is the marks stamped into them, their convenient size and regular weights, and the fact that their denominations were independent of the intrinsic value of the metals used to mint them. Taken together, these factors amount to a revolution.

How the idea of issuing such standardized symbols of value germinated, from what combination of prior habits, has also perplexed scholars. The Aegean coast of modern Turkey, populated then by Greeks, stood in the cultural tidal zone where Near Eastern and Greek civilizations mixed, like salt and fresh water in uniquely lively coastal wetlands. Money may be their fruit. To the east, in Mesopotamia, gold and silver had been means of exchange for two thousand years. Greece, less developed, had a more cumbersome convention: kitchen utensils served, including spits or skewers—the pointed rods we still use for barbecuing meat.

It seems an odd choice. Such spits, then as now, were a no-frills item, dull beside the timeless mystique of silver and gold. And yet, in archaic Greece, these humble rods were thick with meaning. That meaning touches the heart of Greek democracy and the paradoxical nature of money.

Spits were used in religious sacrifices, a central ritual of Greek culture. The entire community would gather to honor the god of the place, or one they wished to placate or petition. Typically, the liver or some other morsel of the slaughtered animal was set aside for the god. But the bulk of the meat was shared among everyone present, equally. "The ancient, regular, and highly ritualized slaughter and distribution of the animal," explains British classicist Richard Seaford in *Money and the Early Greek Mind,* "ensures . . . that there is an 'equal feast.' Equal distribution to all and (especially) collective participation . . . are persistently emphasized in . . . references to the animal sacrifice." In other words, the sharing of meat is what really mattered.

This ceremonial use suggests several qualities of spits that might make them a functional currency. Their nondescript interchange-ability is a plus. A spit is a spit, just like a dime is a dime. They are portable; it's easy to grab a handful and pass them around. And their symbolic worth is independent of the value of the metal used to make them.

What I mean is this: the best way to ensure everyone gets—and is seen to get—an equal share of meat is if the same number of chunks is put on every spit. In that way each similar spit, whatever its precise length or weight, is "worth" the same amount of meat.

But let's pause a minute on the ceremony itself: this equal-sharing thing. It is important. For Seaford, the "main purpose of the ritual" is not so much the offering to the god, who lives on ambrosia any-way. The high point is rather "the equal distribution and communal eating of the meat." By bringing all members together, in public, to share in eating meat, this sacred ritual integrated the community, across whatever internal divisions roiled it. The "communality and equality of sacrificial distribution," Seaford argues, were "crucial to the cohesion of the polis," the democratic city-state.

As I read these sentences, an image sprang suddenly to mind: a vivid scene from my young adulthood. After college, I served in the Peace Corps in rural Morocco. We ate seated in a circle around a single clay platter mounded with food. Crowning the dish were succulent chunks of lamb or chicken that had slowly simmered over charcoal in olive oil with a luscious accompaniment of spices and vegetables. I could suddenly see the merry eyes of my favorite neigh-bor as she leaned forward to break the tender meat into morsels and place an equal portion in front of each person she was hosting. That gesture, launching our meal, bound our fellowship.

Morocco lies westward across the Mediterranean from Greece, so perhaps the custom originated there. But this solemn, public div-vying up of meat was no Greek invention. The practice reaches far deeper into prehistory. In fact, it may have helped make us human.

Christopher Boehm is a primatologist and anthropologist who has spent much of his career exploring the origins of the human sense of right and wrong—our distinctive conscience. A change in the eating habits of our archaic ancestors, he argues, may mark a decisive turning point. Chimpanzees and our other primate cousins are mainly vegetarians. They enjoy the flesh of game (including smaller monkeys) and sometimes go hunting in groups. But meat is only an occasional treat.

Early humans developed a different diet. Animal protein became a staple food, essential to their very survival. This was in the age of giant, sometimes ferocious mammals—woolly mammoths and saber-toothed tigers. The only way archaic humans with their primitive weapons could kill them was if several hunters cooperated.

To cement the solidarity of their hunting parties, says Boehm, so all members would keep participating in the arduous and risky expeditions, members shared equally whatever meat they bagged—no matter who had delivered the death blow that day, or who had fashioned the spearpoint.

The closest analogue to these lifeways may be found not among our primate cousins, in fact, but among wolves. In his luminous book *Of Wolves and Men,* Barry Lopez compares the practices of Inuit hunters and of wolves. He thinks "a similar sense of social pressure and interdependence operates to hold a wolf pack" and the Naskapi tribe together. In the canines' case, "old wolves and young pups can eat only because the middle-aged wolves are good hunters. During rendezvous season the wolf, hungry himself, having eaten at the kill, returns home from ten miles away with a haunch of meat in his mouth. And he is besieged with as much affection as the successful Naskapi hunter is." This is the crucial point, Lopez emphasizes, with respect to the humans: "The social system of the Naskapi bestows prestige on the successful hunter; that is what is exchanged for meat. . . . The individual ego is therefore both nurtured and submerged. A man's skills are praised, his food is eaten, his pride is reinforced." Sharing, not hogging or hoarding, is rewarded, and the meat taken with reverence, and shared, is sacred. Each such meal is a Eucharist.

Boehm has examined accounts of dozens of different hunter-gatherer tribes whose living conditions most resemble those of very early humans and finds this egalitarianism to be a constant. It is obviously deliberate.

Apes are different. No matter which individual brings down the prey on their hunts, it's the alpha male that snatches it, only doling out some scraps of the feast to stave off insurrection. Human egalitarianism was a social revolution within the primate order.

Boehm has spent years working out how our ancestors did it. How did they keep the strongest in the group from dominating the others? How did they stop sneaks from cheating? How did they stave off nighttime assassinations?

The answer he has come to is quite logical, really. Through rewards and punishments, Boehm argues, humans made clear what types of behavior they approved of, and where they drew the line. "Foragers use social control to keep their societies equalized rather than hierarchical, and they do so quite efficiently," he writes. A set of values "inherent in the egalitarian ethos" is enforced collectively by members of the bands. "Certain attitudes and behaviors are praised, while others are condemned and punished."

By combing through anthropologists' accounts and tracking what gets punished and how often, Boehm was able to rank the types of conduct that are most severely frowned upon. Apart from killing someone, he found, the surest way to be disciplined by the rest of the band is to take more than your share of the game.

The sharing out of meat, in other words—and the egalitarianism it engendered—is part of what turned us from apes to human beings. It remained the pillar of our social organization for about 180,000 years.

If skewers are associated with the Greek reverence for this meat-sharing egalitarianism, and if skewers also lie at the origin of coinage, then a question arises. Are the two phenomena connected? Did the dawn of money have anything to do with that other (relatively) egalitarian Greek innovation, modern democracy?

Indeed it did, according to the classicist Richard Seaford. Solon, counted among the architects of organized democracy in its birthplace, Athens, began reshaping the city-state's laws around 600 BC, just as money was making its way across the Aegean from Anatolia to Greece. He introduced the radical innovation of equal penalty under law for a given crime—regardless of the rank of the wrongdoer or the victim. The fines his texts set forth were payable in "drachmas," a word that means both a set of six spits and a coin.

Through these laws, in other words, money—like the egalitarian ritual it grew out of—was putting citizens who used it on an equal footing.

The connection between these two powerful intertwined novelties can be seen again in the rebirth of democracy more recently. Money fell out of use in Europe after the sack of Rome in the fifth century AD. So completely did it disappear that when it returned to circulation there some eight hundred years later it was as though newly invented. With it came the first democratic stirrings, such as England's Magna Carta, forced on King John in 1215.

The next spurt in the circulation of money in the West came in the sixteenth century, with the Spanish conquest of the Americas. Huge amounts of silver—wanton quantities, disgorged by armies of captive human bulldozers dying at their labor, by the snuffing out of incomparable civilizations, and the demolition of sacred forestland and mountains—were vomited onto the world market.

Outside its land of origin, that silver had a more salutary effect. "For the first time [since Antiquity]," writes historian Jack Weatherford, "large numbers of people could buy large amounts of goods, and private citizens could start their own hoards of coins." As in ancient Greece, whose mints punched out tiny denominations, the money glut was such that even village craftsmen and small shopkeepers could adopt the innovation. "The new coins," writes Weatherford, "helped to wash away the old aristocratic order in which money games could be played only by the privileged few."

It was during this same sixteenth century that the northern provinces of the Spanish Empire—today's Netherlands and Belgium and a chunk of France—rose up against the Habsburg crown. In 1588, they declared an independent republic, along lines imitated two centuries later in America. Trade-based seafaring communities, with bustling towns like city-states, the Dutch provinces bore a resemblance to ancient Greece. As part of Spain, they experienced the full force and the equalizing effects of the sudden flood of money, like ancient Greece. Nobles and wealthy merchants led the rabble of wage earners in demands for limited government, subject to law and local consent—"an office, not an empire." They turned an insult thrown at them—that they were nothing but a bunch of bums and hobos (*gueux*)—into a badge of pride.

Money, likewise, impregnated American democracy. The future United States was founded as a profit-making venture, to deliver dividends to the shareholders of large corporations. Over time, colonists grown wealthy themselves chafed at laws designed in London to benefit the moneyed English at their expense. Theories of popular sovereignty and ideals of religious liberty helped prompt the American Revolution. But so did the pecuniary interests of merchants on the northern seaboard and the owners of vast cash-crop factory farms across the South.

In the decades immediately before and after the war, privateering, slaving, and land spoliation—at the price of the lives and loves and living cultures of the peoples who made and were made of those lands—founded the fortunes of such Founding Fathers as John Adams, John Hancock, Patrick Henry, and George Washington. Meanwhile, a burgeoning religious ideology equated the wealth such practices generated with moral rectitude.

It was this era of political revolution, too, that helped spawn the next revolution in the Western history of money. To guarantee a market for her own finished goods, England put curbs on American manufacturing. The colonies, forced to buy English products with cash, suffered shortages. There was simply not enough coinage available to pay for needed merchandise. How did Yankee ingenuity solve that problem? By pioneering the use (outside China) of paper money.

In this new form, currency was suddenly available to everyone. Another abrupt democratizing glut hit. The revolution put so much into circulation as to spark that other terror of money hoarders: inflation. "Paper Money, Paper Money, and Paper Money!" wrote Thomas Paine in 1786, "is now, in several of the states, both the bubble and the iniquity of the day."

"Americans," sums up historian Gordon Wood, "seemed to be a people totally absorbed in the individual pursuit of money." A powerful adhesive gluing the new country together, moneymaking became a republican virtue. Commerce and the quest for gain were "the *'golden chains,'*" Wood quotes eighteenth-century patriot and industrialist Samuel Blodget, *"the best social system that ever was formed."*

Money, in other words, is rooted just as deeply in the American identity as democratic principles are. In fact, the two are entangled.

Still, a great paradox of money is this: despite its democratizing start, once people get their hands on it in quantity, they turn it into the basis for a new aristocracy—one no better than the old, and maybe worse.

2

Jesus

That is just what had happened when a drama played out on a fraught piece of rocky ground at the eastern fringe of the Roman Empire. The events underlie one of the most consequential sacred stories in human history. For most Americans, it is far more familiar than the myth of Midas.

"And Jesus went up to Jerusalem." So starts its climactic episode, as related some decades later.

> In the temple he found people selling cattle, sheep, and doves, and the money changers seated at their tables. Making a whip of cords, he drove all of them out of the temple, both the sheep and the cattle. He also poured out the coins of the money changers and overturned their tables.

It is a remarkable event on Christ's journey toward crucifixion. And money is center stage.

Nearly three-quarters of Americans attend church at least a few times each year. Many of us reflect on episodes from the Bible to help understand our world and shape our own behavior. Religious or not, almost all of us have absorbed New Testament stories. We've heard the narratives, taken names in vain, seen a painting in a museum or on the glossy pages of a book. We have watched a movie, gone to Sunday school, prayed on Fridays. Approaching my fellow citizens as

Rembrandt van Rijn, *Christ Driving the Money Changers from the Temple*, 1635.

I would Nigerians, I decided to seek out some elders who could help explain the significance of this sacred story for this society.

I found some at the Emmanuel Episcopal Church in Cumberland, Maryland. Hosted by the rector, Martha Macgill, I met with several local pastors over lunch. Macgill had told them I was seeking insight on the cleansing of the temple. She had printed out the verses from the four canonical Gospels.

It is one of the few happenings in the life of Christ that appears in almost identical terms in all of them. Mark, Matthew, and Luke place the episode toward the end of the tale, when Jesus enters Jerusalem for the last time, the prelude to his Passion. He does this thing shortly before he is tried and convicted and crucified. John, who wrote later and rearranged events in order of their importance as he saw it, puts this drama right up top.

I watch the pastors reading over the verses as they dig into their sandwiches. Despite its obvious weight in the sacred story, they seem not deeply familiar with the passage. They read carefully.

They don't preach on it often, they explain. It comes up only once every third year, during Lent. At length, Macgill puts the trouble on all their faces into words: "I don't think we're very comfortable with it," she confesses.

Puzzled, I wait for more.

"You've got Jesus," she gropes her way, "who is the Prince of Peace—" Her voice fades.

"Who's whuppin' everybody." Marsha Bell, a Texas native, finishes the thought.

So that was it: the violence. In a set of sacred texts devoted to the virtues of mercy and forgiveness, the immortal who embodies them suddenly loses his cool. Over money. It's the only time such a thing happens in the Gospels.

More frankly than her colleagues, Bell appreciates this militant Jesus, his choice of targets, too. "As opposed to going after some individual kingpin," she explains, Jesus "is going after the system. The whole operation, the whole temple setup being a den of thieves. They've lost the plot. The poor can't participate," can't even be considered righteous, because "without money to pay for the sacrificial animals," they can't uphold the law.

Another pastor I spoke with some weeks later dwelled on this aspect of the episode: how distorted the ancient ritual of sacrifice had become. Rich Wright ministers at the Church of Christ in Paw Paw, West Virginia. Under ancient Hebrew law, he told me, you offered up a lamb at Passover that you had raised yourself. It had to be a beautiful lamb, that spring's most flawless. Maybe you had helped the laboring ewe, sliding your hands inside her body. You lavished care on that lamb. But no other would do. The point was not the market value of the offering, it was that loving care.

And what about the meat? I asked. I explained the ancient Greek ritual with its spits, the prized food evenly apportioned, and how the ceremony tied its celebrants back to the primordial egalitarian roots that made us human.

"That's just it," Wright exclaimed. "Under Levitical law, the priests got their share. But the rest of the sacrifice was for the people. By Jesus's day, that tradition had fallen away." You didn't raise your lamb, you bought it. You no longer gave a tenth of your annual yield as a sacred offering to the whole community on that holy day. You had to count out its equivalent in coin. Some small farmers had to mortgage their crops or their very land to get the money. Some had no land to mortgage and, penniless, were in effect excommunicated: excluded from the polis.

The new rules, says Wright, meant "everyone was robbing God. The high priests and the Sanhedrin [the high court], because they were organizing the trade. The market people, because they were cheating. And the comfortable classes, because they liked the convenience." Those with means no longer had to bother with the nurture of a newborn sheep. For those without, the monetary obligation was so heavy as to end their lives as independent members of the community: a degree of suffering surely pointless to any ambrosia-fed immortal.

This system, which drove an outraged Lamb of God to commit a violent act, had turned a sacred, deeply humanizing ritual on its head. Instead of bringing the community together on a basis of sharing and equality, it had become a brutal portcullis locking most members out.

Just as in the case of Midas, science has a lot to say about this sacred story. History and archaeology put Christ's conduct in an instructive light.

The temple Jesus stormed, they reveal, was the most magnificent building complex east of Rome. It was "a project of unparalleled size and magnificence," writes Lee Levine in *Jerusalem: Portrait of the City in the Second Temple Period.* Within its precinct stood the lofty Antonia Tower, which garrisoned Roman troops. There were buildings for worship, of course. There were other buildings for government, such as the high court's chambers. There were rows of towering pillars and "an immense basilica hall, the largest known in the East at the time."

"On entering the Temple, no matter from what direction," elaborates another historian, "a man . . . would have to pass through double gates covered with gold and silver."

I stopped reading. Glinting walls of precious metal in the Temple of Jerusalem? Parallels from today jostled to mind. I saw the online images of Ukrainian potentate Viktor Yanukovych's gaudy pleasure palace. The pictures had gone viral after the 2014 revolution there. I thought of those gold-plated bathroom fixtures that appear whenever the ways of the superrich are depicted. I thought of the signature gold trim on Trump Tower condominiums. The temple gleamed with gold?

That meant this place of worship was no community gathering place, welcoming to all. Its lavishness intimidated.

It was also where the most important judicial matters were decided, where law was handed down. And troops were quartered there. What other functions did that temple complex perform? What manner of men set up shop in its precinct? The historical texts and archaeology provide consistent answers.

"Owners of capital had always been attracted to Jerusalem; wholesalers, tax collectors, Jews of the Diaspora grown rich."

"An important function of the Jerusalem Temple . . . was its role as a bank for both personal and public funds."

A bank.

"In Jerusalem sat the customs officials, not only those in charge of the market dues of the city, but also those in control of much greater levies. . . . Such people . . . often established themselves as bankers in the capital, and they must have been those who . . . mortgaged the land and crops of the needy peasants. The money was deposited in the Temple, where . . . myriads of private fortunes were kept."

Next come the references to corruption. To make their Passover offering, it wasn't enough for pilgrims to bring their hard-won coins. They had to go through more steps, exchanging money for special tokens and then trading the tokens in for the required lamb or dove. Who knows what sleight of hand multiplied the cost at each transaction? For the yearly tithe, people had to convert the local currency they had scraped together into the shekels from a neighboring country, Tyre. It would be like Americans being required to pay the IRS in euros.

By ignoring the pagan images on these coins—because they had the purest silver content—temple rules made millions for the money changers. No wonder the priestly aristocracy coveted jobs on the trading floor and "filled the post of Temple treasurer from the younger members of its families." Often the families purchased the positions.

That's another pattern I've observed in modern-day kleptocracies: the jobs that offer the best opportunities for extorting bribes or stealing public money are bought and sold.

Now the picture was clearer. In today's terms, the temple Jesus took on might be understood as some unholy combination of Washington, DC, the Vatican, Wall Street, Fort Knox, and the military base in Qatar. When he roared that this den of robbers was supposed to be a house of prayer, we're told, "The whole crowd was spellbound by his teaching."

No kidding.

Indeed, the Gospels frame this episode as the fatal turning point in Jesus's career. It was not his summons to ordinary people to love their neighbors that enraged the power structure. It was not his own version of the archaic sacrifice: the egalitarian meat-sharing ritual at which miraculous loaves and fishes were divided up among his followers, thus forging them into a community. It was this dramatic act. It was only after the Prince of Peace threw their money on the ground that the high priests and the bankers "started looking for a way to kill him."

But they couldn't, not just then. For Jesus was surrounded by that great crowd of worshippers, drinking in his teaching. As humans had done for tens of thousands of years, those ordinary people were coming together in a wide gathering of equals. As a group, they were capable of reining in their would-be dominators: the leading members of society who were snatching far more than their fair share of its meat.

Reverend Martha Macgill and I closed the day in Cumberland at a potluck supper with members of her congregation. Seated at the same U-shaped table where we had met her pastor colleagues, we returned to the topic of the cleansing of the temple.

A good Christian's aim, as I understood it, should be to seek to emulate Jesus in his or her own life. If that is so, I asked these observant laypeople, what example do they draw from this story? "Who would the money changers be today?"

"Bankers," came the immediate reply. "Credit card companies."

"Big Pharma," someone else suggested, because those companies foster an epidemic and then supply the cure, making money on both ends—more money the more people they sicken.

And the company heads "have the politicians in their pockets," one woman added quietly. Meaning, as a man sitting next to her expanded, "there's no way we're breaking into that system to get a solution."

An older gentleman compared drug companies to cigarette manufacturers, whose leadership was aware for years that their product caused deathly illnesses but tried to hide the findings.

A young woman with striking black hair and eyeshadow added the processed-food industry to the list.

After a time, I saw a hand go up in a corner. Shoshana Brassfield, a philosophy professor at nearby Frostburg State University, has a soft and thoughtful voice. "I want to add another piece to this," she said. "The problem with the money changers wasn't just that they were corrupt. The problem was that they were being brought into the temple—into the sacred space. So I've been thinking: not just who are the money changers, but what is our temple now? And are we bringing the corruption into our own temple?" She paused. "And . . . pick your temple, right? Your home, your school, your church, your doctor's office . . . what are we bringing in?"

And, I thought, our government. If we are, in this country, a civic communion—down to the sacred architecture of our public buildings—what manner of corruption have we brought inside our temples?

Brassfield and Rev. Wright were probing at a very deep problem. Centuries before Jesus threw it out there, in bleating, squawking pandemonium on the temple's marble paving, this question troubled ancient Greeks, as they learned to live with the new phenomenon of money. What values do we consider sacred? What goods are so unique, or do we hold so dear, that there is no putting a monetary price on them? What happens when we do? What gets defiled if that thing is subjected to the buying and selling of the marketplace?

Spurred perhaps by the twin revolutions of democracy and money, Greece entered a great age of thought and creativity about a

century after the first coins arrived from nearby Lydia. Money preoccupied the great thinkers of this time. Anguished tragedies, philosophical disputations, and plays filled with farts and foul language
were devoted to it. Their authors were taken aback by the effect this
thing was having on their culture.

In recent memory, the items Greeks had given one another as gifts,
or the prizes bestowed on victors of athletic bouts or poetry contests,
were never judged by their exchange value—their weight in bronze
or silver. What mattered was their peerless qualities. Two foes might
trade sword belts before joining battle, as a mark of their esteem. The
prize at stake in a wrestling match might be a fine-wrought drinking
bowl or, as in Homer's *Iliad,* the horses and chariot of Achilles himself. Or, fatally, a woman. Those horses had been a gift of the sea god
Poseidon to Achilles's father. No steeds could rival their immortal
value. The bowl might be the work of a famous artist, a master in a
far-off land. Perhaps the belt had served in noted feats of arms.

Here's a less lofty example. I have a kitchen counter. The boards
came out of my friend Gail's barn—the oldest building around. My
neighbor Ronnie spent hours trimming them and sanding off the
four coats of grey paint. He found buckshot embedded in the wood,
where someone had fired at the side of that barn, or at something in
front of it. Ronnie and another neighbor, Randy, built struts against
the kitchen wall and decided which side up to put the boards, so
the beautiful knots would show. Then I took my tiniest carving tools
and picked out the grain—every wavy line. Now the surface is gently
furrowed, like hard sand at low tide. I rubbed it silky with steel wool
and soaked that counter with coats of linseed oil. When my friend
Sebastian came to visit one weekend, we cut edging for the side—
angling two of the mitered corners in the wrong direction, I realized
later. I love that counter.

Items like this are meaningful; there are no others like them. They
draw their value from the stories they incarnate, the admired people and deeds associated with them, the unmatched quality of their
craftsmanship (well, normally). It was through the exchange of such
priceless articles that the egalitarian Bronze Age Greeks wove elite
social networks.

Gaining membership in these circles was not just a matter of wealth
or even bloodlines. A set of values defined Greek aristocracy—even

if many members failed to meet them. Those values included excellence in every endeavor, be it physical strength, making music from the strings of a lyre, fine weaving, craftiness or courage in battle, or the sacred responsibility for the people that a political leader was expected to shoulder upon ascending to high rank. To win a matchless gift, one was expected to behave in ways that made one worthy of it.

Money is the opposite of unique. The whole point of its regular size and weight, the instantly recognizable stamp, is that a dime is a dime. No matter who spends it and the exact metallic content of the coin, a dime is a dime. Money tends to bring the things it buys—and their buyers—down to its own indistinguishable level. The upside of this effect is democracy. But there is a downside.

"Not for nothing, Wealth, do mortals honour you most of all," reads a poem from this period, "for you easily put up with baseness." "Baseness" here was not just the usual aristocratic put-down of the poor. In democratic Athens, it meant something qualitative.

If you can go to a cattle broker and buy Achilles's horses, then they are hardly different from any other high-priced steed. And you, with your bags of money, need not be a skilled and valiant warrior, or a person of great intellect or honor, to make them yours. This "universal value," applauded by modern economists, disturbed philosophers like Aristotle. By making objects interchangeable, by giving people access to the most prized privileges without having to live up to the standards of excellence and ethics that earn the right to them, money debases those values themselves.

This is the real meaning of the myth of Midas. It wasn't just that the king might starve to death through blind greed. It was that everything he touched lost its incomparable properties and turned into cold, hard cash.

Nathaniel Hawthorne told the tale for children, imagining a daughter for Midas named Marygold. Next to the precious metal, she was what he loved the most. As the king is realizing the danger of the fatal gift he just received, his child rushes over to comfort him:

> He bent down and kissed her. He felt that his little daughter's love was worth a thousand times more than he had gained by the Golden Touch.

"My precious, precious Marygold!" cried he.

But Marygold made no answer.

Alas, what had he done? . . . The moment the lips of Midas touched Marygold's forehead, a change had taken place. Her sweet, rosy face, so full of affection as it had been, assumed a glittering yellow color, with yellow tear-drops congealing on her cheeks. . . . Little Marygold was a human child no longer, but a golden statue!

That laughing, sparkling creature had been transformed to metal he could take to market, but his special girl, the light of his life, was no more.

This ability to debase things and people is why many Greeks saw in money "mankind's most deadly invention," as Sophocles has his King Kreon exclaim:

> It plunders cities
> encourages men to abandon their homes,
> tempts honest people to do shameful things.
> It instructs them in criminal practice,
> drives them to act on every godless impulse.

Upended by the onslaught this innovation unleashed on everything their culture honored, Greek thinkers struggled to draw the line between value and value: the material measure of what can be bought, and inestimable qualities or principles. And, as Jesus would do centuries later, they struggled to protect the latter from the former.

We are engaged in the same struggle.

3

Aristotle

Those Greek thinkers also grappled with this question: What made wealth in the form of money so different from the other types of riches that had come before? One who took that question on was Aristotle.

In *Politics,* the philosopher tries to distinguish between two modes of "property-getting." One, in his view, is "in accordance with nature." In that category he places gathering the goods needed to ensure that the family or community has a comfortable standard of living. "Goods, that is, which may be stored up, as being necessary for providing a livelihood, or useful to household or state." Wealth of this sort—jars of oil, flocks of sheep, shoes, or building stones—might be considered "natural" wealth.

To Aristotle, "wealth in the true sense consists of property such as this. For the amount of property of this kind which would give self-sufficiency for a good life is not limitless."

That idea is key. The wealth that matters, Aristotle is implying, is a good and fulfilling life. And there's only so much stuff you need to fashion one. This is also the type of property that requires loving care, like God's lamb. A fig tree won't produce sweet fruit if it isn't tended. Could that tending itself have a place in the good life?

There is a different "technique of acquiring goods," however. This other is "concerned primarily with coin." The aim is to "enabl[e] one to see where a great deal of money may be procured." Not just to acquire something you need, but to discover "where and how the greatest profits might be made out of the exchanges." What had been a means—for facilitating the trades that a good life might require—becomes the end in itself.

And here's the crucial difference: "There is indeed no limit to the amount of riches to be got from this mode of acquiring goods." For Aristotle, this is the terrible aspect of what he calls "unnatural wealth," or money made from money. There is no getting enough of it.

It is a face of money that horrified his contemporaries. Unlike any other pleasure, money provokes a bottomless desire. Aristophanes was a playwright born around 450 BC, about sixty-five years before Aristotle. A routine in his slapstick comedy *Wealth* puts it baldly.

"No one can ever get enough of you!" the main character, Chremylus, exclaims to the god Wealth, who doesn't seem to understand his own power. "You can have too much of everything else," he tries to make Wealth see, then launches into a duet with his slave. You can have too much sex, he says. Too many rolls of bread, counters his slave. Too much music. Too much lentil soup. But no one can have too much money. "So far, there's never been anyone who ever had enough of you! Give someone thirteen talents and he'll want sixteen. Put sixteen in his pocket and he'll yell for forty. . . . Then he'll start [whining] that he can't survive on that!"

This same phenomenon is horrifying Americans today.

I met with another group of citizens to discuss corruption, in Lexington, Kentucky. I began that conversation, like this one, asking about money.

"I don't think there's enough for some people." That is how Debby Eddy, a nurse in charge of health and safety at the J. M. Smucker Company, described the role it has come to play in our society.

When people thought about money in the past, agreed her neighbor, Deborah Knittel, the concern "used to be about having enough to be comfortable and safe. It wasn't ever-growing wealth."

As though to illustrate her point, a business self-help book, by the CEO of the largest private security firm in the United States, came out not long after that conversation. It was titled, in all seriousness, *No Off Season: The Constant Pursuit of More.*

In 2014, a recovering Wall Street banker described the problem as crudely as Aristophanes had, minus the dirty words. "In my last year on Wall Street my bonus was $3.6 million," wrote Sam Polk in the *New York Times,* "and I was angry because it wasn't big enough. I was 30 years old, had no children to raise, no debts to pay, no philanthropic goal in mind. I wanted more money for exactly the same reason an alcoholic needs another drink: I was addicted."

Polk describes walking onto the trading floor for the first time and seeing all the screens and knobs and buttons: "It looked as if the traders were playing a video game inside a spaceship; if you won this video game, you became what I most wanted to be—rich."

When he landed a job, Polk "worked like a maniac." He became a trader in credit default swaps—one of the unregulated derivatives that helped bring on the stock-market crash of 2008—and rented a $6,000-a-month apartment. He was making $1.75 million. "I felt so important," he confesses. "At 25, I could go to any restaurant in Manhattan. . . . I could be second row at the Knicks-Lakers game just by hinting to a broker I might be interested in going."

Yet Polk was "nagged by envy. . . . When the guy next to you makes $10 million, $1 million or $2 million doesn't look so sweet." He went to work for a hedge fund. Why? "I wanted a billion dollars."

So powerful has this fixation become it is shoving other precious values aside.

That's just what the ancient Greeks saw money doing when it took hold in their society. "Nothing else after all is of use," laments a poem written probably in the 500s BC—in the earliest years of coinage on that side of the Aegean. Other once-prized virtues did not seem to have much standing anymore. Not the knowledge or good judgment of the gods, not the silver-tongued eloquence of a Nestor (the *Iliad*'s elder statesman), not fleetness of foot to rival the winds. "No," concludes the poet, "store up this thought: that for all people, wealth has the greatest power."

I have heard this ancient lament voiced countless times today.

"If you're penniless, people won't even see you," an office worker told me in January 2018, in Kathmandu. I had asked her if the role of money had changed in Nepalese society during her lifetime. I've put the same question to people all around the world. The replies are immediate—and never complimentary.

In the past, other Nepalese told me, the oldest son of a high-caste family in the Himalayan foothills would feel it a duty and an honor to become a teacher in the local school. Now he would be more likely to sell the piece of land the school is standing on to developers.

A village elder in southern Nigeria answered my question this way: "You know the truth, but then they use money, and everything changes."

That was deep. I wondered what exactly he meant.

"Once they give you money," the old man replied, "you can't criticize them anymore. You can't decide a case against them. Money makes liars out of people."

Many Nigerians emphasized how much it used to matter how a person got his or her wealth: where the money came from.

"In the past, money was generally from reliable sources, so it had value, whether it was a big or small amount," Fisa Nyoni Obasogie, another older man living near the southern town of Benin City, explained. "The elders would assess your farm, what you grew there, to see what kind of income you should be earning. Parents would question their children if they found money in their hands. No one wanted their name dragged in the mud."

Several people I met had searing memories of such interrogations. Some told of being beaten for bringing something home they had bought with money they could not convincingly explain. But now, interviewees agreed, any kind of money wins more respect than the qualities their people used to value: truthfulness, objectivity, considering the good of others, hard work, education or the wisdom of old age, humility, and open hearted generosity.

"People judge you by your wallet," concluded filmmaker Abdulkareem Mohammed, in the northern city of Kano.

When I asked a similar set of questions in Norway in 2018, I heard that not so long ago, people with a lot of money were looked at sideways. It was almost shameful to be rich.

"But that has changed," said Trond Eirik Schea, Norway's chief prosecutor for white-collar crime.

"Once the question was, 'To be or not to be,' " agreed Øistein Akselberg, a senior loan manager at DNB bank. "Now it's, 'To have or not to have.' "

I was struck by the date Norwegians placed on this change in attitude. The clear consensus: it was around 1980. For Nigerians, too: "When money became everything was in 1985." Egyptians I interviewed identified a similar shift in the 1980s. That is when new and flashy types of cars started showing up in their neighborhoods.

Of course, the infamous 1980s were hardly the first time in history that money became a kind of virtue—the measure not just of value in the marketplace, but of the value of a person. After the Reformation in the sixteenth century, for example, many Protestant communities saw monetary wealth as a sign of God's pleasure. In the new Dutch Republic—that precursor to the United States founded by merchants and burghers in 1588—Rembrandt and other great artists painted portraits by the dozen. The leading citizens they so beautifully depicted are draped in the black garb of good Puritans, and they are grasping sacks of money. Both accoutrements were on display, as equal signs of godliness.

That idea, that God signaled his "election" of a person by showering him or her with money, followed the Dutch and English Protestants to the New World and became a central strand in America's own mythology.

Still, over the course of history and around the world, the intensity of people's obsession with money has not been constant over time. It waxes and wanes. The 1980s marks a waxing phase.

In the United States, both the type of transformation and the time frame of the change echo what I have heard elsewhere.

"When I was growing up in the forties, there was a pride in being poor. I don't see that anymore." Lawyer and former county official Jon Larson was sharing his perspective with the group of neighbors I met with in Kentucky. But he could have been one of the Norwegians I had spoken to earlier that year. To illustrate his point, Larson did not cite a campaign slogan or new government regulations. He pointed to Hollywood. The change came, he said, "after that movie, where greed is good . . ."

He meant *Wall Street,* and that was 1987. Larson may have been off by a few years. But he was on to something.

In the 1980s, Americans still made a family outing of a movie. What we saw on the big screen both reflected and shaped our worldview.

Judging from the cinema of those years, the money addiction was already epidemic by the time *Wall Street* came out.

The 1983 youth flick *Risky Business* led the way. A nubile Tom Cruise gets the run of his parents' opulent house while they are on vacation. The dress, the demeanor, even the way shots of those overbearing parents are framed—everything about them is loathsome. They are fish-cold and obsessed with their precious things—Porsche, sleek stereo, crystal egg—and the dogma that their son Joel's future lies by way of high test scores and Princeton University.

At a fast-food joint, Joel and his high-school friends discuss the earnings prospects for different career tracks. Business school ranks high. "Doesn't anyone want to *accomplish* anything?" he bursts out. "Or do we just want to make money?"

"Make money," comes the chorus. "Make a lot of money." When Joel suggests helping other people, his friends laugh out loud and start throwing food.

Under the tutelage of a beautiful young prostitute named Lana, Joel quickly comes around. "It was great the way her mind worked," he reflects. "No guilt, no doubts, no fear. . . . What a capitalist."

While his classmates in a semester-long private-enterprise workshop are earning a few hundred dollars selling prosaic gadgets they dream up, he turns eight thousand dollars in a single night, using his parents' house as a brothel—an activity he brands dealing in "human fulfillment." The Princeton admissions officer interrupts the lewd festivities to conduct Joel's interview, leaves much later with a girl, and decides that—despite a mediocre high-school record— "Princeton can use a guy like Joel."

The message is clear. Learning and making things are for chumps. Anyone who plays by the rules and builds a comfortable life by way of ordinary privilege is contemptible. The only admirable choice is to "say what the fuck"—as a friend urges Joel—and make it big. " 'What the fuck' gives you freedom. Freedom brings opportunity. Opportunity makes your future."

As President Ronald Reagan was making freedom his trademark, *Risky Business* was redefining the concept.

The movie ends with the business students giving their pathetic presentations, while a dapper Cruise strolls away with Rebecca de Mornay and the secret to infinite wealth. The making of money by criminal means is anything but shameful. For a whole generation of 1980s adolescents, Cruise and his shades and Elvis dance moves made it cool and sexy.

Wall Street, the 1987 blockbuster my Kentucky interviewee Larson mentioned, was intended as a cautionary tale. Director Oliver Stone has said he meant to shine a light on the dangers of a world in which monetary returns to shareholders took precedence over any other corporate aim. "The point is, ladies and gentlemen," Michael Douglas lectures a spellbound board of directors, "that greed, for lack of a better word, is good. Greed is right. Greed works. Greed . . . captures the essence of the evolutionary spirit . . . the upward surge of mankind. And greed, you mark my words, will [save that] malfunctioning corporation called the USA."

The lines were meant as satire. But they were lifted from a real speech by a real person. The graduating class of the business school at UC Berkeley, famous as a liberal bastion, rewarded them with cheers and laughter. Stone's movie, instead of shaming Wall Street as intended, inspired flocks of young adults to drop their prior plans and head right there to make some money.

I witnessed this brain drain. I graduated from college in 1984, ten months after *Risky Business* was released. I watched dozens of my highly motivated, highly educated classmates opt not to "*accomplish anything*"—serve their community, or invent or create something useful or beautiful—but instead go make money where the money was to be made: in the financial-services industry. No other endeavor seemed to them as worthy.

That was new. To the same crop of graduating seniors just a few years earlier, striving baldly for money would have been the opposite of cool. It would have been tacky. It would have been servile conformity to the System. Between 1977 and 1987, according to Robert Reich, "employment in the securities industry . . . increas[ed] by an average of 10 percent a year, compared with average yearly job growth of 1.9 percent in the rest of the economy."

Maybe my classmates got what they wanted: more money than they could ever use, and applause for making it. But did the rest of us? Is this what we want our smartest people doing? Don't we want more great epidemiologists and social workers? Some visionary city planners, with the weather we've been having? Did my classmates enjoy the lives they wrought?

Taken together, the impact of the personal choices my peers made was gigantic, if uncounted. Brains and talent were sucked onto Wall Street, while other things that contribute to a country's greatness were starved of air. That's called an "opportunity cost," and it was huge.

Starting in those same years, rewards in the form of our national prosperity—the meat, if you will, that we hunted together—began landing in huge chunks on banks' and bankers' plates. It was no longer being shared as equally. Nor was it invested in ways that benefit the whole of the tribe that is our nation or that honor values other than itself: the making of money. The vicious circle was engaged.

With the spread of this culture around the world, money has come to serve an unintended purpose. It has become the most important social measuring rod. That is how it shoves other values aside: society stops rewarding them. People cease competing over the quality of their craftsmanship, or the care they show their friends, their helpfulness, their courage, integrity, or humility, or cultivating the kind of foresight that might save lives. Instead, if they make a lot of money through a "What the fuck" *lack* of foresight—shattering lives in the process—they are still considered heroes. These days, as Nigerian filmmaker Mohammed summed up, "The first index to judge the quality of a person is money."

If you are an individual, you are ranked—and you rank yourself—by your salary. If you're a corporation, share prices and profits are your measure. If you're a country, you are evaluated, constantly and incessantly, by your gross domestic product. These monetary figures, easily graspable and stackable, define our social worth. They tell us if we've got respect. They tell us if we're winning.

A friend saw this up close when she hired two local handymen to do some work on her mother's house in rural Texas.* She asked the first his rate. He told her fifteen dollars an hour. When she brought the second on to help him, she paid him fifteen dollars, too. A few months later,

---

* The location of this story and two other details have been changed to keep it anonymous.

the first man came to her, seething. "We need to talk," he announced. She motioned to a chair beside her at the kitchen table. "I just found out you're paying Pete as much as me. I'm a little upset," he declared. "The carpenter is supposed to make more than the assistant."

My friend was startled. She had paid what this man had asked for, rounding up the number when she counted out the cash. More importantly, she considered him a friend. Nothing in his life had come easily. Sometimes he had confided in her. She admired him and, she thought, had always shown it. But once money entered the picture, none of that mattered. Pay was how he ranked himself.

At the bottom of the social ladder, this use of money as a stand-in for respect is particularly harmful, for one sacred value money undermines is solidarity. It corrodes the tendency to share with other people and look out for them. Just as the monetization of the ancient Greek economy broke down the tradition of gift exchanges that kept elite networks bonded, money—an innovation born of meat sharing—ironically undermines the solidarity that binds egalitarian communities together. It is another of its terrible paradoxes.

The examples of how this happens are striking. When asked how money was changing their society, Norwegians described a tradition common until recently. It's called *dugnad*. "It's when you call on all your family, friends, and neighbors to pitch in with some big task, such as building a house," explained prosecutor Trond Eirik Schea. Sort of like a quilting bee. The family receiving help cooks a feast, and the shared labor becomes a celebration. Participation is such a social expectation that in Norway, "no one doesn't come."

Until the 1980s, that is. That's when respect for money began swamping such traditional values. Now, Schea and several compatriots explained, *dugnad* is felt to be a tiresome chore. People try to get out of it.

Researchers in psychology have conducted experiments to learn how even subconscious reminders of money affect people's willingness to help others. The experimenters brought money to some participants' minds by asking them to count banknotes, while another group counted blank sheets of paper. Or some subjects were seated in front of a computer with money floating across the screen. The experimenters found that even the glancing thoughts of money triggered this way made participants less likely to help someone they encountered during the experiment. Fewer of them stooped to pick up a handful of pencils a stranger had dropped or stopped to help her understand a set of instructions. Participants who had seen money were also more likely to keep their physical distance even from friends and loved ones.

The irony these findings reveal weighs especially heavily on the poor. Reflexes and traditions of solidarity are especially necessary to them. These practices help people on the edge survive. They can make living there not just bearable but joyful, sometimes. Yet money makes people who are merely reminded of it *less* likely to share and help one another out.

There is no way to live in the United States today without being reminded of money.

In his 2016 book *Tribe,* about the ethos of interdependent communities like platoons in combat, Sebastian Junger argues that one cause of many modern mental health and social problems is the extreme lack of community in contemporary urban society. Reliance on money, according to the social science research cited above, aggravates the tendency to isolate ourselves. Subjects of experiments who had counted money or seen it on their computer screens placed chairs farther away from other participants than those who had not been triggered. They reported preferring solo leisure activities instead of things you do with others, like playing horseshoes or meeting for a coffee.

But the more isolated people are—the less sense of community and responsibility for one another they feel—the more they turn to money for their comfort and survival. Sebastian and I have been friends since we were four. He has spent years thinking about community and how the lack of it is damaging people. I have spent years thinking about money and the dangers of its excesses. Now we learn that our two obsessions feed each other. They are locked together in another vicious circle.

Among the rich, the use of money as a proxy for winning has a different destructive effect. It means, as Aristotle understood, that there is no such thing as enough. "When the guy next to you makes

$10 million, $1 million or $2 million doesn't look so sweet," as that
Wall Street trader Sam Polk put it. If one man has a lot, his rivals will
want to beat him. And on and on. If money is the yardstick for measuring success and social value, then enough has nothing to do with
it. It is a race with no finish line. Whatever number *Forbes* magazine
puts after a person's name just becomes a challenge to outdo.

What Aristotle had not discovered was another great paradox of
money, which has now been demonstrated amply. It's not as if the
contestants in this infinite race are relishing his good life and just piling
up useless excess wealth along the way. For most of them, pursuit of
money is preventing them from tasting that good life at all. Like Sam
Polk, they work like maniacs; they're constantly comparing themselves
with others and feeling that they come up short. Multiple experiments
have demonstrated that—above a certain amount for comfort—more
money does not make those who have it happier. Instead, it often
leaves them feeling unfulfilled and ratchets up their stress.

And yet we keep desiring more.

Economists have contributed to this problem by indoctrinating us
with an irrational reverence for growth. It's not just a high GDP that
has become a synonym for a country's economic health, it's how fast
that number is getting bigger. Economic growth has become a mark
of countries' virtue. And what goes for countries goes for people. It's
not enough to have high net worth anymore. What matters is the rate
of increase—that is, "ever growing wealth."

The contestants in this ghoulish marathon may suffer, but they
are not the ones who suffer most. For money is not conjured out of
nothing. This race among the superrich—for zeroes in their bank
accounts—means a race to transform items of inestimable value into
cold, hard cash. The land, what's on and under the land—all that
vibrant life—human effort and creativity, our friendships, our health
and the "statistical value" of our very lives, all are being converted
into money. We have even equated speech—that unique human gift—
with money.* Just like the gifts Greeks once gave one another, or like

---

* In a momentous 5–4 decision in 2010, the Supreme Court ruled that for the purposes of the constitution, spending on electoral advocacy equates "speech" and is
thus guaranteed the robust protections enshrined in the U.S. founding document.

the Marygold of Hawthorne's Midas, these items are irreplaceable. Once the cash is spent or banked, there's nothing left but zeroes.

In the Bible—that so often contradictory anthology of sacred stories—there seem to be two different attitudes toward wealth. The Old Testament casts it mostly as a positive, a sign of God's favor. Only meat hogging—extortion and other types of "unjust gain"—are singled out for shame. Puritans and many of their Protestant successors found in this teaching a rationale for seeing money as a synonym for virtue. This Old Testament tendency has also been used to build a bigoted caricature of Jews as money-loving misers. Jesus, by contrast, is often seen disparaging wealth and those who love it. And he threw all those coins on the temple floor.

What may explain the difference is the timing of the texts. The Old Testament dates from before the days of money. Back then, only pharaohs hoarded wealth, in weights of gold or copper, or as heaps of grain in vast storehouses. Ordinary people did not run in the endless race. By the time of Christ, however, coins were in. And the traders were making money from their money. In the process, they were stripping members of their own people—their own hunting band—of their good lives, indeed their very livelihoods. The money changers were violating their culture's deepest principles, defiling their own most sacred values.

Aristotle, in other words, had it right. He put his finger on the key distinction. A generous living for households and communities is indeed a blessing. Gaining that is a natural ambition contained within natural limits. It entails lavishing loving care on the sources of the abundance. It calls for foresight, the knowledge of how to nurture and help regenerate those sources, not just use them up. Nothing about this kind of wealth threatens us today.

It is the "unnatural" ambition, the one Aristotle found to be "concerned primarily with coin," that is the mortal danger to us all: the ambition of the speculators and the superrich to keep making money from their money, to achieve infinite, ever-growing wealth. Left to

---

[There are some caveats, such as, the spender is not allowed to coordinate directly with a political candidate or his or her campaign, but these have proved flimsy.] This decision, allowing for unlimited spending, has upended U.S. political campaigns.

them, our one planet and all its life and its loves and beauties will be chewed up and spat out as cold, hard cash. Or, these days, as flashing electronic signals.

Though many of us bemoan the role money has come to occupy in our culture, I'm still not sure we understand the true dimensions of the peril. In 2012, Donald Trump coauthored a book called *Midas Touch: Why Some Entrepreneurs Get Rich—and Why Most Don't.* Like Trump, we have misunderstood the myth. Americans have contracted the Midas disease, but we haven't realized it's a curse.

II

CRAZY MONEY

1873–1935

1

Europe

The Midas disease was like one of those highly contagious and rapidly mutating viruses. Once it was transmitted, instilling unlimited moneymaking as a virtue around the globe, it quickly morphed into an epidemic of corruption. People in revolt against kleptocratic governments can readily date the change from ordinary corruption to something different—something unbearable. The pins in the calendar cluster around the mid- to late 1990s.

Corruption is as old as government. No period in history is free of bribe taking, sweetheart deals between public officials and their pals in business—or even joint ventures with out-and-out criminality. Yet when people tell me that, and then cite some specific scandal to support their point, the examples they choose are not evenly scattered across time. The events almost always fall within another specific span of years: the era in the late nineteenth and early twentieth centuries known broadly as the Gilded Age. The brazenness, the method, and the global spread of the practices that are sparking indignation today were last seen a century ago.

Like myths, perhaps this history has something to tell us.

It was Mark Twain (with his coauthor, Charles Warner) who gave the period its name. Their 1873 satire was called *The Gilded Age: A Tale of Today*. The plot follows the antics of an extended family of country bumpkins peddling a land-speculation scheme for a railroad and riverboat hub on a muddy little tributary of the Missouri River. They want some bank to sponsor a bond offering—that is, a way for them to borrow money from everyday investors, as if they were a company or a government. But to entice the banks, they need a congressional appropriation to dredge and widen the river.

Incarnating the fast-money Washington elite that the book parodies is one "Patrique Oreillé (pronounced O-re*lay*)"—aka Patrick O'Riley. He's a former New York alderman, writes Twain, a job that

> was just the same as presenting him a gold mine. . . . By and by he became a large contractor for city work, and was a bosom friend of the great and good Wm. M. Weed himself, who had stolen $20,600,000 from the city and was a man so envied, so honored—so adored, indeed—that when the sheriff went to his office to arrest him as a felon, that sheriff blushed and apologized. . . . Mr. O'Riley furnished shingle nails to the new Court House at three thousand dollars a keg, and eighteen gross of 60-cent thermometers at fifteen hundred dollars a dozen; the controller and the board of audit passed the bills, and a mayor, who was simply ignorant but not criminal, signed them.

Wm. Weed, no reader of the time will have missed, rhymes with William Tweed, the boss of New York City's infamously corrupt Tammany Hall machine.[*]

In 2000, New York mayor Rudolph Giuliani approved a project to restore the courthouse that this passage winks at, which had come to symbolize Tweed's graft. The modern job was initially budgeted at $35 million, grew to more than $80 million—and the number kept rising.

And in 1984, O'Riley's descendant stepped out of the pages of fiction to sell real hammers to the U.S. Navy at more than five thousand dollars a dozen, and toilet seats for six hundred dollars each. Twenty-five years later, not even a blushing sheriff could be found to arrest the authors of the global financial meltdown of 2008. "So honored" were those authors, "so adored, indeed" (at least by their friends and relations in U.S. political

---

[*] These patronage-driven urban power structures dominated local politics in such cities as Philadelphia, New York, Chicago, and Boston. Famous for their graft and cronyism, usually run by immigrants from Ireland or Italy and their descendants, they were often (but not always) connected with the Democratic Party. They provided jobs and often sustenance to the urban poor in return for votes.

and economic leadership), that several were awarded senior government positions, a privilege that would allow them to design the conditions under which their former institutions were offered approximately $73 billion of our money. A dozen years later, some played a similar role in the award of trillions in emergency coronavirus loans and corporate bond purchases, including of low-grade junk bonds.

Flush with cash, Twain's O'Riley "retired from active service and amused himself with buying real estate at enormous figures and holding it in other people's names." This pastime has become a signature occupation of the global kleptocratic class today. New York condominiums at addresses like the Time Warner Center, whole streets of mansions in London's most elegant boroughs, are held in "other people's names." Those names are usually of some limited liability company domiciled on a Caribbean island and represented on the documents by a lawyer. The private equity funds operated by public figures from Madeleine Albright to Steven Schwarzman are deep in real estate speculation of this sort, buying and selling marquee properties "at enormous figures" for undisclosed investors. Another former New York mayor, Michael Bloomberg, loudly encouraged such distortions of the property market, calling on billionaires to buy New York's buildings.

The Gilded Age was well timed. As traveling booksellers were delivering the tooled-leather volumes to homesteads across the United States that spring of 1873, the stock market in distant Vienna collapsed—due to precisely the type of corrupt railroad and real estate speculation the book lampooned.

The details differed, of course. The land that Vienna's speculators were feverishly racking up debt to buy was no wilderness backwater. It stood under the fashionable faubourgs that were being laid out in the Austrian capital, and in Berlin and Paris too. Amid an orgy of a new kind of paper money—recently invented (and as yet completely unregulated) financial instruments like stocks and bonds—building booms were lining newly surveyed boulevards with the latest ornate edifices. The supply of housing and office space was far outstripping demand.

So many joint stock companies, especially banks, were incorporated in the years leading up to the crash that the whole period is called the Gründerzeit, or "The Founders' Period." Nobles and government officials jostled for their piece of the action. They joined company boards to bolster investor confidence. They used their official positions to manipulate markets—and even diplomatic negotiations—to lock in their advantage and keep the helium pumping into that balloon.

"So many and doubtful have been the new speculative enterprises presented to the German public," editorialized the conservative *New York Times,* "that the word *gründer,* or 'founders,' has become synonymous with swindlers."

On May 9, in the midst of what was billed as a magnificent world's fair, putting Austria's prestige on display, the bottom fell out of the market. "The panic," reported the *New York Times* correspondent on the scene, "was fearful. About the doors of the Bourse there was a group of some 200 speculators in a state of wild excitement, and at every moment news came that some other house had closed its doors." A last-ditch effort to bail out top banks could not stanch the hemorrhage of bad loans. The crash brought down dozens of banks, hurtling hundreds of other companies into insolvency.

It took four months for the shock waves of this disaster to ricochet across the Atlantic. They struck an economy whose foundations were already shuddering.

Just a year before, Americans had discovered that their greatest technological triumph, the Transcontinental Railroad, was also "the most damaging exhibition of official and private villainy and corruption ever laid bare to the gaze of the world." In September 1872, *New York Sun* investigative reporters revealed that the Union Pacific Railroad, responsible for the eastern third of the line, had created a shell company by which it had robbed the U.S. government of $40 to $50 million (equivalent to as much as $1 billion in 2020). It had bribed dozens of top officials to ignore the ongoing heist, in just one scandal that wracked the notorious Ulysses S. Grant administration.

With a name as elegantly European as Patrique Oreillé's, that shell company, the Crédit Mobilier of America, was captained by one of the scheme's masterminds, a U.S. representative from Massachusetts. Bribes in the form of discount prices on stock went to Speaker of the House and future vice president Schuyler Colfax, future president James Garfield, and senator and vice-presidential candidate Henry

Wilson. Coming just months before an election, the scandal and the three federal investigations it spawned touched off a furor.

Much of the frenzied rush to blast rock and lay iron across the American West had been financed by European bond purchases. So when—on top of this Union Pacific scandal—Austrian and German banks collapsed amid a fire sale of U.S. securities, the blow was too powerful to absorb. Railroad companies still racing one another to span the vast wilderness went under, together with their Wall Street backers.

On September 18, the doors of one of the most prominent among them, Jay Cooke & Co., failed to open; on the nineteenth, Fiske & Hatch sent word to the exchange floor that it too could no longer cover its obligations. "For a moment," wrote Elisha Andrews, an economist and historian, some years afterward, "there was silence; then a hoarse murmur broke out . . . followed by yells and cries indescribable, clearly audible on the street." Throngs choked the corner of Wall Street and Broad (where J. P. Morgan was just opening his office) and brokers nearly came to blows on the exchange floor. Bank branches were besieged by desperate depositors. On September 20, the stock market suspended trading for the first time ever and stayed dark for ten days.

The Panic of 1873 set off an economic depression that lasted years. Much of central Europe took a generation to recover. Some high-flying speculators committed suicide. Many were ruined. So were thousands of ordinary people who, trusting what they thought was expert advice, had traded coins in their mattresses for now worthless securities.

But perhaps the hardest hit on both sides of the Atlantic were just bystanders: store clerks, factory hands, laborers, their families. In the American West, camps scattered across the wilderness emptied, as railroad gangs were called off the job. Tracklayers and cooks and stevedores, their lives upended, took to the byways as hobos—as did their Depression-stricken children and grandchildren a half century later. With demand and prices collapsing, small farmers revolted and shops and factories closed. Unemployment touched 25 percent. It was a time of pitched battles between the police and mobs of protesters demanding work, a time of food lines and bitter strikes, of epidemic addiction to opium.

In neither Europe nor the United States did this calamity jolt decision-makers into much soul-searching. Explanations emphasized impersonal forces of economic structure or policy, such as falling international commodity prices, and the comparative virtues of paper money or the gold standard, one of the big political debates of the day. The incestuous relationships between public officials and the financiers and industrialists who had brought the panic about did not draw much comment.

Within elite circles, challenges to what one historian calls the "epidemic desire to become rich" were expressed indirectly. They resonate in the shocked tone of some newspaper reports or the work of Mark Twain and his towering French counterpart, Émile Zola, who wrote two acclaimed novels about banking and real estate speculation, *L'Argent (Money)* and *La Curée (The Spoils)*.

In fact, far from marking a turning point in the ethos and behavior Twain's novel ridiculed, 1873 is usually considered the *start* of the Gilded Age.

Or, as it is known in France, La Belle Époque, the Beautiful Era. And beautiful it was, for some. This was the period of the great Impressionist painters. Floral motifs inspired by medieval tapestry and newly available Japanese art, later dubbed art nouveau, twined across wallpapers and jewelry. Craftsmen labored to tool them into blocks of stone or to bend steel to their sinuous shapes for the railings of new bridges across the Seine.

But like meteors colliding with the lush surface of those years came scandal after scandal, crash after fiery crash.

In 1882, l'Union Générale bank cratered. Speculation was already back to its feverish pre-1873 pitch by the late 1870s, when this smug start-up added commercial banking to an investment fund—allowing it to gamble with ordinary people's money. "A whole aristocracy, fascinated by dreams in which pecuniary interests seemed to intersect with political or religious ambitions, dashed blindly into mad financial escapades," wrote *Le Temps* newspaper afterward.

Zola's 1890 novel *L'Argent* depicts these characters with merciless realism. They are consumed with competitiveness. They force inside information from relatives in government. They skid headlong into fraudulent reporting and stock manipulation. They know everything has its price. Wrenching scenes draw out the anguish of ordinary people overriding their better judgment to throw their meager savings onto the pile.

In one, an impoverished noblewoman whose lands have dwindled to a single failing farm comes in, "so sad, so pale," with her daughter, to see the founder of the Universal Bank. She murmurs an idea "repugnant to her until then": to make money with money, by buying his shares with her tiny stash of gold.

In another, a silk manufacturer from Lyon—where incomparable fabrics flowed like shining water from looms that were the city's pride—pours contempt on his own life. "What's the use of slaving thirty years to gain a paltry million," he wonders, "when in a single hour, one stock market operation can bring in the same amount? . . . It's enough to disgust a person with legitimate gain."

La Banque Universelle's founder "had sold himself," his loyal assistant at last realizes, and was selling her and her brother too. He was "minting coins out of their hearts and brains."

He was Midas; she was Marygold.

The very year these words appeared in print, 1890, another crash hit. The corruption that triggered it implicated dozens of members of Parliament, three ministers, and none other than Gustave Eiffel, the engineer whose iconic tower symbolizes Paris itself.

A delusional scheme to dig a canal across the Isthmus of Panama was the basis for repeated bond issues, netting hundreds of millions of francs from small-time investors. But a canal without locks, as per the initial design, was a mechanical impossibility given the Central American terrain.

According to official investigations after the fact, about 60 percent of the capital raised was lavished on bribes for public officials, bank fees, and payments to newspaper editors and reporters to ensure the glowing coverage that lured investors. Shares and seats on the board of directors were also doled out, just as in the Union Pacific scandal, weaving the company into the fabric of French ruling networks. Fat executive salaries and grossly inflated bills for supplies ate up the operating budget. "The Panama Canal Company," writes historian Frederick Brown, was "whale blubber for every shark in the water." On the isthmus itself, money changers were busy scalping workers, more than twenty thousand of whom died of tropical diseases.

Perhaps the most fantastic of these scandals was one I discovered almost by accident. In the early days of my work on this period, I went over to some friends' place for dinner near the Place de la République in Paris. I had lived partly in France for twenty-five years, but I knew little about the Belle Époque. So I asked. Apart from all that art and architecture, the urban redesign of Paris, what had that time been like?

"Are you kidding?" my friend exclaimed. "It was *l'argent fou:* the crazy-money time!" And he jumped up to pull a slim volume off his bookshelf.

It was the spellbinding biography of one Thérèse Humbert, daughter of illegitimate parents, orphaned at fourteen, an impoverished nobody from a nondescript village. So hypnotic was her talent for spinning tales, however, that from her teenage years to her eventual disgrace in 1902, she bamboozled whomever she met into giving her whatever she desired, from stylish hats to huge cash loans. She always promised to repay with interest well above the going market rate.

For collateral, as Humbert and her schemes matured, she would brandish the reputation of her father-in-law (and accomplice), a member of Parliament and justice minister. And she spun elaborate stories of a promised inheritance. Proof of her future vast fortune, she insisted, was there in black and white on securities and other papers she kept locked in a safe. Except no one had seen the inside of that safe.

By the time police and prosecutors raided Humbert's opulent Paris apartment—and broke open the safe and found an old newspaper and a button—she boasted multiple châteaux across France; a flock of admirers including several French presidents and magistrates and the country's top police brass; and a roster of creditors ranging from the thousands of small-time investors in a bond issue the family floated, to the major banks, to the jewelers who crafted the exquisite art nouveau pieces she displayed on her person.

In Third Republic France as in the United States today, huge

"LA PLUS GRANDE ESCROQUERIE DU SIÈCLE"

The Swindle of the Century–period postcard illustrating the Thérèse Humbert affair. Her apartment was raided and she was finally arrested in 1902.

sums of money—even fictitious money—commanded the utmost admiration.

Past my incredulity that such a house of cards could possibly have been bewitched into solid stone and priceless gems, I could not shake the sense that there was more to this episode than it seemed. This was not just some fascinating circus exhibit, an outlandish exaggeration of the excesses of a bygone era. The method that Humbert so expertly made her own brings to mind current examples.

There were those two billion dollars that Commerce Secretary Wilbur Ross persuaded *Forbes* magazine to add to his net worth, which reporters could never track down. The magazine finally concluded he had simply made them up.

There were Donald Trump's depositions exaggerating his wealth. Jonathan Greenberg, a reporter at *Forbes,* was just one of those taken in. The main source for his story on Trump's net worth was Trump, who sometimes posed as someone else on the phone. He was bleeding money at the time and, in the words of Bob Garfield, the host of the radio show *On the Media,* "wanted the world to see not a house of cards, but a gilded palace."

Greenberg recalled that in 1982 he and Trump settled on a number for the mogul's net worth: $100 million. It was overblown, Greenberg later worked out, by at least 2,000 percent. The real number was less than $5 million. And there is Trump's obsession with keeping his tax returns locked away, like the button in Humbert's safe.

The results are similar. The Trump family has had as little trouble as the Humberts in securing new loans—even after numerous defaults. These fabrications are not just an ego thing, I realized. They are integral to the business model.

I confess I found the parade of nineteenth-century stories perversely addictive. So many of their plots seemed familiar. As I drank in one improbable episode after another, a few themes began to emerge.

First, the twists and turns are so extravagant that it is easy to get drawn into any one story. They can seem to be separate incidents, their culprits just grotesque aberrations. But across the whole series, the same names keep appearing. These repeated debacles were the work of an interwoven coalition. Often fierce political or economic rivals on the surface, the members of this gang were co-conspirators in perpetuating a syndrome.

Inside the cabal, the bylaw was an unspoken guarantee of impunity. While a handful of perpetrators suffered disgrace and a few years in jail, the "blushing sheriffs" of the day did not arrest their friends—or even their competitors. The guilty survived with their prominent reputations undented. And reputation was essential to prolonging the heist.

To these men, citizens and consumers counted as no more than suckers for fleecing. In the same way that millions of Americans were duped into buying preposterous houses in the early 2000s, so ordinary Europeans—"seduced and reassured" by wealthy investors and respected professional advisors—kept staking money they could not afford to lose.

The Gilded Age financial institutions that lured them to buy all those dodgy securities were at least as concentrated, multinational, interpenetrated—and overleveraged—as ours are today. The large French bank Paribas, for example, was founded in 1872, in a merger between a French and a Dutch bank.* It had stakes in Vienna-based Wiener Bank-Verein, as well as the recently established Deutsche Bank—which in 2017 was fined $7.2 billion for its role in helping to trigger the Great Recession, and is the Trump Organization's most loyal lender. Junius Morgan and his son John Pierpont provided a key bridge for such establishments to the United States.

Underlying most of the speculation these banks promoted were giant infrastructure projects, partly government funded, or at least officially supported. L'Union Générale, the bank whose collapse set off the 1882 crash, was founded to make fortunes on railroad deals— precisely what had wreaked havoc in the United States a decade earlier.

Such public-private partnership arrangements crop up all the time in corrupt developing countries. A chief way the networks I examined siphoned funds out of government budgets was to earmark them for road projects or sports stadiums, to be built by construction conglomerates. Once the money was moved off-budget, private contract law hid the details of how it was spent.

The useless hulks that usually result are known as "white elephants." They are not designed to work; they are designed to enrich people. In "Power Failure: How Utilities Across the U.S. Changed the Rules to Make Big Bets with Your Money," the Charleston, South Carolina, *Post and Courier* investigated changes to state laws across the country that shifted the cost of building new power plants from electric companies to ratepayers. "Utilities tried to build plants with unproven technology," reporter Tony Bartelme found. "They launched projects with unfinished designs and unrealistic budgets; they misled regulators and the public with schedules that promised bogus completion dates; they hid damning reports."

In this context, bipartisan plans for major infrastructure spending bills may be cause for concern, not celebration.

A disturbing realization I came to was this: the late-nineteenth-century syndrome, like the contemporary version, was nonpartisan.

---

* "Netherlands" in French is "Pays Bas." So the bank became La Banque de Paris et des Pays Bas, eventually shortened to Paribas.

The Midas disease and the systemic corruption it bred flourished in the German and Austro-Hungarian empires and in the left-leaning French Third Republic—just as it flourishes today under Egypt's or Pakistan's military regimes, and in both free-market conservative and post-socialist democracies. Without explicit measures to keep it in check, no system of government or political party is inherently immune.

But even the cumulative magnitude of the repeated disasters, the suffering caused to unwitting victims and active participants alike, and the trials inflicted on millions as the price for the luxury of a very few do not seem to have generated many such measures.

The reflex instead was to seek scapegoats. When l'Union Générale bank went down, "an explosion of anger swept the conservative upper classes against the Jews, who had, it was said, caused the disaster," wrote a contemporary reporter and politician known as Mermeix. He dates the rise of organized anti-Semitism in France to that financial disaster. The Panama Canal scandal, in which several Jewish financiers and intermediaries had played key roles, bolstered the blame shifting. "It seems that all of Jewry, high and low, congregated beneath the udder of this milch cow," editorialized the caricature-filled *Libre Parole* (*Free Speech*), a popular anti-Semitic broadsheet launched in 1892. "In the disaster that cost so many French their savings and so many good deputies their reputations, one encounters Jews wherever one turns. They were the authors of this foul mess." Personified by the great Rothschild banking house, Jews, went the stereotype, were too urbane, too comfortable in the cosmopolitan capitals, too close to the money everyone craved.

They were the perfect lightning rod for deflecting public indignation away from the rigged system and its elite beneficiaries.

2

The United States

The best-served beneficiaries were the CEOs of the biggest corporations. Picking through the wreckage in the throes of each panic, they snapped up ruined companies (known today as distressed assets) at a fraction of their worth. Desperation and shock made their victims buckle to brutal terms. In this way, these nineteenth-century vulture capitalists pieced together conglomerates of dimensions unseen in living memory.

In the United States, they are better known today for their works of philanthropy and their art collections than for the way they amassed their fortunes. Even in my mind, when I began exploring this period, Carnegie, Rockefeller, Morgan, and Mellon rhymed with dignified respectability as well as wealth. That confusion was precisely the objective. Also, by founding universities, they shaped mentalities in favor of their business model. John D. Rockefeller's money built the University of Chicago, a leading force in reviving Gilded Age economic thinking and legal norms today.

Several of these men got their start as barefaced war profiteers. For example, Jim Fisk, a broker in gold and railroad stock, won contracts to supply blankets and uniforms to the Union army for Boston's Jordan Marsh Company. For the cloth to fill the orders, he smuggled Confederate cotton through the lines. One of John Pierpont (J. P.) Morgan's youthful crimes was to help flip five thousand breech-loading carbines that the U.S. Army had condemned as obsolete and defective and unloaded for $3.50 each. After getting them

John Pierpont Morgan, at seventy-
five (a year before his death), 1912.

sketchily retooled, Morgan and partners sold the guns right back to
the army for $22 each, for use on the western front.

I couldn't help picturing the scene: young farmhands or schoolteachers, some with the first tufts of beard on their jaws, huddle
behind a chunk of granite. Their bodies reverberate with the din of
a Rebel advance. And in their frightened grip are guns that might
spurt fire at the breech when they pull the trigger, burning or blind-
ing them.

The weapon Jay Cooke sold to the U.S. government during the war
was different: money. (This was the Cooke whose bankruptcy a decade later would trigger the Panic of 1873.) Leveraging a home-state
relationship he and his brothers had cultivated with Treasury Secretary Salmon Chase, he gained exclusive license to market Union war
bonds.

The Cookes were hustlers. They dreamed up the mad idea of mass
marketing securities. Instead of meeting privately with select top
investors to sell the bonds, as was the norm, they turned to small
farmers and clerks on city side streets and village pastors, appealing to their patriotism. While Jay Cooke & Co. was racking up a
prodigious commission on all those small sales, it was also securing
prime access to the only risk-free investments of the age: "those that

Banker Jay Cooke on an 1876 certificate of stock for the Northern Pacific Railroad, a venture that helped bring down Cooke's bank, as the Panic of 1873 struck the United States.

grow out of our connection with the govt," as Jay Cooke wrote to his brother Henry in 1866.

By far the most valuable returns the company reaped from its Civil War bond operation were three intangibles, secured by that same "connection with the govt": first, insider information to manipulate for market advantage; second, influence over government decision-making; and third, a rock-solid public image in turbulent times.

With its Washington office planted opposite the Treasury Department, Jay Cooke & Co. seemed to reflect the power and resources and permanence of the U.S. government itself. So bolstered, it was easy to go back to people who had bought bonds during the recent war, show them some pamphlets glossy with good news, and sucker them into buying shares this time. In particular, Cooke hawked yet another corrupt Pacific railroad: not the Union, but the Northern.

Here was the Humbert method again, something Wilbur Ross and Donald Trump understood perfectly, but that I had not picked up in all my work on developing-country kleptocracy. Here was exemplified the vital importance to the whole operation of a projected image of wealth.

These men were geniuses, obviously. But not the type of genius they are often made out to be. They were the kind of genius brought to the screen by Lana, the prostitute in *Risky Business*. These were criminal masterminds. Indeed, they were far more dangerous than the stagecoach robbers whose capture sometimes competed for space on newspaper front pages with trials of railroad executives.

With no compunctions, these men took actions that maimed soldiers or got them killed, that destroyed businesses employing millions of machinists and carpenters and clerks and shopkeepers. They took actions that led to the near extermination of the original human inhabitants of the land, and of bison and wolves, whose lifeways incarnated and nourished Native Americans' opposing worldview, actions that robbed tens of thousands of settler farm families of their savings and property—and of items of greater, if unseen, worth.

These latter victims were the people whose way of life had been foundational—in the national mythology, and in fact—to American democracy. These were families proud of their autonomy, their ability to provide for themselves, with meat they had raised and cured, with vegetables that took planning and placement and tending and hours of processing for the winter, with fruit in season, and with grain that they could sell, even overseas. They were families who loved the landscapes they were part of, as indigenous peoples had long before them, who loved the homes they had raised and beautified with whittled carvings, curtains, a treasured photograph. They were families proud of the independence that this hard-won self-sufficiency afforded them. That freedom was part of who they were.

Through the actions of men like Jay Cooke, these families were abruptly insolvent. The places they had tended for so long were foreclosed, the acreage, like that on the native nations' steadily dwindling reservations, bought up by speculators or large out-of-town concerns. The crafted objects, the memories and the learning of generations, had no market value. People whose grandparents had cleared the slopes and bottoms, or who, freed from slavery, had somehow managed to buy the ground they tilled, often found themselves working the same fields as before. But now they were reduced to peonage or wage labor, subject to the boss. Millions of other evictees—who had themselves evicted the first lovers and tenders of this land—packed their scattered belongings and joined the faceless men and women who were being swallowed by the steel mills and factories of the burgeoning industrial towns.

What was being enacted through this process was a vast transfer of monetary wealth, but also of other intangible and sacred values deeply embedded in the American identity: the grappling with a still wild place; the belongingness to community, small, interdependent, and egalitarian; and, not least, liberty. The megacorporations of the Gilded Age were creating and enforcing a gaping imbalance between laborers and employers in freedom. Slaves so recently released were finding that the change meant not so much. Even wage earners were coerced into selling what they held to be their "selves"—the strength of their bodies, their creativity, their diligence—at rates and terms they could not affect.

As early as 1861, with a baleful and potentially nation-ending war already strewing Americans' entrails on the dirt within a few hours' horseback ride of the capital, President Abraham Lincoln took time to warn of this danger. In his first State of the Union address, he used vocabulary that today might be considered socialist. He wished, he said, to draw his listeners' attention to "the effort to place capital on an equal footing with, if not above, labor in the structure of government." But labor, the rail-splitter-turned-lawyer declared,

> is prior to and independent of capital. Capital is only the fruit of labor, and could never have existed if labor had not first existed. Labor is the superior of capital, and deserves much the higher consideration. . . . Let [workers] beware of surrendering a political power which they already possess, and which if surrendered will surely be used to close the door of advancement against such as they and to fix new disabilities and burdens upon them till all of liberty shall be lost.

Men like Cooke and Morgan and Carnegie were forcing the surrender Lincoln warned of. They fixed those new "disabilities and burdens" on their fellow Americans. They rigged the system.

Then these moguls unleashed savage violence against the laborers who did the work upon which their stock-market returns were based, because a few more cents per hour, or minimal safety measures in the mines or the plants, or lower freight rates for farmers, might cut into the money that was already so plentiful in their hands that they wrapped it around cigarettes and smoked it.

Without considering consequences, they unleashed an orgy of exploitation of the land and its resources—achieved at the price of a genocide—that in a brief century would alter the chemistry of the planet.

For this type of sociopath, two obvious career tracks lie open: organized crime or systemic corruption, whereby the wrongdoers participate in making and enforcing the rules, so their crimes gain cover of legality. The second is rather less risky.

That is the course the American titans of the Gilded Age chose. In the drama that unfolded during those last three decades of the nineteenth century, I discovered a process that I recognized, because I had lived through something like it in Afghanistan. Beneath what is usually framed in economic terms as corporate consolidation, I saw clusters of people sorting themselves out into relatively stable, rival—yet often allied—corruption networks.

First came the free-for-all. That reminded me of the years right after the United States toppled the Taliban government in 2001, when I lived in their former capital, Kandahar. Those were days of chaotic and sometimes violent clashes among warlords seeking to capture the juiciest revenue streams. Their webs of kin and friends included government officials, the heads of private companies that implemented foreign-financed development projects, and the opium dealers who for many months kept shop in stalls clustered in a corner of the bazaar not far from where I lived. Once, police officers were ambushed by a private militia loyal to the governor.

The ambitious industrialists in the United States of the 1870s and 1880s may not have brandished rocket launchers and AK-47s. But, as former steamboat man Cornelius Vanderbilt and his sons squared off against Jay Gould and partners Jim Fisk and Daniel Drew, or Gould took on legendary trader James Keene, the combat was equally bitter.

Blood was not the substance spilled in these knife fights. The wounds bled what had become an even more prized life force: money.

Erratically, but almost inevitably, this competition gave way to covenants among rivals. Early—often temporary—rate-fixing pools, especially among railroad bosses or steel manufacturers, spawned more permanent agreements. Rockefeller's careful moves with a clutch of allies to force rival oil refineries out of business gave him control of that entire, soon-to-be-essential industry. Pacts among salt, beef, or whiskey producers to fix prices and output and divide up orders attracted attention too, in time. It was a somewhat later, fully transnational cartel of lightbulb manufacturers, called the Phoebus cartel, that gave the world planned obsolescence. Its members agreed to deliberately reduce the average lifespan of their product to boost sales. Starting from an average 1,500 to 2,000 hours, engineers trained themselves to design mediocrity, rather than valuing excellence, in order to meet the new standard of 1,000 hours.

Before long came more structured trusts. Their aim was to consolidate decision-making for a large number of interlocking companies in the hands of a few super-shareholders. With J. P. Morgan's purchase of Andrew Carnegie's steel empire and then of land rich in iron ore that Rockefeller owned, a super-trust was born. U.S. Steel, the world's first billion-dollar conglomerate, welded several leading industries to the country's top financial institution. To my eyes, that looked like a thick private-sector strand of a Gilded Age kleptocratic network.

Then, as now, three sources of revenue dominated all these activities: finance, energy, and high-end real estate.

Many histories of this period focus on the business transactions and individual members of the new big-money aristocracy. It is in passing that the accounts reveal how purposefully the financiers and industrialists braided themselves into networks. They married their children into one another's families. They exchanged positions on boards of directors, so each had some say in how his allies operated. They leaned on hometown connections. The dense fabrics they knit in these ways were flexible enough to adapt to changing situations and to withstand the snapping of a few threads.

Public officials did not just lurk around the edges, pocketing a few bribes. They were woven tight into the fabric, no less active than their industrialist partners. The Cooke brothers' long-standing relationship with Salmon Chase is one example. President Ulysses S. Grant was another Cooke friend. Woodrow Wilson was connected (and indebted) to several top Wall Street financiers, some by way of his years at Princeton University. Vanderbilt lobbied the New York State legislature side by side with Tammany Hall's Boss Tweed.

According to historian Matthew Josephson, "The masters of business who sat in the upper chamber of Congress (or 'Millionaires' Club,' as it was humorously called), or their close associates who became Representatives or governors of states, make up a long and distinguished roll." It takes him the rest of the page to reel off even some of their names.

This interpenetration allowed the networks to leverage the agencies and functions of federal and state government. They secured laws made to order. They got protective tariffs slapped on goods they produced. In contracts with the United States, they got terms unfavorable to the government—that is, to their fellow citizens. Government negotiators were acting on behalf not of those citizens, as their positions required them to, but of the networks.

Another scientist who explores the origins of human morality is primatologist Richard Wrangham. Like his colleague Christopher Boehm, he notes the way coalitions enforced egalitarianism by slapping down their domineering would-be alphas—if need be, by executing them. But Wrangham spends more time on what happened later in the human story. What was it that, with the spread of agriculture perhaps ten thousand years ago, caused humans to go back to dominating and submitting, like apes? Again, the answer seems simple: "They do it via coalitions." Would-be dominators saw they could get back on top if they formed a coalition of their own.

As primates, moreover, we carry within us a latent tendency toward submissiveness, more pronounced in some individuals than others. Dominator coalitions reinforce that tendency.

The results, in the Gilded Age, shaped nearly every aspect of political and economic life. Members of an emerging "money trust" were able to design the Federal Reserve System to their liking—with big financiers largely in control. When workers protested wage reductions, twelve-hour shifts, or the deliberate elimination of their jobs, or when they tried to band together in unions the way their bosses were organizing in trusts, "the army of the Nation, and all its militia" was called in "to compel obedience to its laws."

Those words, which approved a bloody crackdown on railroad strikers in 1894, came from the Supreme Court's opinion in *In re Debs*. Rulings like this, which supported the corruption networks' interests, came down year after year from courts at every level.

Despite the Interstate Commerce and Sherman Antitrust Acts, for example, monopolies and "conspiracies to control domestic enterprise in manufacture, agriculture, mining, production in all its forms, or to raise or lower prices or wages," were declared perfectly legal. But, citing the very same laws that they refused to apply to corporations owned by members of their networks, judges fired off injunctions like a "Gatling gun on paper," as one of them put it, against striking workers. Workers who applauded the actions or helped organize them were jailed for the crime of conspiracy.

Thanks largely to Supreme Court justice Stephen Field, railroads even succeeded in wrenching one of the great post–Civil War constitutional amendments away from its initial purpose. Designed to guarantee newly freed slaves the right to legal recourse ("due process of the law"), and the same protection under the laws that other citizens received, the Fourteenth Amendment was applied in practice not to freedmen and -women at all, or even to people, but instead to corporations.

Field was a friend of California railroad magnate (and Stanford University founder) Leland Stanford. Several years before railroads brought any of the key cases, Field surreptitiously slipped statements on corporations' Fourteenth Amendment rights into rulings on matters not directly relevant. That way, he created precedent.

According to a 1912 study, less than 5 percent of Fourteenth Amendment cases decided by that year concerned freedmen—who usually lost. Megacorporations, on the other hand, had used the amendment hundreds of times to overturn laws guaranteeing minimum wages or worker protections, or imposing meaningful taxation on businesses.

Charles Francis Adams, a railroad executive himself, but born to a house of public servants, leveled this scathing assessment of the Gilded Age:

The offices of our great corporations appeared as the secret chambers in which trustees plotted the spoliation of their wards; the law became a ready engine for the furtherance of wrong, and the ermine of the judge did not conceal the eagerness of the partisan; the halls of legislation were transformed into a mart in which the price of votes was haggled over, and laws, made to order, were bought and sold; while under all, and through all, the voice of public opinion was silent or was disregarded.

American citizens—those men created equal for whom the Republic had been founded—were stripped of recourse. In such situations, I have found, victims go to extremes.

These perversions of the American ideal of government by and for the people, "this evil," wrote Adams, had "its root deep down in the social organization." It lay in the most ferocious case of the Midas disease yet contracted in the United States. It is not that Americans hadn't lusted for money before that. But the accounts of the extreme displays of riches during those years—down to the cigarettes rolled in hundred-dollar bills and diamond-studded dog collars—are hard to read.

Equally striking is the apparent indifference of these nineteenth-century Midases to the worth of what their wealth got them. They did not care much for the incomparable works of art they stuck up on their walls, or even for the social relationships to which they gained access. What mattered—all that mattered—was the money. "The acquisition of wealth," Adams observed, was "the single worthy aim of life."

What other lacks did these men suffer? What gaping hole were they trying to fill by shoving fistfuls of dollars down it? What hunger was this addiction failing to address? Where were their hearts really broken?

Their obsession was stoked by a public opinion that was, in Adams's view, "diseased." People failed to see the money infatuation's menace. Americans of all classes adulated the superrich, no matter where their money came from. Everyone could see the destruction the mania was wreaking. Everybody knew that many of these men lacked honor, integrity, education, even decent table manners. And still, writes historian Matthew Josephson, the magnates' money bathed them in "almost universal esteem." It gained them unquestioned entrée into the highest social circles.

That approval is curious in a species that for millennia survived and made its mark by sternly slapping down bullies who tried to grab more than their fair share of game all had hunted together. How is such admiration possible in a primate that still abhors an unfair advantage?

For, if this plunge into the history of the Gilded Age delivers one certainty, it is this: there is no way to access infinite wealth without rigging the system. No one becomes a billionaire honestly.

The Late-Born Baron

There is someone who worked this rigged system with special skill. Rarely mentioned in the same breath as a Mellon or a Carnegie, he was one of them, or tried to be: Joseph P. Kennedy, father of future president John F. For reasons more to do with timing than religion, he never made it. He is worth a pause, however, because his career is so illustrative of the era—and how it ended.

Born in 1888, when the Gilded Age money-and-corruption syndrome was at its height, Kennedy was a product of the local version of the period's kleptocratic networks: the machine politics that dominated every major city. At his birth, his father, Patrick, was a state representative and rising ward boss in East Boston. A gnarled finger thrust into Boston Harbor, the neighborhood bristled with the wharves and docks where so many Irishmen found work.

Making of his saloon a trusted meeting place for local politicians, Patrick (P. J.) Kennedy had entered their ranks. On the side, he bought into the standard Gilded Age industries, if in a modest way. He became a whiskey wholesaler during the reign of an infamous trust in that industry. He invested in coal. He founded a bank.

For a bride, his son Joseph set his heart on the most eligible Catholic girl in town: the daughter of two-time mayor John Francis Fitzgerald, or "Honey Fitz." While the Boston machine never became as large or as powerful as New York's Tammany Hall, the Honey Fitz administration was wracked by all the same vices as Tweed's: vote stealing and intimidation by local gangsters, real estate purchases by officials while they planned public development projects for the same parcels of land, the award of city jobs to patently unsuitable cronies, extortion, and ostentatious graft in public procurement.

Standing in for her austere mother, young Rose Fitzgerald (soon to be Kennedy) served as the mayor's consort on the galloping whirl of his public activities. After she married Joe, he joined his father-in-law's coterie, helping with Honey Fitz's 1918 congressional campaign. The razor-thin election was so visibly fraud-laced that Congress immediately investigated and expelled Fitzgerald from its ranks.

The Kennedy couple was forged in the crucible of Gilded Age corruption.

Being Irish—and well-connected Irish—Kennedy did not have to work to weave a network. In the face of ugly discrimination and brutal working conditions, the Irish immigrants who landed in America's burgeoning cities in the middle and late nineteenth century depended on ties of family and county of origin to survive and gain a foothold—and for some, as they moved on to control the city, to extract profits by rigging the system.

But Kennedy added another, quite different, network to the one he came into by birthright. Very unusually for an Irish Catholic, he attended Harvard University. Friends he made there became lifelong collaborators.

In keeping with his time—and more fully than his father did— Joseph P. espoused his era's guiding principle: the glorification and pursuit of infinite wealth. Upon graduation, his entire ambition was expressed in those reductive terms. No thought of contribution to his or any other community seems to have entered his mind. At twenty-five, Kennedy boasted he would make his first million before a decade was out—more than $26 million in 2020 dollars. (He almost did.)

The Gilded Age had generated a defining sector. Logically, it was banking. J. P. Morgan had consummated the consolidation of U.S. Steel a decade before, and the vertical integration of the conglomerate with his banking house. Finance was now fully established as the economic force in the country, controlling most major industries. "The turn of the century," Doris Kearns Goodwin writes in *The Fitzgeralds and the Kennedys,* "was the age of the banker."

Banking is where Kennedy went.

A few weeks before his 1912 graduation, the House Committee on Banking and Currency opened a high-profile investigation into excessive concentration in the financial-services industry—otherwise known as monopoly. Collusive speculation and stock manipulation on the part of an insidious "money trust" were exposed to view. Though the investigation and report sparked national outrage, the noise did not register with Kennedy. He remained transfixed by the underlying reality—the power of finance. That reality survived the uproar essentially unchanged.

At twenty-five, Kennedy staved off a hostile takeover of his father's bank by feverishly tapping members of his two networks for loans. Then he elbowed his father aside and took over the establishment. Kennedy became the youngest bank president in the state, basking in the media attention.

A minor Irish institution in a sector locked up by Boston Brahmins, Columbia Trust was a bit player in this world. Still, the title of bank president and lavish coverage in the *Boston Post* gave Kennedy those three key elements of the Gilded Age business model: the appearance of wealth, a supply of other people's money to speculate with, and a dignified reputation.

At Columbia and especially when he joined a brokerage firm later, Kennedy trained himself in the skills that guaranteed outsized returns. This was during the 1920s. Gilded Age speculation fever was spiking again, after the sobering blow of World War I.

Kennedy grabbed distressed assets when mini-bubbles burst. He aggressively pursued insider information—an unfair advantage that was legal at the time. He bought stock for himself under cover of other people's names. He tried to divine which industry might be the epoch-changing—and capital-hungry—innovation that the railroads had been fifty years before, and the technology sector was to become in the 1990s. Settling on the fledgling motion picture industry, Kennedy led Wall Street's invasion of Hollywood, just as J. P. Morgan and other bankers had taken over railroads.

As with the railroads, what followed was the merciless consolidation of independent studios amid stock profiteering. Kennedy's fortune was made.

The same sharp nose prompted him to begin selling down his portfolio in early 1929. The sobriety of World War I, like a morning fog long burned away, Wall Street blazed. Top bankers jubilantly swallowed their own line of jive. The words spoken that year, the mouths that uttered them, the tones of confidence were nearly identical to what we heard in the lead-up to 2008. "I know of nothing fundamentally wrong with the stock market," proclaimed Charles E. Mitchell—the man at the helm of the precursor to Citi—a week before the 1929 crash.

But Kennedy broke with such "self-hypnotized spellbinders"—as another of his biographers, Richard Whalen, calls them. By November, he had eased himself out of the market.

Then, with pandemonium all around him—but with his faith in his own abilities reinforced by having gotten right what so many who looked down on him had gotten wrong—Kennedy planted himself in an office on Wall Street and commenced trading. He methodically decided "which stocks to sell short and why."

He engaged, in other words, in precisely the conduct that would prolong the Depression and the miseries it visited on so many of his neighbors and others around the world. Those miseries, many argue, helped make Germans receptive to Hitler's message and helped bring on World War II.

There was almost certainly one further dimension to Kennedy's activities—one other strand to his personal integrated network. Though it rarely arises in accounts of the major Gilded Age moguls, it is a strand I fully expected to see in my survey of this era.

Every kleptocratic network I have examined, from Afghanistan to Honduras to Central Asian or African countries, has included a skein of outright criminals. Drug traffickers sit down with the brothers or the sons of presidents, at tables lavishly set with lunch, and strike business deals. Smugglers move taxed consumer goods, uncounted and unweighed, across borders for a network that may include the head of customs enforcement. Or they move guns or sex workers. Self-styled militias, or assassins or straight-up thugs—often former military or police officers—place chilling calls or smash kidneys or fire predawn shots into a warm bed—not just for their private purposes, but on behalf of integrated networks.

It is highly doubtful that none of the U.S. railroad barons took part in any of the profitable vices that oiled the lawless West. It may be that—many of their criminal beginnings behind them—the Morgans or Rockefellers of the day gained so much legal cover for practices that were so much more lucrative that the most successful had little need for outright, violent criminality. Persistent rumors, however—and also real evidence—suggest that Kennedy did.

Investigative journalist Seymour Hersh has looked most deeply into this issue. In *The Dark Side of Camelot,* he draws on years of interviews with Kennedy aides, former government officials, mafiosi speaking at the end of their lives, or their biographers or confidants, as well as congressional testimony and FBI documents. I am not equipped to corroborate this reporting. But Hersh makes a convincing argument that Kennedy frequently did business with organized crime.

Marshaling votes for Honey Fitz in his early days, he probably called in muscular help from recently arrived Italian immigrants. His lucrative post-Prohibition liquor importing business may have built upon bootlegging operations during the dry years. It certainly ended with the sale of the Kennedy enterprise, Somerset Importers, to a well-known crime family. And there are strong indications that in 1960, Joseph P. helped his son gain the delegates needed to win the Democratic nomination, and the electoral votes to gain the Oval Office, by asking the Giancana Mafia family to weigh in with allied unions, especially in West Virginia and Illinois.

If Kennedy differed from most of the earlier Gilded Age figures in his likely flirtation with wrongdoing that was nakedly criminal, there was something else that marked him out. That thing was desperately important to him. Unlike the previous generation of banker-industrialists, money alone never gained Joseph P. Kennedy the entrée into America's highest social circles that he craved.

His many biographers unanimously emphasize Kennedy's desire for status, his insatiable need for social standing. "If an Irishman could not wrest social acceptance from the unbending Yankees, who were tightfisted with that commodity even among themselves," writes Richard Whalen of the start of Kennedy's career, "Kennedy decided he could earn respect in the marketplace." "With all his growing success in the world of business," Doris Kearns Goodwin recounts, describing an episode in the early 1920s, "he was still denied the taste of the full sweetness of social acceptance." After World War II, writes Whalen, "an empty title and the notoriety bestowed by riches could not satisfy his hunger for prestige."

None of the authors quite spells out *why* Kennedy could never achieve this overriding ambition.

Perhaps the problem was his Irish and Catholic heritage, an identity that no Harvard diploma, no clothes or cars or zero-stuffed bank account could make haughty Protestants overlook. But that does not quite sound right. Andrew Carnegie was born to a hand-loom weaver in a Scottish stone cottage; his mother helped the family skirt starvation by working as a cobbler's assistant. Did Americans really make such fine distinctions between two famished eastern Atlantic headlands? And anyway, Joseph Kennedy was hardly scraping sod off his boots when he entered business. He was the Harvard-educated son-in-law of the celebrated mayor of one of the nation's founding cities. Could religion alone make such a difference?

Perhaps it was his birth in Boston, not New York. By Kennedy's day, the seat of banking power had migrated south and north from Boston and Philadelphia, respectively, to Manhattan. No Boston-based investor, the suggestion goes, could stand side by side with Wall Street giants.

Or maybe it was Kennedy's loner temperament. He only ever bonded with his own family or a few retainers. Another possibility some biographers suggest is hubris, his decision to leave banking for diplomacy on the eve of World War II, as though the skills and judgment of the one would easily apply to the other.

There may be another reason, however. It has less to do with Kennedy's personality than with changing times. What if Kennedy was welded to the ethos of an earlier time, when the world around him was at last transmuting? What if Joseph Kennedy was born twenty years too late for a man of his Gilded Age ambition and principles? Perhaps by the time Kennedy reached manhood, the Midas disease was going into remission. Perhaps just being filthy rich was no longer what it took to make a person's fellow citizens, low and lofty, bow down in adoration.

Kennedy's choices later in his career do suggest an intuition that the country's mores had changed. The intense desire for a position in the Roosevelt administration that he displayed, after throwing himself into the campaign, marks a pivot from his prior single-minded pursuit of wealth. Stung by the silence that emanated from the new president long months after his inauguration, Kennedy sent hinting letters and telegrams, chatted up Roosevelt's secretary, paid an inconclusive visit, and, insulted, even considered suing the Democratic National Committee for repayment of a loan.

A plum appointment was hardly an unfamiliar aim for men like him. Private-sector members of Gilded Age networks had secured key posts in government in earlier years. In fact, doing so is central to kleptocratic networks' operating system.

Richard Olney, for example, was still drawing a salary as a lawyer for at least one railroad company after he was sworn in as attorney general in 1893. Pulling the levers that position offered, he plunged the federal government into the bitter Pullman railroad strike. He appointed one of the affected railways' general counsel as special prosecutor in Chicago. He got federal troops sent in against the workers. That was the bloody crackdown the Supreme Court applauded in *In re Debs*. It was Olney who promoted the use of court injunctions as a pretext for pitting the U.S. Army against American citizens. Or there was Andrew Mellon, bank president, financier-owner of conglomerates in aluminum and electricity as well as such Gilded Age standards as shipbuilding, railroad, and coal, who was the pre-Depression secretary of treasury.

But such men's objective was different from Kennedy's. They were not in government to enhance their social status. They had social status. They were there to weave the threads that would tie the government into their networks, to use its powers to protect and facilitate their operations. They were there to aid in the pillaging of the public purse, to harness the powers of their agencies to serve their networks' purposes: to rewrite the rules. They were there to rig the system.

Like many of them, Kennedy did use his proximity to power to make some money. He cultivated a cynical friendship with Roosevelt's son, for example, and sailed with him for London in Prohibition's waning days. Impressed by this sign of the new president's friendship, deferential distillers made Kennedy their exclusive importer. Later, as ambassador, he used the diplomatic pouch to ship product for Somerset Importers.

But it does not seem that Kennedy sought government office primarily as a moneymaking venture. Nor is there much evidence that his aim was to fix the game in favor of himself and others like him. In office, he did not do that—on the contrary.

When he did finally get a job offer, it was a stunner. To the consternation of Roosevelt confidant Louis Howe and dedicated New Dealers such as Harold Ickes, and Roy Howard of the Scripps-Howard newspapers, the president named Kennedy chairman of the newly minted Securities and Exchange Commission. As his first game warden, in other words, Roosevelt chose an accomplished poacher.

And yet, far from protecting his erstwhile friends on Wall Street, Kennedy reined in the speculators' worst excesses—practices with which he was so familiar. By all accounts, he acquitted himself with distinction.

His objective in seeking public service, it seems, was to gain not more zeroes in his bank account, but rather the social acceptance that money alone had not delivered. That was new. In the high Gilded Age, no mogul saw public service as a potential badge of honor. By the mid-1930s, something was changing.

In the end, Kennedy failed spectacularly at this foray onto what was such unfamiliar ground for him: the public interest. After running the SEC and the Maritime Commission—a critical post with a war looming—he won what was the highly prestigious position of ambassador to London. But Kennedy proved incapable of living up to the values and principles of the emerging public-spirited ethos.

Finding in British prime minister Neville Chamberlain a kindred business-oriented mind, Kennedy championed his desperate effort to avoid hostilities with Germany. Growing ever more intimate with the embattled British prime minister, Kennedy violated a rule he had lived by all his life: avoiding personal attachments that might entail risk.

Joe Kennedy's fateful final foray into public service: being sworn
in as U.S. ambassador to the United Kingdom. He resigned the
position in disgrace in 1940.

Kennedy had always been opposed to war. In war he feared the
bogeyman of destruction—not so much of human life, but of wealth
and property. He dreaded that inevitable result of a generalized conflict with Germany. Kennedy also recoiled at the "collectivist demands" that another vast war might unleash, and their effects on what
was left of the Gilded Age version of capitalism. Even "Nazism—
with all its objectionable features—was, to him, preferable" to a whiff
of such communistic principles.

After Kristallnacht, a nightlong orgy of murder, rape, and looting through their ghettoes, Kennedy gave his name to an idea for
deporting German citizens of Jewish faith or background to Africa
and Latin America. In effect, he was a proponent of ethnic cleansing. In the spring of 1939—against Roosevelt's orders—he met with
Goering's right-hand man to discuss a large loan of gold to Germany.

Before long, Kennedy was backstabbing his erstwhile friend
Roosevelt to British officials, in terms that were relayed back to
Washington by embassy staff.

After Chamberlain announced London's declaration of war, terminating public ambivalence, Kennedy told anyone who would listen that his host country didn't stand "a Chinaman's chance" of beating Berlin. He redoubled his lobbying to keep the United States neutral. Secretly, Roosevelt opened a direct channel to Winston Churchill.

When Churchill became prime minister in 1940, Kennedy could not quite grasp why he was no longer welcome at 10 Downing Street. Roosevelt took to working around him. In February 1941, Kennedy resigned, never to play a public role again. The path of public service, on behalf of a more egalitarian society than the one that flourished in the Gilded Age—as well as the prestige to be gained from such a career—was a destiny left to his sons.

III

THE HYDRA

1980s–

1

———

"Eight Mortal Heads"

Thus, in the Gilded Age, was spawned in Europe and the United States precisely the species of network I have studied in developing countries. "Network" may not be the right word. Sometimes they seem like living organisms that coil across and through the recognizable sectors and institutions of society—the ones with names, like "political parties" or "the nonprofit sector." They grasp key instruments of state, enhancing their own powers, and digest others down, till all form or function is lost.

The creature that may capture this notion best comes not from current zoology, but, again, from Greek mythology.

In the swamps of Lerna, goes the lore, where the three fingers of southernmost Greece hang into the Aegean Sea, dwelled a monster. She had the body of a serpent, but where her head should be, her torso sprouted not one, but nine. Her "eight mortal heads" formed a writhing thicket, "with a ninth in the middle that was immortal." So recounts a Greek compiler of such treasured stories, writing in the second century AD. But who could even tell the number of heads? Another author puts it at a hundred.

This "Hydra, many-necked, flickering its dread tongues" exhaled poisonous gas with its very breath. Anyone who ventured near would perish. Its blood was a flesh-liquefying toxin.

But the worst feature of this creature was the behavior of its heads. Sprouting from a single body, they struck with apparently independent design. Yet all their several actions served one common pur-

Hydra, many-necked. Etruscan black-figure vase, attributed to the Eagle
Painter, ca. 520 BC.

pose: to sustain the Hydra as a whole. One account includes this
further detail: "the middle head . . . was of gold."

The Hydra has remained a potent image into modern times.
"There is no terrorist organization more malevolent, nor influential,
than Hydra," Marvel Inc. says of a 1960s series. Its fictional network
is bent on establishing a neo-fascist order across the globe. Of ancient
origins, it was restructured by a Nazi genius after World War II,
using his personal fortune and wartime plunder. "Hydra's power lies
in its hundreds of leaders, operatives, and supporters," Marvel tells
us. It "has allied itself with other criminal organizations, including
A.I.M. (Advanced Idea Mechanics)," and even "Norman Osborn's
law enforcement agency."

The Hydra is an apt metaphor for the elusive and dynamic kleptocratic structures I am talking about. Or you could see them as
primatologist Richard Wrangham's dominator coalitions. Another
helpful way of understanding them is, indeed, as a particular species
of social network. I will use all three.

I first started thinking about networks in Afghanistan. Advising the
military, I would get invited to forward bases to share my unusual

street-level perspective. Clumping in my stiff boots across gravel likely bought at a ridiculous price from a cousin of the local strong-man to a plywood shack festooned with the latest electronics, I'd be treated to an intel-ops brief.

The young intelligence officer would click through slides depict-ing local Taliban commanders' networks of associates. They would show headshots of some men, wearing beards and turbans like all my friends, and baleful black silhouettes standing in for targets not yet photographed. Branching lines connecting the pictures indicated the relationships.

Afghans, I realized, as I contemplated the slides, think in network diagrams. If I ran into a friend standing on a street with someone I didn't recognize, my friend would not introduce the man by telling me what he did for a living. He'd say: "Sarah, meet Ahmad Shah. In fact, you know him! He's Shir Khan's brother-in-law." Inside my mind, a line would shoot out from this man's face to a picture—one of those blank silhouettes—marked "Shir Khan." My friend would read my puzzled expression, and add, "Shir Khan, remember? Muhammad Ibrahim's cousin." Or he'd give me the name of a tribe: "His people are Barakzais, in Arghandab District." There aren't many Barakzais in Arghandab, so I'd chime in with a name, which my friend's companion would recognize, and he'd launch into a story about that person.

In other words, my friend would give me the clues I needed to ex-tend the network map I carried around in my head until one of its branching lines touched the man standing beside him, who was sud-denly no longer a stranger to me. Knowing where that man fit in the local networks told me a lot about him.

This process—called "link analysis"—is a science. Police depart-ments use it to help understand organized crime gangs. The branch-ing lines may extend across oceans. Today's analysts scrape social media and other big data sources and run specialized software to sort for patterns. Using techniques of this type, political scientists John Padgett and Christopher Ansell showed how, in early 1400s Florence, Cosimo de' Medici built a crosscutting network like the ones that dominate so many corrupt countries today. It survived for three hundred years and helped launch the modern banking industry.

After the intelligence officers showed me their slides, I would ask if they had worked up a different diagram, one featuring the local political and business leaders, the contractors or heads of NGOs with which the base did business. That slide would show how enmeshed those seemingly separate spheres of activity were, how network members or their cousins played roles in the different sectors. It would show how a single integrated web was snagging all the benefits the Americans brought and was wielding the American military as a weapon against its rivals. Some of its branching lines would even reach across to the officers' Taliban diagram. "Good guys" and "bad guys" would be knitted together.

No such diagram was ever plotted.

For the United States, two books provide this type of analysis. *Dark Money,* by *New Yorker* staff writer Jane Mayer, and *Democracy in Chains,* by historian Nancy MacLean, are must-reads for any American citizen. Through painstaking, even dangerous sleuthing, the authors chart the development of a U.S. integrated kleptocratic network like the ones that dominate so many developing countries. It is the most sophisticated, powerful, and threatening such organism to anchor itself in the United States since the Gilded Age.

Swaying like the thicket of its hydra necks are captains of the most lucrative industries in the country—fossil fuels, private investment firms (especially those specialized in distressed assets), the tobacco industry, and such trademarks as Amway, Home Depot, and Coors. This many-tentacled entity has twined outward over the past several decades. At its center, like the Hydra's golden head, rises the multi-billionaire energy, mining, and chemical mogul Charles Koch.

His network has created or at least partially absorbed dozens of special-purpose nonprofits, from the Cause of Action Institute to the Federalist Society to the Independent Women's Forum and the State Policy Network. Sowing bewilderment, many of these entities frequently change their names.

Koch and his network allies have financed programs or whole schools within leading universities, such as the Mercatus Center at George Mason University, or Stanford's Hoover Institution. And the group has seated thousands of public officials, from state legislators and members of Congress to judges to the bureaucrats who do most of the work in federal, state, and local agencies.

Career paths of network members snake through these different entities and sectors, knitting them together. The aim is "to get top operatives exposed to the different elements," MacLean told me. "People shuttle from one to another: the corporate side, various non-profit advocacy groups, the leading academic centers, and government itself." The result, boasts an operative quoted by Mayer, is "a fully integrated network."

I asked one former insider what this hydra wants. Though its serpent heads weave and strike independently, he told me, they have a "common cause. And it is frightening. They want private, not democratic, control of the country's resources."

MacLean puts it this way: "They want to protect their infinite wealth-accumulation from democracy. They want permanent, radical rules changes that would shackle the majority's ability to chart our collective future. Up to and including changing the Constitution."

"I've heard that for years," confirms the former insider. "They are pushing for a Constitutional convention so they can rewrite the Commerce Clause, to make federal labor laws like child protections or the minimum wage impossible." The aim, writes MacLean, is to lock in "the kind of political economy that prevailed in America in the opening of the twentieth century"—that is, the Gilded Age.

This network operates on the terrain of ideas. And it plays a long game. Capitalizing on calls for civics education in high school, for example, members are moving to reorient the nation's moral compass. "They want to imbue kids with market-based morality," says the former insider. That is, the notion that everything is worth, in moral terms, the price it can fetch—that there is no such thing as a sacred value.

For now, young adults seem perhaps to be leaning in the opposite direction. But this goal suggests one reason why privatizing education is such a hotly contested issue.

In the shorter term, a rewrite of the Constitution may seem fanciful. But thirty-three states have applied to Congress in one form or another to convene a convention, though some have retracted. It takes two-thirds, or thirty-four.

Thanks to the work of investigators like Mayer and MacLean and a growing counternetwork of campus and other activists, this Koch web and its success in shaping the political economy of the United States is finally gaining attention.

But it is not alone. Interweaving with it is a coalition of CEOs of the top companies in the U.S. Chamber of Commerce. Like a fairy-tale cloak that confers invisibility, the Chamber's mainstream aura makes it easy to overlook, especially in light of the apparently more extreme Koch entities. While these allies may compete or disagree on tactics, the groups' playbooks and overall objectives largely align.

The personal relationships I learned to scan for in Afghanistan—marriage and kinship ties, the intimacy born of war horrors endured side by side—may not be the vital ligaments connecting U.S. networks that they are elsewhere. Better anchored U.S. institutions do more of the binding. And then there's money, that leveler. In the United States, where money is like blood, the main requirement for membership in these variations on the foreign kleptocratic networks I studied is lots of zeroes in one's bank account. And the obsession to keep adding more.

Still, a few minutes clicking internet links can give way to a compulsive hunt for headshots and the branching lines that link them.

Take former secretary of state Madeleine Albright. She presides over two allied entities. One is an international consulting firm, the Albright Stonebridge Group. Its business model consists mostly in leveraging Albright's reputation and the relationships with developing country leaders she gained as secretary of state to win favors for large U.S. corporations.

On the advisory board of this company sits someone I did not expect to find: Thomas Donohue. President of the U.S. Chamber of Commerce since 1997, Donohue is the man who converted what had been a loose trade association into a structured network allied with Koch's.

A repeat client at Albright Stonebridge is an investment fund called Elliott Management. Its "Who We Are" page proclaims that it is run by sometime Koch network acolyte Paul Singer, his son Gordon, and a second Koch network regular, Steven Cohen. Elliott is known for buying up the debt of corrupt third-world countries at a discount, then filing lawsuits to get payment in full—out of strapped budgets that are supposed to provide clean drinking water, schools, and health care to impoverished populations.

Albright's other business is a hedge fund. It is run by her son-in-law, Gregory Bowes. Close family ties do keep showing up in U.S. networks after all.

In 2011, Albright Capital Management bought APR Energy, which specializes in pop-up electricity plants. I remember one of those from Afghanistan. It ran on filthy diesel that had made its way across the Pakistani desert, swapped en route for a lower grade than what had been purchased. I would go over for dinner with the South African engineers who maintained the behemoth and listen to them curse having to change its $30,000 filters every week or so.

APR promotes itself to the mining industry in Africa, where resource extraction enriches a handful of kleptocratic elites and leaves local people mired in pollution and conflict. Many of APR's contracts are with the U.S. Agency for International Development, which reports to the State Department, where Albright was secretary.

So just visualize the network map for a moment. Its branching lines connect the U.S. government and people who control a hefty budget line, kleptocratic networks from some of the most notorious countries in Africa and Latin America, the conservative Koch network and its allies in the U.S. Chamber of Commerce, and the top reaches of Democratic Party leadership.

Or here's another map, built around Treasury Secretary Steven Mnuchin.

He got his first job out of Yale at Goldman Sachs, the investment bank that has been fined a dozen times for just the type of Gilded Age malfeasance that left the wreckage of stock-market crashes and depressions in smoking heaps across the late nineteenth century. The list includes trading violations, foreign exchange manipulation, illicit political contributions, and Goldman's "conduct in the packaging, securitization, marketing [and] sale . . . of residential mortgage-backed securities (RMBS) between 2005 and 2007"—that is, helping to cause what could be called the Panic of 2008.

Yet Mnuchin was proud to single out his early mentors, Lewis Ranieri and Michael Mortara, to the Senate Finance Committee during his 2017 confirmation hearing. Those are the men, he beamed, "who started the mortgage backed securities market."

More recently, Goldman has been found woven into a klepto-cratic network I encountered in my international work. With the Malaysian prime minister and a jet-setting financier (now in hiding) as its central golden head, this hydra set up a public infrastructure investment fund with the aim of pillaging it. Like Jay Cooke & Co. and the shady Union Pacific Railroad, Goldman sold bonds for this scam, charging bloated fees for its services. More than $2 billion disappeared from the 1MDB fund, in a scandal that toppled the Malaysian government.

Given their repetition across the years, such practices must be understood as part of Goldman's business model. It is for all intents and purposes a criminal entity.

The bank was close to home for Mnuchin. There he joined his brother Alan, a vice president, and his father, who was a general part-ner. Robert Mnuchin reportedly mentored another future treasury secretary, Robert Rubin, and former Treasury official and Democratic New Jersey senator and governor Jon Corzine, among others.

On a historical network map, the lines connecting Goldman Sachs and the U.S. Department of the Treasury would thicken starting in the 1960s. Three decades later, the bank was running Treasury, as first Robert Rubin under President Bill Clinton, then Henry Paulson under President George W. Bush, became secretary. Former and future Goldman Sachs employees stud Treasury's lower ranks, but also regulatory agencies and other parts of the government, weaving a seamless fabric.

Men like Rubin and Mnuchin built their careers athwart public and private sectors. Given the prestige of banking today, it is doubt-ful they sought government office as a way of gaining personal status, as Joe Kennedy did. Instead, their purpose was to do this weaving at the very highest level, in order to make the government serve their network.

In the prime of life, Steven's father, Robert Mnuchin, left Gold-man to launch an art gallery. Maybe he was bored with finance and, content with his riches, decided to devote himself to a personal pas-sion for art. A *New York Times* portrait suggests as much. Mnuchin, comments another gallery owner, "comes to art dealing through col-lecting and through the absolute love of art."

Maybe. But the stories of Gilded Age magnates throwing money at paintings give pause. So does the fact that corrupt officials the world over buy art, often anonymously, as a way to launder money. The uber-rich use it to dodge taxes. Warehouses in Geneva and New York are stacked with specially conditioned safes. There, great works are reduced to the equivalent of zeroes in anonymous bank accounts.

A picture in the article shows a bearded and bespectacled Robert Mnuchin, gesturing at a set of what looks like red shelves on the wall behind him. Except they are set too close together to be useful for putting books or knickknacks on. "I've kind of fallen in love with this color," Mnuchin tells the *Times*. "It's endeared itself to me." The shelves, it seems, are art. A set has sold for more than $10 million. Mnuchin finds something about them "even romantic."

I read on. When he opened his gallery, his second wife, Adriana, was head of the acquisitions committee at the Whitney Museum. His first wife was a director of the Solomon Guggenheim Museum, with its galleries in New York, Venice, and Bilbao. Mnuchin, that is, was applying the method—in fact, the only method, and a guaranteed

Robert Mnuchin with Donald Judd's *Stack,* in 2013. Similar pieces sold for between $7 million and $9 million in that time frame.

one—for making money on contemporary art. That method is Joe Kennedy's old favorite: insider information.

Through their networked relationships, dealers get an advantage in what remains a completely unregulated market, writes Maureen Mullarkey, in a 2006 takedown of the contemporary art scene. Such practices, and the resulting windfalls, are now the norm within a web that connects parts of the contemporary art world, philanthropy, and investment banking. "Trustees know ahead of time which artists will have their work exhibited or acquired by which museum" and can calibrate their purchases or sales accordingly.

Treasury Secretary Steven Mnuchin served on the Whitney's board too, as well as that of the Museum of Contemporary Art in Los Angeles. The wife of his longtime business partner Daniel Neidich became co-chair of the Whitney board in 2008. Mnuchin's 2019 financial disclosure lists two "interests" in a painting by Willem de Kooning, worth between $5 million and $25 million. In other words, Mnuchin holds shares in a work of art—shares that can be leveraged, or securitized, like subprime mortgages.

Thus does the Midas disease, touching one of the most irreplaceable human values—their artistic creativity—transform it to lifeless gold.

With Neidich, also of Goldman, Mnuchin set up a private investment firm, after leaving the house in 2002. It's then that an unexpected face takes its place beside his on the link-analysis diagram: liberal financier and currency speculator George Soros. Mnuchin worked for Soros. The new venture, Dune Capital Management, was a spin-off of a Soros subentity.

Alongside Soros and a few others connected by those branching lines, Dune bought the bank IndyMac, which had crashed in the Panic of 2008 and was in federal receivership. The investor group secured generous FDIC terms: taxpayers would assume liability for about 80 percent of loan defaults, the new owners only 20 percent. With its name changed to OneWest, the bank joined the ranks of the post-crash mortgage foreclosers.

The heads of private equity investment firms specialized in deals on distressed assets of various types—bankrupt coal or chemical plants, failed banks and foreclosed properties, or whole swaths of the economy in the wake of economic meltdowns—which feature prominently in the ruling networks that have taken hold in the United States.

Trump confidant Tom Barrack launched his Colony Capital by buying up bankrupt savings and loan institutions in the early 1990s, with the help of the Resolution Trust Corporation, a U.S. government entity. Later, Colony used the same tactics in Japan, South Korea, and Taiwan amid generation-altering economic meltdowns in those countries. After 2008, it turned to foreclosed properties, converting them to rentals. Since then, tens of thousands of families have been subjected to robo-evictions. In 2010, Colony sold a Beverly Hills hotel to the Malaysian prime minister's partner in the 1MDB scheme, undoubtedly pocketing pilfered public funds. A decade later, Barrack lobbied the Federal Reserve to expand its already unprecedented coronavirus emergency powers to purchase risky *commercial,* as well as residential, mortgage-backed securities. His strategy may even include investing in distressed people—as a business proposition. Among those who received a timely Colony investment was Michael Jackson, when his ranch Neverland was underwater, and Paul Manafort, former advisor to kleptocrats in Ukraine.

Commerce Secretary Wilbur Ross also pursued financial crises across Asia, like those lawyers who post their numbers on highway billboards and make their living chasing ambulances. There is a difference though: the accident lawyers rarely get to write the traffic laws in such a way as to make the accidents more likely.

Once you start looking, the sinews of these networks appear everywhere, entwining institutions or individuals that are uncomfortably familiar—some that we may revere, some whom we know personally.

If there is one such sprawling organism that exemplifies this entire phenomenon, and how far its tentacles can lead—a mythological archetype of horror come to life—it is this one, which I edged into sideways, scratching around some of its less-well-known members.

School ties, top judicial clerkships, work side by side at the Chicago law firm of Kirkland & Ellis, or in government or the impeachment investigation of President Bill Clinton, bind Health and Human Services secretary Alex Azar to Kenneth Starr and to Supreme Court justice Brett Kavanaugh. He was a year behind Azar at Yale Law

School and was his colleague on the Starr investigation. When Starr was President George H. W. Bush's solicitor general, Kavanaugh had also worked for him, and the three overlapped at Kirkland & Ellis.

Kavanaugh attended a small prep school in Washington, DC, with his future High Court colleague Neil Gorsuch. In 1993, the two clerked together for then-justice Anthony Kennedy. This is the same Justice Kennedy whose son Justin was President Trump's loan officer at Deutsche Bank, and whose own early retirement gave Trump a surprise second Supreme Court slot to fill. And here the branching lines link into the network map above: before joining multi-recidivist Deutsche Bank, Justin worked at Goldman Sachs for none other than future Treasury secretary Mnuchin.

Trump filled Kennedy's seat on the Supreme Court with the justice's protégé, Kavanaugh. Trump's prior pick, Gorsuch, is the son of Anne Gorsuch, who was President Ronald Reagan's EPA administrator. She and her soon-to-be husband, Bureau of Land Management chief Robert Burford, worked to dismantle and weaponize their agencies, in ways that prefigured today's gutting of the EPA and use of the BLM to swiftly auction off public land to fuel and lumber interests. Anne Gorsuch had to resign in 1983 under a barrage of corruption allegations.

But there is more. With yet another Kirkland & Ellis attorney and mentee of his, Jay Lefkowitz, Starr anchored the original defense team of one Jeffrey Epstein, the late suspected child sex trafficker. Starr and Lefkowitz and a high-profile colleague, Harvard law professor Alan Dershowitz, achieved a now-criticized nonprosecution agreement for Epstein in 2008. It allowed him to serve a comfortable thirteen-month work-release sentence on state-level charges, instead of life in prison for running a vast sex-trafficking operation. He kept raping children while serving this sentence.

It must have helped that the man with whom Starr and Lefkowitz negotiated this deal was their friend U.S. Attorney Alex Acosta. Between 1994 and 2001, Acosta (who was Trump's secretary of labor until he resigned over this episode in 2019) overlapped with both of them—and with Azar and Kavanaugh—at Kirkland & Ellis.

And so we have arrived at Jeffrey Epstein, hedge fund high roller and compulsive pedophile. And the network map starts shooting out in all directions.

But before we start tracing lines, let's listen for a moment. U.S. district judge Richard Berman barred recording devices from his courtroom on August 27, 2019, for an unusual hearing to allow those who would have testified against Epstein to speak. A few have given extended interviews, however. Their poise and composure is remarkable, but they can't quite get through it. At some point the anguish spills out.

Maria Farmer was a painter, completing her studies at the New York Academy of Art in 1995, and already making a name for herself. At the school's graduation exhibit, the dean introduced her to someone who wanted a painting of hers, of a nude young woman reclining on a couch while a man in boxers regards her from the doorway. The buyer was Epstein, accompanied by the woman frequently seen at his elbow, Ghislaine Maxwell.

Maxwell, a well-known socialite, was the doting daughter of English publishing mogul Robert Maxwell, who looted hundreds of millions of pounds from the pension funds of several of his companies, including the Mirror Group, and was broadly suspected of working for Israeli intelligence. His naked body had been fished out of the Atlantic off the Canary Islands four years earlier.

Epstein hired Farmer as an art consultant—the kind Gilded Age tycoons sent off to scour Europe for masterpieces. But she wound up a receptionist, checking in visitors in his cavernous Upper East Side foyer. A stream of young girls burbled past her and up the spiral staircase. "Hundreds," Farmer told the *New York Times*. "Hundreds. Hundreds. Hundreds." They were auditioning for modeling jobs with Victoria's Secret, she was told, whose founder was close to Epstein.

And it goes on from there. Maria's kid sister Annie gets involved, accepting gifts and trips. But not till Maria travels to Epstein's Ohio residence to work on a commission does her world shatter. Epstein and Maxwell appear, and, like so many other girls, Farmer finds herself the object of their attention.

Like a shard of exploding glass, the implications pierce her: "What happened to Annie?" The anguish still lacerates her voice. "Was Annie hurt? Was Annie hurt?"

She wasn't, but Maria has only begun to recover.

Jennifer Araoz was a ninth grader at a distinguished public high school for the performing arts when she was introduced to Epstein in 2001. She makes it through several long minutes of an NBC *Today* interview. But then, asked if she had realized that what she went through was rape, she cracks. "No," she says. "I just thought, like, 'It's my fault.' I was, like, *obligated.*"

These voices bring surging to mind the Midas story, in Hawthorne's version—with Marygold. "Her sweet, rosy face," the poet wrote, "assumed a glittering yellow color, with yellow tear-drops congealing on her cheeks." At Midas's touch, "little Marygold was a human child no longer."

What grotesque forms today's Midases take. There were hundreds of Marygolds—who were touched and touched and touched.

This is the context to keep in mind in considering the networks that twined around Epstein. His unctuous welcome at the New York Academy of Art parallels his involvement with higher-profile educational institutions, notably the Massachusetts Institute of Technology and Harvard University. One enabler who ushered him into that world was that Harvard law professor and tabloid attorney, later part of the defense team at President Trump's Senate impeachment trial, Alan Dershowitz.

A 2003 portrait in Harvard's student newspaper, *The Crimson,* drips with praise from academics who received Epstein's money. He is "brilliant," exclaims Dershowitz. "One of the brightest people I've ever known," echoes noted psychology professor Stephen Kosslyn. He must be brilliant, they seem to be saying, because he can keep up with me, and I'm a Harvard professor. This self-gratifying logic is even more explicit in a later quote, in which an unnamed source discusses a big Epstein donation. For Epstein, the source says, "there was not a choice between Harvard and another place; there isn't another place that exists."

Thus does a deft combination of ego stroking and cash work just as effectively on Harvard professors as on teenage girls.

Other academics in Epstein's stable include Lawrence Summers, former Harvard president and current professor, also Treasury secretary under President Clinton and chairman of President Obama's Council of Economic Advisors. His wife, Harvard English professor

Elisa New, was another Epstein beneficiary. The New York literary scene helped Epstein meet celebrity scientists, thanks to agent John Brockman.

But it is Dershowitz who looms largest in this circle. A devastating 2019 *New Yorker* magazine portrait details pages of disturbing behavior: his constant use of rape examples in class, his "pretty close to indefensible" legal stances; his apparent intimidation of police investigators and victims in the Epstein case.

I find this information unnerving. I know Dershowitz, or almost. My father taught law at Harvard for half a century. I always sensed his distaste for Dershowitz but never probed it. "He thought the man was a crook!" my mother burst out when I asked her. "I mean, he never came out and said that, but I gathered."

Today I am left wondering: Why not? What made my wonderful, ebullient dad so reticent? Why, over the course of three decades, did he never question his beloved institution's service as validation and platform for Dershowitz? Tenure may be an impregnable fortress. But concerned colleagues could at least have increased the friction Dershowitz encountered as he violated his community's stated principles.

It's not just Harvard, obviously. I am emphasizing my alma mater precisely to make it personal. If my own father did, what manner of corruption have I enabled—is each of us enabling—by not asking probing questions of people we work with, support, or admire?

Epstein's highest-profile public-sector contacts were Presidents Clinton and Trump. Both outsized figures loudly distanced themselves upon his 2019 indictment, playing down the length of time they associated with Epstein and the depth of the relationship. Their statements are false.

In Trump's case, a close social relationship lasted more than a decade. He and Epstein shared two dominant traits: the Midas disease—an obsession with infinite wealth and its vulgar display—and compulsive sexual behavior.

Both had a hand in fashion industry offshoots that offer contact with exceptionally beautiful, often young and disadvantaged, women. In Epstein's case it was Victoria's Secret and French mod-

eling agent Jean-Luc Brunel. Trump had his own modeling agency
and the Miss Universe pageant. The moment I heard he brought it
to Moscow with the help of Emin Agalarov, my suspicions flared. A
former son-in-law of Azerbaijan president Ilham Aliyev, Agalarov is
deeply entwined in that potentate's kleptocratic network. Former
Soviet republics have been sex-trafficking source countries since the
empire imploded, and fashion shows have served as a cover.

Trump and Epstein fell out in 2004 when they competed to purchase a foreclosed Palm Beach mansion. That's the mansion Trump
unloaded a mere four years later for more than twice his purchase
price to a member of Putin's kleptocratic network named Dmitry
Rybolovlev. In November 2018 he was charged by prosecutors in
Monaco in relation to a probe into corruption and influence peddling in his long-running commercial dispute with Geneva art dealer
Yves Bouvier.

As for Clinton, he shares with Epstein and Trump a long-
standing and well-known pattern of predatory sexual behavior
and, more recently, a fixation on money. Fundraisers and several
White House visits prove intersections with Epstein going back
at least to 1993, including by way of Clinton's college friend Paul
Prosperi. Prosperi remained friendly enough with Epstein to visit
him multiple times during the sex offender's thirteen months of
work release.

Then there are Clinton's rides on Epstein's private jet, "a total of
four trips," according to a spokesman. The publicly available flight
logs are incomplete, contested, and often illegible. But by my reading, they indicate twenty-six flights grouped into seven separate trips,
including a multicountry Africa trip, one from Rabat, Morocco, to
the Azores, and two to Asia.

Would this connection be less damaging to Clinton if the trips'
main point was to further Clinton Foundation? Not much. Even
without adding sexual exploitation, doubts have swirled around
the foundation since its launch into global philanthropy in 2001.
An Epstein connection only adds a grotesque twist. Proudly mixing
business, splashy humanitarianism, image enhancement, and personal enrichment, the Clinton Foundation is known for its unsightly
smudge of financial and personnel practices. Among its donors and
beneficiaries, corrupt and abusive developing-country politicians rub

shoulders with Western business executives angling for sweetheart deals, and members of both groups hoping to curry favor with the Clintons. It—and the lower-profile Trump Foundation, closed in 2018 due to "repeated and willful self-dealing"—are the U.S. versions of the "charities" run by corrupt ruling families from Honduras to Uzbekistan.

In other words, *both* presidents hung out with Epstein. Dedicated right-wing lawyers and liberal academics alike defended and praised him and happily banked his money. The staggering point here is how effortlessly Epstein's network wove between America's supposedly warring political camps.

"Money washes hands," said my West Virginia interlocutor. Overshadowed by his sex trafficking and inexplicable death, Epstein's money—which cleaned him up in so many people's eyes—is shrouded in just as dense a fog.

After an inexplicable stint at investment house (and 2008 fire-bomb) Bear Stearns, he joined a debt-collection agency, at which point it commenced fashioning a colossal Ponzi scheme. CEO Steven Hoffenberg spent eighteen years in jail for it—Epstein, not a day. "I thought Jeffrey was the best hustler on two feet," Hoffenberg told the *Washington Post* in 2019, a "criminal mastermind."

Criminal masterminds share a trait with other psychopaths: they are expert manipulators. Psychologically impaired by an inability to feel empathy, they learn to mimic its signs. The best of them can fool almost anyone.

There is nothing intrinsically immoral about a network, of course. We are all embedded in networks of family, friends, and colleagues. The diving ducks on my river live in a network. A former police chief I know draws "integrity network" maps of constructive public officials in Mali. But when a network is structured and organized around a purpose, it can become a beast—multitalented, elusive, and relentless.

Epstein's demonstrates the twists such a network can take. It also demonstrates the intertwining of public, private, and criminal sectors and the globalized, border-crossing agility. Yet, illustrative as it is, Epstein's was not exactly the type of network in focus here.

It was a corrupt network to be sure, but not a kleptocratic one, and that is a crucial distinction. Though it intersected with kleptocratic networks and funneled money to some of their members, its purpose was not to re-engineer the nation's institutions. Its primary purpose was to sexually gratify the insatiable Epstein.

The networks at issue here are pursuing an intent of a different order: to rewrite economic, political, and legal rules around the world—permanently, in the United States, through changes to the Constitution. They mean not just to pleasure themselves in the short term, but to bend the power of government away from the public interest and make it serve themselves and their like, forever.

2

Powers Wielded: The Scales

The job of the members of such networks who hold public office is to do the actual bending of the instruments of government. Like rogue gunnery sergeants, they grip their agencies and authorities and swivel them in a new direction, to fire upon targets that were not in the original plans.

It was these activities that caught my attention when I was working on developing-world kleptocracy. Gathering groups of journalists, members of civic associations, and a few former officials, I'd set up flip charts and use different colored markers for the different network strands: blue for public-sector agencies, green for businesses and nonprofits in the private sector, and red for out-and-out crime. We would start by working through the government institutions the local ruling networks had denatured.

Debate often swirled around the details. Was the Anti-Corruption Commission actively weaponized—aimed like an artillery piece at threats to the network? Or was it just made ineffectual? Was the Education Ministry primarily a source of revenue—through bribes for grades, consulting positions for professors, accreditations to substandard for-profit schools? Or did it provide some other service, such as a badge of credibility for unqualified network members or the ideas they were peddling?

In Nigeria, the education system—disdainfully called "boko" even by people who treasured learning—was widely seen as the corrupt intake valve into a viciously corrupt civil service. Considering it

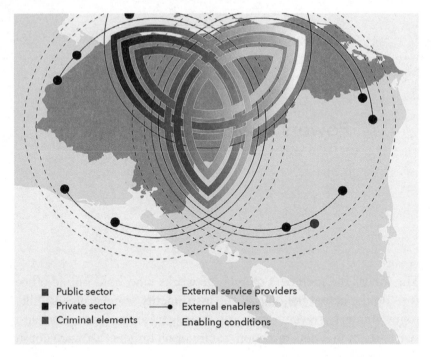

Infographic illustrating kleptocratic capture analysis as applied to Honduras.

in that light gave me a startling insight into the attacks on schools by the Boko Haram militant group. Maybe Western learning and culture wasn't what made people so mad. Maybe it was the role schools played in the structure of Nigerian corruption.

Unexpected examples always turned up. In Tunisia, even the water department was made to serve. Lacking the fossil fuels that lubricate the bedrock of neighboring Libya and Algeria, this chip of a country, set sparkling between the desert and the Mediterranean Sea, prizes more poetic exports. Its northern plains are covered in the glossy green of orange groves. Orange blossom oil, distilled in artisanal alembics, is sent to perfumeries in the south of France. At the other end of the country, oases rise like misplaced tropical forests from the Saharan sands, shade-loving fruit trees growing lushly beneath the date palm canopy. Persian Gulf families break their Ramadan fast with those dates when the sun finally completes its arc.

What is the limiting factor on date cultivation? It had not dawned on me until I visited an oasis that water, that precious liquid, reaches the palms not just naturally through the soil, but in pipes. And those pipes are controlled by the water department. A buyer connected to former ruler Zine el-Abedine Ben Ali could force down the price for the choicest dates by threatening to close the spigot and parch the seller's lovingly cultivated trees.

In drought-threatened regions of a warming and eroding planet, gaining chokeholds on water sources will be a prime goal of corrupt officials.

Different assortments of such public powers are in the hydra's grasp in different countries. But everywhere, I have found one that kleptocratic networks must control: the justice function.

The administration of justice is synonymous with sovereignty. The most radical act that rebels against divine-right monarchy did when the Middle Ages were waning was to apply the law to the monarch himself. So revolutionary was the very notion that when an insurgent English Parliament dared to put King Charles I on trial in 1649, he refused to enter a plea, even knowing he would therefore die. Silence, under English law, was the equivalent of confession, and he was accused of capital treason. But declaring himself innocent meant recognizing the court's jurisdiction over his divine person, and for Charles, a king who did that was no king. He was king in name only—"but the outside, but the picture, but the sign of a king."

Subjecting a ruler to the rule of law was the first way a coalition of subordinates successfully slapped down its apex alpha dominator in a modern, complex society. It was the first step humans took to reassert their unique egalitarian ethos after centuries of submitting to apelike hierarchy in kingdoms and empires. The second cornerstone of democracy—the vote—came only later. Kleptocratic networks seek to suborn both.

U.S. presidents—whose very office was invented to contrast with kingship—have fought this constraint just as kings did. Far be it from modern presidents to hint that they consider "the President a Kind of Sacred Person." That was still a phrase that could be uttered when the Constitution was being debated, but it would shock U.S. citizens today.

Yet President Richard Nixon's claims of executive privilege to avoid turning over his recordings of Oval Office conversations were not that far off. They implied that a sort of fairy dust glitters upon the elected executive. Presidents Thomas Jefferson and Bill Clinton made a more practical argument: that they should not be distracted from their urgent presidential duties by the whine of judicial inquiries.

This is largely what Supreme Court justice Brett Kavanaugh contended in a 2009 law review article. Having helped investigate Clinton, he proclaims that future presidents should be free from such interference. Attorney General William Barr, yet another Kirkland & Ellis alum, also worked to free presidents from the law. He took office just as his new boss was making his own expansive claims of executive privilege.

Charles I's refusal to plead, back in 1649, casts an instructive light on President Donald Trump's across-the-board rejection of congressional subpoenas. Current Justice Department policy holds that—unlike the precedent English commoners sought to establish back then—a sitting president cannot be prosecuted. That leaves the House of Representatives, exercising its impeachment authority, as the only body that can subject a president to the law. To refuse to acknowledge the legitimacy of its proceedings is to assert a kind of "divine right" of presidential rule.

As coalitions of would-be dominators, kleptocratic networks must disable legal constraints—and not just on behalf of the lone individual on top. They work to protect all their members from judicial repercussions, even the lowliest. For that is the deal holding the networks together, the same deal that made the strength of the Mafia: protection for lieutenants and foot soldiers in return for a constant flow of spoils up through the ranks. If any revelation emerged from years of working on corruption cases in Afghanistan, that was it. That bargain is essential to the functioning of a kleptocracy. President Hamid Karzai made no bones about his direct interference in judicial proceedings. Indeed, he wanted it publicized—so network members could be sure he was still honoring the deal.

So far as we know, it did not take a phone call from on high, like the ones Karzai made, to ensure protection for Epstein. Then–U.S. attorney Acosta and the defense team were close-knit. When the 2008 nonprosecution deal gained national attention after Epstein was indicted again in 2019, media coverage emphasized the pressure on Acosta, how Epstein's riches gained him the best lawyers money could buy. No one examined Acosta's personal relationship with those lawyers (though Julie Brown's groundbreaking *Miami Herald* investigation did note that they were "colleagues").

There is little evidence in the record of those lawyers' great skill. There is abundant evidence of their connections to Acosta, and of tactics worthier of mafiosi than fine legal minds. Those tactics, however, seem to have been deployed not against Acosta, as he later claimed, but against teenage victims and blue-collar law-enforcement officials—ones outside the network. The Palm Beach police chief and lead detective, according to the *Herald*'s Brown, found their trash searched and their grade-school teachers contacted; they had to dodge tails as they worked. "Dream team" defense attorneys threatened repeatedly to smear the victims.

When Acosta announced his resignation on July 12, 2019, his friend Kenneth Starr, a Fox News contributor, defended him on *The Ingraham Angle*. Acosta, the former Clinton prosecutor and Epstein defense attorney said, "took one for the team today." It was Acosta and his office, insisted Starr, "who were playing tough" back in 2008. He ridiculed the notion—repeated that day by Brown herself—that Acosta had been "bowled over" by high-powered defense attorneys. "The idea that anyone was bowled over is absolute nonsense."

That much is true. No one was bowled over. They were teammates. They had one another's backs.

Another member of this team is fellow Kirkland & Ellis and George W. Bush White House alum William Barr, now attorney general. It was his father, Donald Barr, who hired Epstein back in 1974 to teach math and physics at the prestigious Dalton School in Manhattan, the job that launched his career. And it is Barr who has responded to pressure from Trump that is every bit as direct and public as President Karzai's was, including asking a judge to mete out a more lenient sentence to a convicted network member than his department's own lawyers recommended.

At a breakfast in Kathmandu in early 2018, two former supreme court justices reeled off the techniques Nepal's networks use to hamstring the judiciary. Via a majority on the Judicial Council, corrupt officials control appointments. If "pliable" candidates are lacking, the council leaves gaps on the bench. A huge case backlog has developed. Lawyers loyal to the networks add delays. They make frivolous requests for adjournments. They multiply procedural maneuvers. They even agree to argue cases before judges to whom they are related—knowing the opposing side will object and a different judge will have to be chosen and the whole case start over.

Egyptian president Abdel Fattah el-Sisi, who took power after police gunned down hundreds of protesters in the streets of Cairo in 2013, used a wholesale method. As a former top general, he can influence military courts. So, pushing laws through parliament, he expanded those tribunals' jurisdiction while taking cases away from the civilian judiciary.

As that example suggests, kleptocratic networks rarely stop at sabotaging the justice sector's power to rein them in. Legal action can be a weapon as flexible and lethal as a rapier. They seek to wield it.

The justice system also rakes in cash for kleptocratic networks. Nigerian cartoonists lampoon the misuse of arrest and bail as extortion. Almost every stage in a judicial proceeding can serve. Defense attorneys may even hit up their clients for extra money to bribe the judge and then pocket some of it. The proceeds are shared up the ranks. In the United States, economist Thomas Ferguson has exposed how bribes for public officials who are also lawyers can be hidden as fat retainers for legal services.

The method by which the Fourteenth Amendment was deliberately twisted away from its purpose of protecting freed slaves to shield corporations instead illustrates a judicial power that is especially important in the United States. Courts can interpret the words of the most solemn laws to mean almost anything. A network armed with that weapon hardly needs to control the legislative process. U.S. networks began a campaign to regain that power of the scales in the early 1970s.

Washington's very architecture seems aimed at keeping the justice function sacred. If any building in the U.S. civic communion is a temple—is built explicitly to look like a temple—it is the Supreme Court. One man more than most ushered today's coalition of money changers inside: Justice Lewis Powell, who officiated there from 1972 to 1987.

Powell "cultivated a reputation as a swing vote with a penchant for compromise." That's what a lot of quick-look-up online bios tell us. For the casually curious, those are the words that until recently would have stuck to Powell's name.

But Justice Powell was a radical.

He entered the Supreme Court's temple precinct after a career dedicated to an industry that put love of lucre above every other value, including life: tobacco. Though internal documents prove companies' knowledge of the carcinogenic effects of smoking back to the 1950s, the industry constantly contested those findings in public. It lobbied hard against warning labels. It aggressively marketed its product to children. In later years, R. J. Reynolds and Philip Morris organized and funded phony grassroots "smokers' rights" groups to fight smoke-free zones and other protections. Sharing this model with Koch-network affiliates such as Americans for Prosperity and FreedomWorks, these companies helped jump-start the Tea Party.

Leaving his seat on the Philip Morris board and his long legal service to tobacco companies, Powell ascended to the highest bench with a sweeping plan in hand. Its aim was to help such corporate giants gain more leverage over American courts—and American politics, and even the way Americans think.

Just months before his appointment, Powell delivered a detailed memorandum to the U.S. Chamber of Commerce. It warned of what he described in apocalyptic terms as an "assault on the enterprise system." The blitz, he insisted, was "broadly based and consistently pursued." Yet, in the face of this "massive" "frontal assault" (Powell kept the volume high), whose like had never been seen in American history, boards of directors and top executives had responded with "appeasement" and "ineptitude."

Then comes his blueprint for going on the offensive. First, Powell said, weave a purposeful network. "Strength lies in organization, in careful long-range planning and implementation, in consistency of action over an indefinite period of years, in the scale of financing available only through joint effort, and in the political power available only through united action and national organizations."

That network, urged Powell, should revamp what is taught in high school and especially college, via a staff of scholars and speakers, textbook evaluation, demands for "equal time on the campus" for theories useful to the network, and the "balancing of faculties" toward professors supporting corporate interests. It should target the media and the political arena.

And crucially, the network should regain the courts, for the judiciary "may be the most important instrument for social, economic and political change." As Powell was readying to take his place on the highest one in the land, he showed the Chamber how to help him to rule in its favor. Powell clearly understood the advantages of weaponizing the justice function.

The Powell Memo should be understood as one of the core documents shaping American political and economic realities over the past half century. For decades, the Chamber of Commerce implemented it like a military campaign plan.

Allied organizations, especially Koch's constellation of donors and entities, also took Powell's cues. They applied his education strategy to his objective of gaining control over the justice function. "Outsmarted and undermanned in the 1970s," the legal movement they supported "became [a] sophisticated and deeply organized network," writes Steven Teles in *The Rise of the Conservative Legal Movement,* the most detailed examination of this process.

Works like his and *Dark Money* and *Democracy in Chains* chart how proponents of a new school of legal thought landed grappling hooks on the decks of prestigious law schools, under cover of the deliberately bland moniker "law and economics." Harvard University, roiled in the mid-1980s by a controversy surrounding the esoteric critical legal studies movement, was an early success. Koch funding helped build George Mason University's entire law school into a bastion. It became one of the prime organizers of a regular series of seminars for judges and other legal professionals. For years, often in luxurious settings, these trainings have been inculcating legal arguments in favor of network priorities and market-based ethical standards and denigrating the very notion of the public interest.

Since 1982, the Federalist Society—conceived initially by Yale law students but quickly adopted by network members, including Judge Robert Bork and President Ronald Reagan's energetic attorney general Edwin Meese—has comforted anxious young law students. Yale's chapter, enthuses a post on the law school website, has "stepped in . . . and has created a school within a school." The second-year author, identified only by his or her initials, talks up the chapter's well-attended speaker series, mentoring, and social and networking activities, meant to bind members into a "close community."

The weaving of this subnetwork of legal scholars and practitioners has been crucial to the hydra's ability to weaponize the justice function. In the past decade, the Federalist Society has become the primary clearinghouse for federal judicial nominees. No similar organization serves the same function on behalf of ordinary citizens.

The results are measurable. More—and younger—jurists who align with the hydra's worldview and priorities have been appointed and confirmed in the past ten years than ever in living memory. "Trump judges are very different from Reagan appointees or either of the Bushes'," says Daniel Goldberg, legal director of the Alliance for Justice. "They are much, much, much more radical. They are much more willing to use the court to delete the last century of jurisprudence, especially New Deal era legislation." These judges don't just hold conservative views on social issues like abortion or gay marriage. They take radical positions on corporate rights. What American citizens don't realize yet, Goldberg points out, is that "this will make it very hard for future democratically elected institutions to govern."

Some of the novel ways members of this subnetwork have been hustled into justice-sector slots have shocked my lawyer friends. No president until Trump has personally interviewed nominees to the top prosecutor position (U.S. attorney) in jurisdictions where he or members of his family may face litigation. None has leveled such virulent attacks on justice-sector personnel and institutions. To my eyes, however, such antics are familiar. They're exactly what Hamid Karzai would do.

Other changes to the way justice is dispensed have been less glaring—and less partisan. In a series of cases decided between 2010 and 2015, the Supreme Court upheld contracts that disempower ordinary people. They prevent credit card holders, cell phone subscribers, small business owners, or employees such as restaurant workers or NFL cheerleaders from banding together to sue a company as a group if they have all suffered similar abuses.

Imagine finding several two-dollar roaming charges on your phone bill when you can prove you were home those days. Or finding penalties on a bank account you never opened. Who could afford the legal fees to win back such tiny sums? But if tens of thousands of customers found the same error, together they could foot the bill. They would represent the modern version of the kind of egalitarian coalition anthropologist Christopher Boehm describes ostracizing or even expelling a greedy meat hog from hunter-gatherer bands.

But buried in the eye-crossing contracts we all sign when we start a new job, or subscribe to a streaming service, or—hearts in the dirt—move an elderly parent into a care facility are clauses telling us we can't join with others in such class actions, or sue in court at all. Instead, if several of us find bedsores on our loved one's hips, we have to submit our complaints separately to private arbitration.

It is such clauses that the Supreme Court has repeatedly upheld. So is the power of numbers weakened, while the power of money is enhanced. So are we barred from reconstituting that great human innovation, the egalitarian coalition.

This series of cases is just the type of litigation Justice Powell urged the U.S. Chamber of Commerce to launch: "where the purpose is not so much to represent the client as to change the law." According to a meticulous *New York Times* investigation, a team of attorneys for such Chamber stalwarts as Citi, Toyota, and General Electric devised the strategy.

The first petition to reach the Supreme Court was on behalf of Discover Bank—another repeat offender. Its attorney was John G. Roberts. He was hoping to revive a 1925 federal statute recommending arbitration for disputes between two quarreling companies and swivel it, to aim it at a different target entirely. Roberts maintained that this law also guarantees companies' right to force ordinary people—their customers or employees—to submit to arbitration instead of getting their day in court. The Supreme Court declined to hear the argument.

Three years later, Roberts was chief justice of that same Supreme Court. The cases came rushing in.

As it happened, federal regulatory agencies—the FDIC and the new Consumer Financial Protection Bureau—went after Discover and Wells Fargo. But at the heart of democracy is the right of citizens to petition courts themselves to right their wrongs. That is the whole purpose of democracy: to subject the powerful to the law, to provide citizens with a means of redress. Now, under contracts we have no choice but to sign, we are deprived of that right. Now citizens are barred from the temple, while the money changers wear the robes.

In Washington, that temple to justice lacks something I expected to see. There is no great statue of the goddess to proclaim its august function. There is no Justitia holding her impartial scales aloft, blindfold across her eyes to prevent personal knowledge of the parties from influencing her. Instead, on a frieze in the back of the courtroom, a muscular Justice with stars in her hair leans on her threatening sword, while an epic battle rages.

The justice function has become a new theater of partisan civil war.

But the point here is this: the tendency to see its skirmishes in political terms, as contests between opposing armies labeled "D" and "R"—the tendency to obsess over each 5–4 decision and the party affiliation of each nominee—blinds us to a deeper reality. That reality is reflected in the 8–0 ruling in the *McDonnell* case. The hydra has already seized the scales.

Justice leaning on her sword, from a frieze along the top of the west wall of the Supreme Court's courtroom. (Farther along the frieze to her right, Divine Inspiration—not Justice herself—carries the scales. Among the forces of evil arrayed against the two goddesses are Crime, entwined in Hydra-like serpents, and Corruption, with his bag of money.)

3

Powers Wielded: The Pen and the Mace

In August 2009, I walked with members of my skincare cooperative through Kandahar to the dusty school where they would cast
their ballots in the presidential election. Afterward, they stopped and
squatted at a gutter to scrub the purple ink off their fingers. None
intended to vote a second time that day. They were afraid of running
into Taliban and being shot for having cast a ballot at all.

In Afghanistan I learned that elections are not stolen on voting
day, by individuals cheating. They are stolen well before and often
afterward. That July, the Afghan government—a hydra with President Karzai as its golden head—became obsessed with electoral districts. Maps dominated every meeting I attended. Cabinet members
browbeat the U.S.-led military to change districts' color: from black,
meaning too dangerous for polls to open at all, to red, meaning just
very dangerous.

Eventually, the U.S. officers in charge of the forces, which were
responsible for election security, complied. Here's how that decision
helped Karzai steal the election. Villagers in the remote electoral
districts that had been switched from black to red were so terrorized
that the Taliban did not need to commit much violence to keep them
away from the polls. Warnings were sufficient. That left truckloads
of ballot boxes empty, in places no international election observer
could go.

Then the stuffing began.

An international investigation later found that about a third of

Karzai's votes were fakes. In some cases, whole pads of ballots were jammed into the boxes, the sheets not even separated. In others, zeroes were added to the count penned on the outside of the boxes.

Instead of refusing to recognize the results of this farce, the U.S. government dispatched then-senator John Kerry to sort things out. He spent long hours with Karzai negotiating over the size of his victory.

In Afghanistan, only the presidential election was worth such effort. Parliament has no power. But kleptocratic networks want the power of the pen—the power to write the rules of the collective game. That power, in the United States, is largely held by Congress. And in many U.S. states, congressional elections are rigged.

*Ratf**ked: Why Your Vote Doesn't Count* chronicles a brazen, multistep strategy for rigging them, launched in 2009. Just as in Afghanistan, it was all about the districts. Republican strategist Karl Rove even broadcast the principle in a 2010 *Wall Street Journal* op-ed. It was subtitled "He Who Controls Redistricting Can Control Congress."

So proud of his handiwork was the plot's mastermind that he walked *Ratf**ked* author David Daley through the blow-by-blow:

- The realization that the 2010 election would be key. The census is taken each zero year. Afterward, the number and shape of congressional districts get changed, according to the new population figures. And, in Rove's words, "he who controls redistricting can control Congress."

- The selection of states where the legislature (not an independent body) runs this redistricting process, and where Republicans might gain a majority.

- The blast of money and effort at these state-level targets—at "107 seats in 16 states," Rove helpfully signaled to absent-minded Democrats.

- The 2010 electoral triumph—not so much Republicans' 63 U.S. House gains, but the 680 seats they won in state legislatures.

- Then, the new state-level majorities' use of big data and advanced map-plotting software to slice out contorted congressional districts that would guarantee Republicans more seats in the U.S. House of Representatives than their share of the vote entitled them to. The acrobatic boundaries either crowd as many Democrats as possible into a small number of districts, so lots of votes produce only a few lawmakers, or scatter likely Democratic voters across many different districts, so they can't obtain a majority in any of them. Informed by all the data routinely captured about anyone who clicks an internet link, the maps could be drawn with laser-like precision.

Though the intent was unfair, it was perfectly legal to give Republican voters extra representation this way, in the states where it was done. And it's not just Republicans who resort to gerrymandering to cement their hold on elective office. Take a look at the congressional districts in Illinois, for example, especially the Fourth and the Eleventh. Or Maryland's. A Democrat representing one of those admitted to me it's misshapen. He is pushing for a law that would mandate redistricting by nonpartisan commissions nationwide. But in the meantime, "we are not going to unilaterally disarm," he said.

Still, David Daley sees Democratic gerrymandering as scattershot, mostly opportunistic. The 2009 REDMAP effort, he writes, was different. It was "the most strategic, large-scale and well-funded campaign ever to redraw the political map coast to coast." On June 27, 2019, the Supreme Court ruled 5–4 that it could not intervene in partisan redistricting. The maps stand.

Some wonder whether it took a plan to achieve this result. Or have we, the American people, homogenized our congressional districts ourselves? Lilliana Mason, author of *Uncivil Agreement: How Politics Became Our Identity,* argues that Americans' political leanings have come into line with other traits and preferences. They fuse "a variety of social, economic, geographic, and ideological cleavages" into one powerful affiliation. So aligned, Americans now "seek comfort in increasingly homogenous neighborhoods . . . sort themselves into geographically isolated groups that share their culture, values, race, and politics."

She's right, Daley concedes. "We have surrounded ourselves with people who agree with us." But that fact does not explain the lopsided results REDMAP achieves: "435 sets of lines, drawn by experts, informed by more data than ever before, have *sorted us* into congressional districts. Those districts, intended by the Founders to be directly responsive to the people's will, have now been insulated from it."

Whatever color manipulation like that paints the map, Americans don't like it.

Among the financiers of the 2011 redistricting push are some familiar names: the U.S. Chamber of Commerce, Walmart, AT&T, and—you may have guessed it—two tobacco companies.* For their modest investment, these members of the U.S. kleptocratic coalition tightened their grip on the power of the pen.

And yet, as in the case of the courts, the blue or red glare lighting up squares on the map blinds us to a deeper reality. The "money primary"—the shocking cost of elections—already blocks anyone who is not part of the dominator coalition, or is not at least comfortable around its members, from entering the race at all. Whatever letter follows their names, whichever regular folks our members of Congress claim to represent—coal miners or suburbanites or single mothers from Detroit—most serve the networks first. They have to, once they've taken the money.

Economists Thomas Ferguson, Paul Jorgensen, and Jie Chen have demonstrated what most Americans suspect: money buys political outcomes. That's what those residents of St. Marys, West Virginia, kept telling me. This state of affairs, the economists note with dry sarcasm, "is hard to miss without special training." They mean the kind of training that muddies plain reality with head-swimming details and jargon.

The authors wade right into the details. Using data from the IRS as well as the Federal Election Commission, checking for people who made several contributions listing different addresses or spellings of their names, and linking individuals back to their corporate employ-

---

* Which that same year had won one of the Supreme Court cases barring customers from suing as a group, or "class."

ers, Ferguson et al. gained a picture of the true pattern of campaign contributions. Then they compared the money flow to the results of every House and Senate race between 1980 and 2016. The graphs their computations spit out look eerily alike. For every race but one, almost perfect diagonal lines denote a direct relationship between money spent and the outcome of the vote. Americans are right to believe their eyes.

Campaign contributions rarely land in candidates' pockets. As part of this work, the three scholars burrowed behind other façades that can disguise direct payoffs for elected officials who are network members. Banks, for example, may provide loans at discount rates, or offer unusual mortgages, like the one Senate majority leader Mitch McConnell obtained on his house in 2008. Some retainers for supposed legal services (about a third of members of Congress and half of U.S. senators are lawyers) are really just payoffs, as are outsized consultants' fees and honoraria for speeches, stock tips, and insider information. Perhaps the spectrum should also include the employment public officials take up after leaving government.

This research has brought Ferguson and his colleagues to a stark conclusion. Elections don't really reflect a clash between voters with different visions for improving Americans' lives. Elections boil down to "conflicts within the business community"—or, framed another way, to rivalry among kleptocratic networks.

In Honduras, a group of villagers told me that after years of watching how different parties in power treated their lands and their lives, they "realized none of the political parties really represents us. They just come in and divide people. The aim is to pit us against each other." Native North Americans refer to "settler infighting."

Another map that circulated in the wake of the 2016 election conveys a similar sentiment. U.S. states are colored not just red and blue but, in boxes down to the county level, red, blue, and black. Using census data, an amateur cartographer counted all American citizens above the age of eighteen—that is, all eligible voters. Then he treated not voting in the 2016 presidential election (including by not being registered) as a vote for candidate Nobody and colored Nobody's votes black. Great splotches blacken this map. My state, West Virginia, is one of the blackest. But so is New York. So is California. The Electoral College results are even more startling. Counted this way, Trump would have earned 21 electoral votes, Clinton 72, and Nobody would have walked to victory with 445 Electoral College votes.

Most U.S. citizens sense that elections no longer have much to do with them. So they disengage. That gesture both reflects and enables the hydra's capture of the power of the pen.

The mace is a metaphor—for the use of force by kleptocratic networks. But it's not that far off the reality. The black-and-white photograph I'm looking at shows well-dressed marchers filling a city street. The men wear hats, bowlers mostly, and skinny ties knotted at their buttoned collars. A few kids in front are smartly dressed, too. Above their heads hang black pennants, and this sign: "They asked for bread. They received bayonets." In another picture, the bayonets are arrayed on one side of a ditch; the men in their hats crowd the other, behind two huge American flags.

These are photographs from a strike that silenced the clatter of textile mills in Lawrence, Massachusetts, for sixty-three days in early

The Lawrence, Massachusetts, textile workers' strike, 1912.

1912. Women, much of the workforce, with their children, "were strikers as well as wives," wrote organizer Elizabeth Gurley Flynn later, "and were valiant fighters." The mace was employed along with the bayonet, or at least, as testimony to Congress later put it, "an exceptional club . . . not the ordinary club."

In February, troopers fell upon strikers at the train station: "Children were clubbed and torn away from their parents and a scene of brutal disorder took place." An avalanche of telegrams thundered into Congress: "Whereas, the mill owners . . . have called in their police, thugs, and military forces," reads one, the Cigarmakers Progressive International Union No. 90, of the city of New York, "condemn[s] the illegal and brutal acts . . . of the governor of Massachusetts in sending the State militia to do the bidding of the mill owners, magnates, and employers of Lawrence." Railway workers, mixed trade unions, and citizens' committees across the country echoed the cigar makers' outrage.

For at least forty years, since the Panic of 1873, strikes had convulsed the country. Determined, sometimes festive, often bitter protests demanded an end to the wringing of infinite wealth from human deprivation and suffering. The lopsided use of government force became central to the grievances. In what manner of democracy, strikers wondered, are police and hastily deputized sheriffs and even federal troops deployed not to protect the people, but to protect the wealth of the infinitely wealthy *from* the people?

The congressional Strike Commission, convened to investigate the 1894 Pullman Strike, noted this disturbing fact: "United States deputy marshals . . . selected by and appointed at request of the . . . railroads . . . acted in the double capacity of railroad employees and United States officers." Their deployment came at the request of Attorney General Richard Olney, who was drawing a salary as a lawyer for those railroads while he was United States attorney general.

"We are American citizens," the *New York Times* reported striking miners insisting that year, "and demand the [same] protection that is afforded the company." But "the governmental apparatus in most localities acted as a handmaiden to business," writes historian Robert Goldstein. Two decades later, all-out war—including aerial bombing—was waged against miners in West Virginia.

One of the most soulless uses of government force by the Gilded

Age kleptocratic coalition was the re-enslavement of thousands of African Americans to toil for new industrial barons in the South. Arrested under vagrancy laws, "capriciously enforced by local sheriffs and constables," writes Douglas Blackmon in *Slavery by Another Name*, "adjudicated by mayors and notaries public," former slaves and their children were leased or sold back to cotton plantations, but especially to such Gilded Age titans as U.S. Steel and the Georgia Pacific Railroad. Blackmon found records detailing "almost animalistic mistreatment": women stripped and beaten, "workers perpetually lice-ridden and barely clothed." All the partners in this scheme—the industrialists and their friends or relations, the sheriffs and wardens—cashed in.

The mace was not always glad to be wielded. When gangs of such mostly black detainees were hustled to Briceville, Tennessee, to work in idled coal pits, striking miners sent food to the guards and set the prisoners free. Militia units kept melting away from the picket lines they were supposed to police; troops would hand over their ammunition. During the epic 1892 Homestead strike at the Carnegie Steel works in Pennsylvania, Pinkerton private security guards had to be shipped in at gunpoint.

The U.S. Army was more reliable. Court injunctions applying the Sherman Antitrust Act to workers instead of to the trusts it was meant to curb provided the excuse to deploy it. Several late-nineteenth-century presidents sent troops but left local officials or the corporations themselves to decide how to use them. "No president deemed it wise or necessary to send independent observers," writes Jerry Cooper, in *The Army and Civil Disorder,* "to report on the advisability of a federal presence."

Today, these Gilded Age practices bring to mind the example of Uzbekistan, a Central Asian dictatorship. There, forced labor is still shipped to the cotton fields—not from prisons, but from schools and government offices. And there, a dispersing crowd was fired upon in 2005 at the end of a demonstration—almost exactly what happened in Chicago at the end of an infamous rally in 1886. The Uzbek version came to be called the Andijan Massacre. The death toll dwarfed Chicago's. Its victims were branded religious extremists. In reality, they had been speaking against government corruption.

This kind of naked government violence seems hard to imagine in the United States today. Yet, here and now, sheriffs' deputies and state troopers from as far away as Louisiana flocked to windswept North Dakota bluffs in 2016 to join forces with local cops and private security agents against a ragtag encampment protesting a gas pipeline under the Missouri River. North Dakota proceeded to pass no less than four laws expanding what counts as criminal trespass and allowing the state attorney general to badge out-of-state law-enforcement officers to help curb it.

The Louisiana connection may not be a coincidence. In a similar pipeline fight deep in the bayous, Louisiana state probation and parole officers pulled security for Energy Transfer, the company behind both pipelines. The men acted, as the Gilded Age Strike Commission report would have put it, in the double capacity of pipeline employees and state officers.

At least in some parts of the United States, the hydra is closing its tentacles around the mace. Where it does, in a democracy, it gives people reason to hate their government.

Still, it would take a lot, today, to make U.S. Army units fire into a protest by American citizens. So a question arises: Should a kleptocratic network be considered more frightening, or less, if it has so altered people's mind-set, so addicted them to material comforts and to a race for success counted in dollars, that it no longer has to use violence to maintain control?

4

Powers Wielded: The Purse

Not needed to quell internal insurrection or repel a foreign invasion, the U.S. military has come to serve another function typical in kleptocracies: as a revenue stream to be pillaged by network members.

This phenomenon was on display, on three distant continents, in 2015.

The jouncing video shows men in turbans sprouting from the turret of a U.S. tank, their arms up in a victory V.

Four thousand miles south and west, screams shatter a Sahara night, as children are yanked from dormitory beds.

On the flank of a windswept hill far off to the north and east, kerchiefed women pick their way, carrying basins of potato soup for soldiers huddled in fraying tents.

The militaries of Iraq, Nigeria, and Ukraine all collapsed in 2015, in the face of grotesquely less equipped and organized enemies (respectively ISIS, Boko Haram, and Russian-backed rebels). The insurgents did not win their stunning victories. The opposing armies—hollow shells of armies—lost.

In late 2014, a Nigerian general risked his career. He wrote to his commander in chief: "Please Mr. President, Save the Military and Nigeria from Collapsing." At the time, defense spending in his country was on the order of $6 billion a year, astronomical for Africa.

"Commanders see . . . [the] NE operation," meaning where the army was battling Boko Haram, "as a personal money making venture," the officer declared. Details follow. "All the units in NE are understaffed, but on [the] payroll their strength [is] complete."

By way of that fraud, unit commanders were pocketing the pay and food and fuel allowances of their nonexistent soldiers, while the real comrades of these phantoms were doing twice the work. Equipment was sold off or not even purchased. Commanders took the money and soldiers took to the field unarmed.

"When a unit is attacked and [overrun] by the BH not because the soldiers are unable to fight, but lack of weapons, ammunitions and communications equipment, the soldiers on many occasions will [run] away." Such men were being court-martialed for cowardice.

In the United States, the heist is less brazen. And the men and women who help perpetrate it are rarely on the front lines. They sit in offices stringing unintelligible acronyms together into contracts for substandard goods and services. Or, perhaps "simply ignorant but not criminal," as Twain put it in *The Gilded Age,* they sign those contracts where indicated by a yellow tab. Readiness is preserved. But no war is won. In this process, funds are being pumped from the public purse into private hands on a scale that dwarfs Nigeria's.

Cast your mind back to the days after the 9/11 terrorist attacks. Dick Cheney, who has just left his position running a major defense contracting firm, is vice president of the United States. In Manhattan, a wind is up. A woman pulls a roll of packing tape from her bag. She's trying to stick down the corner of a sheet of paper to the glass wall of a bus shelter. It has the words of a song on it, and a photograph—of her sister, lost in the fiery hell. The bus shelter is covered with such memorials. The pall hangs heavy on the city. In Washington, that same day, a subsidiary of the vice president's former company submits a bid for a contract with the U.S. Army. The document runs to dozens of pages. Despite prior cost overruns of nearly a third in the Balkan wars a few years earlier, the vice president's company wins.

The contract is built like one of those expandable suitcases. It allows the army to order as-yet-unspecified services, for which the company can bill at as-yet-unspecified rates. No military action has been announced. Americans are still blind with grief.

As I scroll through a version of this contract, looking at all the rows marked "to be determined," images surge to my mind. I think of what those TBDs translated to on the ground: the bases I toured in my ungainly boots; the tactical operations centers packed with fully rugged laptops, the giant screens and satellite links for simultaneous secure video conferencing the length and breadth of Afghanistan. I think of those delicate electronics, requiring a separate army of IT people just to keep them running in the talcum powder dust. I think of the Stryker vehicles, taller and wider than normal Humvees and fitted out with high-tech communications. They were deployed to Arghandab, a place of walled pomegranate orchards and irrigation channels and dirt passages too narrow for such lumbering vehicles. I remember the treated-lumber boardwalks that made bases into shopping malls; the mess halls serving up gloppy trucked-in food—while platoons taking fire in forward posts went hungry. I think of the supply chains all this required, the dependence on yet more contractors to protect the convoys of gaudily painted trucks, the fantastically complex logistics and maintenance: the sheer effort of keeping this top-heavy tangle in existence.

My eyes refocus. The date at the bottom of the page is December 2001. The United States is still only engaged in a limited intervention in a bereft, rock-strewn place where Usama bin Laden set up shop. Unbeknownst to American citizens (but perhaps not to executives at the vice president's former company), plans are already afoot to pivot the full force of their nation's power against a different country, which had nothing to do with the recent terrorist attacks.

The vice president—decisive, explosive, riveted to details—is driving this change of course. That other country is awash in oil and natural gas. His former company is an energy services provider. The invasion is launched on the basis of a lie.

The wars in Afghanistan and Iraq are a glaring example of the abusive transfer of public wealth into the hands of private individuals, and of the consequences. But the methods used were old. They have continued largely unchanged for decades—across administrations of both political parties.

Dina Rasor is the one who found out that the U.S. military was paying $436 for an ordinary claw hammer and $600 for a toilet seat. Also $74,165 for a retractable ladder aboard a Lockheed military transport plane. That was in 1984.

Rasor would write up memoranda explaining arcane costing

mechanisms and staple them to budget and contract documents whistleblowers had provided, and hand the packets to select journalists. In those days, she says "everything was procurement. We had mutually assured destruction"—the nuclear standoff with the Soviet Union—"and people were still burnt on Vietnam. No one in the Pentagon wanted a war. They just bought weapons."

Reporters pounced on the issue, political cartoonists too. In December 1985, the *St. Louis Post-Dispatch* published an eight-part series titled "Arms Costs: A Wasteland?" Contracts were signed with no audit of the cost projections. Pentagon representatives on the factory floor were "getting chummy with the very companies they're supposed to monitor"—where they often later went to work. Decisions canceling contracts or suspending companies for malfeasance were waived.

Worse: many of the weapons systems did not work. Some of the stories are collected in *More Bucks Less Bang: How the Pentagon Buys Ineffective Weapons.* A radar broadcasts the position of the unit deploying it. A tank must stop every seventy-five miles for an air filter replacement. Ammunition that has fouled rifles since Vietnam is still in use.

The profiteers were as active as in J. P. Morgan's day.

Coverage like this and public outrage did compel some reform. Audits and inspections were stepped up in the mid- to late 1980s. Pentagon employees had to wait a few years before taking a job at a company they had dealt with while in office.

But shortly after taking the presidential oath in 1993, Bill Clinton put Vice President Al Gore in charge of a grand initiative "to redesign, to reinvent, to reinvigorate the entire National Government." With the stated goal of increasing efficiency, says Rasor, "the Pentagon was able to get rid of those pesky investigators and auditors" and loosen contracting standards. Efficiency became the new morality.

Sick at the sight of years of effort undone, Rasor turned to health care for some years. Now, she says, the situation "is worse than I've ever seen it."

One difference is the sheer scale of the looting. Even with two long wars wound down, the defense budget keeps ballooning. For fiscal year 2020, it reached $738 billion.

The Navy's six-hundred-dollar toilet seat became a millstone around Defense Secretary Caspar Weinberger's neck.

I teeter here at the edge of a cliff above a river of numbers. That's what would normally come next in an analysis like this. But who is moved by a number? Who tells a sacred story about one? The whole point of numbers is to exclude imagination. To erase the moral choices. Let's put imagination back in. What could you make whole, right now, with $738? Whom could you delight? Give the billion of us in all the Americas—every person from the Arctic to Tierra del Fuego—that opportunity.

Nearly half this unfathomable sum went directly to private companies. Add to that another $7 billion or so—more than Nigeria's entire defense budget. That's what the State Department pays defense contractors in a year for the training programs and weapons it gives governments as bad for their people as Nigeria's: Sisi's in Egypt, for example, or the Philippines'.

On those contracts, on every "CostPlus" or "Firm Fixed Price—as appropriate" entry for a "Fly Away Communications Package" or for "propulsion and engineering change order," the totals rise with each renewal. Projected costs, still unaudited, are based on historical data—with the waste and overruns Rasor found in the 1980s baked in, year after year. "Things are astronomically overpriced now," she says.

In other words, the U.S. government is creating a vast artificial market, where a handful of repeat offenders can fob off shoddy or defective products on American citizens at ever-increasing prices, without suffering any market consequences.

Patriotism keeps us from quibbling. Fear, too: What would you not spend to stay safe? Another powerful pretext for this larceny is jobs. Defense contractors, we are told, employ people. Oh? So we as a country believe in a government-funded jobs corps? Then let's choose together what work we want those subsidized employees to do. Perhaps they should rebuild failing water systems instead of building failing fighter jets. Perhaps they should run rural bus services, care for the elderly, or revive lands polluted by the industry of an earlier era. Maybe their cutting-edge engineering powers could invent new modes of transport.

Numbers erase choices. They erase competing values.

Another transformation grew out of that contract inked while the 9/11 dust still hung acrid in the air. Weapons procurement is no longer everything. Today, nearly half the $320 billion or so paid to private defense contractors goes not for hardware but for labor. "The war services industry has exploded, and that contract was the rocket fuel," Rasor judges. "Service contractors are the new four-hundred-dollar hammer," agrees Scott Amey, of the Project on Government Oversight (POGO). "At least when you're talking planes, trains, and automobiles, you can break a bottle of champagne over the latest ship. Labor hours are much harder to track." In 2014—like those Nigerian officers who kept ghost soldiers on their budgets—Military Professional Resources Inc. billed the U.S. government for hours supposedly worked by employees who were actually home on leave.

Reporters investigating these doings back in the 1980s never used the term "kleptocratic network." They described the structure as an "iron triangle." In the words of the St. Louis Post-Dispatch: "Key members of Congress, Pentagon officials and defense contractors share powerful common interests and are locked in an 'iron triangle' of mutual support."

The post-9/11 contract applies the soothing language of partnership. "Partnering," it reads, "requires the parties to look beyond the strict bounds of the contract in order to formulate actions that promote their common goals and objectives." Those common goals and objectives, that is, eclipse the rights of taxpayers and the law. "It is a relationship that is based upon open and continuous communications [and] mutual trust and respect."

The networks woven by such relationships get thicker every time people switch places, landing jobs in the private sector in return for ignoring contract terms, or going back inside government after a stint with a contractor. This dance is called the "revolving door."

But I'm not sure that's the best way to think about it. Isolated individuals are not pushing a door between two separate sectors. These people are members of an integrated network. They perform different tasks at different times to promote the network's "common goals and objectives": maximizing members' wealth.

Combing through years of records, POGO has built a database documenting hundreds of instances when officials left government to work for defense contractors. Mandy Smithberger, who designed and manages it, notes that the flow goes the other way, too. "Now more than ever before, executives and lobbyists from defense contractors have taken the reins of the department itself."

President Obama quickly waived the binding commitment against lobbying he issued as his first executive order to appoint

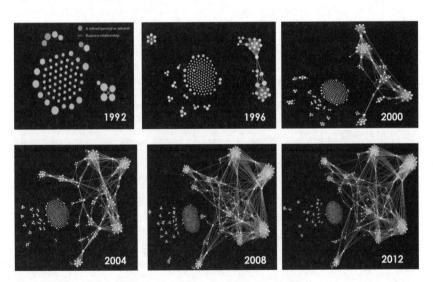

This link-analysis map depicts business ties among retired generals and flag officers—the vast majority of them in the defense industry. Each dot represents an individual retired officer. Lines represent business connections.

former Raytheon lobbyist William Lynn deputy secretary of defense. Former Lockheed vice president James Comey became FBI director.

Under President Trump, at least three-quarters of top DoD appointees hailed from industry, including former General Dynamics board member James Mattis as secretary of defense, former Boeing vice president Patrick Shanahan, who took over as acting secretary when Mattis quit, and former Textron CEO Ellen Lord as undersecretary in charge of acquisitions. "This interpenetration of the private and public sectors is unprecedented," says Rasor, "and it has become acceptable. Cronyism is now seen as a positive good."

The hydra holds the strings of the purse.

Which example to write of next? Who blinks anymore when public property is deeded over to private interests? Who weighs the worth of what is lost?

French economist Thomas Piketty has highlighted the sell-off of publicly owned capital in Great Britain and France after 1980. The 1990s fire sale of public assets in the former Soviet Union helped incubate a virulent new strain of kleptocratic network with nodes in Russia and other former republics and twining branches that soon reached around the world.

The United States never kept so much capital in public hands. But there is one irreplaceable asset that American citizens do collectively own: our land. Few countries on earth contain the forests and floodplains, the towering peaks and stretches of tundra, the rock formations and rippling prairies that grace the United States.

When America was conquered, land was wealth more obviously than it is today. The breathtaking value of what was here was lost on no one—the teeming aliveness of the land, invisibly tended by "savages" who knew it was sacred. A genocide was perpetrated over it. Our most honored Founding Fathers were rapacious land speculators. "Obsessed with the idea of amassing land in the West," George Washington, for example, made his first purchase at age eighteen. The objective? "Wealth, possessions, and status." He aggressively parlayed his surveyor's expertise into personal landholdings estimated in the hundreds of thousands of acres.

In the Gilded Age, much of the frenzied stock-market speculation depended on huge federal land grants to railroad companies.

Today, infinite wealth is still tied, in the end, to land: energy production and transport occupy terrain like an invading army; rare earth metals for information technology are "blasted and hauled" up from land; industrial farming erodes and sterilizes mile upon mile.

No wonder familiar players keep clamoring to possess what land remains in the public domain. A 1976 law shifted U.S. policy emphasis from "disposing of" this real estate to stewarding it in the broader public interest. Big-money logging, mining, and energy magnates lurched into action. Huddling with ranchers and other locals who had made their lives on the weathered western landscapes and who mistrusted distant Washington, they helped fire up a so-called Sagebrush Rebellion. The movement's goal was to force the federal government to hand over the public lands it was now bound by law to protect.

The campaign foreshadowed the Tea Party. Legitimate grievances and local pride nourished it, but it was funded behind the scenes by members of the then-emerging hydra. Like that monster, it belched up a fetid breath of violent intimidation. It tolerated joy in laying waste to the very land it was fighting over. Art left on timeless stone architecture by our human forebears was defaced, or pried right off the rock.

For nothing has standing, has reality, except my wants—now—and their market value.

This attitude reaches far outside the federal domain. It infects all of us, and our own use of lands in our own care. The U.S. kleptocratic networks want us locked in an economy—and a culture and morality—in which value is what can be most efficiently extracted and transformed to cash. Everything else can be spoiled. We leave the wreckage behind. We move on to the next parcel, open it up. Subject to this indoctrination, we are logging and farming and building on land in ways that spoil it. We are taking joy in the spoiling.

But this is not the only option. It is possible to construct a culture and an economy that honor the use of land in ways that revive and enrich it—and revive and enrich the people too, offering them other sources of joy.

After 1980, efforts to divest the nation of its public lands gained more outside money, as well as a coordinated legislative and litigation strategy. The sponsors? People and groups now familiar from the Koch and U.S. Chamber of Commerce networks: Joseph Coors, for example, and the American Legislative Exchange Council, which writes model state laws for passage by network members who hold state office.

The "rebellion" flamed up again in the early 1990s and the 2000s, paralleling spurts in Koch activity. In 2015, three dozen bills on transferring lands to state control were introduced across the West. Two years later, Utah's Jason Chaffetz submitted one in the U.S. House. It required the secretary of the interior to auction off more than three million acres of our collective property. The outcry was so blistering that Chaffetz hastily withdrew it.

Those behind this agitation—who were not, obviously, average American citizens—tried other strategies. One is to delegate management to the states, while leaving the federal government to cover the cost. Another is to accelerate leasing—instead of outright sales—the way an auctioneer's chant accelerates the English language.

"There is a rush to offer acreage," says Autumn Hanna, of Taxpayers for Common Sense, who attends meetings of the Interior Department's Royalty Policy Committee. "They are fast-tracking permitting, streamlining procedures." Working hand in hand, she says, companies and officials "are weaponizing the Department of the Interior to essentially privatize the land without the cost of ownership." Leases even come with subsidies, such as logging roads constructed and maintained at government expense.

Oddly, Hanna and her colleague Ryan Alexander have found, the lands the Interior Department has prioritized for leasing "are the hardest to develop: in Alaska, in Nevada—remote, wild, sensitive land, with no infrastructure, and where there is a public appetite to protect. They are giving these lands away to industry for next to nothing. It makes no economic sense."

These are the last frontiers. These are the sacred places, deliberately defaced.

There are other anomalies, like a single company submitting requests for the lease of acreage in Montana, but then not bidding at the auction it requested. A few days later, for the selfsame parcels, the company gets the much lower prices that apply to "unwanted" land. American citizens lost about $30 an acre, or more than $3 million total just on these Montana deals.

I see why advocacy organizations try to convert their objections into market terms this way: to calculate taxpayers' loss in dollars. The World Wildlife Fund has even put a dollar number on the oceans: $24 trillion. I understand the strategy. Yet, in doing so, they succumb to market-based morality. Great chunks of meaning are effaced.

Meaning is expressed in choices. Deliberately, like the Sagebrush vandals, the Interior Department has chosen to lease acreage near revered places. Not only where the bones of ancestors lie, or elk or wild birds congregate, but places where "wisdom sits." For wisdom is stored in sacred stories—in myths—whose drama unfolds within specific landscapes. You pass that butte and catch its color in the slanting light, and the scenes of the story spring to life. You are struck by the dart of its wisdom.

How are we valuing wisdom?

I found an answer in a jumble of internal rules the U.S. House of Representatives adopted late at night on January 2–3, 2017. Among clauses on how many subcommittees a committee may form and whether "the Speaker shall rise to put a question [or] may state it sitting," come these words: transferring federal land "shall not be considered as . . . decreasing revenues, increasing mandatory spending, or increasing outlays."

In other words, for budget purposes, the value assigned to our land—and the wisdom it contains, and all its teeming life—is zero.

In the absence of much other public property, the power of the purse is wielded as the Defense Department wields it: to purchase goods and services from members of the kleptocratic network. For safeguarding our health, for educating our children, for helping house our poorest neighbors, for punishing our neighbors who have done wrong, the contracts look much like the one signed in the wake of 9/11. Their terms boil down to "pay or die." Their line items are marked "to be determined." Repeat offenders keep winning the bids.

It's not just our lands we are ceding to this hydra. We are giving over our bodies and our minds. What value are we assigning to them in this process? Is it zero, too?

5

Powers Sabotaged

What manner of beast would willfully break its own legs? It seems unnatural. Yet that is what the hydra does. I have seen it around the world and I am seeing it in the United States. Once inside government, it deactivates powers and spikes those tools that are meant to serve and protect the public. The hydra will expend significant effort and resources to vandalize equipment and individuals it deems a threat.

The push to strip the United States government of its authority to manage lands it holds for all of us and future generations—and to further disinherit those who have loved those lands time out of mind—provides a small example. After Chaffetz's effort failed, bills flooded Congress to give the states "exclusive jurisdiction" over the most important aspects of what happens on and to that earth. Other bills created sanctuary zones where the writ of U.S. law could not reach.

With that legislation making little headway either, then–interior secretary Ryan Zinke started giving powers away unbidden. In a September 2018 memorandum, he recognized "the States as the first-line authorities for fish and wildlife management," including on federal lands. The federal government would "hereby . . . defer to the states." He gave Interior Department bureaus ninety days to bring their guidance, regulations, and policies into line with state provisions, wherever those provisions were *weaker* than federal law.

That order got me reaching for the United States Constitution.

"This Constitution, and the Laws of the United States which shall be made in Pursuance thereof," reads Article VI, "shall be the supreme Law of the Land."

I thought so. A beast sworn to support and defend the Constitution can't just abandon its supremacy. It can't subordinate the Laws of the United States to weaker state provisions.

Yet that is the tack the Environmental Protection Agency has also been taking since 2017. Its mission is to maintain standards of good neighborliness in the use and disposal of dangerous chemicals, radioactive materials, and solid waste so as not to poison the air, water, and soil upon which life within and even outside the United States depends.

I have a friend who works there.

He's shouting into the phone: "I've never experienced a guy with such stupid, harebrained ideas!" Most of our conversations start with some version of this sentence. For the past few months it's been about water pollution. "The states are supposed to implement the Clean Water Act *under federal guidance* and subject to *minimum* federal standards!"

Those standards apply to how much toxic waste may be leached into our waterways; states can't set lower numbers. But also, my friend explains, the standards apply to state agencies' enforcement practices: how hard they try to investigate or prosecute violators, or if they waive the standards instead or turn a blind eye. "Now someone has ginned up a draft regulation that says the states don't have to maintain federal standards, they can have their own standards. That's just insane! It's illegal!"

"I don't think it's insane," I counter. "I don't think this guy is harebrained. This is strategy. I've seen it too many times. This is corruption."

The EPA is in part a law-enforcement agency. But that is not the kind of mace the hydra wants to wield. The platoon-sized round-the-clock security detail that helped make former administrator Scott Pruitt the butt of jokes was staffed by veteran criminal investigators. It's hard to chase bad guys when you're babysitting the boss. Even before the coronavirus pandemic hit, prompting a moratorium on most enforcement, EPA investigators across the country had to check with Washington before even requesting information from suspects or ordering laboratory tests that might prove a crime has been committed. At headquarters, prosecutors are assigned to write regulations they know are invalid, instead of building cases against violators of the legal laws.

Though inevitable, the impact of such self-sabotage on both enforcement actions and the sums recovered still made me catch my breath. In the first two years of the Trump administration the numbers just collapsed—compared to the Obama and George W. Bush administrations alike. At the Department of Agriculture, to take just one other example, fines levied on meat and processed food conglomerates for cheating contract farmers and other violations plummeted by 2018 to a tenth of 2013 levels. Imagine if a local police department reported that its arrests for assault and battery had suddenly plunged by 90 percent. What questions would it be scrambling to answer?

A stone in free fall accelerates. This trend is accelerating like that, only faster. A December 2018 study found that the EPA had cleared about half as many cases nationwide as it had just the previous year, FY 2017.

So enfeebled, what do the enforcers still enforce? With limited resources, they go for smaller fry. My neighbors out fishing are more likely to get a citation for a leaky outboard than the insulation factory a few towns over is for swilling gallons of formaldehyde into a river. No wonder people hate the EPA. They never see it helping, only harassing people like them.

Exploiting this sentiment, the Trump administration promised to cut regulations to the bone, and is doing so. Career EPA lawyers, as instructed, have cranked out revised rules by the ream. Nearly every one challenged in court has been overruled. By late 2018, the score was 18 EPA losses in 19 cases. But new measures weakening regulations totaled a staggering 143. It's the strategy of the archers' volley: the arrows don't have to be aimed. Some will lodge.

Much of the EPA's mutilation is happening as though under a microscope, invisible to the naked eye. Just adjust how things are counted or words are defined, and thousands more kids can't catch their breath at recess; your cousin has an enlarged liver; a vibrant ecosystem is laid waste, depriving the sickening earth of another vital organ.

For the purposes of required cost-benefit analyses, what dollar amount should be entered for the harm caused by an additional ton of carbon dioxide belched into the saturated air? When assessing the risks posed by the use of a certain chemical, do you calculate only the danger to those who actually handle it? Or do you add everyone, non–*Homo sapiens* included, likely to be exposed when it spills? What do the words "ambient air" mean? Is air no longer "ambient"—does it stop circulating—if the public is instructed by "signage" to avoid the patch of ground beneath it? What happens to the neighbor's crops and to the living soil when what's in that air rains down on them?

These questions are not the arcane technicalities they are disguised to be, dressed up in their chemical symbols and impenetrable vocabulary. They are moral choices. And they are being made by a self-dealing network whose private-sector members have been handed control of the public trust to a degree unprecedented in the United States, even in the Gilded Age.

The foreign kleptocracies I have examined don't bother with such minutiae. They can starve government institutions in plain sight.

One major focus of international development assistance is "capacity building"—trying to improve the performance of third-world officials by providing computer software, for example, and training. The premise seems to be that officials lack the education and the office equipment to handle the complexities of their jobs. I interviewed a European Union functionary who conceded that in the twenty years since she first worked on Honduras, its government's "capacity" to serve its citizens had not improved.

Why did she suppose that was? I wondered. Did she suppose Hondurans were just stupider than other people—than she was, for example? Or could the "capacity deficit" be deliberate?

An official at a major development bank, which makes about $2 billion in loans per year in Central America, lamented the constant turnover at the government agencies the bank was assisting. "When you're trying to improve the capacity of local counterparts," he said, "the problem is rotation. You can waste a lot of time and money training units, creating systems," and then the people get transferred.

As he spoke, I remembered the valiant and lovingly mentored

anticorruption prosecutors in Afghanistan who were abruptly reassigned to districts infested by Taliban.

There are other ways the networks can reduce the capacity of inconvenient agencies. When I arrived in Honduras to ask questions like these in the summer of 2016, the employees of the Instituto Nacional Agrario were picketing. They had not been paid in weeks. The INA was one of the few offices that village *campesinos* and indigenous people could access to register claims to the lands where their families had lived forever. And that was the specific agency that lacked budget for salaries.

Corruption in the United States, of course, is subtler than this, goes the consensus. But then again, for a month starting in December 2018, federal government offices in every state in the Union were locked. Meat and poultry inspectors worked without pay. Public servants were forced to join lines at food banks. They swallowed that humiliation. The detailed information on prices and crop futures that small farmers stake their lives on each spring, the loans they need to buy seed and new fencing, were not provided. Securities and Exchange Commission investigations into fraud on Wall Street were frozen. But at the Bureau of Land Management, preparations for the next land lease auction went forward.

An across-the-board federal hiring freeze proclaimed when Trump took office lasted only a few months, to be replaced by a "more strategic, more surgical" approach. I'm not suggesting there aren't too many bureaucrats in too many offices making track changes on the latest version of some document. I know—I was one of them.

But the life of the patient depends on who's in the doctor coat doing that surgery. We in whose name the flesh of our government is being carved should look for patterns in the incisions. Which agencies are shedding people? Which people? How many of those public servants are being replaced with higher-priced private contractors who answer not to us, even theoretically, but to a CEO wasted by the Midas disease?

Since 2017, the number of unfilled vacancies in top federal positions has been unprecedented, including the at least one additional federal election commissioner required to reach a quorum. Currently, without one, the FEC cannot enforce U.S. election laws. Just imagine if this year's Super Bowl game were set to kick off without an umpire. Infinitely more is at stake in our elections. In spring 2020, two dozen ambassadorships lacked nominees, including to such vital places as the Central American countries of Honduras and Panama, as well as Afghanistan, Qatar, and Norway. There was no secretary of homeland security; no director for the Office of National Drug Control Policy, in the middle of a historic addiction epidemic; no commissioner of customs and border protection, Trump's signature issue. Indeed, a striking number of top executive branch positions were held by "actings," or formally low-ranking subordinates to whom the director's duties have been "delegated," but whose names had not been submitted for the Senate confirmation required by the Constitution. Below them, such key offices as the National Security Council's Directorate of Global Health Security or the Centers for Disease Control and Prevention lost resources or were disbanded entirely. Other agencies, such as the Consumer Financial Protection Bureau—which defends Americans against predatory loan sharks and exploitative banking practices—are piloted by people whose role is to break their legs.

Where the cutting has been wholesale, and has lasted, is in Congress—Congress: the first branch of government, closest to the people; Congress, which on our behalf keeps an eye on all those un-elected bureaucrats. Congressmen and -women have sabotaged their own institution's ability to do that for us. They have smashed the tools it possessed to help fashion laws in the public interest. They have crippled their own capacity to come to independent conclusions as to the nature of the problems such laws would address. Congress has been disabled from inside.

Most of this happened in one of those revisions of the House of Representatives' internal rules when an election flipped the majority party. It was January 1995, and a last-minute geyser of campaign cash had delivered an upset Republican victory two months before. Newt Gingrich held the gavel. The very first provision of the new rules he hammered through on January 5 reads: "In the One Hundred Fourth Congress, the total number of staff of House committees shall be at least one-third less than the corresponding total in the One Hundred Third Congress."

Congressional staffers are the citizens' subject matter experts. Over years, these scientists and auditors and lawyers and military veterans build up historical knowledge on the complex issues that jostle for House and Senate attention. They help members, who have to be generalists, drill down into specifics. Cut staffs, and members lose the bandwidth to craft wise legislation, the expertise to ask telling questions in hearings—the ability to hold oversight hearings at all. The Congressional Research Service, the Government Accountability Office, the Congressional Budget Office all suffered the cuts. The Office of Technology Assessment was abolished—because, in 1995, what new technology could possibly be poised on the horizon?

Democrats, when they regained control of the House, did not repair the damage. Today, the number of staff fielding thousands of corporate lobbyists or fact-checking their jive remains lower than it was a quarter century ago. For example: at least 6,243 highly paid professionals lobbied Congress on the sweeping 2017 tax overhaul. Opposite them, representing taxpayers, stood 130 members of the Senate Finance and Joint Taxation Committee staffs. The House Ways and Means Committee held zero hearings on that momentous bill.

Fumed a former staff lead on security issues for the top House Republican: "They say, 'We have to be good stewards of taxpayers' money,' so they cut staff. The Armed Services Committee has sixty staff and they're overseeing a Department of Defense budget of nearly seven hundred billion dollars. It's just optics! If you want to be good stewards of taxpayer money, you hire seasoned forensic accountants, people who have been in DoD for twenty years, and pay them decent salaries. You call an undersecretary in for a hearing? You grill him on discrepancies in the budget. But they're staffed by twenty-four-year-olds making forty thousand dollars who have never set foot in the Pentagon. No one will say this. No one will say, 'Triple Congress's personnel budget.' They're too chickenshit."

A new college graduate serving a fellowship with the Republican majority on the Senate Transportation Committee recounted his experience in this vein. The twenty-two-year-old said he was one of two staffers working on the committee's probe into the design flaws and lax enforcement that led to the crashes of two Boeing 737 MAX jets, grounding the fleet worldwide for months. The committee has requested upward of a million documents from Boeing—with just the two staff-members to comb through them. The young man recalled one recent meeting at which he and his colleague sat across the table from seven senior Boeing executives plus their lawyers. The two are tasked with not just this case, but all the oversight duties for the whole committee, whose purview includes the nation's commerce and scientific affairs.

Democrats who gained the Speaker's gavel after Gingrich must have enjoyed the powers he had stripped from committee chairmen and vested in his own office, for they kept them. Now a House Speaker can project herself as a kind of national gladiator, facing off against a president.

Democrats also copied the internal pay-to-play system Gingrich invented, whereby choice committee chairmanships and leadership positions were essentially auctioned off. In *Money in the House,* political scientist Marian Currinder published the 2008 price list: "The five chairs of the power committees," for example, "must contribute $500,000 [each] and raise an additional $1 million" for congressional campaign funds. Big donors thus get to choose not just who runs for office, but who, once elected, leads.

Through such acts of sabotage, more powers of the pen fall to the hydra. More and more of our laws are simply cribbed from drafts prepared by members of kleptocratic networks or their large staffs.

Starved of funds or obstructed or ridiculed, other government research functions—at the National Institutes of Health, for example, or the National Oceanic and Atmospheric Administration, or the Centers for Disease Control and Prevention—are being sabotaged, too. Even the leadership of the nation's numerous and well-endowed intelligence agencies must now consider which findings to convey— and how—to the members of government they serve, after acting director of National Intelligence Joseph Maguire endured a tongue-lashing and an early termination because Trump disliked a briefing a member of his staff gave to the House Intelligence Committee in February 2020.

The hydra is crippling our collective power to know, and to communicate and share our knowledge.

Along with egalitarianism, these abilities are what make us human.

In Congress, it is not just anonymous staffs that are hobbled. Members have been dispossessed of their primary function: voting on laws. Senate and House leaderships—super-empowered since Gingrich's day—spend much of their time preventing measures from ever reaching the floor. Far more than selling votes for bribes, this is the form corruption takes in the United States Congress today.

This seems, in fact, to be the purpose for which the hydra seized the power of the pen. The creature seems to prefer rewriting the rules by way of the elite and durable institution of the federal courts, rather than through the people's elected representatives—no matter how the elections are manipulated.

One wholesale method for thus crippling the nation's ability to make law is the Senate filibuster. The Constitution requires a supermajority—more than half of the members who are present in the chamber and voting—to pass measures of special consequence: treaties entered into by the United States, for example, constitutional amendments, the conviction of impeached federal officials. All other laws were to be passed by simple majority.

The filibuster came into being in the early nineteenth century, by way of another of those rules changes, in the Senate this time. It permitted debate with no time limit on any measure. If a determined minority could find enough senators willing to take turns talking (about anything at all) for long enough, they could delay a bill—and all other business—till the end of the session. In effect, they could talk a measure, even a popular one, to death. A 1917 reform allowed the majority to end, or "cloture," such antics. To do so requires a vote of three-fifths of elected senators (normally sixty).

Back in the day, senators actually had to filibuster. They had to stand up there for hours on end, droning on about whatever they could think of, reading recipes out of cookbooks, napping right there in the chamber while a colleague relieved them. They had to make the effort, make fools of themselves. Everyone could know, by name, who was obstructing the nation's business. Constituents could confront those individuals.

But no more. Now just the threat of a filibuster keeps nose counters from bothering with proposed legislation unlikely to clear the sixty-vote bar. The majority no longer rules in the United States. A forty-one-person minority can run the show.

That is a wholesale method for crippling the legislative power. Senate majority leader Mitch McConnell has perfected the retail method: refusing to permit his fellow senators to debate or vote on bills he dislikes, even if they have passed in the House and enjoy broad support—because, as majority leader, he can. Casualties have included the Violence Against Women Act, which was passed in 1994 and reauthorized every five years with bipartisan majorities, through 2013, and bills to address prescription drug prices or to secure U.S. election systems after overwhelming evidence emerged of foreign efforts to subvert it in 2016 and since.

Or, here is a perplexing example. For years, bipartisan measures were floated to take some of the money that is set aside for reviving land scarred by now-abandoned coal mines and use it to shore up miners' health-care or pension funds. McConnell—a senator from coal-rich Kentucky—refused to bring them to a vote until December 2019. His retired mineworker constituents, many disabled or wheezing with black lung disease, lived for years in fear of losing their pensions. They draw an average of about six hundred dollars per month.

McConnell countered that troubled pension systems across all industries should be addressed in one comprehensive law. In May 2019, a new Senate-confirmed presidential appointee was sworn in as head of the Pension Benefit Guaranty Corporation, the government agency that would handle the multibillion-dollar cash transfusion needed to backstop the hundred or so underfunded multi-employer pension plans nationwide. That appointee, who took office well before his respected predecessor's term was up, was McConnell's brother-in-law Gordon Hartogensis.

Network maps are a perversely gratifying kind of maze, in which every turn leads closer to the center. Instead of miners' pensions, here is what McConnell did get the government to spend $4 million of that mine cleanup money on. In October 2018, he announced a grant to prepare an eastern Kentucky industrial park for the construction of a huge aluminum plant. But no such plant existed. It was a notion, unfunded. What followed was a contorted sequence of events typical of today's era of transnational kleptocratic networks.

While McConnell was working to divert mine cleanup money to the imagined plant in 2018, a top staffer, Brendan Dunn, left his office to join a K Street lobbying firm, where he soon began harrying Mnuchin's Treasury Department to lift sanctions on a mammoth Russian aluminum conglomerate. The sanctions had been placed on Rusal and several dozen other Russian individuals and entities that spring because of their involvement in Moscow's occupation of Crimea and efforts to subvert democracy, including in the United States.

Within nine months, the lobbying effort succeeded: sanctions on three of the entities—including Rusal—were lifted. Senators across parties fought to reverse Treasury's decision, eventually voting 57–42 to keep the sanctions in place. In a floor speech lambasting this effort as "political theater," McConnell vaunted his party's tough line on Russia but pushed the body, "in this narrow case," to allow sanctions to be lifted. The majority did not reach the sixty-vote threshold to end a filibuster that no one was actually conducting, and, with McConnell's strenuous assistance, the measure failed.

Three months later, Rusal announced a $200 million investment in that Kentucky venture. One of Rusal's top shareholders (a 26 percent share, held with sanctioned oligarch Viktor Vekselberg) is multibillionaire Leonid Blavatnik, a Kremlin-linked mogul, who founded his fortune in the 1990s free-for-all that followed the collapse of the Soviet Union. It is widely understood among Russia experts that Putin helps such barons consolidate their booty on condition that they spend some of it furthering his causes. Blavatnik has spent around $7 million of his since 2015 on campaign funds controlled by Mitch McConnell.

Let's keep tracing those branching lines. Another major (21 percent) shareholder in Rusal is the Kremlin-linked bank VTB, also under U.S. sanctions. Since 2015, VTB has been joining forces with a Chinese counterpart, China Eximbank. In October of that year, China Eximbank announced a $37.5 million loan to a U.S. shipping company named Foremost, to order two cargo vessels from the China Shipbuilding Industry Corporation (CSIC). Foremost is the shipping company owned by the family of McConnell's wife, Transportation Secretary Elaine Chao—who was present at the Beijing signing ceremony. The activities of this company, and anything Chao or McConnell might do to facilitate them, would be subject to the oversight of that twenty-two-year-old temporary Senate staffer. If he had any time.

And so we have arrived in the world's most populous kleptocracy, China. In 2019, CSIC merged with China's other state-owned shipbuilding mammoth, China State Shipbuilding Corporation (CSSC). Chao's sister served on CSSC's board of directors, and the family has had most of its ships, which are all foreign flagged, built in China, by CSSC and CSIC.

Thus have the branching lines led independently from Kentucky to McConnell's in-laws, and their multiple business and political links in China. A proper network map would examine the boards of directors of each of these entities, their long-standing relationships and patterns of transactions. Still, there is enough in the public record to raise serious concerns. These are the Chaos, for example, who bailed out their son-in-law to the tune of between $5 million and $25 million in 2008, when he had to mortgage the couple's house for campaign cash. It is the family that has contributed generously to the majority leader's coffers. It is the family whose company McConnell's wife has used her public office to promote.

Today's kleptocratic networks are transnational.

The family's second most prominent member is Chao's sister Angela, now Foremost CEO and married to billionaire investor Jim Breyer. Along with her stint on the board of China's state-owned shipbuilding behemoth, Angela Chao is also a director of the Bank of China. In 2016, the Bank of China loaned more than $2 billion to the state entity at the center of Putin's network, Gazprom. It has a partnership with major Rusal shareholder VTB.

So, to recap. While single-handedly denying aged former coal miners their meager pensions for years, McConnell steered the money that could have gone for that purpose to a prospective factory whose product—rolled aluminum—is vital to the construction of U.S. military seagoing vessels and aircraft. That plant would be largely owned by a Russian conglomerate tied in several ways to Vladimir Putin and—like McConnell's in-laws—to the Chinese politico-military hierarchy, both U.S. adversaries.

I am, among other things, a national security professional. For that category of people, this tangle raises red flags. One—call it a "hard" security threat—is the vulnerability of a strategic raw material, as well as part of the merchant marine fleet built in China, to U.S. adversaries. A second has to do with constraints on national security decision-making. The more embedded entities like Rusal and Chinese state banking and shipbuilding concerns become in the U.S. economy, the more difficult it is for Washington to use tools like sanctions on those entities, for fear of hurting that precious U.S. economy.

But the security threat that scares me the most might be considered "softer." It is almost invisible. In whose interest is it to vandalize that symbol of modern democracy, the United States Congress? A clique of billionaires? Or totalitarian regimes like Russia's and China's?

Or both?

6

Bowing to the Money Changers

All of this hardly compares to what the money changers have done.

In no other industry have the private- and public-sector strands of our kleptocratic networks been so entwined for so long. In no other industry have the consequences for the public of the resulting damage been so widespread, so punishing—and so repetitive.

"We conclude this financial crisis was avoidable," declared, in 2011, the commission charged with investigating the 2007–2008 financial cataclysm. That event caused more people to take their own lives in the United States than the 9/11 terrorist attacks caused casualties. It triggered what would be considered a humanitarian crisis in any African or Middle Eastern country, as millions of Americans, forced out of their homes, became internally displaced people.

In a chapter entitled "Before Our Very Eyes," the report lists just some of the warnings that went unheeded ahead of the crash. The cofounder of a California community organizing and policy research group "began meeting with [Federal Reserve chairman Alan] Greenspan at least once a year starting in 1999" to explain predatory lending to him. Nonprofit housing advocates from a dozen states, besieged by desperate homeowners, showed regulators sample mortgages riddled with irregularities. In 2000, Cleveland's county treasurer begged Federal Reserve officials to write rules to curb the "rings of real estate agents, appraisers, and loan originators" feeding big banks' craving for loans. Those rules were called for under a six-year-old reform, but the Fed refused to write them. State attorneys general battled U.S. regulators in court for the right to rein in the dangerous practices themselves, and lost.

The prophets were banging on the temple doors and they were scorned.

But the warnings don't just start on the eve of the collapse. The Great Recession was foreshadowed and predicted by crises going back to the Panic of 1873, when speculators in Vienna and Berlin used new types of loans to flip unfinished buildings, heaping up debt they could never repay and sending prices rocketing.

In the late 1970s, powers wielded by the U.S. government still protected the country from this type of behavior. Then, beginning in the Reagan administration, came the sabotage. By law and by willful inaction, by rewritten rule and by instructions to focus enforcement efforts on some criminal behaviors and not bother with others, constraints on the type of bank that is closest to American communities were disabled. Such establishments were offered a potent cocktail of the new "What the fuck" freedom of *Risky Business*. Taken together, the measures:

- Allowed federally chartered savings and loan institutions (S&Ls, or "thrifts") to increase the interest rates they could offer, to attract depositors.

- Expanded the types and size of loans S&Ls could make, especially for commercial real estate, including interest-only loans for which no down payment was required.

- Allowed thrifts to accept deposits bundled by brokers into big $100,000 packages—precisely the size of the upper limit for federal deposit insurance. Shares of these could be bought. So what used to be personal savings accounts became a new kind of speculative investment.

- Dropped the requirement that a chartered savings bank have a minimum number of shareholders. After 1982, a single individual could own a federally insured bank, even staking noncash assets for the founding investment, such as (easy to overvalue) land.

· Reduced the mandatory net worth of an S&L—that is, the positive value that had to be left over if all the liabilities on the books were subtracted from all the assets.

· Relaxed the accounting standards by which these assets and liabilities could be calculated.

· *Reduced* the number of examiners and the budget for watching how bank managers were handling all these new temptations.

Alongside such moves "emancipating" thrifts to engage in foolish lending and to falsify their books came one that shielded them from likely negative consequences. As part of the 1980 Depository Institutions Deregulation and Monetary Control Act, federal insurance coverage was *increased.*

No member of Congress voted on that change. In the version of the bill the Senate approved, the total balance a depositor could recover if her bank defaulted went up to $50,000, just a $10,000 increase. The House version left the limit where it was, at $40,000. Yet, when a joint committee got finished merging the two passed bills into a single law, a new number had appeared: $100,000. Plot the link-analysis map for key members of that conference committee. The lines branching out from their photos lead to pictures of top S&L executives.

This change shifted most of the risk for what banks did with depositors' money onto taxpayers. Under cover of protecting depositors, it protected bankers.

There was a more insidious effect. "Higher deposit insurance diffuses the impact" of bank scandals, reflected former top S&L regulator William Black when I asked about this in 2015. If fewer victims suffer personally, then outrage is less widespread. It is harder to bring a broad-based coalition together to slap down the banker–meat hogs.

In combination, these measures jacked up the payoff for bank managers who robbed their institutions from inside, while decreasing the repercussions they might face. The immediate result: an epidemic of criminality in the savings and loan sector.

The basic fraud was the same as the one perfected by scam artist Thérèse Humbert in Gilded Age France: point to a locked safe, tell everyone it contains a juicy inheritance—that you have huge assets on your balance sheet—then borrow real money on the strength of that fable. The assets the S&Ls could now declare were just as fictitious as Humbert's inheritance. Like her, the delinquents used part of the money they got today to pay interest to yesterday's creditors—aka depositors—so the bank would look solid enough to prolong the heist. To bring in that fresh money, they dangled the newly legal high interest rates before potential depositors.

The details of the thefts took different forms. An S&L could *charge* high interest, too, for loans it approved. So, using deposit money, you could offer someone who called himself a developer a no-down-payment loan for a building project, charging some absurd interest rate, say 20 percent. You'd agree that if the borrower failed to pay it back, you couldn't sue him. You'd fatten the total loan amount to include not just the purchase price of land and building materials and construction workers' wages, but also the bank fees and a generous salary for the "developer," plus several years' interest on the loan itself. Your "developer"-accomplice would send some of that loaned money back as interest payments for a few months, then walk away from a debt he never intended to honor. He couldn't honor it even if he were actually doing any building, because the interest rate was too high for the project ever to break even.

But those interest rates looked great on banks' plus columns. The whole arrangement would be booked as an *asset,* not the liability it really was. Stock prices were buoyed. Executives paid themselves whopping salaries and perks. When the loans defaulted, the bank took the losses, not those delinquent executives.

To make this fraud work, bank owners needed co-conspirators. They needed developers who didn't know or care much about construction—or their reputations. They needed appraisers who would overestimate the value of building projects to make them look like solid collateral for the outsized loans, and accountants who would bless the books. They needed fellow S&L executives to keep values inflated by trading projects back and forth at ever higher prices, or to serve as one another's "developers," or to make personal loans, disguising the use of bank funds for tawdry details such as mansions or Mercedes sedans.

The criminal CEOs were infecting whole communities. Honest bankers were derided as chumps—just like Joel's fellow students in *Risky Business*. The weakened standards schooled accountants to line up numbers that veered farther and farther from reality—that is, to lie. Appraisers couldn't get work if they wouldn't play. Ethics were unlearned.

By sabotaging government powers, in other words, the hydra was not just protecting wrongdoers. It was instigating wrongdoing. It was corrupting us.

What helped was a sudden shift in culture. "It was all a metaphor about risk," recalls former regulator William Black. "It was a macho, adolescent culture. To take huge risks meant having cojones, a big swinging dick." The *Risky Business* culture was taking hold.

The problem with that metaphor, Black points out, is that the delinquents risked nothing. Applying these methods, they were guaranteed to get rich. The *banks* were being pushed into peril. So were their depositors and their neighborhoods and taxpayers. But for the executives, "it was a sure thing." Just like their assets, their courage was fictitious.

Economists George Akerlof and Paul Romer have modeled different possible strategies for S&L owners during that period. They found that some CEOs were indeed taking risks on high-stakes bets they hoped their banks would win. But those executives "would be concerned about the quality of their loans and the size of the operating expenses that they incur." The new breed of highflier displayed the opposite behavior. The result that got them richest—their "preferred outcome," Akerlof and Romer conclude—"is the one in which the thrift goes bankrupt."

A new business model was born: bankruptcy for profit.

This has become a prevailing business model in the United States, whereby the person most highly rewarded is he who extracts the maximum current value out of his enterprise and then moves on—leaving the wreckage, the salted earth, behind.

The criminality at the root of the savings and loan crisis was only discovered and punished due to a mistake. In 1983, the network behind the fraud chose the wrong member to take up public office on its behalf. The nod for chairman of the Federal Home Loan Bank Board went to Edwin Gray, a thrift executive and Reagan insider who had lobbied for deregulation. But the network had misjudged Gray's character. He soon had misgivings.

A year into his job, in 1984, he watched some footage sent by Texas examiners of streets of pocked and weed-choked office space. In a few short years the dereliction had spread out from Dallas like a strain of leprosy. Already concerned and now nauseated, Gray changed directions. He and his team, including Black, started enforcing fraud laws and repairing some of the rules governing banking practices.

Gray's term ended in 1987. His banker friends ensured he did not get another. Still, by the early 1990s, the crisis was spent. The Financial Institutions Reform, Recovery, and Enforcement Act of 1989 had restored crucial regulations. More than one thousand banks had gone bust. The board had made more than thirty thousand criminal referrals to the Department of Justice. A thousand-plus felony convictions resulted. A lot of meat hogs were punished.

And all those cases provided a data set revealing a pattern of systemic fraud.

Attention to patterns helped the team spot the crimes in the first place, Black told me. He used an analogy to explain. "When there was a spike in airplane crashes in the early seventies," he said, "the Federal Aviation Administration started doing autopsies, to see if there were any repeating problems." When the same maintenance gaps kept cropping up, the FAA designed tailored rules. "Like you can't move a plane till the chief mechanic signs off. He's personally accountable, and he knows if he's wrong, three hundred and fifty people die."

Imagine that kind of personal accountability applied to bankers. (By the 2010s, it had been badly eroded at the FAA, too, and, in 2018 and 2019, about 350 people did die.)

Black said the Bank Board imitated the (earlier) FAA: "Our litigation staff did systematic autopsies. It was hard. Two banks were failing per week. You had to force yourself not to deal with them and look at the past instead." Practices that "popped up recurrently" included forged documents and blanks in the records where bad loans had been removed from the file. "We trained examiners to look for those."

The Bank Board's work revealed another pattern: abnormal growth. Three white-collar criminologists who compiled and studied S&L crisis data put it this way: "The most catastrophic thrift failures [were the ones that] grew the fastest and consistently reported the highest profits." In a sample of three hundred failed savings and loans, the average growth rate was more than 50 percent.

That pattern hides a paradox. Economists tell us, and we have believed, that growth is a synonym for health. We score countries by their GDP growth, economies by rising stock markets, companies by their ballooning size, societies by their growing populations. The thrifts' rapid growth was seen as a sign that they must be sound. That bias stalled action against them, Black told me. In reality, like a cancer, sudden exponential growth of an S&L meant the patient was terminally ill.

What manner of fright will it take to sear us with this knowledge: unlimited or unnatural growth is an omen of impending disaster.

When President Bill Clinton took office in 1993, it was well documented that fraud had exploded as soon as banking regulations had come down in the 1980s. The pattern of the crimes was clear. The laxest states, California and Texas, were the worst affected. A comparison between S&Ls and similar institutions that had remained regulated, such as mutual savings banks, proved that stricter rules led to fewer bankruptcies. Prosecution and reregulation had contained the epidemic.

Any rational public servant would have responded to that kind of evidence by continuing to repair the broken fences and spiked tools that had protected the country from such disasters prior to 1980. Instead, the Clinton administration dismantled those protections even further.

Remaining checks on consolidated interstate banking were removed. Through waivers and then the repeal of the 1933 Glass-Steagall Act, commercial banks were invited to merge with brokerages—just like l'Union Générale in 1880s France—so insured deposits could be used for speculating. Meanwhile, the minimum net worth (the positive balance that had to be maintained to cover bad bets on mortgages and mortgage-backed securities) was reduced. Supervision of trading in the most complex and opaque of these, known as derivatives, was lifted. Whereas, complex as they were, it seems their market might need more supervision, not less.

Federal Reserve chairman Alan Greenspan—a Reagan appointee, reappointed twice by Clinton—flatly opposed government supervision of the banking sector. Despite the criminality that had caused the S&L crisis, he refused to use his authority under a 1994 reform to do what the FAA did after the 1970s crashes: make the mechanics abide by stricter rules. That was what the Cleveland county treasurer begged him to do in 2000. But it was Greenspan's view that fraud should not even be prohibited by law.

As part of that "Reinventing Government" initiative that Clinton asked Vice President Gore to manage, scores of additional rules were shredded in the cause of efficiency, such as one on underwriting that required certain forms be filled out for each loan. Missing documents or forgeries, Black reminded me, had constituted much of the S&L fraud. Now banks were legally allowed to "reduce their paperwork." Even so, "liar's loans," for which still-mandatory records were falsified, were rife by the early 2000s.

One argument for gutting all these rules was that bankers weren't complying with them. In other words, the high crime rate meant the wrongdoing should be legalized. What an interesting principle. People shoplift, but we haven't made that legal yet. As for what was still considered criminal, enforcement plunged. Hundreds of FBI agents were reassigned from bank fraud to health-care cheating, and after the 9/11 attacks, to terrorism.

Marietta Parker was an assistant U.S. attorney in Kansas City, Missouri, who switched from drug offenses to bank fraud in 1991 and recalls the transformation. "We were heavy into prosecuting savings and loan cases and all that fraud and malfeasance," she told me. "We worked hand in glove with regulators, who were inside the banks." But some years after Clinton's election, she stopped seeing an FDIC examiner she had loved working with, because of his rigor. "The bank fraud units went away," including hers. Her supervisor was demoted to a regular line prosecutor. "Health-care fraud got really sexy for a while. After 9/11, the FBI transferred all kinds of resources to terrorism. Other agencies tried to pick up the slack, but it wasn't the same. The best prosecutors started fighting to get on the terrorism unit."

These momentous changes that took place across the 1990s and into the new millennium multiplied the incentives for exactly the kind of fraud that had produced the S&L crisis starting 1981. Only this time, mortgage lenders were not stuck with the bad loans they made. With new ways of combining and packaging loans into derivatives, speculators were clamoring for raw material. Lenders could fob off whatever they signed. Now they booked real, not fictitious, profits at each handoff of their lousy loans. Purchasers, by chopping them up and packing the mincemeat into sausage casing, could disguise the offal and sell it on to someone else. Chances of prosecution fell to statistical zero.

That a crash of epic proportions would result wasn't just predictable, it was inevitable.

What then is to be said about the architects of this edifice—the presumed public servants, such as Roger Altman, Timothy Geithner, Alan Greenspan, Henry Paulson, and Robert Rubin? Most of these men collected tens of millions of dollars per year in compensation as Wall Street executives before and after their stints in public office—during which they busied themselves changing the rules of the game to benefit bankers like them. These men commanded such salaries, we were told, because of their specialized knowledge and unusual abilities, because of the economic value they created.

Yet, given the data they possessed and the scale of the social consequences they had witnessed over the preceding decade, I am having trouble finding gentle words for the way these men responded in the 1990s and early 2000s to the recent S&L experience. Either they were exceptionally dim-witted, or they were sociopaths.

And they were left in charge.

A Nigerian once answered a question about the social significance of money with an enigma: "People use money to intimidate people," he stated.

I knew what he meant, but I made polite conversation: "Really? How?"

"By giving it to them."

That was not the answer I expected. I waited.

"Then they can tell them what to do."

Afghans said the same, I remembered: "When someone eats your food, he should obey you. You don't obey him."

And yet, in the Great Recession, the power to make those who ate our collective food obey us was not wielded. Under neither the George W. Bush nor the Obama administrations were conditions attached to the taxpayer-funded assistance banks were handed. No one leveraged the collapse of the banks' moral authority. The U.S. government chose not to use our money to intimidate the banks.

Neil Barofsky, who was the special inspector general for the $750 billion Troubled Asset Relief Program launched in 2008 to rescue them, wrote a searing book, *Bailout*. It details the fierce opposition he encountered when he tried to pay attention to how that money was spent. Making banks adhere to safer standards and treat their victims decently in exchange for the free money was out of the question. "Given the amount of risk it was assuming," he told me in 2019, "the government should have gotten way more return. But the Democratic administration . . . flat-out broke its promise in order to bend over backwards to make it as soft as possible for the banks. It could have, should have, was supposed to help struggling homeowners. [But it] didn't care about homeowners, it cared about the banks."

For Barofsky, the damage reaches beyond even the devastating material fallout: "There is the destruction that comes to market discipline—to the very essence of capitalism"—from the reinforced "notion that government was a backstop, would not let them fail. How do you assess the cost of banks being able to get bigger and bigger and amass more and more political capital?"

A former top Obama administration Treasury official corroborated Barofsky's experience: "In negotiations with the banks, discussions on helping homeowners kept falling by the wayside," she recalled in 2019. "Things like giving people thirty days' notice before a foreclosure. That never happened."

Imitating the still-revered Greenspan, banking regulators refused to write the new rules that the Dodd-Frank Wall Street Reform and Consumer Protection Act called for. The Treasury official recalls Obama calling them into the Oval Office to push them. "They kept nodding politely," she told me. "But they never did anything."

President Obama's regulators could have imposed some decency. They could have rewired the incentive structure that had turned young traders into improvised explosives. They did not.

Unlike the Home Loan Bank Board and the Department of Justice in the 1980s, they did not investigate or prosecute criminal bankers, either. Likely crimes included violations of the Securities and Securities Exchange Acts (15 USC 77 and 78), making false statements to an agent of the federal government (18 USC 1001), honest services wire fraud (18 USC 1343 and 1346) in those pre-*McDonnell* days, accounting fraud (various chapters of USC 15, 18, 27, and 28), and criminal conspiracy (dozens of statutes, most of which do not require the crime actually to take place), not to mention potential income tax fraud (26 USC 7201) or violations of the Controlled Substances Act (21 USC 13 and other chapters) if reports of widespread use of cocaine on Wall Street are to be believed. But bank regulators made no criminal referrals to the FBI, compared to thirty thousand in the 1980s. Under Attorney General Eric Holder—as under his George W. Bush predecessor Michael Mukasey—the Department of Justice pressed no charges against an officer or former officer of a major bank. "We were picking off the little guys," recalls Marietta Parker, the former assistant U.S. attorney. "We were waiting for Wall Street indictments. But they never came. That's when I realized it doesn't matter which party is in power."*

---

* Holder represented the Swiss bank UBS at the Covington & Burling law firm, where he returned after his stint as attorney general. A month before being elected president, then-senator Barack Obama said this on the Senate floor in support of the Economic Stabilization Act, which bailed out the top Wall Street banks via the Troubled Asset Relief Program: "While there is plenty of blame to go around—and many in Washington and Wall Street who deserve it, all of us—all of us have a responsibility to solve this crisis, because it affects the financial well-being of every single American. There will be time to punish those who set this fire, but now is not the time to argue about how it got set, or did the neighbor sleep in his bed, or leave the stove on." (Barack Obama, "Senate Floor Speech in Support of the Wall Street Bailout Bill," October 1, 2008). "Did the neighbor sleep in his bed, or leave the stove on" is the type of language often used to downplay corruption.

Under President Trump, nothing changed.

Alongside the familiar crop of Wall Street personnel on loan to Washington, the administration did welcome an unusual number of private equity CEOs with a background in high-end real estate, who had benefited personally from both the S&L and Great Recession panics. Private equity firms are like investment banks, only less regulated. "I was pretty surprised to discover how thin the rules are," the former Treasury official confessed when she looked into it for me. With no requirement to disclose even the names of investors or non-voting owners, these firms are perfect vehicles for money laundering.

Casinos, among the high-end properties in several cabinet secretaries' portfolios, are also ideal for money laundering. Just walk in with some dirty cash, buy chips and a bottle of champagne, stake a few bets or don't bother, and convert your stash back into money. Now you can call it gambling winnings.

Trump's private equity blowflies made their careers buzzing around distressed assets and the special opportunities they offer. Commerce Secretary Wilbur Ross partnered with a corrupt South Korean president when he went shopping for bankrupt businesses during the Asian financial crisis of the 1990s. With his launch of the International Coal Group in 2004, he became a giant in that limping industry. Two years later, a disaster at his Sago Mine in West Virginia killed twelve miners. In the wake of the Great Recession, Ross bought two mortgage servicing companies, creating American Home Mortgage Servicing, Inc., the largest post-crash debt collector on subprime mortgages. The company was repeatedly sued for a plague of illegal debt-collection tactics, including harassing homeowners, failing to credit them for payments and then slapping them with late fees, as well as illegal foreclosures. In 2011, Ross got a controversially low price for the recently bailed out Bank of Ireland, sparking allegations of insider trading. In 2014, he allied with Deutsche Bank to buy out the collapsing Bank of Cyprus, widely known for laundering the money of members of Russian kleptocratic networks.

In 2006, treasury-secretary-to-be Steven Mnuchin's Dune Capital, with some Goldman friends, bought out Capmark Financial Group. It became a leading originator of commercial real estate loans and collateralized debt obligations in the lead-up to 2008. The FDIC assumed nearly 80 percent of the losses when Mnuchin bought Indy-Mac in 2009. Renamed OneWest, it enriched him on homeowners' distress. Mnuchin knew what he was doing: he got his start scooping up failed S&Ls on similar terms for Goldman Sachs.

Trump confidant and Inauguration Committee chairman Tom Barrack did the same at the Robert M. Bass Group, taking advantage of strikingly favorable terms granted select buyers of collapsed S&Ls in Texas (the federal government assumed all the losses, but the buyers still got to take a tax deduction for those losses). With Texas oil heir Bass as an investor, Barrack launched his own Colony Capital in 1990. There, "the ethical and moral tombstones we abide by," he told a reporter, were those "learned at Bass." (Taking a page from Mark Twain, Barrack has disguised his Arabic last name—which is the same as President Obama's first name—by pronouncing it BEAR-ack.) Like Ross, Barrack went ambulance chasing in the 1990s in Asian countries where he had ties with corrupt leaders. In the Great Recession he partnered with Ross to purchase loans from the FDIC at twenty-seven cents on the dollar, and he bought up foreclosed homes and ran the rentals like tenements, helping spur the growth of what has become a rental eviction industry. Amid the 2020 coronavirus pandemic, Barrack urged the Federal Reserve to expand its emergency purchases to low-grade commercial mortgage-backed securities, off limits even in the Great Recession. Admiring portraits in financial journals paint Barrack, like Ross, as a steely nerved risk-taker—just like the S&L frauds.

Private equity funds also specialize in requiring companies they buy to take on excessive debt, in order to pay high management fees to their new owners. If struggling but sound, those companies often go under. Employee pension funds are wiped out and those obligations are assumed by the taxpayer, via the Pension Benefit Guaranty Corporation. The result has been an economy-wide explosion of corporate debt since the Great Recession, making the real economy, instead of the financial services industry, vulnerable to the next major economic shock.

"It used to matter where a person's money came from," Nigerians told me. With so much of it coming from bankruptcy and financial crisis, a question has formed that I can't shake: Would a rational economic actor *seek* to bring crisis on? Would he deliberately create the conditions for it?

Once in office in 2017, the Wall Street contingent sabotaged the government's powers yet again. They cut holes in the fencing that had been welded back in place during the brief window for reform after 2008. They changed the rules for counting the higher positive balances now required to offset bad bets, encouraging fudging. Internal Department of Justice guidance instructed investigators to focus on smaller fry. It limited fines that could be sought against delinquent banks.

After the crash, a new agency had been set up as the cop on the bankers' beat. Called the Consumer Financial Protection Bureau, its mandate was to defend customers' interests and patrol for crimes. It was kneecapped, its very right to exist challenged in court.

Then came coronavirus. Designing the rescue package—and thus perfectly positioned to serve their networks—were these same people, plus some more familiar faces from 2008. The unprecedented loans and Federal Reserve securities purchases that were authorized dwarf the 2008 bailout. And Trump swiftly kicked down even the flimsy guardrails attached to some of the measures.

These moves seem purpose-built to instigate wrongdoing, even reward it, as banking deregulation did in the 1980s. The dimensions of the transfer of national wealth to a small group of networked insiders will haunt us for generations.

The only reason no evidence emerged of widespread fraud in the 2008 calamity, in contrast to the S&L crisis, is that no one looked. No autopsies were performed on the approximately five hundred banks that failed, no search for patterns. There were no prosecutions; there was no meaningful deterrence. No one slapped the meat hogs down. Just a handful of banks were fined. That is, the sacred value of justice was monetized.

In the context of bankruptcy for profit, fining a bank is nonsensical. The institution does not commit the crime. It may even be the victim of its self-dealing executive. The only criminals are those executives. And thousands of them, now experts in complex fraud, remain at the controls of America's banks.

7

Tactics and Countermoves

There is one last thing about the Hydra. The reason Herakles was summoned—the reason no other hero could slay it—lay in this ghastly fact: even with gore spewing from the stump of a hacked-off head, it would not die. Two new heads would bud from its writhing torso. "Restoring itself by its own destruction," the Hydra "throve on wounds."

Today's hydras, too, seem to "branch with serpents sprung from death."

Three years after a once-a-century revolution in Egypt dislodged a military dictator named Mubarak and the kleptocratic network his son had spawned, the country was again ruled by a military dictator, Sisi. Freed of competition, the network he revived grasps what is valuable and beautiful in Egypt with a grip more bitter than before. The breath of this hydra, exhaled in decrees and rulings by military tribunals, has withered the heroes of 2011.

In Guatemala in 2015, voters, with some foreboding, flocked to a hastily staged election and made a television comedian their president, on the force of his anticorruption platform. Crowds had packed the streets for months in festive and fierce demonstrations to support criminal investigations into the prior administration. A special counsel's office of sorts, composed of Guatemalan and international sleuths and prosecutors working side by side (known by its Spanish acronym, CICIG), had unearthed proof that top officials were entangled in a vast kleptocratic network with organized crime bosses.

Military officers who, in the 1980s, had committed what is deemed a genocide against the heirs to the Mayan civilization constituted another strand in this network.

Braving the haunting memories, indigenous people joined a truly crosscutting coalition in 2015 to insist that some of this hydra's heads must come off. The then-president was impeached and resigned. His vice president resigned and was convicted of corruption, with three hundred other officials.

But less than two years later, former comic Jimmy Morales, now president and no longer so funny, spiked the anticorruption body. The hydra had sprouted a new head.

Anticorruption protesters, in such differing and distant countries as Burkina Faso, South Korea, Iceland, Malaysia and Brazil, have fixated on their country's topmost official, the man or woman who seems to personify the blight on their political system. If the impossible happens, if that president falls from office, they usually stack their arms and disperse, high on their historic achievement.

That is a mistake. Hydras don't stay dead.

Kleptocratic networks use several deft tactics to cheat their fate. Perhaps the most unexpected is the one featured in the examples above. When the threat is grave enough, they will detach a few of their own heads—let them be lopped off. Or, to switch to the link-analysis metaphor, they will allow a few faces to be torn out of the diagram. New faces are taped in. The connecting lines reconfigure and the network lives on.

But to stave off threats that extreme, kleptocratic networks deftly execute other maneuvers. They disguise their members and activities, for example. They distract and disorganize potential grassroots opposition.

In an examination of seven anticorruption insurrections on five continents, the tactic I found to be most common—and most effective—was to deliberately enflame identity-based divisions that could pit groups of the population against one another. This is how a vastly outnumbered dominator coalition defeats the rest of us.

Lebanon—a synonym for factionalism—provided the most poignant example. Its allied kleptocratic networks had divvied up the spoils of public procurement along party lines, privatizing key public services to crony businesses. Garbage collection can be a gold mine if done poorly enough. The main dump for the capital, Beirut, was spilling into the surrounding neighborhood. Bound by contract to find an alternative, the waste-disposal company ignored one deadline, then another. Stomachs heaving, residents blockaded the entrance, halting garbage collection throughout the city.

It didn't take long, under the Mediterranean sun, for the heaps of refuse lining the streets to dissolve into putrid muck. The symbolism, like the smell, was overpowering. As Nizar Ghanem, a young protest organizer, put it, "You're going to rob the country, then you're going to throw garbage in our face?"

The You Stink movement that sprang up that summer of 2015 cut across the sectarian and political fractures that had splintered Lebanon for decades. "It was the first time since the civil war you saw anything like it," one protester told me. "All these Lebanese in the streets, and no party flags, just the Lebanese flag." Signs and banners read: "All Means All." That is, no more pointing fingers just at an opposing camp. People would no longer let party loyalty shield their own side's leaders from their wrath.

Then those leaders started working the media, and the phones. They branded the demonstrations with the sectarian party labels the protesters rejected: "That's a Hizbullah demonstration," Sunni leaders would lie. Veiled threats went out on the radio, recalled Alexandra Tohme, who lives in the northern mountains: "We can't promise your village will be safe from the Druze in the next valley if you leave to join." Others described text messages sent right to their phones.

Soon the broad-based coalition broke down.

Humans are highly vulnerable to tactics like these—for reasons rooted in evolution. It has hardwired us to organize into groups that bristle with mistrust for anyone understood to be "other." This tendency is so powerful that the objective characteristics such an understanding is based on can be nonexistent. Think of sports fans.

In *Uncivil Agreement,* political scientist Lilliana Mason describes an experiment from the 1950s in which two groups of similar white middle-class boys from Oklahoma City were sent to adjacent summer camps. After a week, when the groups of boys had bonded and named themselves—the Eagles and the Rattlers—they were told about the other camp. Never even having met, the boys slapped ugly labels on their counterparts. A baseball game was scheduled; they hurled insults. Within days, Eagles and Rattlers were shoving and punching and throwing stones. It got too dangerous. The experiment was stopped.

That's how bad it got with no material difference separating two gangs of fifth-grade boys. In Beirut in 2015, distinctions were real. The mostly urbane and well-educated You Stink protest organizers, struggling to cross sectarian lines that were inked in their parents' blood, fell right into a chasm they had failed to consider: class. When scores of impoverished youngsters from the city's southern slums took real risks to join the movement, the well-to-do organizers shunted them off to a separate city square—as though they stank. Hurt feelings stoked the kids' indignation. Store windows got smashed; cars got torched. The broad-based coalition had fatally divided against itself.

The trouble was compounded in this case because separate and deeply felt identities were fused. The south Beirut kids weren't just poor; they also belonged to the Shi'ite branch of Islam. Most of the more affluent or rural protesters did not. So geography and class combined with religion to reinforce the divides.

This grouping of different parts of our identities—often under a political party banner—is what Mason sees happening to Americans. And the more our political labels braid together with other aspects of who we are—the food we like, the car we just bought, our skin pigment and all its history, our slang—the more tightly we cling to those political loyalties.

As we do, Mason's findings demonstrate, the relationship between our red or blue feeling and our specific policy preferences gets *looser.* It does not, of course, disappear. "Those with intense conservative [or liberal] identities do tend to have more intensely conservative [or liberal] policy positions," she emphasizes. But when different aspects of our identity join within a liberal or conservative affiliation, as ours increasingly do, we grow more tolerant of the gap between the policies we were hoping to see and what our favored leaders actually do in office. We ignore—or make excuses for—their deviations.

That is a wonderful state of affairs for kleptocrats. Waving a red or blue flag, they hold on to camps of ardent loyalists while betraying them to serve the network instead. Most Americans disapprove of policies that benefit the superrich at everyone else's expense. Both parties pursue such policies. We find reasons to vote our colors anyway, or opt out of the conversation.

There's a related benefit to these tendencies, from the hydra's perspective. In his research on hunter-gatherer societies, Christopher Boehm found that the techniques for curbing alpha dominators only work if the egalitarian coalition using them has reached consensus. The teasing or cold shoulder directed at an arrogant meat hog must express a universal disapproval. If the coalition splinters, the band descends into factionalism, each side rejecting the legitimacy of the other's point of view. The meat hog goes unpunished.

By shackling our attention to identity divides, that is what our meat hogs achieve. They are manipulating us into an angry factionalism that defeats any hope of bringing them to heel. While they're off chasing zeroes in bank accounts, they have us chasing other zeroes. They have us mired in a contest over suffering, and whose is valued most.

All means all. This tactic is not the purview of just one side. Like those secular, educated, broad-minded Beirutis, many people who believe in tolerance spend a lot of time fixating on differences.

This issue is so polarized that even broaching it is polarizing. Having done so, I won't get much more specific. There is no question that most of us have spent centuries callously dehumanizing our neighbors. We have used them as less than human, and benefited from that use. We still do it. There is no question that whole histories of suffering are shrugged off, and so perpetuated. The urgency—the nobility—of working to bind the gash between All Men Are Created Equal and reality is unquestionable.

What I also know from my work overseas is that kleptocratic networks disorganize their opposition by playing up identity divides.

I wish it didn't work so well. I wish our struggles didn't so often collapse to a ranking—my gender, my history of slaughter and crippling slights, my people's right to cross borders or stop others from crossing—ahead of the damage the kleptocracy is doing to everyone. Let's tackle both. Let's expand the egalitarian coalition to mean all of us. When the hydra manipulates our loyalties, let's recognize the tactic.

We might explore how the networks of a previous era, bent on personal enrichment, deliberately invented and kept enflaming the same identity categories we fixate on today. We might explore how those outside our camp, and their ancestors, were mauled too.

We might think beyond the obsessive policing of language. Training our ears in other directions, we might hear stories of the care with which those we consider "other" treated a person or a place or a piece of work they could have ignored.

We could consider whether victimhood equates to virtue. Or ask ourselves whether binding our identities to a wound, no matter how grievous, leaves much room for healing.

We might encourage personal growth by welcoming it, by offering and accepting genuine apologies, in words and changed behavior, and by not imposing abject humiliation as the price of redemption.

We might take in the shock of our own blindnesses to the attempted extinction of others and their worldviews: of Native Americans by all of us settlers, for example, or of the white agrarian class by those of us who live in cities. Not to mention the actual extinction of countless entire species, precious to this planet and its health. We might consider our own acts of commission and omission—all of us.

"All means all" is not the same as false equivalency. It means ideology is not an extenuating circumstance.

Breathing on the embers of a carefully lit empathy, we could forge the consensus required to bring today's meat hogs back to a shared standard of decency. Failing that, if the early twentieth century is any guide, we are all in for devastating consequences.

I am sitting in a padded chair, my arms strapped to the armrests. There is a band around my head, electrodes at my temples. Electrodes are clipped to each finger; bracelets grip my ankles.

Every time I think seriously about secrets, I land back in this nightmare: the polygraph test I had to endure as part of the process for getting a top secret security clearance. Even now, I break a sweat. Secrecy is emotional. And secrecy is a tactic.

There can be good reasons for keeping secrets. Facing an enemy, it is essential he not know your plan of attack or the assets you array against him. There may even be times to keep secrets from friends. That's why I was disturbed when, in 2010, WikiLeaks began dumping more than 250,000 U.S. diplomatic cables into the public domain. Imagine you are an ambassador meeting the interior minister of an allied country, about whom you recently provided the secretary of state a candid assessment, via a classified cable that is now available on the internet. If two or more people are trying to think through the most constructive way of approaching a colleague, they must be able to communicate confidentially.

Still, during the months I spent reading and writing secret documents, and exchanging often trivial email on the SIPR (Secret Internet Protocol Router) system that was reserved for classified communications, I found that there was less weightiness to all that Pentagon secrecy than I had expected.

That may be part of the point. The comparative mythologist Joseph Campbell thought deeply about secrecy and initiation rites, and the psychological impact they are designed to achieve. He writes of an Aboriginal boy in Australia. After being seized and dragged terrified to a ceremonial ground, he watches strange dances, doings he has never seen before. Men then lead him into some bushes and paint on his skin: a star, for example, or some colored bars, to signal his new status. They warn that "he must never disclose to any woman or boy any of the secret things that he is about to see and learn." (Thus is freedom of speech relinquished as a price of in-group membership.) After some days, the youth is circumcised, in a ceremony blaring with traditional noisemakers. And he becomes a man.

For the women and children banned from these rites, the roaring is the voice of a terrible spirit, Twanyirika, who has whisked the youth away and replaced him with an adult. But the initiate learns the truth. The elders give him the noisemakers and show him that these objects made the sound, not the mighty spirit he had feared all his life.

Screening allegories, as Campbell calls the Twanyirika story, help "exclud[e] those not eligible for initiation." They busy the minds of noninitiates, suggests French anthropologist Gilbert Bochet, with something intimidating but tantalizing. Reading his words, I remembered how General David Petraeus would load think-tank scholars into deafening helicopters for visits to the Afghan theater.

"In its most extravagant form," writes Belgian anthropologist and art historian Anne-Marie Bouttiaux, "the ideal secret is one that consists in nothing. Initiates alone know that what they must cloak in silence doesn't exist." This paradox, a bit of which I experienced in the Pentagon, points to a deep purpose of secrets: to protect knowledge, perhaps, but also to shut people out of a group. And being shut out of a group inflicts on humans an acute variety of emotional pain.

Bearing this interpretation in mind, it is important to greet secrets with two questions: What is being hidden, and who is it being hidden from?

That second question offers a suggestion as to why the private email server that then–secretary of state Hillary Clinton used for most of her official work sparked such an intense reaction. Attention focused on what classified information might have been accessible to noncleared "noninitiates." But the real problem was not that too many people might gain access, but too few. If the business being done was the public's business, why was Clinton using personal infrastructure to shut the public out?

By the same token, why is obsessively secretive President Trump trying to shut the public out of public business by making White House staffers (whom the public pays) sign restrictive nondisclosure agreements? Why is no American present to interpret or take notes at some of his most important meetings with foreign counterparts? Why is he refusing to disclose his tax returns, to comply with lawful subpoenas? What is it Trump is keeping secret, and from whom?

If money is speech, especially when applied to the public business of politics, then why isn't the public allowed to know who is "speaking" in the form of campaign contributions? The recipients are initiated into the secret. The public is kept away, listening to noisemakers. Why? Is the business being transacted not public, after all? Is it private? If so, why is the money that changes hands protected as speech in the name of the public interest? Is that whole legal story a screening allegory?

The list of secrets goes on. Defense Department budget numbers for classified programs can legally be fudged. CIA activities can be off-budget altogether. The Federal Reserve was not required to disclose the beneficiaries of its trillions of dollars of purchases of questionable securities during the coronavirus pandemic.

The private-sector strands of kleptocratic networks use secrecy, too. In the Gilded Age, big bankers scheming up the design for the

Federal Reserve System did so in secrecy. They used code names. They met off the coast of Georgia. "I was as secretive—indeed, as furtive—as any conspirator," recalled one participant.

Members of today's kleptocratic networks who incorporate companies under fictitious or borrowed names are using a modern screening allegory on law enforcement and the public. Only initiates learn where the money comes from, how much there really is, and how much is being stolen from fellow citizens in the form of unpaid taxes.

One entity has been particularly effective in its use of secrecy: the Koch network.

In *Dark Money*, Jane Mayer quotes a former employee commenting, "To call them under the radar is an understatement. They are underground!" Koch staff conducted background checks on managers and bartenders at the resorts where donor summits were held. Participants were told to destroy meeting notes. "Audio technicians planted white-noise-emitting loudspeakers around the perimeters" of meeting rooms.

The philosophy can be summed up in a remark attributed to the family patriarch: "The whale that spouts is the one that gets harpooned."

"They can generate an unlimited number of entities with similar names that they move money to," marveled the former insider I interviewed, "depending on which is getting too exposed. Sometimes the only way to tell companies are related is to look at the name on the 'contact' line. There is a core administrative team handling activities for a hundred different organizations. You can't file a suit against an entity. It no longer exists. You can't research it. You keep hitting dead ends just a few months old. It's like the burner phones drug dealers and terrorists use: one call then you throw it away. These guys have burner entities: use them and get rid of them."

So effective has the Koch entities' secretiveness been that as late as 2010, few American political leaders—let alone American citizens— had heard of them.

That's the year their money delivered a historic sixty-three-seat midterm "shellacking" to President Obama, the year their patient efforts were rewarded by a Supreme Court decision—in *Citizens*

United v. Federal Election Commission—explicitly validating the principle that in American democracy, those with more money get more influence over politics.

That year, 2010, was more than a decade after Charles and his brother David first pulled the lever sending hundreds of millions of their and allies' dollars pumping into all the shifting, interrelated organizations that execute their strategy. Some have kept their names over the years: the American Legislative Exchange Council, which drafts many state laws; the Federalist Society, which chooses our judges; the group Citizens United, which brought the Supreme Court case; and the Tea Party. For fifteen years, these appeared to be independent organizations, their interrelationship and central planning invisible. They have revolutionized American politics and transformed much of American thinking.

If these men wished to influence ideas and public policies, why the secrecy? Isn't that what people do in a democracy?

In a 1997 speech, historian MacLean found, Charles Koch provided an answer: "We are greatly outnumbered." Meaning, most Americans don't want what they want. Democracy can't work for them.

That comment suggests another insight about secrets. Secretiveness is not just about exclusion; it is about hierarchy. Initiation rites, with their psychologically searing drama, are designed to imprint a new mind-set on those who undergo them. It is a mind-set of elitism. The group within the cloak of secrecy is superior to the rest. Those not eligible for initiation are at best inferiors. They may be the enemy.

Inferiors or the enemy: that is how Koch seems to view the American people. Behind all that sneakiness is a fixation that goes far beyond snobbery and screening allegories. As grimly as on a battlefield, Koch and his inner circle are determined to keep us from glimpsing their war plan or their assets.

And with good reason. That plan aims at nothing less than dismantling our democracy. We, the excluded, are right to get emotional about it.

Similar to secretiveness are ways the hydra throws the public into doubt about its practices. The most common of these is obfuscation. Use big words. Make the public comment process so byzantine no ordinary citizen would bother. Drown people in details and complex chemical formulas, when the concepts are simple. Or jumble unlike things together under one heading, such as "deregulation"— as though big and small businesses, and the rules that should apply to them, are the same. Downplay important matters: corruption, fraud, tax evasion, campaign financing. Fade them down to inaudibility. These are tactics. Heroes hoping to defeat the hydra must get good at spotting them.

Another is to deceive.

One of my favorite museums on the National Mall in Washington is the Arthur M. Sackler Gallery. Its main wall is set with a diamond-shaped window that invites a filtered natural light to bathe the treasures of Asian jade and porcelain inside. But that museum is a part of the deception tactic.

According to a court filing stamped January 31, 2019, "Defen-

The Sackler Gallery, Washington, DC.

dants Richard Sackler, Beverly Sackler, David Sackler, Ilene Sackler Lefcourt, Jonathan Sackler, Kathe Sackler, Mortimer Sackler, and Theresa Sackler . . . directed deceptive sales and marketing practices" to push the synthetic opioid OxyContin. The objective was to sow doubt about the dangers of the drug and to build incentives that transformed doctors into killers.

The results have laid waste to communities across the United States. In hospital neonatal intensive care, infants enter this world convulsed with the tremors and fierce abdominal spasms of opioid withdrawal. Middle-school teachers permit students to lay their heads on their desks during class—when they know those students huddled under a car the previous night, or were made to pose for pornographic videos that their addicted parents filmed, or were just taken from their grandmother's house and thrust into foster care. In War, West Virginia, about half of middle school students live with a relative not their mother or father, or with a foster parent, or are constantly shuttling from one to another. Large cities are witnessing mass homelessness. In smaller towns, "once thriving communities . . . people are just walking around in a daze and picking through garbage cans and falling out and overdosing in public parks."

The Sacklers and their obfuscation decimated an entire generation.

And they were not alone. Ironically, by plastering their name on museum walls, they attracted attention. In the shadows by their side were lesser-known pharmaceutical magnates, such as Mallinckrodt CEOs Richard Meelia and Mark Trudeau (who registered the company's legal headquarters in tax-free Ireland in 2013), or John Hammergren, who ran the bulk distributor McKesson for twenty years, or countless anonymous marketing directors.

A secondary harvest of the seeds of doubt these executives sowed is less visible: the collapse of trust in the medical profession. Who can really blame a person for not vaccinating her children or shirking that diagnostic exam when so many white-coated medical professionals abused so much trust?

The Sacklers "always knew that [their] opioids carry grave risks of addiction and death," reads the Massachusetts filing. Nevertheless, they made employees design pamphlets, websites, and videos featuring counterfeit testimonials. Sales staff had to meet an aggressive schedule of door-to-door visits to doctors' offices—more than

150,000 just in the state of Massachusetts in the decade *after* a Massachusetts court ordered the Sacklers' Purdue Pharma to stop. In-state, 11,431 people died of opioid-related causes over the course of that decade, according to the Department of Public Health.

The Sacklers and their subordinates "falsely denied the risk of addiction, falsely implied that addiction requires patients to get 'high,' and falsely promised that patients would not become addicted if they took opioids as prescribed."

And yet, in the excerpts from internal documents included in the filing, it is hard to find an outright lie. The genius of the campaign lay in the confusion it spawned. Like the blaring of those Aborigines' noisemakers, it masked the views and practices the Sacklers promoted.

This generation of Sacklers doubtless learned from their father, Arthur M., whose aggressive marketing of Valium in the 1960s led to massive overprescription and widespread dependence, especially among women. Perhaps the family also learned from sugar producers. Beginning in the 1950s, industry-funded research linked sugar to heart disease. Court filings in that saga don't say sugar executives denied the findings—but that they smothered them, and pointed at fat. Fat, most of us grew up believing, is fatal. It took years of painful diabetes deaths for sugar's toxicity to be widely recognized. By that time, many of us were hooked. The behavior of tobacco majors— assisted by the likes of Lewis Powell—was even more egregious. Prosecutors identified a "lengthy, unlawful conspiracy to deceive the American public."

Together, sugar, tobacco, and opioids have killed and crippled hundreds of thousands, maybe millions of people. But the sickness we are inflicting on our planet—that miracle—is of a different order entirely. However humans respond to the ecological crisis that is now under way, we are in for sudden, hugely disruptive changes. We can take the initiative, imagining economies and lifestyles that restore the earth's living tissue and offer a sense of purpose and fulfillment. Or we can mouth the excuses and suffer the blows that collapsing habitats and an altered earth chemistry will inevitably deliver.

Our very thinking on the most prominent dimension of this problem has been addled by CEOs in pursuit of infinite wealth.

"When public opinion on the big social and political issues

changes," writes Naomi Klein, "the trends tend to be relatively grad-
ual. Abrupt shifts, when they come, are usually precipitated by dramatic events. Which is why pollsters were so surprised by what . . .
happened to perceptions about climate change in just four years."

In 2007, 71 percent of Americans thought that burning fossil
fuels affects the climate. The next year, the then current and former
speakers of the House of Representatives, Nancy Pelosi and Newt
Gingrich, teamed up to deliver a public service announcement. "We
don't always see eye to eye," Pelosi launched, in an understatement.
Gingrich responded: "But we do agree that our country must address
climate change." Nevertheless, by 2011, only 44 percent accepted
the connection to fossil fuels. During that time, computer modeling
got better; predictions by climate scientists came true. Opinion has
shifted back a bit since but has not recovered.

It is now clear that for years, ExxonMobil, among other oil companies and Koch-network affiliates, has been doing exactly what Big
Sugar and Tobacco and Pharma did: deceiving the public about scientific realities their own research uncovered. The objective, according to one participant in the campaign quoted in a *Washington Post*
exposé, was "cacophony."

This time it was not the businesses themselves but a shifting web
of nonprofits that took the lead in throwing sand in Americans' eyes.
Taking a page from Lewis Powell's 1971 memo, organizations such as
the Competitive Enterprise and Heartland Institutes—most of them
extensions of the Koch network—churned out spurious research.
Under U.S. law, donations to these organizations, whose function is
not to serve the public but to defend their donors' wealth *from* the
public, are tax-exempt.

The deceptively stirring names of those organizations, such as
"Heartland Institute," bring us back to the beginning of this section:
to the Sackler Gallery. They too aim to deceive. That building bathes
the name hanging above its doors in a glow. It confuses people—
including perhaps the Sacklers themselves—about what the family
really does.

"People tend to accept theories and statements of 'fact' because
of who states them," reads a paper Charles Koch delivered in 1976.
"Therefore, it is essential to develop the image and credibility of the
movement's leaders." It is harder to imagine that the Sacklers com-

mitted mass manslaughter if you associate them with a wonderful museum. Andrew Carnegie and other Gilded Age barons made good use of this tactic.

Like them, today's Sacklers and their counterparts—at Teva Pharmaceutical Industries or Cardinal Health; the Koch family with its fossil fuel, pipeline, and paper pulp companies; the executives of sugar and processed food conglomerates; agribusinesses like Monsanto that drive farmers worldwide to plant only the mutant products of their laboratory experiments; the biggest banks; not to mention the latest behemoth, the tech industry—all stand behind another giant deception. They proclaim that business—all business—is inherently good, while government, by its very nature, is "the problem."

The evidence, not to mention common sense, proves that is ridiculous. But the idea has taken hold.

This list of tactics kleptocratic networks use to forestall or counter opposition is hardly complete. Some leading members seem scatterbrained, even crazy, inviting observers to underestimate them. President Hamid Karzai and his older brother Qayum perfected this act: one playing the frighteningly unbalanced variation, the other the absentminded professor version. U.S. commerce secretary Wilbur Ross, even Trump, may have adopted a similar approach.

There is intimidation—the physical variety remains rare in the United States, though not unheard of. Police dogs, threats, or back-alley bullying, while on the rise, aren't the weapon of choice for U.S. kleptocrats. They prefer to use the legal system, to tie challengers up in endless proceedings.

Even when the defendants win—which they usually do if they can find the means to fight—they may emerge from the delirious march of accusations and depositions and media exposure and insulting settlement demands as stress-wracked heaps. They may regret they ever filed that complaint or organized their neighbors to challenge that town council decision. "Lawsuits," as Ian MacDougall noted in a *Harper's Magazine* investigation, "have a tendency to haunt the people subjected to them, like trauma or an inauspicious omen."

One last, potent tactic must be mentioned. Today's kleptocratic networks—both Republican and Democrat—stymie some of their ablest potential opponents by infecting them with their own illness: the Midas disease. They inject a dose of money into their victim. Or perhaps you prefer the addiction metaphor. As crack dealers used to say, "The first hit is free." Today's money-pushers like to disguise their drug as something wholesome: "Think of your kids' education," they murmur while writing out the check.

Once hooked, public officials will introduce legislation allowing foreign corporations to confiscate their neighbors' property. Former diplomats will market weapons systems to the governments of impoverished countries they know need running water. University presidents, who are increasingly compared to corporate CEOs, will find reasons to host research they know will be colored by the money that funded it.

Perhaps the most gut-wrenching example is the exodus of Drug Enforcement Administration prosecutors from jobs tracing the drug manufacturers and distributors that were sending millions of opioid pills to small-town pharmacies. Firing off suspension orders, DEA officials had stopped many shipments. But then, several found new jobs within the very drug industry they had been pursuing. They applied their brains and insider knowledge to protect the pharmaceutical industry from the strategies to restrain it that they themselves had devised. They helped inflict 200,000 deaths on their own communities.

Like a drug, money can make its addicts betray almost anyone.

8

Colluders

The headquarters of the Jones Day law firm, set on an angle in front of a park overlooking the U.S. Capitol, could be a government building. It is a hulk of tawny sandstone, griffins flanking the broad stairs. Inside, busy with words, work some of the colluders.

A legion of colluders assists the hydra. It would languish without their multitude. They sell condominiums for unlikely prices, open accounts for unnamed depositors, stamp A's on unsound investments, proffer their podiums, pen awed portraits, greet drifts of dollars with an absence of wonder as to the source—investing university endowments in hopes of an outsized return, or polishing brass names over plate-glass doors. They use national security pretexts to open land and sea to energy exploration. They find, and they cling to, justifications. The services they render are irreplaceable.

It can be hard to distinguish between colluders and full-blown members of a kleptocratic network. It may be a matter of degree. How much money can they be satisfied with? What decisions can they make?

Take former Obama White House counsel Gregory Craig, who banked more than $4 million for his firm by helping launder the reputation of Putin-linked kleptocrat Viktor Yanukovych in 2012, just two years before an irate population ejected him from power in Ukraine. Craig took that account on a nudge from the notorious Paul Manafort, who helped disguise the payments via offshore accounts, and whose daughter Craig pushed his firm to hire in return for the lucrative account. Craig was on the board of trustees of the Carnegie Endowment for International Peace when I went to work there that year.

Or what about former Jones Day partner Noel Francisco? Representing Bob McDonnell, he won that unanimous 2016 Supreme Court decision against the United States. Now he is United States solicitor general. His job is to argue on behalf of his onetime adversary, those United States. Society has authorized lawyers to switch sides this way, to make their best argument in favor of whomever they are paid to represent. Still, I wonder: Is Francisco a colluder or a network member?

Like other categories and metaphors used here, this one blurs at the margins. In the effort to impose exactitude, some meaning is lost. Still, I would rate Francisco a mere colluder. He sells his services, as authorized.

One essential service is the mincing of words. Economist Thomas Piketty wrote that the persistence of extreme inequality will depend, "primarily, on the effectiveness of the apparatus of justification." Lawyers make their living mincing words. Many devote their skill and hard labor to constructing the apparatus of justification.

Spry, sandy-haired Don Ayer, now retired, worked inside Jones Day's headquarters when I interviewed him. He helped his colleague Francisco prepare for the oral argument in *McDonnell.* "We had a client, and that's part of representing a client. I was happy to play the part of a judge. You're asked to be a hostile judge, find the holes in the argument."

Ayer was a good pick for this part in the role-play. *McDonnell,* like many momentous Supreme Court decisions, didn't just happen. It came at the end of a series of cases, stretching back years. Almost three decades earlier, Ayer had argued the first of them: *McNally v. United States.* Back then, as a federal prosecutor, he argued for the United States, against the corrupt state officials.

They were James Gray, Kentucky's secretary of public protection, and Howard "Sonny" Hunt, who, as powerful chairman of the state Democratic Party, decided on the state's behalf where it would buy its insurance policies. Gray, the official, and Hunt, the party boss, incorporated a phony insurance agency. Charles McNally was just a colluder. He let Hunt and Gray put his name down as CEO.

Hunt made a deal, on behalf of Kentucky, to let one Wombwell Insurance Company of Lexington be the state's broker. But Wombwell would have to share the commissions Kentucky paid it with a few other insurance agencies—selected by Hunt. He listed his own, naturally, to get some of the kickbacks.

The defendants were convicted, and their convictions affirmed on appeal, for violating the federal mail- and wire-fraud statutes. Under the terms of these laws, U.S. mail or wire communications, including broadcasts, can't be used to further "any scheme or artifice to defraud, or for obtaining money or property by means of false or fraudulent pretenses, representations, or promises."

The defendants, Ayer's argument contended, had done both. Not only had they "obtained money or property" in the form of kickbacks from Wombwell, their scheme had also "defrauded" the people of Kentucky of something essential to government in the public interest. It was, in the words of the original indictment, the citizens' "right to have the Commonwealth's business and its affairs conducted honestly, impartially, free from corruption, bias, dishonesty, deceit, official misconduct, and fraud."

In other words, what Hunt and Gray stole was an endowment of immeasurable worth: Kentuckians' right to the honest services of their public officials.

This time, the Supreme Court did not rule unanimously in favor of the corrupt politicians, not quite. The vote overturning their convictions was 7–2.*

"The words 'to defraud,' " the justices opined, "commonly refer to wronging one in his property rights by dishonest methods." Then they minced "commonly" into "only." "Defraud," they decreed, could *only* mean "obtain money or property" by fraud, nothing other. The American people were stripped of their actionable right to the basic integrity of their public servants.

Thus did the Midas disease, in 1987, reduce a treasure of inestimable value to mere money.†

---

* Justices Blackmun, Brennan, Marshall, Powell, Rehnquist, Scalia, and White in the majority, O'Connor and Stevens in the minority.

† The court went on to find that even though Hunt and Gray had deceitfully "obtained money or property," that still did not constitute fraud, since there was

Justice John Paul Stevens was one of the two who recoiled at what he called his colleagues' "crabbed construction" of the law. "Can it be," wonders his indignant dissent, "that Congress sought to purge the mails of schemes to defraud citizens of money, but was willing to tolerate schemes to defraud citizens of their right to an honest government, or to unbiased public officials?"

"It was a meat-axe opinion," Ayer maintains today. "I think we should have won. But the train was rolling. This was what they were going to do." In fact, Ayer had steeled himself for such a result. His boss, pleading the expected arrival of a new baby, had passed off the case. "You're going to get your head handed to you," he graciously informed Ayer.

Proving Stevens right about its intentions, Congress quickly passed an amendment to the mail- and wire-fraud statutes (18 USC 1346), spelling them out. "For the purposes of this chapter, the term 'scheme or artifice to defraud' includes a scheme or artifice to deprive another of the intangible right of honest services." The citizens' invaluable but invisible possession was restored. A string of convictions over the years guarded it.

Ayer left the Department of Justice and joined Jones Day. He argued his first case on the other side—against the amended statute—in December 2009.

That was just three months after the justices heard a different case attacking the "intangible right to honest services." The petitioner was no obscure state official this time, but one of the most notorious white-collar criminals in the country: Jeffrey Skilling. This "incandescently brilliant" "visionary" had joined the Houston-based energy company Enron in 1990. Skilling made Enron what it became, and made CEO in 2001.

The division he ran first was called Enron Finance. It did with natural gas what Gilded Age barons had done with railroads. It shifted the heart of the business from the laying of steel to specula-

---

no proof the people of Kentucky had *lost* any money through the dishonest scheme. Italics throughout are the author's.

tion in securities. Skilling, via Enron, created a new market in pieces of paper: the contracts to provide gas to an end user. Enron took the lead in buying and selling them.

That was the business model. Then came the inevitable abuse. Boiled all the way down, the Enron scandal was a retooling of that other Gilded Age artifact, recently revived in the S&L crisis: the Humbert method. Like the 1980s thrift managers, Skilling updated Humbert's trick a bit, pointing not at a locked safe, but at spreadsheets. Thanks to one of those accounting gimmicks (called mark to market accounting), Enron's rows and columns indicated vast assets in the form of projected future profits. But they were made-up assets, which did not, and would never, exist. Enron's shares were propped up by the equivalent of a fictitious inheritance.

For his role in the transnational swindle, Skilling was convicted, among other crimes, of "engaging in a wide-ranging scheme" to defraud Enron shareholders of the intangible right to his honest services. On June 24, 2010, the Supreme Court overturned his conviction. The vote was 9–0. Ruth Bader Ginsburg wrote the opinion.

The decision returned to the original *McNally* question: Of what right, exactly, had shareholders been defrauded? How *much* honesty can people legally expect of those who are paid to serve them?

Since 1988, when Congress amended the law to spell out that "intangible right to honest services," prosecutors had usually gone after clear violators. Most cases involved outright bribes, or kickback arrangements like the Kentucky insurance scam. They were the easiest to prosecute. In *Skilling,* the Supreme Court ruled that since *most* of these cases were heaped up around those two misdeeds, then they were the *only* misdeeds that counted. Once again, "commonly" had been minced to "only." Henceforth, the only honesty to which people had a legal right was that measure of honesty needed to avoid outright bribery or not demand cash kickbacks on procurement contracts.

"Construing the honest-services statute to extend beyond" those two crimes, Ginsburg wrote, "would encounter a vagueness shoal. We therefore hold that [the statute] covers only bribery and kickback schemes." Skilling, though he had clearly deceived his shareholders, had committed neither.

Here was the court, back to "only." And here was Americans' right to integrity back to mere money. *Only* if an official had taken dollars and cents—and *only* if she had done so by means of one of two narrowly defined crimes—had she violated anyone's right to her good faith in performing her duties.

In the wake of this decision, some in Congress tried to do what had been done after *McNally:* fix the statute.

Noah Bookbinder is another former federal prosecutor, but he went on to serve as chief counsel for criminal justice on the Senate Judiciary Committee after his years in the Justice Department. At DoJ, he says, he was "the honest services guy": the expert in what malfeasance could reasonably be charged under the mail- and wire-fraud statutes as revised after the 1987 decision in *McNally.* By the time *Skilling* was decided in 2010, Bookbinder had moved on to the Senate staff. So he helped draft a second clarifying amendment, to list what other types of dishonesty the statutes covered, beyond "*only* bribery and kickbacks."

A bill that included his amendment passed the Senate with ninety-six votes. It went to the House of Representatives. Bookbinder heard from contacts that Heritage Foundation personnel spoke to then–majority leader Eric Cantor. "Heritage was huge on this," he recalls.

When the House voted on the bill, the honest services language had magically disappeared from the text. So *Skilling*'s crabbed construction stood. Only kickbacks and bribery could be prosecuted.

Now the campaign to legalize corruption could move on to mincing down the definition of bribery. That is what was accomplished six years later in *McDonnell:* the case against the former Virginia governor who got all those gifts from the manufacturer of tobacco-based pills.

And it was a campaign. As a "friend of the court" (or amicus curiae), the U.S. Chamber of Commerce had submitted a written argument to help the justices deliberate on *Skilling.* So did the Cato Institute and the Pacific Legal Foundation, entities largely funded and directed by the Koch network—which, back in 2010, was still almost invisible to the naked eye.

In the 2016 *McDonnell* case, the last phase of the campaign, the same kind of amicus brief was submitted by the Citizens United group. That's the organization that won the more famous 2010 decision allowing for unlimited campaign contributions by corporate entities. Citizens United was joined by the Gun Owners of America and affiliates. And Citizens' lawyer, James Bopp, wrote a separate brief, on behalf of an entity called the James Madison Center for Free Speech. Cofounded by Senate majority leader Mitch McConnell and funded to the tune of $400,000 (as of 2012) by Koch allies Walter Kohler and Betsy DeVos, this nonprofit is a shell to collect tax-free financing for Bopp's work. DeVos was a founding board member.

"There was clearly a concerted campaign," Bookbinder reflects. In his long years working criminal justice reform, he says, he sometimes found himself side by side with Koch-funded groups, fashioning a joint approach. There was always some kind of horse-trade. "They'd say, 'Sure we'll help with drug sentences,'" for example, "'but here's what we want.' And they would point to reducing the number and type of white-collar offenses on the books. Honest services fraud was certainly one" to whittle away, says Bookbinder.

Here is an unexpected place where word-mincing matters: in the bargaining, and in the weighing that takes place before the bargaining even starts.

Tens of thousands of drug offenders, disproportionately persons of color, languish behind bars in the United States. The injustice in who gets arrested for what, in the length of the often mandatory sentences, is vast and visible. Place that weight in one pan of a balance. If "fraud" or "corruption" is the stone in the other pan—and if those words can be shaved down to just a few tawdry bribes or kickbacks—that pan will rise. It may become justifiable to well-meaning reformers to bargain away punishment for that sort of distasteful misdeed in exchange for relief for so many disadvantaged nonviolent offenders, now and future, so ill-used.

But these other nonviolent offenders benefiting from the new leniency may include the type of banking executive—perhaps once a former Treasury official—who brought down the world economy and shattered as many lives as there are drug offenders in jail. They may include senior managers of a chemical company that spills rank spume into a river that crosses two states, who walk away from the bankruptcy. Different weights allow for different justifications. Shaving the weights helps lure decent people into colluding.

The *McDonnell* case attracted a raft of those amicus briefs from outside experts. One was the "brief of 77 former state attorneys general"—Republican and Democrat—in favor of McDonnell. A second begins, "We are former federal officials with first-hand knowledge of the types of interactions that routinely occur between government officials and members of the public." The signatories, also supporting McDonnell, boast of their service to "every President of the United States since Ronald Reagan."

That one is quoted in the court's opinion, a rarity. The justices took to heart its warning: that to let McDonnell's conviction stand would "chill federal officials' interactions with the people they serve." Citing the brief even during the oral argument, Chief Justice Roberts exclaimed, "Now I think it's extraordinary that those people agree on anything!"

I glanced through the names of these officials. My eyes lit on one: Lanny Davis. He is a notorious Washington lawyer-lobbyist, close to the Clintons, who more recently represented Trump's fixer, Michael Cohen, and another well-known member of Putin's network. I had encountered his activities in my recent work on Honduras. He is the man who influenced Hillary Clinton, then secretary of state, to bless a 2009 military coup there, which helped that country's hydra spring back to life. There was that former Obama White House counsel, Gregory Craig, who had worked to burnish the image of Ukrainian potentate Viktor Yanukovych. Former George H. W. Bush White House counsel C. Boyden Gray was there too, and former U.S. attorney Harry Litman. Part of a left-leaning coalition of organizations and individuals dedicated to holding President Trump accountable under the law, he did not respond to repeated requests to discuss the brief.

Only two names on that list are of people who had ever been elected officials. All but one, Litman, are lobbyists—meaning they make their fortunes on pay-to-play politics. Their business model is based on buying access and influence. But they presented themselves as servants of the public. And the court took them at face value, as experts in matters of representative government.

On the other side, amicus curiae briefs were sparse. One of only two was submitted by Citizens for Responsibility and Ethics in Washington (CREW), a research, advocacy, and strategic litigation nonprofit. At its helm by then was the "honest services guy," Noah

Bookbinder. Jennifer Ahearn cowrote the brief. I asked her why no public servants had spoken up alongside CREW.

"I don't know how successful we would have been at drumming any up." She sighed. "Even the other nonprofits in our community were not that interested in getting engaged." Her colleagues underestimated the gravity of the issue, she suspected. They had "given up on criminal public corruption statutes," what with the string of Supreme Court decisions.

And other stones weighed heavier in the balance.

Jones Day's Ayer thinks the court got it right in *Skilling* and *McDonnell.* "The law needs to give fair notice that if you commit a crime, you can be punished," he told me.

I looked at him, my face blank.

He plunged on. "In our system, people are supposed to behave aggressively in their self-interest. But they can't do certain things. Well, you have to tell them what they can't do."

Telling them they can't serve their constituents or shareholders dishonestly, using artifice or false pretenses, doesn't apparently cut it. "You don't have a way to distill out a rule that shows an aggressive, hurly-burly 'I'm going to do the best I can for myself' person where the line is."

This was Ginsburg's "vagueness shoal."

"Fair warning," wrote the U.S. Chamber of Commerce, quoting several past Supreme Court decisions, "should be given to the world in language *that the common world will understand.*" Emphasis in the original. Cato and the Pacific Legal Foundation went further. "When statutes are so vaguely worded that the public finds them incomprehensible, voters will not be able to . . . discipline the conduct of government officials." By "government officials," here, Cato does not mean venal governors and party bosses. It means power-mad prosecutors lusting to put respectable people in jail.

But here's the thing. This was Enron. This was Jeffrey Skilling. So whopping were his crimes that his lawyers gave the Supreme Court a second reason for overturning his conviction: he did not get a fair trial because of the widespread outrage; no neutral juror could be found. The public, it seemed, was having no trouble comprehending the dishonesty of his doings. The "common world" was not having a vagueness problem.

"You have a good point there," Ayer conceded, unmoved.

I'm looking at two branches of a river diverging. Regular people have a pretty firm grasp on dishonesty in public office. That grasp may not be based in fine definitions, but rather in "vivid intuitions," to use the words of poet Mary Oliver. Bereft of intuition, perhaps, elites find the public dishonesty concept knotty. They need it parsed out for them, minced finer and finer. Observing this curious disability, regular people become suspicious of elites.

Perhaps, in this matter, elites' judgment is impaired. After all, they are in the balance. Almost by definition, corporate crimes and corruption can only be committed by elites. Only those who hold public responsibilities can abuse them. When Bookbinder went around Capitol Hill in 2010, advocating for the attempted post-*Skilling* amendment, he got peppered with a type of question that is rare in policy discussions.

Instead of deliberating the possible effects on the public interest and the conduct of government, says Bookbinder, legislators and judges started thinking back over things they had done, wondering, " 'How could this affect me personally?' I saw this at every level."

He described senators reaching for far-fetched examples, asking if they'd have to start checking receipts if they took this trip or let someone pick up the tab for that gourmet meal. "We ended up putting in a bunch of exceptions for little things, just to get people over that hump—even though prosecutors are not charging that stuff." Bookbinder added wryly, "The reason the prisons are overcrowded in the United States is not because there are too many CEOs and public officials in them."

I never accused Ayer of switching sides. I did not call him a colluder. But a raised eyebrow, the lean of the question mark left in the air, must have conveyed the thrust of the query that underlay the conversation—the reason I had sought him out in the first place. How did the guy who thought he should have won *McNally* find a way to applaud the decisions in *Skilling* and *McDonnell*?

It comes down, he offered, to the American system. We've "gone off the cliff," he said. "Money is everything, the key to the castle. If you've got money, you can do practically anything, except outright pay to get a contract. It's a total disaster. But if that's the way we want our system to run, I don't see a practical way you criminalize" the details.

There it was, that explanation of the justices' thinking. So Ayer applied himself to ensuring those details were not criminalized.

"We." I considered his word. I remembered the polls showing, again and again, that the vast majority of Americans—in the 80 percent range—disapprove of the weight of money in our political life. About the same percentage of registered voters would roll back the *Citizens United* decision. I thought about the half of the electorate that doesn't vote, like those residents of St. Marys, or my neighbor, who told me, "The fat cats will put who they want in anyway." Even senators overcame worries about their own potential liability and voted to restore citizens' legal right to the honest services of public and corporate officials.

"Who's we?" I asked Ayer.

"We," he replied, "means the whole country. The whole picture that emerges from decisions construed by interpretation."

As though the two were the same. Pressed, he conceded: "I agree there were some unfortunate Supreme Court decisions."

I did not ask how the investment of his intellectual gifts, his honed skills and prodigious work ethic in support of those decisions had helped deliver their "unfortunate" outcomes.

"It's a complicated question to see how we got here," Ayer concluded. "Our historical national philosophy of individualism is at the root of it."

Thus is constructed the apparatus of justification.

And yet, perhaps I had better put down that stone in my hand. Who among us doesn't, at some point, grab the crutch Ayer helps fashion? Who doesn't find a reason to keep banking at Wells Fargo? Or to vote for lower taxes, if ours are lowered too?

Who doesn't moon over the pictures of an idolized president, on "the coolest vacation of all time," surrounded by stars aboard a $590 million yacht that belongs to billionaire *Risky Business* producer David Geffen? Who among us in the other camp doesn't keep finding reasons to forgive an idolized president who stiffs his workers and owes his fortune to bankruptcies and cheating?

Which of us doesn't shop online or at a giant chain, because it's just so much more convenient? In the grocery store, who doesn't insist that products once prized as holiday delicacies be in stock for supper every day? Who wonders how those delicacies got there, what happened to people and places en route? Who thinks about the "blasted" landscape from which the minerals in our cell phones were "hauled," or the conditions of the hauling?

This is how culture is made. The hydra thrives in this culture.

And I am still left pondering the question, "Who's we?"

IV

IT THROVE ON WOUNDS

1870s–1945

1

Fighting the Hydra: The Cities

"The strike swept through this country like a flame. It leaped from town to town and from state to state. . . . Over the wide expanse of this country one could see the most dramatic thing in the world—thousands on thousands of patient men doing nothing."

So wrote war reporter Mary Heaton Vorse, describing the mass work stoppage that shut down half the steel industry in the United States in the fall of 1919.

If the parallel I have been drawing is sound, if the last time transnational integrated networks of corruption gained the kind of control they have achieved today was in the Gilded Age, then a question presses: What broke the grip of that era's hydra? What sparked the transformation in governing structures, in standards of public integrity, in attitudes toward excessive wealth that took shape with the New Deal and in the early 1940s? Given that both the Gilded Age syndrome and its significant if imperfect repudiation unfolded throughout the industrialized world, should we not be on a quest for the answer?

"Answers" might be a better word, for they are multiple. One of them, clearly, is heroism.

"These workers were slenderly organized," Vorse found over weeks traveling the steel towns of Ohio and Pennsylvania. She threaded through narrow alleys and refuse dumps to visit homes, depicting the overflowing privies in smoke-blackened back lots shared by several families of six or ten, the patched and darned curtains kept white by the incessant labor of steelworkers' wives. She recorded earnest conversations over whether the family could hold out just a few more days before drawing a ration of potatoes and milk from the precious supply at the commissary the strikers had pooled. The food was for those who were not just deprived but treading the borderlands of starvation. She stood for hours in union offices, where chairs were not allowed, because men sitting would constitute a banned meeting. She described the open-hearth furnaces, where "the red flames seem dark. The red flames seem to be the brothers of smoke, beside the white incandescence of the molten mass that will become steel." She stood on picket lines and spoke to scabs. The strikers, she wrote, "were separated by distance. They were divided by race and language, but for months they thought together, they starved together, they suffered terror [and] doubt."

Her account details methods used to stamp down the workers, and a viciousness in their application that some historians judge to be unparalleled in the West. Gatherings of families on church steps after Sunday mass were broken up. Mounted police patrolled residential streets, yard-long clubs in leather holsters at their thighs. They forced mothers standing on their own stoops with infants crooked in their arms to scramble for the door. Sometimes the police rode their horses into the houses after them. Workers were arrested by the score, then released days later without charges, but fined nevertheless. Or they were held without booking, handcuffed for hours in painful positions. "The stories of beatings and arrests came in an endless flood. There was no end to them. Within two days one was drenched with them." Committees of vigilantes were organized. Paid informants sidled into step with strikers on an hours-long trek to a permitted meeting, infecting the air with mistrust. "Each man gutted of his self-respect was a victory for the Steel Companies," writes Vorse, of methods that were pervasive throughout the United States for decades. "Strikes are broken by breaking men's courage; strikes are broken by making men play traitor to what they believe."

It is against this backdrop that we should consider the heroism of those who stood up to the Gilded Age syndrome. Over the nearly seventy years that it held sway, from the early 1870s through the 1930s, defiance persisted. It plunged on in three broad currents,

The Great Railroad Strike of 1877, which broke out in Martinsburg, West Virginia.

each with its distinct character, yet in aspirations, basic principles, and often personnel, intermingling.

One was the industrial labor movement, restless in the steel and textile mills, in railroad and lumber yards, in mines and on docks—in places where "Man is puny; Industry great." Vorse keeps returning to the gargantuan scale of the industrial landscape, how humans within it are as ants. "The mill gates open up in the morning and suck the men in and at night they open up again and spew them out."

The most apt imagery to depict the rising of those men is similarly titanic: Vorse uses that of a wave. "The mass of workers heaved and swayed . . . like the heaving of mid-ocean." Again and again during those seven decades, the wave crashed against unyielding rocks. In the years around 1877, 1886, 1892, 1902, 1919 and '20, and 1934, massive swells rose and then broke.

Demands changed little in all that time. Wages were cut, routinely, 10 to 25 percent a slice; workers struck to keep their pay. They wanted relief from measures that compelled ever more speed and prodigious effort for the same or less pay, an end to child and convict labor, and the enactment of at least rudimentary safety protections. Perhaps most significantly, they wanted the right to organize—to form a coalition, just as industries were banding together against the employees they wished to dominate. The reduction of the workday from a typical twelve hours or even sixteen to a more humane eight was a rallying cry throughout the nineteenth and early twentieth centuries.

But these specifics were embedded within a broader challenge to the whole Gilded Age ethos. Even the call for an eight-hour day was framed as part of a yearning for the opportunity to fulfill more of one's human potential. An early workers' confederation, the Knights of Labor, placed this longing within an expression of democratic citizenship. "The toilers," its 1876 platform stated, sought

> more of the leisure that rightfully belongs to them; more soci-
> etary advantages; more of the benefits, privileges, and emolu-
> ments of the world; in a word, all those rights and privileges
> necessary to make them capable of enjoying, appreciating,
> defending and perpetuating the blessings of good government.

The intent "to elevate workers' moral, social, and intellectual condition," as the Amalgamated Association of Iron and Steel Workers put it that same year, and to "raise ourselves to that condition in society to which we . . . are justly entitled" was central to the demand for a shorter workday.

A reverence for other values was there, too. "We want to feel the sunshine," went the lyrics to the Knights' anthem, "We want to smell the flowers; / We're sure God has willed it. / And we mean to have eight hours."

The Knights' 1878 platform identified—and denounced—the central component of the Gilded Age syndrome:

> The recent alarming development and aggression of aggregated wealth, which, unless checked, will inevitably lead to the pauperization and hopeless degradation of the toiling masses, render it imperative, if we desire to enjoy the blessings of life, that a check should be placed upon its power and upon unjust accumulation.

The first objective following this preamble was to make "industrial and moral worth, not wealth, the true standard of individual and national greatness." The Knights aimed to eradicate the Midas disease.

The Knights of Labor was the first and arguably the most dynamic and successful major drive to organize workers across identity divides. Those divides splintered their class into sharp fragments. Conflicting interests pitted craftsmen who had mastered their specialties through long apprenticeship—many of whom belonged to jealous little unions of their own—against the unskilled who fed and tended the new machines that were replacing the craftsmen. Americans of British or Irish descent resented the more recent influx of immigrants from continental Europe. Those speakers of German, Italian, Polish, Swedish, or Yiddish could hardly even exchange greetings. Women were everyone's inferiors, demeaned and excluded. The expertly manipulated race divide was a devastating rift, still unhealed.

The Knights of Labor and a similar confederation that came after it, the Industrial Workers of the World, as well as hundreds of "central" or "amalgamated" unions in a single town or city—and the periodic general strike or revolt that ripped across a vast, far-flung industry, like the 1919 steel strike—sought to weld these cracks. Organizers traveled with translators. Proclamations, meeting readouts, digests of breaking events in an ongoing confrontation were copied late into the night in half a dozen languages. Resolutions urged "steel, coal, and the railways," for example, "not [to] settle their difficulties independently." Objective thirteen on the Knights of Labor's 1876 platform was "to secure for both sexes equal pay for equal work." Women were seen and heard on the front lines, and were revered by embattled workingmen.

Across three generations of sludge-smeared days and tragedies gulped down, a striking feature that emerges is the cultural vitality of this movement. Images captured in accounts of the period are indelible: hundreds of Slovaks on a hillside, breaking into polyphonous chant at the start of an outdoor strike meeting; amateur theater groups at local halls, composing and performing comedy for an audience of neighbors; orchestras and singing clubs, even acrobatics teams practicing at community gyms; a few dozen men rolling cigars in a shop, while one reads aloud from a book they all chipped in to buy, then debating what they heard.

The debates were often fierce. Their bitterness shattered strikes. Still, a kind of curriculum was thus developed, a shared arsenal of ideas, a language and vocabulary that merged current European thinking with the principles laid out in American founding documents. It armed a diverse and far-flung population with a common framing of its predicament and aspirations.

This effervescence was on boisterous display in the big cities, magnets as they were for talent and ambition of all kinds. Here, labor unionism most closely overlapped with a second current of defiance against the Gilded Age system: revolutionary political movements such as socialism of various stripes, or anarchism.

Chicago, a burgeoning metropolis that incarnated the new West—with its man-dwarfing rail yards and steel mills and slaughterhouses—served as a crucible where anarchist ideals and industrial labor organization could meld and fuse. One remarkable figure was a

Lucy Parsons, one of the great anarchist and labor leaders of the nineteenth and early twentieth centuries, in 1886.

Texas-born former slave of mixed lineage named Lucy Parsons. With her husband, Albert, a Confederate veteran who converted to the cause of African American citizenship after the Civil War, she helped blend this potent alloy.

The couple's greatest triumph came in 1886, when they united anarchists and laborers in helping organize an unparalleled wave of strikes for the eight-hour day. It shut down much of Chicago—and spread through the country, intersecting with other walkouts, as far as the Parsonses' native Texas. "Nothing like this had ever happened in America, or in Europe," writes historian James Green. "These huge protests stunned observers like Friedrich Engels," who exulted at "the vastness of their movement." Employers began meeting some demands, inspiring other laborers to join. By linking workers across their internal elite-versus-plebeian divide, the Parsonses helped forge "a new kind of labor movement," judges Green, in which "working people believed they could destroy plutocracy, redeem democracy and then create a new 'cooperative commonwealth.'"

The euphoria lasted only days. Chicago's elites had been beefing up public and private security forces for years. On May 3, police shot strikers at the gates to the McCormick harvester factory. On the fourth, as a huge nighttime protest rally at Haymarket Square was breaking up in the gathering rain, a company of police under that same belligerent commander marched into its midst, ordering the last few hundred stragglers to clear the square. And then someone—to this day no one knows who—lobbed a bomb at the men in blue.

A year and a half later, Albert Parsons, swathed in white, dangled beside three of his comrades at the end of a rope, convicted and hanged for inciting the bombing. Parsons had been in Ohio for most of that tumultuous day, and no evidence linked any of the condemned to the crime. But the massive crackdown and Red scare that followed the Haymarket bombing broke the wave of labor defiance of the mid-1880s.

Until Lucy Parsons's death in 1942 at nearly ninety, she kept it up, galvanizing people to fight the "wage slavery" she found little better than the "chattel slavery" she had witnessed as a child, inspiring them to seek autonomy and human development as individuals, while join-

Execution of the men found guilty in the deaths of policemen at the Haymarket rally, May 4, 1886, including Lucy Parsons's husband, Albert. The Red scare that followed crushed mass labor and radical political activism for a decade.

ing together in new inclusive structures that made decisions democratically and shared ownership of key resources.

Anarchists, in other words, were not proponents of unbridled violence and chaos, as their name suggests. Having never experienced
a government that did not serve a kleptocratic network, they turned
their backs on centralized government altogether, and its means of
coercion. "Such concentrated power," Parsons wrote, "can be always
wielded in the interest of the few and at the expense of the many."
How else a society might in practice be structured, however, is not
clear to me from her or any other leading anarchist's writing.

"We can judge from experience that man is a gregarious animal,
and . . . works to better advantage combined with his fellow man
than when alone," Parsons hazarded, in a pamphlet from about 1905.

> This would point to the formation of cooperative communi-
> ties, of which our present trades-unions are embryonic pat-
> terns. Each branch of industry will no doubt have its own
> organization, regulations, leaders, etc. It will institute methods
> of direct communications with every member of that indus-
> trial branch . . . and establish equitable relations with all other
> branches.

"When once free from the restrictions of extraneous authority,"
hoped New York–based anarchist leaders Johann Most and Emma
Goldman in 1896,

> men will enter into free relations; spontaneous organizations
> will spring up in all parts of the world, and every one will con-
> tribute to his and the common welfare as much labor as he or
> she is capable of, and consume according to their needs. All
> modern technical inventions and discoveries will be employed
> to make work easy and pleasant, and science, culture, and art
> will be freely used to perfect and elevate the human race, while
> woman will be coequal with man.

In the clogged streets and tenements of Goldman and Most's
New York, anarchism often took root in the sweatshops that took
in piecework from the garment industry. That is where many Jewish

immigrants, fleeing pogroms or discriminatory legislation in Russia or eastern Europe, landed. They developed a vibrant anarchist community on Manhattan's Lower East Side.

It is worth pausing to consider the profound culture shock that hit such people. The workplaces most of them left—like the farms and fishing boats and small shops that American-born workers and other immigrants abandoned for industrial jobs—were scaled to the dimensions of the basic human social unit: the extended family or tribal band. Those workplaces may well have been stifling or deprived. Perhaps it was no longer possible to earn a living there. Yet a certain band ethos—valuing equity, shared resources, and the contributions of individual talents to the welfare of the group— permeated social relations.

The conditions into which industrial-age workers were thrust savagely violated this ethos. Lined up by the maws of the mines or steel mills or the endless rows of factory looms, by a system that "transmutes human lives into gold, gold, countless gold," men and women were stripped of personhood. They did not matter.

In the narrow shops of the Lower East Side, the shock may have been worse. Often set up in private apartments, run by people who shared the background of those they exploited, these workshops mimicked extended families. The cruelty that reigned in them was a traumatizing betrayal.

Disappointment lay heavy on many migrants when they finished their arduous journey. "So we have crossed half the world for this!" Marie Ganz remembers her mother flinging at her father when he showed her into the miserable tenement that would be her New York home. Thousands, who could, returned to Europe.

Instinctively, those who remained in the United States tried to fashion new forms of extended family in the contrary circumstances. Often the effort passed by way of language. In a study of anarchism in New York, New Jersey, and San Francisco, historian Kenyon Zimmer describes how Italian and Yiddish—sometimes learned in the United States—served as lingua francas for communities that shared a culture but were divided by local languages or dialects.

The radicals flung themselves into the exuberant working-class cultural life. Performance art, writes Zimmer, was central. Food, too.

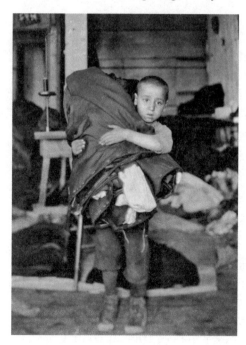

The intimate scale of many New York City tenement sweatshops—both managed and staffed by Jewish immigrants—may have added to their cruelty.

Yom Kippur balls, violating the penitential gloom of that religious observance, and festive picnics on made-up holidays added layers of shared experience.

Such scenes might be seen as modern versions of the initiation rites that comparative mythologist Joseph Campbell studied. From the most distant prehistory, masked dancing and dramatic art have woven the fabric of group life. Declaiming and performing myths was a way of reinforcing a common worldview, bringing it to embodied life, imprinting it in members' subconscious. That is what the anarchists were doing.

And then, what are picnics but meat-sharing rituals? Those ancient Greek religious celebrations, with their distributions of smoke-fragrant skewers, were held outdoors. They featured theater and athletic games. Similarly, on the northern shore of the Sea of Galilee, Jesus of Nazareth bid the multitude that had followed him to that lonely spot to be seated on the ground—in groups of fifty or one hundred, the size of a typical hunter-gatherer band. All present, he promised, would share in a picnic. From a few loaves of bread and some fish, enough was provided. By this miracle a motley crowd became an egalitarian coalition. Its new sacred stories were being enacted—performed—in real time.

Like Jesus, the anarchists faced a daunting challenge: how to unite such a coalition on a scale and across a welter of affiliations unimaginable in hunter-gatherer days. Even abandoning their native tongues for Italian and Yiddish helped little. "This world," writes Zimmer of the tight-knit Jewish anarchist community, "was an insular one, bounded geographically by the borders of Jewish neighborhoods and linguistically by the use of Yiddish, limiting interethnic and interracial collaboration."

Nevertheless, anarchists did insist on a stated ideal of inclusivity. So doing, they echoed in their way the Torah's ancient injunction to "love thy neighbour as thyself", which Jesus too recalled in his teachings and urged his followers to espouse anew. The hope was that the shared dream of an egalitarian and cooperative society—human but scalable—might form the basis of a new type of large community, extending beyond the bloodlines of clan or tribe or color.

Unlike the recorded teachings of Jesus, however, anarchist ideology embraced the considered use of violence. Lucy Parsons avowed that had she been at Haymarket Square when the police arrived, had she seen their behavior and heard what transpired, she would have "flung the bomb [her]self." In "the voice of dynamite," Parsons heard "the voice of force. The only voice which tyranny has ever been able to understand."

Most anarchists did not translate such talk into action, but enough did—especially after 1890—to light a thirty-year fuse of panic across much of the industrialized world. Assassins struck throughout Europe, cutting down chiefs of state in Russia, France, Greece, Italy, Portugal, and Spain. Bombs blew out the windows of cafés and concert halls. They strewed grotesque images, along with debris, upon the public imagination: a horse on its back, three legs sticking up in the air; half-naked bodies, some burning, some still flopping; a woman's shoe on a window ledge, foot and ankle inside; a man whose head, scalped, rained blood; another whose head was severed.

On July 23, 1892, Emma Goldman's companion Alexander Berkman entered the Pittsburgh offices of Carnegie Steel and pulled a revolver. Henry Clay Frick, Andrew Carnegie's right-hand man and the living personification of the Gilded Age syndrome, sat on a swivel chair behind his heavy desk. He was in the process of crushing the steelworkers' union, at the cost of a bloody battle between Pinkerton private security guards and strikers at the nearby Homestead plant. Berkman shot and wounded Frick, though not fatally. Nine years later, an anarchist-inspired man of unstable mind killed President William McKinley.* Police infiltration—and even active participation in some conspiracies—not to mention fevered press coverage, whipped up the confusion.

It was in a similar context—in the midst of a terrorist insurgency with parallels to that one—that I began thinking about systemic corruption in the first place. In Kandahar, by 2008, grotesque images like decapitated heads had become commonplace. I once found myself coldly considering the *lack* of one as evidence that a remote-controlled device, not a suicide bomber, had killed a friend of mine. Through conversations with my neighbors and later research, I reached the conclusion that systemic corruption helps fuel violent ideological extremism. Gilded Age anarchists provide a further example.

German-born Johann Most was an explicit conceptualizer of such terrorist violence—what he called "action as propaganda" or propaganda by the deed. "When modern revolutionaries carry out actions," he wrote, "what is important is not solely those actions themselves, but also the propagandistic effect they are able to achieve." He is speaking of performance art.

It is a concept I kept trying to explain to brass in Afghanistan. They would conduct operations mobilizing thousands of troops, while a few officers on the side were tasked to develop "information

---

* McKinley was also emblematic. In 1896, awash in corporate money, he had defeated a political insurrection mounted by the fused Democratic and Populist Parties, which had backed William Jennings Bryan. By then the Populist movement had been battered by a savage campaign of vote rigging and intimidation in the elections of 1892 and 1894, and its fusion with the Democrats diluted its platform. Still, it represented enough of a threat to mobilize an overwhelming reaction to ensure McKinley's victory. See below, pp. 217–28.

operations," such as radio shows. Actions were meant to change situations. Information operations were about words, and were afterthoughts.

Meanwhile, a few hundred Taliban would swoop down from the mountains and occupy a whole district, almost bloodlessly. Then they would withdraw. NATO commanders would applaud themselves for pushing the insurgents out. Except the Taliban had not intended to occupy the district—at least not that way. Staged largely for "propagandistic effect," the attack itself was an information operation. It was a kind of theater. On a level deeper than language, it transmitted a clear message to its intended audience: local villagers. It told them they were vulnerable, and when the Taliban began quietly filtering back over the winter, they had better offer food, a place to sleep.

And that is just what happened, in the example I'm thinking of. By the next spring, the Taliban controlled the district.

It is possible to consider Jesus's dramatic confrontation with the money changers in a similar light. The passages in the Gospels relating it are brief. Upright amid the sprawled tables, the coins spinning across the paving stones, in a din of squawks and bleating, Jesus utters a single sentence. Who could even hear him? What mattered was not the words, but the gesture. Jesus was engaged in "propaganda by the deed"—or, if you will, in performance art.

It was nearly two thousand years later, on a September day, that a volcano of fire and smoke and plate-glass missiles and sizzling chunks of metal erupted within the precinct of what the United States had made its temple: Wall Street. That attack, on September 16, 1920, came amid anarchist plots across the United States. Nerves were raw. The number of Wall Street victims, always cited, and the scale of the damage don't convey the point. The point was the wordless symbolism; it was those images, shock branded into millions of brains. Targeted at the very emblem of Gilded Age abuses—the offices of J. P. Morgan—the attack was a perfect piece of "propaganda by the deed."

As was another one, on the very same spot, eighty-one years minus five days later. Aimed again at the money changers in their temple, 9/11 might be understood as the most stunning example of propagandistic performance art the world has ever witnessed. Some of the motivations—when we overcome our anger and revulsion to tune

September 16, 1920, outside the offices of J. P. Morgan, Wall Street and Broad.

in to them—are uncomfortably familiar: "We hate the corruptive financial lifestyle that does not please God," al-Qaeda member Abd al-Rahman Atiya explained, years later. "It is a corrupt, wayward, and unjust system . . . based on . . . greed, gluttony, injustice, selfishness, [and] extreme materialism."

There is a crucial difference, of course, distinguishing Jesus's "propaganda by the deed" from such later, bloodier examples. It is the level of violence. And also the sequencing.

Anarchists imagined that a few heroic assassinations of the architects of suffering would infuse the sufferers with courage and spirit and ignite a mass movement. Egalitarian hunter-gatherers knew better. They knew a sneak attack to kill even an unpopular meat hog would never forge a consensus; it would destroy any hope of ever building one. It would shred the band in endless rounds of vendetta. So, faced with a would-be alpha whose domineering behavior needed curbing, their first step was to gather a consensus—about the severity of the problem, about what to do. Only then, and only as a group, would the band rebuke the offender.

That is the sequence Jesus followed. First, by exhorting the plain people of his community to love their neighbors, by sharing bread and fish among them in that most profound of human rituals, he built the egalitarian coalition. Only once that was achieved, and only in the thick of a great crowd—a stand-in for the consensus of society at large—did he publicly shame the dominators. Having opened the eyes of the blind, he showed them where to look.

By getting this sequence wrong, modern terrorists doom themselves and their cause. Their bloody versions of "propaganda by the deed" almost always produce the opposite of their desired effect. Instead of awakening and inspiring the victims of corruption, they frighten them into the arms of the corrupt.

Red scares united Americans against not just the handful of violent anarchists, but against the hundreds of thousands of labor activists who were tarred with the same brush. Instead of precipitating a movement against the plutocrats, the shock yanked people's gaze in the wrong direction. Similarly, after 9/11, the terrorism fixation swiveled Americans' heads away from what the attacks aimed to highlight—and what was arguably the principal danger to American society.

Only now, as I write this, do I realize how I too was fooled by that optical illusion. I went halfway around the world in my compulsion to respond to 9/11. But the greatest national security threat was not terrorism, it was right here on Wall Street.

Fighting the Hydra: The Countryside

Just because a movement gets the sequence right, however, does not mean it will prevail. That fact was demonstrated by the third major current of resistance to the Gilded Age networks' stranglehold on America. From the mid-1870s through the mid-1890s, an insurrection swept the back-country of the nation's South and West. Though disfigured by the white supremacy derived especially from its southern roots, this vast stirring in coveralls and calico, of sod houses and village schools and covered-wagon encampments across thousands of square miles, was the most significant mass democratic uprising the United States has ever seen.

From a twenty-first-century perspective, two elements defy the possible. First, a population that was more scattered and solitary than we can imagine—lone farmsteads tossed on an ocean of grass, or clinging to a riverbank down miles of dirt trail, or cupped in a meadow half-way up some mountain—mobilized to take coordinated joint action, without benefit of social media. And kept at it for years. Second, the most penetrating critique of the Gilded Age syndrome and the most thorough and forward-looking proposed alternatives emerged not in one of the burgeoning modern urban centers, but from the brains and dedication of country people, who were then, as they are now, scorned as backward, lazy, and stupid.

The initial phase of this revolt was the Farmers' Alliance movement, born on the Texas frontier. The core problem faced there came down to money. Farmers' labor in the dirt and the rocks, mending fences and scraping gore off their arms after slaughtering a pig, did not deliver much they could use. Like farmers today, they were engaged in commodity agriculture. They couldn't eat the cotton or tobacco they raised any more than mill hands could eat molten steel. Their effort and creativity and the earth's fertility were being converted to someone else's infinite wealth. And they had no control over the terms or the timing of the conversion.

Farmers needed money for everything—even, ironically, food. They needed it worst at the end of the winter, just when they were poorest in every way. But they had no hope of earning any till harvest, when markets for their crops were glutted and prices low.

As one correspondent put it in the pages of the North Carolina *Progressive Farmer* in 1886, "It is only a question of time how long the farmer who stakes his all on cotton and tobacco, and has his smoke house in Baltimore and his corn-crib in Chicago, will hold out. Time-buying at from 40 to 100 per cent and a lien on the crop to be sold when everything is the lowest, is sure ruin."* The author—doubtless a landowner—argued for crop diversification, for raising only "a little cotton and tobacco made by using your own compost" to bring in "some money to school your children and pay the preacher." He still had some choice in the matter. Most did not.

For what kept the vast machinery of low-priced commodity production running was a form of servitude called the crop lien system. Banks—where they had a presence—weren't handling the small loans dirt farmers needed; the local merchant was. When those farmers came to him for supplies in the spring, he demanded their fall production as collateral for his loan. Five or so months later, having shouldered all of the risk, the farmers owed the benefit—their harvest—to the merchant. They lost even their say over what their families could plant. The merchants insisted on a cash crop; in the South, that meant cotton.

I came upon this system in the opium economy of southern Afghanistan. Farmers, faced with a major expenditure, turned to the only source of credit available: the opium dealer. He insisted on

---

* Translation: buying spring supplies by means of a loan at 40–100% interest, with the crop as collateral, to be paid off at harvest time—meaning the farmer is obliged to sell just when the glut of harvested grain is driving the price down—is, in the letter-writer's view, "sure ruin."

repayment in opium—no other crop, not even cash. If the farmer failed to pay in full, he owed double as much opium the next year. This is why vast campaigns to destroy poppies in the field never solved the opium problem. Most farmers weren't choosing to plant poppy. Till their debt was cleared, they could not switch to another crop.

At least my Afghan neighbors did see cash money. At least there were plenty of opium dealers who might make competing bids and competing merchants from whom to buy. In nineteenth-century rural America, most farm families were at the mercy of a single "furnishing merchant."

That merchant kept the books. A fictional exchange, from the later novel *Blood on the Forge,* puts it starkly: "Mr. Johnson keeps the book," a black tenant farmer tells a stranger. "He don't let us see what's writ in it. . . . He say what we made, and what's writ against us leaves us owin' him." By underweighing and undervaluing cotton at harvest, and by marking up the prices of the goods provided to farmers on credit, the furnishing man could reap as much effective interest as the opium dealers' 100 percent.

But he rarely advanced actual money. He advanced the supplies. And if "what's writ against" the farmer left him too deep in debt, the furnishing merchant would decide what supplies the farmer could have, what food he would eat, what color of cheap cloth his wife could use to patch the family's clothes. He looked at the farmer's list, then pulled whatever he wanted off the shelves. For borrowers who owned their land, the merchant was soon taking that in payment for the outstanding debt, reducing the family to tenancy.

African Americans had the unspeakable worst of this system. Lacking reparations for their prior forced labor, or earned cash, most families started out in debt if they were lucky, more likely as tenants. To that starting handicap was added most of their inability to read "what's writ" in the book, and their lack of standing to ask to see it if they could. Racism, the unwillingness of poor white farmers to be in last place—and the manipulation of these sentiments by white planters—crippled hopes of advancement.

African Americans did not suffer this system alone, however. Tens of thousands of white tenant farmers, cash-poor landowners too, were caught in the same spiral. "Once a farmer had signed his first crop lien," writes historian Lawrence Goodwyn, "he was in bondage to his

merchant as long as he failed to pay out. . . . In ways people outside
the South had difficulty perceiving, the crop lien system became for
millions of Southerners, white and black, little more than slavery."

And so, apart from the land's generosity and people's labor, the
thing of inestimable value that this version of the Midas disease converted to gold may be the most priceless of all to human beings: their
autonomy.

Gold itself, fittingly, makes an important appearance in this story.
Needing money to finance the Civil War, the U.S. government had
printed paper "greenbacks." And it had sold war bonds, the ones
banker Jay Cooke marketed. Most buyers purchased them with those
new paper greenbacks. Members of the Gilded Age networks, especially bankers, bought in bulk. After the war, they demanded repayment not in the same plentiful—and thus cheap—paper currency,
but in gold. In fact, they wanted greenbacks retired altogether. They
wanted the country back on the gold standard. For, when money is
limited, he who holds it is powerful. It is when money is abruptly
abundant that it democratizes societies. This insistence on gold,
which carried the day in that infamous year of the panic, 1873, added
to farmers' difficulties—as they learned.

That is the first thing the Farmers' Alliance set out to do. It began in
1877 as a local club, complete with passwords and secret handshakes.
But the objective was democratic: the embryonic Alliance sought to
expand its members' knowledge. As the movement took root and
grew, with hundreds of communities clamoring for "sub-Alliance"
charters, it got better at it. One or two nights a week, throughout
the South and western Great Plains, parents found seats on their
children's schoolhouse benches. They avidly studied new scientific
farming techniques but also the latest international prices for their
production, and the various reasons they were not receiving those
returns. Traveling lecturers instructed them.

What remarkable organization. Alliance leaders developed a standard curriculum, with lessons including "history, statistics, finance,
economics, and government." They screened and trained new lecturers. They fostered a network of thousands of weekly newspapers,
which, thanks to the U.S. Postal Service, reached the most far-

flung communities. Farmers flocked to weekly meetings from miles around and afterward discussed the lessons or lectures, the wisdom of some new farming method or proposed joint action, or questions they themselves submitted to the group, such as this mix, from the May 12, 1886, issue of *The Progressive Farmer:* "Is it wise or safe to give crop liens or mortgages? . . . Is the extensive use of commercial fertilizers, as now practiced by our farmers, a benefit or an evil to the agricultural interests? . . . What benefits can farmers derive from organization?"

The constant and vigorous local input, the "small stories of personal tragedy" absorbed every day by the traveling lecturers and reported back to headquarters or printed in letters to the editor, exerted an ongoing pressure that shaped the movement's practices and its political vision. "Education may not at first appear to be an effective fulcrum for a protest movement," writes historian Charles Postel. "But education served to agitate, mobilize, and organize" farming families.

Around these intellectual pursuits, the Farmers' Alliance, like the era's other protest and reform movements, birthed an exuberant culture.

It extended to frequent Alliance meetings . . . where the whole family came, where the twilight suppers were, in the early days, laid out for ten or twenty members of the suballiance . . . but which soon grew into vast spectacles; long trains of wagons, emblazoned with suballiance banners, stretching literally for miles, trekking to enormous encampments where five, ten, and twenty thousand men and women listened intently to the plans of their Alliance and talked among themselves about those plans. At those encampments speakers, with growing confidence, pioneered a new political language to describe the "money trust," the gold standard, and the private national banking system that underlay all of their troubles with the lien system. . . . Grounded in a common experience, nurtured by years of experimentation and self-education, [this culture] produced a party, a platform, a specific new democratic ideology, and a pathbreaking political agenda for the American nation.

In other words, a broad-based egalitarian coalition was coming together and reaching consensus—about the nature of the problems it confronted and what to do about them.

That consensus was far from complete. In a region where most, and the poorest, farmers were African American, they were ultimately excluded from the Farmers' Alliance and had to build a separate and terribly unequal version, the Colored Alliance. The Farmers' Alliance forced the Knights of Labor to abandon its rule welcoming members of all races as the price of a merger, and Alliance ideas contributed to the racial subjugation that came into force across the United States in the 1890s, descending into a campaign of state-sponsored terrorism that lasted for eighty years—the hydra's most devastating manipulation of the identity divide tactic.

On the white side of the line, opposing interests made for awkward fellowships between landholding Alliance members and their own tenants, who brought conflicting aspirations and needs to those shared school benches. The ugly scars of Civil War wounds made

THE BLUE AND THE GRAY.

Former foes clasp hands as equals in the light of a Populist dawn. Trampled at their feet, unfortunately, were the rights of African American farmers and laborers, sacrificed for the sake of bridging this chasm.

organizing across the Mason-Dixon Line searingly hard. Gut loyalties to the parties that matched the blood-soaked armies—grey Democrats in the South, blue Republicans in the North—blinded many farmers to those parties' joint service to the very networks of bankers, railroad executives, and large manufacturers that were making profits on their misery. "Sectionalism" was the other main identity divide protecting kleptocrats. Both parties cynically manipulated it.

Still, like industrial workers, Alliance members had no problem answering the *Progressive Farmer*'s question. The benefits to be derived from organization were capital. In fact, the only possible way to better their lot was to build a vast coalition, the way the moneyed interests had built their small and powerful one. "All are fighting unsupported by each other and remind me of a scattered army," one correspondent complained to the *Progressive Farmer,* when "every one knows how important it is to keep the lines closed up to insure success in battle."

Apart from sacrificing African American farmers, the way to close the lines, at least initially, was to remain nonpartisan. So the Alliance focused on economic action. Its first battle was to sidestep the furnishing merchant by combining individuals' supply needs into bulk orders, which an agent for the group could purchase directly at urban wholesalers. Alliance headquarters would pay on credit. The organization would secure that credit—for the total sum, including tenants' orders—using landowning members' holdings and current crop liens as collateral. Then everyone's harvest, also combined in bulk, would be sorted and graded in a common warehouse. Farmers with surplus could store it there to gain higher prices out of season. The crop would be offered for sale directly to bulk purchasers in the North, or England or Germany.

It was an experiment much like what Lucy Parsons and other anarchists had envisioned. Local cooperatives, based in a single "branch of industry," had, as she put it, "instituted methods of direct communication." And they were taking collective action.

These farmers, note, were no throwbacks. The pages of their newspapers display the same enchantment with scientific progress and modernity as their urban compatriots'. But they were experimenting with a different configuration of modernity than the one industrial giants offered. They were groping for a modern order that allowed citizens to participate in the new economies of scale instead of being subject to them, one that offered more freedom of choice to more members of society. Theirs was a version of modernity based on grassroots cooperation, not zero-sum competition.

It worked brilliantly—at first. It saved Alliance members several million dollars collectively on their supply purchases the first planting season. But that very success sparked the hydra's countermoves. In Texas, local merchants and banking executives met and decided that the banks should deny credit, whatever the value of the collateral offered. As Alliance president Charles Macune put it in 1888, after knocking on bank doors across two states, "Those who controlled the moneyed institutions . . . either did not choose to do business with us, or they feared the ill will of a certain class of business men who considered their interests antagonistic to those of our order." The coalition of the dominating few overpowered the coalition of the egalitarian many.

It was this stinging setback that forced the Farmers' Alliance into politics. The drift had begun earlier, piloted by some of the more radical traveling lecturers. In 1886, a county sub-Alliance voted to boycott the southwestern railroad system in support of a walkout linked to the strike for the eight-hour day that Albert and Lucy Parsons had helped organize. Though hardly punching a clock, many Texas farmers sympathized, even bringing baskets of food to the workers. The strikes were broken in the wake of the Haymarket bombing, and with them that generation's wave of labor activism. But farmers emerged more determined.

That summer, the Alliance adopted a radical platform—over the furious dissent of the old guard, who wished to "eschew all political questions, resolutions, demands, or platforms." It was addressed to "state and national governments" and demanded "such legislation as shall secure to our people freedom from the onerous and shameful abuses that the industrial classes are now suffering at the hands of arrogant capitalists and powerful corporations."

With these words, farmers—tenants and landowners—included themselves among "industrial classes," alongside rail-yard workers or mill hands. Demand number one was the recognition of "trades unions, cooperative stores, and such other associations as may be organized"—suggesting an equivalency between urban and rural collective action. Convict labor, read another plank, should be abolished.

The whole thrust of the platform suggests an insight of significance today. The Alliance saw the greatest threat to freedom not in government, but in big business. It looked to government as the only viable counterweight. Among the measures it advocated were an interstate commerce law to regulate railroad freight rates and laws to curb or prohibit financial speculation in railroad stock, agricultural futures, and land, and the strict enforcement of those laws.

In its most political move, the Alliance took up the matter of money. Through their studies, leaders had concluded that when the same number of monetary units was being spent to purchase a growing quantity of goods, prices would inevitably fall—while the dollar sum due on a loan or in taxes did not. Agriculture was thus "the helpless victim of the rapacious greed and tyrannical power of gold." The Alliance called for expanding the money supply, including through a government-issued paper currency, printed in quantities that increased with rising population.

Over the following years, the farmers adopted even more daring political proposals, such as the abolition of private interstate banking; the nationalization of railroads, of urban public transport, of the telegraph and the recently invented telephone; a graduated income tax, the secret ballot, and direct election of senators.

As for their original idea for farm credit and joint sales of agricultural commodities, they asked the government to step in where banks and local merchants had locked them out. A revolutionary "sub-treasury" plan called for government warehouses and grain elevators to be built across the land. Farmers would be able to store their crops and secure loans in treasury notes against their harvest, at an interest rate not to exceed 2 percent. Those treasury notes would amount to a government-issued paper money, "legal tender for all debts, public and private."

Such ideas ran directly counter to prevailing political convention. To provide the type of redress farmers sought, the government would have to be expanded and strengthened, but also its loyalties and personnel would have to be split off from big business. The networks would have to be unraveled.

Not surprisingly, individual Alliance-endorsed candidates who ran for office under either Democratic or Republican banners proved, once elected, less than energetic in pushing the farmers' demands. After fifteen years of trying other solutions, there was no alternative. The logic of Alliance thinking dictated a third party.

And that is what emerged. The Populist Party was born on July 4, 1892, in Omaha, Nebraska, with Alliance members and thinking at its heart. The preamble to the party platform justifies the move: "We have witnessed for more than a quarter of a century the struggles of the two great political parties for power and plunder," it stated,

> while grievous wrongs have been inflicted upon the suffering people. We charge that the controlling influences dominating both these parties have permitted the existing dreadful conditions to develop without serious effort to prevent or restrain them. . . . They propose to sacrifice our homes, lives, and children on the altar of mammon; to destroy the multitude in order to secure corruption funds from the millionaires.

And so, the Populists declared, "we seek to restore the government of the Republic to the hands of 'the plain people,' with which class it originated."

Despite several victories in local, state, and congressional elections, the ultimate fate of this big-chested effort was the same as that of the earlier cooperative purchase and sales idea—only more punishing. Apart from the sectional divide, a challenge the new party faced was the gap between organized, experienced rural Populists and urban workers, who were repeatedly shattered by the savage crackdowns and whose languages and cosmopolitan cultures were foreign to farmers. But the most important factor was elite backlash. Such a threat did this groundswell represent to northern industrialists and southern planters alike, to Democrats and Republicans, that the often rival networks joined forces to defeat it—by any means necessary.

Those means included "wholesale ballot-box stuffing, open bribery, various forms of intimidation, and massive voting by dead or fictitious Negroes." Lynchings soared. Workers who campaigned for Populist tickets were blacklisted and could not find jobs. Barriers to voting, such as the poll tax or education requirements, were stiffened. Press aligned with one party or the other "systematically played on racial, sectional, and class fears to alert readers to the Populist menace." And, especially in 1896, when the Populists reluctantly opted to combine with the Democratic Party and back William Jennings Bryan, unprecedented political spending funded a public relations blitz equating Republicanism with patriotism.

William McKinley—later assassinated by an anarchist—won.

This review of the passionate, brave, creative, disciplined (if sometimes excessive), labor-intensive, and often embittering struggles to rein in the Gilded Age networks is sobering. Most striking is the sheer effort expended: the daily work of preparing and attending gatherings, of listening, thinking, and speaking up, so as to reach a shared understanding and a language for expressing it; the hours and energy eked out around twelve-hour shifts and lavished on decorating halls and painting banners and writing or sitting through long, sometimes boring, sometimes melodramatic speeches; the miles and miles of travel; the creativity to devise new solutions when earlier ones were thwarted. All of this over and over for months and years, as reformers learned from setbacks, regrouped and tried something else, somehow not losing heart. The long view that was required, the stamina and determination, are critical lessons for our generation; the need to build up—in thin, careful layers like the colors of an oil painting—new thinking and organizational structures, an independent analysis, and a new movement culture. A hard lesson, too, is the difficulty and the importance of extending that structure and culture across the inherited barriers that divide the "plain people" in any complex modern society.

But what a powerful inspiration, too, are those seventy years of struggle. There was a place in the effort for everyone. Startling talents emerged. Unexpected people played roles they would never have imagined for themselves. People who had been made to feel they were of no account, that they did not matter, found a meaning in the shared sacrifice and the bursts of imagination that were called for. All those people did matter. With their different gifts, their quirky talents and idiosyncrasies, or just their dogged perseverance, they were needed. In their struggle, they found suffering and disappointment, but they also found joy.

The failure of each of these movements spelled the failure, in the United States, of a certain kind of participatory democracy, in which decisions and actions taken in concert on a grassroots level might contribute to shaping the destiny of the nation. Curtailed, too, were hopes for a similarly democratic economy, based to any significant degree in joint local action in the interests of participating citizens.

And yet, even in "failure," these movements profoundly altered the American system—at least for a time. Almost every demand made by the labor and Alliance movements, from the eight-hour day to a flexible paper currency and the direct election of senators, was enacted.

But it took long enough. In 1933, as he assumed the highest office, President Franklin Delano Roosevelt spoke insights that anarchists had hanged for half a century earlier. "The money changers have fled from their high seats in the temple of our civilization," Roosevelt proclaimed.

> We may now restore that temple to the ancient truths. The measure of that restoration lies in the extent to which we apply social values more noble than mere monetary profit. Happiness lies not in the mere possession of money; it lies in the joy of achievement, in the thrill of creative effort. . . . Recognition of that falsity of material wealth as the standard of success goes hand in hand with the abandonment of the false belief that public office and high political position are to be valued only by the standards of pride of place and personal profit.

Not until the decade opened by his presidency were many of the reforms realized that had been fought for so hard in the nineteenth century. So: Why then?

3

"It Had Needed a War"

In Paris one day, walking past a municipal building, I noticed a public exhibit and veered over for a look. Black-and-white photographs, enlarged and laminated, converted the edge of the sidewalk to an open-air museum. The pictures were from World War II, somewhere in Poland. One was of a young woman standing thigh-deep in a trench, grasping a shovel with one hand, the other flung out toward the sky. Her face shone with a look of incandescent joy.

This picture may hold a hint as to why the sweeping reforms of the 1930s and 1940s came when they did.

This woman was facing mortal danger. Her city was about to be bombed. People she knew would die, perhaps she would too. Life as she knew it was about to be pulverized. And yet, there was no faking—or disguising—the joy on her face. I could not get over that paradox.

It is a paradox that sociologist Charles Fritz experienced firsthand, also during World War II. From 1943 to 1946, he was stationed in England. He married an Englishwoman. What he found in her family and across the country after five years of war was

a nation of gloriously happy people. . . . The traditional British class distinctions had largely disappeared. People who had never spoken to each other before the war, now engaged in warm, caring personal relations. . . . [T]hey gladly shared their scarce supplies with others who had greater needs. . . .

[T]here was an easygoing, friendly intermingling of people of quite different racial, ethnic, class and cultural backgrounds.

Fritz spent the next two decades researching this anomaly. His monograph—only published thirty years after he wrote it—includes this remark from a compatriot of the woman in the photograph: "The country forgot about the division between manor and cottages, and it welcomed with Samaritan help the people of the towns. Men who were very unpopular in the country—tax collectors, policemen, foresters, and other minor officials—now found a warm hospitality in the same houses which they could hardly have entered before the war."

We have all heard striking examples of this phenomenon or lived through them ourselves. Every natural disaster brims with accounts of breathtaking altruism. But still we're surprised. There are the improvised soup kitchens, set up in some tent—or a homeless shelter, as after Hurricane Harvey in Houston in the late summer of 2017. There, "chefs, cooks, bartenders, bar and restaurant owners, . . . barbecue pit masters" pooled supplies and talent to create the Midtown Kitchen Collective, as *Houston Chronicle* food writer David Leftwich recounted. It provided more than 250,000 meals. There are the citizen first responders, like the Cajun Navy of boat owners from Louisiana, who conducted thousands of search and rescue missions. There were the volunteer medical personnel who rushed into the epicenter of the coronavirus storm, the citizen sewing circles stitching masks. Little things can be most striking. When Superstorm Sandy deluged New York and New Jersey in 2012, someone draped power strips over a fence, so people could charge their phones. Taxi drivers gave free rides. Incredulous, the mayor of Newark tweeted, "Police have reported ZERO looting or crimes of opportunity."[*]

Numerous recent studies have confirmed Fritz's 1960s findings. My friend Sebastian Junger anchored his book about community, *Tribe,* in this reality. Rebecca Solnit brought Fritz's work forward

---

[*] Note an important distinction Rebecca Solnit makes in her book *A Paradise Built in Hell,* referenced below, between looting—opportunistic theft for personal gain—and the ad hoc requisition of emergency supplies to fill victims' basic requirements.

to include the 1985 earthquake in Mexico City, 9/11, and Hurricane Katrina, among other examples. Her title speaks the paradox: *A Paradise Built in Hell.* Boiled down, the basic principle is this, in Junger's words: "Communities that have been devastated by natural or man-made disasters almost never lapse into chaos and disorder; if anything, they become more just, more egalitarian, and more deliberately fair."

A number of elements combine in this phenomenon, both resulting from and reinforcing it. One is meat sharing, the loaves and the fishes. Houston food writer David Leftwich describes his arrival in the kitchen of a chic Vietnamese bistro, fragrant with beef and star anise. He's carrying sacks of produce donated by another restaurant. Members of the "food community" pile into the bean sprouts, Thai basil, carrots, and jalapeños, chopping and adding them to the simmering broth. Minutes later, the group is handing out one hundred equal portions of "meat"—aka somewhat unusual Vietnamese pho soup.

Solnit quotes a survivor of the earthquake that struck Gilded Age San Francisco in 1906: "Food was voluntarily divided; the milk was given to the children, and any little delicacies that could be found were pressed upon the aged and the ailing." After 9/11, a cruise ship from Virginia became a floating refectory. "You walked on that boat and you saw this great crowd of people eating together," a chaplain told Solnit, "which was a very Eucharistic image."

Disaster survivors and their neighbors instantly place whatever food they can collectively hunt and gather in common. There is no class, no race, no political orientation. Such meat sharing lies at the root of humans' remarkable egalitarian tendencies. Those tendencies are reinforced every time the ritual is enacted—especially at moments of vivid intensity.

The "strong feeling of mutual suffering," but perhaps more importantly of shared sacrifice—the joint effort to address common problems—may be the most powerful force invoking this ethos during crises. An "emergent community develops," writes Fritz, which "does not have primary reference to the preexisting social system, but to the situations and experiences produced by the disaster." He quotes a 1958 study of tornadoes in Texas: "Persons and institutions submerge their particular aims in a common effort." Suddenly everyone's unique traits and capacities find a use. Shaped by the new values, this "survivor community" is configured along new lines. Level of need and contribution to group welfare are the criteria that count.

Crucially—and the testimony is unanimous—class distinctions evaporate. As a report on a 1955 flood in Connecticut put it, "All the social statuses that ordinarily act as structural divisions in New England communities tended to disappear during the crisis." Or, in this elegant framing: "An earthquake buries rich and poor, learned and illiterate, authorities and subjects alike beneath its ruined houses," a survivor of an Italian quake wrote. "An earthquake achieves what the law promises but does not in practice maintain—the equality of all men."

Amid the ashes of stratified society, the egalitarian consensus can arise.

But for that to happen, Fritz warns, the disaster must be generalized. Crises of more limited scope tend to have the opposite effect. Those afflicted feel "the need to explain having been singled out, as an individual or as a member of a particular group, for special punishment or suffering, and this search for a causative agent often results in aggression."

Indeed, for social solidarity to take widespread hold, it may be especially important that elites—the "rich," the "learned," and the "authorities"—undergo their share of the suffering. At crucial moments, leadership can thwart the upwelling of egalitarianism, as Solnit found after Hurricane Katrina. Occasionally, it encourages it.

One way to understand the Gilded Age juggernaut is to think of the lives of the working poor as constituting an everyday calamity, a disaster in all but name. The punishing conditions helped birth the protest and reform groups' remarkable solidarity. But those conditions were not experienced by—or even visible to—other classes. And the nation's leadership did everything it could to thwart egalitarian tendencies.

Between 1914 and 1945, however, the industrialized world and much of its periphery suffered a series of disasters that were absolutely generalized. These were of the man-made variety. The Gilded Age networks' excesses and self-protective tactics, gone too long unchecked, can be blamed for the unspeakable calamities.

The decades-long debate about the causes of World War I is not typically framed in such terms. But it is hard to argue that Western nations' competition over colonial holdings had zero to do with the voraciously expanding Gilded Age industrial activities, and stock-market speculation on them. In *The First World Oil War,* historian Timothy Winegard argues that World War I and the ensuing peace were largely shaped by the quest for oil. "For the first time in history, territory was conquered specifically to possess oilfields and resources."

Several historians suggest that a resort to jingoistic nationalism to short-circuit the revolutionary agitation of an angry working class helped precipitate the conflict. Arno Mayer calls out Gilded Age networks' "resolve . . . to foster their political position by rallying the citizenry around the flag." He notices that the individuals most sharply criticized for their brinksmanship "were intimately tied in with those social, political, and economic strata that were . . . battling to maintain" the Gilded Age status quo.

The strategy, if it was one, worked. A powerful international labor organization was laying plans for a Europe-wide general strike to deprive the war machine of manpower. On July 31, 1914, one of its leading figures, Jean Jaurès, was assassinated in Paris. The next day, Germany declared war on Russia, and France began mobilizing. In the scramble to defend father- and motherland, labor solidarity was forgotten. Strikes died almost out for the duration of hostilities.

In pursuit of objectives that boil down to infinite wealth, the flower of humanity, the most beautiful young men and women each nation had to offer, were fed into the maw of industrialized war. On those European fields, a grotesque distortion of the human-dwarfing mills and factories that were chewing up laborers chewed through the human sacrifice laid before it. Wantonly, just fodder, millions of human lives were fed to it and spat out in shreds of mud-fouled flesh.

The causal link between Gilded Age practices and disaster is even easier to make for the Great Depression. There is no question that those practices and the policies that protected them brought it on, as they had the string of prior panics.

As for World War II, an instructive comparison is between the proportion of votes the Nazi Party won in the 1928 and 1932 German parliamentary elections. It jumped from about 2.5 percent to nearly 38 percent of the total. Again, multiple factors might help explain this leap. But a big one is the Midas-disease-generated Depression. It hit Germany hard, just when a gifted Social Democratic chancellor (Hermann Müller, 1918–1920 and 1928–1930) had helped steer the shattered country clear of the worst World War I wreckage.

Germany's reaction did not have to cut the way it did. As Fritz and Solnit observed, quite different tendencies well up among ordinary people in times of crisis. Leadership matters. Different leadership pushed the United Kingdom and the United States in a different direction. It might have nurtured egalitarian tendencies in Germany, too.

But as it happened, the disciplined Nazi Party leaped into the confusion with a ready-made scapegoat for the sudden misery. In Japan, similarly, a series of homegrown financial crises, plus the depression that slammed into the archipelago from overseas, made aggressive, nationalistic policies a tempting diversion.

The Gilded Age syndrome is an unspeakable threat.

Stroll through any village lost in the French countryside, and you'll see signs of the heartrending scope of the first of these disasters. Near the stone church, with its round arches and creaky doors, will be a monument to the village war dead. The one in Montalieu, near the border with Switzerland, counts 92 names for World War I. Montalieu's total population, about 3,300 now, barely topped 2,000 at the time. Run your finger down the list engraved in the slate: Chabout, Chabout; Chaillet, Chaillet; Champier, Champier; Guicherd, Guicherd, Guicherd, Guicherd. Whole families were extinguished.

Every monument, everywhere, looks like this.

Lyon, the city nearest Montalieu, spills down from facing hills across the confluence of two rivers. It was an industrial center, a pioneer in aeronautics and the chemical industry, as well as that revolutionary new art Joseph Kennedy exploited, film. Also reputed for its medical facilities, Lyon became, as the mayor is reported to have summed it up, a "vast hospital." Public and private facilities were emptied of civilian patients to make room for trainloads of mutilated soldiers. River barges were requisitioned to provide more beds, a chocolate factory, too—like convention centers across America in 2020. A city of some 460,000 handled 200,000 war wounded between 1914 and 1918, in just one of its manifestations of disaster solidarity.

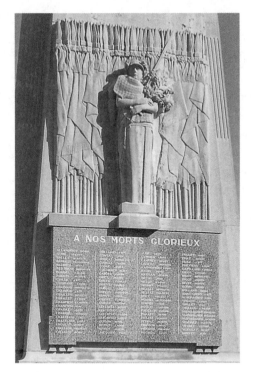

Monument to the war dead
from the village of Montalieu,
in eastern France.

Floods of refugees washed through the town too, and were generously taken in. Frightening shortages hit, of items as basic as salt.
Malnutrition gnawed well into the middle classes. One village peti-
tioned the minister of defense to cut short the military service of its
lone baker, for there was no bread.

Until the coronavirus pandemic, it was impossible for Americans
to imagine such a universal disaster. Since the South in the Civil War,
the United States had seen nothing close. England, entering World
War I later than the continent, still suffered on the order of 420,000
casualties in the Somme offensive alone. It was martyred in World
War II. Germans and their immediate neighbors—not to mention
Armenians and Chinese and Jews and Roma and others singled out
for mass sadism—were raked by every appalling chapter of those
appalling decades.

The United States experienced both world wars more entirely
than it has any war since. The whole population suffered the burden,
at least through wartime production, recycling campaigns, blood

donations, the constant barrage of public messaging, or the loved ones gone perilously overseas. For those who deployed, either to fight or support or report, the experience was life altering. It rearranged their worldview.

The generalized disaster of the era for the United States as a whole, however, was the Great Depression. And, though class barriers hardly disappeared, a vivid sense of sociologist Charles Fritz's "survivor community" feeling does emerge from the words of those who endured it. World War I veteran Jimmy Sheridan, interviewed by Studs Terkel in 1971, recalled "bumming the town" with other destitute veterans from across the country who were converging on Washington in 1932, in what was called the Bonus Army: "We'd go to the different grocers . . . and they would give us sausage or bread or meat or canned goods, and then we'd go back to the railroad yards, the 'jungles' " and cook together. Conductors added boxcars to the trains to accommodate the marchers. "Even the railroad detectives were very generous. . . . Townspeople were very sympathetic. There was none of this hatred you see now when strangers come to a neighborhood."

Sheridan's voice catches, then lights up: "That's one of the things about the Depression," he exclaims. "There was more camaraderie among people during the Depression than there is now. . . . There was a fine feeling among people! You were in trouble; could they help you? Damn it, if they could help you, they would help you, even if they had very little themselves. And that was the feeling that America lost."

The same note reverberates through other accounts: "It was Depression time," recalled waitress Dorothy Bernstein, who, as a child in a foster home, gave her Friday lunches to the knots of homeless drifting through town. "I think there was a whole different sentimentality." Jazz musician Robin Langston's parents had a restaurant, so there was always food. "There must have been ten white families within fifty feet of us. I remember feeding them, I remember feeding little black kids. . . . We had a basement in our home. My father would let people sleep down there, as long as they would keep it up. . . . I met so many interesting people."

By the end of this thirty-year series of mass calamities—each devastating different countries in different ways—just about everyone in the industrialized world, and many beyond it, had been touched. Transformed. Including elites.

Disaster on such a scale does more than spur personal generosity. It has effects that are relevant to the large-scale enactment of regulatory and social welfare measures in the 1930s and 1940s. Disaster "provides an unstructured social situation that enables . . . the possibility of introducing desired innovations," Fritz found. "If paradise . . . arises in hell," concurs Solnit, "it's because in the suspension of the usual order and the failure of most systems, we are free to live and act another way." There is room for improvisation. In fact, it is called for.

In World War I Lyon, the inexperienced young mayor (a future French prime minister) staved off food shortages by launching municipal purchases of wheat and potatoes on the international market, and sales to the public at controlled prices. He opened municipal soup kitchens, a precursor to welfare. He convened a commission to monitor stocks and prices of foodstuffs. The commission enacted an antispeculation tax.

In the United States today, speculation is a virtue.

Alongside new ideas came new people. Sent to the distant front, or elbow to elbow with refugees, people who had never left home were suddenly exposed to new perspectives. It was impossible to ignore the prowess of the "Senegalese sharpshooters" whom the French army recruited in West African colonies, or of the hundreds of thousands of African Americans who fought in World War II. Women kept munitions factories open and flew airplanes. A crippled man proved to be one of the greatest American presidents. It took too long, and has been too imperfect. But such people, their capacities demonstrated, began to gain space in society.

The upheavals, furthermore, supplied daily proof that it was in fact possible to radically transform the system. The sky wouldn't fall. (The sky had already fallen.) Fortified by that proof, hopes long submerged blazed up. At such times, wrote W. E. Hocking in the midst of World War II, "we rediscover humanity and regain freedoms of which we had robbed ourselves through our possessions and habits. We are cured of myopia and the petty bookkeeping with private gains."

It is this shared experience of disaster, and its psychological and social transformations, that helps explain why the radical reforms of the 1930s and 1940s happened, and finally took hold, when they did. Alongside all the other factors—the unrelenting strikes, the emergence of a frightening communist alternative, inspired and determined leadership—the succession of devastating blows built up a critical mass of people who were personally touched and somehow transfigured. Though certainly not universal, a new "survivor community" ethos gained ascendance over the earlier Gilded Age values, which had enshrined money above all else. New practices were admired and rewarded. Some of the old ones were no longer tolerable. As William Sansom wrote in a landmark chronicle of the Blitz, "One was ashamed to reflect that it had needed a war."

Not a war. Two wars, which unleashed two genocides, mass starvation in Europe, and a pandemic of proportions unseen since the bubonic plague; two wars that debased humanity as no events before them ever had. And a global economic collapse. That's what it took. That was the price the world paid to break the grip of the hydra.

For an illustration of the workings of this societal transformation on the scale of a single family, it is helpful to glance back at that emblem, Joseph P. Kennedy.

Just a few years into his career in pursuit of infinite wealth, the country around him became preoccupied, then obsessed, with the first disaster in the series. Like a continent-sized hurricane that had stalled over Europe, World War I was inflicting devastation of an increasingly shocking magnitude. Americans were glued to the news.

Not Kennedy. "As he saw it," his wife, Rose, told historian Doris Kearns Goodwin, "the essence of war was waste and destruction— the destruction of wealth, the destruction of order, the destruction of property and the destruction of lives." Rose listed the casualties in that order.

Her husband fell out with his best friends over it, in a scene she never forgot. Gathered for a Fourth of July weekend two years into the war, the young men could not stop talking about English preparations for what would be one of the bloodiest and least conclusive campaigns in military history, the Somme offensive. At first Kennedy sat silent, as Rose recalled it. Finally, he let loose. He accused his friends of "contributing to the momentum of a senseless war, certain to ruin the victors as well as the vanquished."

Kennedy was absolutely right. There was no justifying the millions of lives and dreams shredded on those blood-sodden fields, the priceless human achievements reduced to rubble. But in a paradoxical way, he was wrong. He missed out on something essential—as he soon began to discover.

One after another, his college buddies dropped their lives and volunteered for officer training. Kennedy was losing touch. Businesses across the nation were retooling—businesses other than banking, that is, which was financing the effort and, as usual, profiting. Soon Kennedy was writing plaintive letters to friends in uniform gone silent. He was "increasingly disturbed by the growing gulf," writes Goodwin. "Their way of life now was so different from his."

In June 1917, serial numbers for a first round of the draft were drawn. Not Kennedy's. He did find a way to join the excitement, however, with a job managing a shipyard that was awash in new orders from the U.S. Navy. It was, according to another Kennedy biographer, "one of the dizziest whirlwinds in the history of American industry."

Demanding, important, frenetic the job certainly was, but it did not expose Kennedy to the vivid realities—or the resulting "different sentimentality"—that transformed the World War I survivor community. The Fore River Shipyard was no volunteer soup kitchen. It was a moneymaking concern, reaping vast income from the war. The ethos was one not of solidarity, but of maximal efficiency. The shipyard had just been bought by Charles Schwab's Bethlehem Steel. A Gilded Age stock character, Schwab was one of the Carnegie lieutenants who had helped Henry Clay Frick crush the steelworkers' union during the infamous Homestead lockout of 1892. Fore River was firmly anchored in the Gilded Age.

Kennedy prospered. Drawing a handsome salary, he still schemed to supplement it. He awarded himself the contract to operate the workers' cafeteria.

Nothing in this experience disrupted his worldview.

In early 1918, Kennedy learned that he was almost certain to be picked in the next round of the draft. Shocked, he got a Bethlehem exec to talk to some people in Washington and escaped duty. While lamenting in letters to friends at the front that he was not in the trenches beside them, in other words, Kennedy was dodging the draft.

His first encounter with Roosevelt dates from this period. Two battleships, commissioned by Argentina, had languished at Fore River for months. Kennedy, the merchant, was refusing delivery without payment in full. Roosevelt, the public servant, was responding to a different set of concerns. Assistant secretary of the navy at the time, he was thrust into the maelstrom of an unprecedented war, whose outcome might hinge on control of the seas. He dispatched navy tugs to tow the battleships away for dispatch to the U.S. ally.

I am reading these two men not just as flesh and blood historical individuals but as the national myths they became—as archetypes of a collective experience. Similar in ambition and energy, those raw metals hammered out quite differently on the anvil of this first global disaster.

After the war, untouched by any disaster-survivor ethos, Kennedy doubled down on the very Gilded Age practices that had helped bring it on. Instead of returning to his community savings establishment, he took up investment banking.

The Depression—caused a decade later by the very type of speculation he practiced—left him unscathed. In fact, it left him wealthier, his family more favored. While his neighbors were savaged by the hardest times they had endured in a hard half century, Joe Kennedy, planted in his temporary office on Wall Street, kept making money.

And yet in 1932, he—along with a crucial minority of other bankers—diverged from the Republican norm and sided with Roosevelt. Kennedy backed the man who was bent on chasing money changers like him "from their high seats in the temple." In fact, he avidly sought a government position.

It is as though Kennedy sensed that mores were shifting, and that in the era now dawning, riches alone would not win him honor. He seemed to know—at least in the abstract—that service to the public was gaining new admiration.

In a September address to the Commonwealth Club in San Francisco, Roosevelt called for just such a "reappraisal of values":

A mere builder of more industrial plants, a creator of more railroad systems, an organizer of more corporations, is as likely to be a danger as a help. The day of the great promoter or the financial Titan, to whom we granted anything if only he would build, or develop, is over. Our task now is not discovery or exploitation of natural resources, or necessarily producing more goods. It is the soberer, less dramatic business of administering resources . . . of distributing wealth and products more equitably, of adapting existing economic organizations to the service of the people.

If Kennedy was intuiting and responding to this shift, however, his premonition was no "different sentimentality." It was calculation. Passed over in the first round of FDR appointments, he went right back to helping deepen the national disaster—to short selling. In fact, he picked as his partner a symbol of the fetid past: Henry Mason Day, one of a ring of oil executives who had bribed the secretary of the interior in the most sensational political corruption scandal of the time, the 1920s Teapot Dome Scandal.

In a ploy favored by dodgy shell companies today, Kennedy hid his participation in the venture by using the name of a flunky on company documents instead of his own. That is, he recognized that the United States was losing patience with stock-market gambling. He recognized it clearly enough to cover his tracks—but not clearly enough to abandon the practice.

Eventually, Kennedy did get Roosevelt's call. The job he was handed, chairmanship of the new Securities and Exchange Commission, was as important as it was surprising.

Kennedy worked his usual punishing schedule at the SEC and frequently entertained the president at evening gatherings in the mansion he had rented in Maryland (which came complete with that apparently mandatory option for the superrich: gold-plated bathroom fixtures). Kennedy did well, too, in his next job: as chairman of the Maritime Commission.

But neither position matched his ambitions. In naming him ambassador to the United Kingdom in 1937, Roosevelt got closer. Given the timing, the role was more critical than Kennedy could have dreamed.

And he used it to try to keep the United States out of the fight against Hitler.

Bathed in her exhaustive reading of primary sources and interviews, historian Doris Kearns Goodwin reflects that "there was in Kennedy's thinking about the war an apocalyptic tone strangely at odds with his fundamental pragmatism. With huge leaps of the imagination, he convinced himself that the chaos of war would bring the end of civilization."

But maybe Kennedy was right. Maybe his premonition was working again. Maybe he understood that a second world war would deal the final blow to *his* civilization: to the Gilded Age world in which he fit. A survivor ethos that put the needs of the community ahead of personal wealth would never hold a man like him in esteem.

Most biographies ascribe Kennedy's spectacular professional implosion to personal failings: diplomatic inexperience perhaps, certainly arrogance and his overpowering self-interest. And yet, at the height of the Gilded Age, those traits had been virtues. They would have stood Kennedy in fine stead had he been born two or three decades earlier.

There is another way to read his personal calamity. It is to observe that in the dramatically changed environment brought forth at last by the succession of generalized calamities and nurtured by Roosevelt's leadership, his Gilded Age reflexes had become shockingly inappropriate. He had intuited that public service was an emerging value, and so his ambitions had veered toward high political office—even the presidency. But, himself untouched by the disaster experience, Kennedy had undergone no personal transformation. So he lacked the reflexes to carry out his public duties in the way that the new situation demanded.

His sons were different. They were of the next generation. Born as the United States entered World War I, John F. may have been as ambitious as his father, was certainly possessed of similar appetites, and would even cheat if necessary. But, exposed to the shock of the Depression in his teenage years, he drank in Roosevelt's words as a young adult and lived through a soul-altering experience his father had avoided. He went to war. Captaining a small patrol boat during

The change of generations: "Honey Fitz" (John Francis Fitzgerald, seated, left) and Joseph P. Kennedy (standing) as the torch is passing to John F. Kennedy (seated right), 1946.

World War II, he confronted life-threatening hardship with a band of comrades. Thus affected, he may have been ripe for shaping by the new ethos and incentive structure that came to predominate in the wake of all the disasters. He—and, perhaps even more, his brother Bobby—harnessed himself to its values.

In the changed world, that was the only way to achieve social standing. The younger Kennedys' prime ambition was not, like their father's, to make money. It was to discover what they could do for their country. That ethos, stunted as it may have been, lasted a generation.

V

THE PATTERN

1980–

1

The Turning (1980s)

And so, together with much of the rest of the industrialized world, the United States entered four decades in which our hydras were—at least somewhat—curbed.

Of course, no society turns on a dime. Gains for ordinary people did not come at once. Better working conditions and wages and the eight-hour day; restraints on banking practices, on stock-market speculation and business monopoly; the right to organize and speak up for workers; safety nets for the elderly, for the very poor and the unemployed; more equal treatment for minorities and women; protections for people and for the land and water and air against dangerous products and poisonous waste—all came. But they came piecemeal, hard-fought.

Nor were the victories free of consequences. Golden age thinking is no way to find lessons in the past. So it is important to take the caveats seriously.

Some of today's most challenging problems are rooted in the very advances made then. Expanding ideas of citizenship and human dignity at home, for example, rarely reached other shores. An intoxication with anything labeled "scientific progress" traded family farming for corporate agriculture and foods assembled in factories. Rising standards of living brought an addiction to convenience and idle distractions. Most urgently, those years accelerated the grievous harm we are doing to our priceless home. The postdisaster ethos of empathy toward fellow humans did not spill over to the earth.

On the contrary, it is as though Gilded Age wantonness was simply democratized.

These reservations are real. They cannot be dismissed. Yet something was different during the postwar years. Even I find meaning in the numbers that reflect the difference. If some are familiar, bear with me. They are worth repeating.

From about 1935 through 1980, they tell us, the incomes of American earners, however much they made, rose and fell at essentially the same rates. If anything, the lot of those toward the bottom of our social ladder was improving faster than that of the most fortunate. Our "meat," in the form of economic growth, was broadly shared, as were the tougher times.

From the end of World War II through the 1970s, according to historian Colin Gordon, average incomes (salaries and bonuses) of the bottom 50 percent of earners rose by 129 percent, doubling and then some within a single generation. During the same three-plus decades, the incomes of the top 1 percent rose less than half as much, by about 58 percent. And the gap between the two groups was narrower than it was before and afterward. After 1980, however, growth for the bottom 50 percent of earners cratered, totaling a mere 21 percent over the next thirty-five years, while the incomes of the top 1 percent of earners nearly tripled (194 percent).

Or, in terms of CEO pay packages: from the end of World War II until about 1990, CEO compensation at top publicly traded companies hovered within sight of median nonmanagement employees' pay. By 2018, bosses were taking home 287 times as much as those workers.

Companies, especially banks, stayed sound during that postwar period. The mass liquidations of the Gilded Age years subsided.

This radical transformation of Gilded Age conditions was not the automatic result of the particular structure of the post–World War II economy. It was produced by the sweeping policy changes inaugurated with the New Deal. The political and economic system, so long twisted to serve the wealth-maximizing objectives of the Gilded Age networks, was straightened out a bit. The results were plain.

Values had changed, too. Though public corruption under-

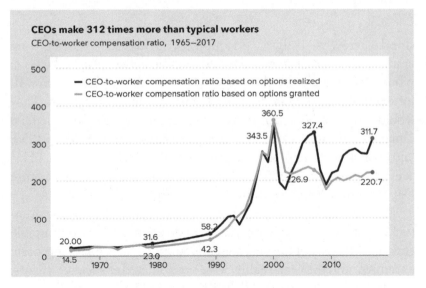

CEOs make 312 times more than typical workers
CEO-to-worker compensation ratio, 1965–2017

The ratio of CEO compensation (including salary, bonuses, and other payouts) to the compensation of the average worker in the same industry. Source: Economic Policy Institute.

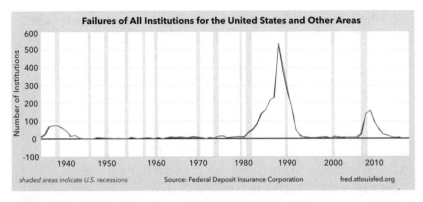

Failures of banking institutions in the United States and territories. Shaded areas indicate recessions. Source: Federal Deposit Insurance Corporation.

stood narrowly—bribery, extortion, or kickbacks—was far from eradicated, a higher standard for acceptable behavior did take hold. None of the generals who led U.S. troops during World War II, for example, worked in the defense industry after retirement. They would have considered it dishonorable. "In my opinion," General Omar Bradley told a House Armed Services subcommittee in 1959, "no former member of the Government should take advantage of his previous position to bring any influence on members of the Defense Department, or any department of Government."

Money, too, lost its spellbinding power. As my Lexington, Kentucky, interlocutor put it, people wanted "enough to be comfortable and safe." It was not the barometer of our personal worth. Corporate executives and the very wealthy were not adulated as society's saviors. Sometimes they were regarded with downright suspicion.

It was these postwar realities that Lewis Powell found so objectionable when he penned his memo to the U.S. Chamber of Commerce in 1971. "No thoughtful person can question that the American economic system is under broad attack," he insisted, suggesting that the economic equality that had been achieved, the policing of corporate crimes against customers, employees, and neighbors, and society's less worshipful attitude toward the rich were dangerous aberrations. Using language chosen to shock, in the midst of the Cold War, he continued:

> There always have been some who opposed the American system, and preferred socialism or some form of statism (communism or fascism). . . . But what now concerns us is quite new in the history of America. We are not dealing with sporadic or isolated attacks from a relatively few extremists or even from the minority socialist cadre. Rather, the assault on the enterprise system is broadly based and consistently pursued. It is gaining momentum and converts.

Powell's readership took note of his blueprint for reversing the values and policies that had taken root with the New Deal and the end of World War II and set about implementing his plan.

Slowly, their efforts bore fruit.

Watergate, the most spectacular corruption scandal of the postwar period, may have horrified the nation and spawned a raft of new ethics rules. But it also set a precedent for breaches of the public trust at the highest level of U.S. government. Wrongdoing was not limited to stealing confidential information from Democratic Party headquarters. It also included massive illegal campaign contributions by top corporations.

As the scandal was unfolding, Pink Floyd sang a deathless song, to the rhythmic clang of cash registers. *"Money!"* it proclaimed, was in. Stop with the goody-goody bullshit.

That decade, families started putting a new form of money in their wallets: the credit card.

The president who started deregulating key industries (airlines, natural gas) and environmental and workplace standards (Occupational Safety and Health, EPA) was Jimmy Carter, elected in 1976. His administration, like those of Presidents Kennedy and Johnson, raised taxes on salaried incomes while reducing them on corporations and on the dividends reaped by the wealthiest Americans (capital gains).

In 1978, a core concept of the fight against the Gilded Age networks came under attack: the understanding that supersized businesses threaten democracy. All the reform movements of the late nineteenth and early twentieth centuries had battled trusts and conglomerates. The concern was their ability to rig politics as well as the market, by stamping out competition in both arenas and rewriting the rules in their own favor. Landmark antitrust laws passed at the turn of the century went largely unenforced at first. It took the post-calamity interlude—from the late 1930s on—for the federal government to get serious about preventing and dismantling monopolies.

It was that keystone of the postwar egalitarian order that Robert Bork, then a Yale law professor, chose as his target. To shatter it, he contended that practices then prohibited—such as integrating conglomerates so they could control entire supply chains, or making deals with competitors to fix prices—"are not illegal under the laws as written." If business concentration improved "efficiency," he asserted, and led to lower prices, it was a positive good. Damage to small businesses and the communities they serve, to jobs, innovation, and democratic government were discounted.

This idea, an irreplaceable ingredient in the potion that revived the U.S. hydra, took hold. By the late 1980s, it had become the standard for launching antitrust enforcement actions. And not just in that domain: marginally lower prices for urban ratepayers became the pretext for allowing power giants to seize land, evict someone's grandma, pile refuse, or spoil a view in what have become this country's sacrifice zones. Bork's doctrine delivered the epidemic of mergers and acquisitions that swept across the 1980s and 1990s, and with it the junk bond crisis, then media concentration, too-big-to-fail banks, and Google and Amazon.

So we arrive at 1980, that fateful turning point. What has come to be called the Reagan Revolution, the great shift in attitudes and in economic and political practices that was inaugurated then, had historical roots. Still, 1980 marks the moment when the postwar ethos of expanding equality foundered. The onset of our current version of the Gilded Age syndrome can be pegged to 1980.

President Ronald Reagan is so associated with the decade's culture of wealth glorification and self-interest that it is remarkable to discover he never articulated such a philosophy. I nearly imagined it was he, not the character Gordon Gekko, who declaimed *Wall Street*'s ode to greed. But Reagan's speeches in his last year as governor through his first year as president don't come close. Entrepreneurs and laborers appear side by side, festooned with the same garlands. The refrain is hard work and its just return. "The freedom to take a risk, to reap its rewards," he told friendly business leaders in the fall of 1981, "to work hard for a better wage, to climb as high as your ambition and effort will take you—that kind of freedom is basic to the dream that is America."

It is only with skeptical hindsight that such words might be parsed for a hidden content. Could the freedom to climb as high as ambition will take you be code for freedom from workplace or environmental safety regulations? Or from paying higher (or any) income tax, if you make more money than you or your children could possibly spend? Did Reagan mean "What the fuck" freedom—for the select few?

Here is another example: Reagan's 1981 announcement creating a new one-time holiday, American Enterprise Day. In light of the

Powell Memo's definition of the "enterprise system," its language is striking. "The unique blend of individual opportunity, incentive and reward that is the free enterprise system," said Reagan, "provides Americans with an unparalleled standard of living. As the foundation of our economic life, free enterprise depends on and serves every American. It is the enemy of poverty."

In fact, it was the *refereeing* of that system, the willingness to call big players offside, that served most Americans. It was the curbs on abuses by too-powerful businesses, the progressive income tax that the Farmers' Alliance had called for—withheld from paychecks starting in 1942—that provided postwar Americans with an unparalleled standard of living.

And those are the measures Reagan set about dismantling.

To get a better idea of his true designs, it is helpful—you may have guessed it—to glance at his network. Many of its members reappear in the orbit of Charles Koch or the Trump administration. What some see as a recent aberration has Reagan-era roots.

Beer magnate Joseph Coors was a loyal and generous Reagan supporter. Coors also contributed seed money for the Heritage Foundation, one of the think tanks inspired by the Powell Memo and now a top Koch beneficiary. Coors underwrote the American Legislative Exchange Council, another Koch favorite, which pioneered the strategy of getting network-friendly rules enacted in select states before taking the campaign to the federal level. Another Coors start-up was the Mountain States Legal Foundation, launched to attack environmental protections in court.

Coors helped its president, James Watt, win the secretary of interior job. Also recommended by Coors, Anne Gorsuch Burford (mother of the Supreme Court justice) got the Environmental Protection Agency. She had to resign in early 1983, amid a storm over her allegedly corrupt management of the Superfund money for toxic waste cleanup.

Her fiancé, Robert Burford, was Watt's director of the Bureau of Land Management. The trio's role mimicked one I saw in developing-world kleptocracies and see now in the Trump administration. It was to disable their agencies—or better, to weaponize them on behalf of fossil fuel, chemical, lumber, and mining interests.

Coors was joined in Reagan's inner circle by Alfred Bloomingdale (of the department store) and Justin Dart (of the Dart drug and processed food conglomerate). Merrill Lynch chairman and CEO Donald Regan became secretary of the treasury, then White House chief of staff.

Another supporting actor was Edwin Meese, first a cabinet-level counselor to the president, then attorney general. A longtime Reagan henchman, he was among the captains of the legal insurgency that has bent the justice sector over the past forty years to the service of the richest Americans. He helped solidify the fledgling Federalist Society, appointing its alums to Justice Department positions and crafting the criteria for judicial nominees used to select Justices Gorsuch and Kavanaugh and dozens of district and appellate court judges. Meese, whose tenure at Justice was beset by scandals over cronyism and influence peddling, left under fire in 1988 to join the Heritage Foundation. He continued to pilot the Federalist Society.

The policies that this Reagan network initiated are well known. Measures requiring corporations to show basic respect for consumers, workers, communities, and landscapes—not to lie or commit fraud or sell defective merchandise manufactured in dangerous workplaces, or disgorge poisonous waste wherever convenient—were berated as "inefficient and burdensome."

The lifting of key restraints on banks plunged the country into the savings and loan crisis. Reagan's home state of California suffered most. Oversight agencies were spiked—budgets and personnel slashed at the Consumer Product Safety Commission, the Occupational Safety and Health Administration, even the Federal Grain Inspection Service. Toxic waste enforcement and cleanups plummeted, while public land and resources such as timber and fossil fuel were practically given away. Apart from the savings and loan anomaly, prosecutions of white-collar crime dropped sharply, in a climate of tolerance for corporate wrongdoers.

Starved of resources, enforcement departments turned against easy-to-catch violators: weekend fishermen, the kitchen at the corner grill, the $30,000 earner's tax filing. Ironically, such tactics choked resources further, since the returns on effort spent chasing such petty violations are so small.

Government spending cuts were selective. Reagan sounded sympathetic when he said it wasn't "easy to restrict benefits . . . in food stamps, subsidized housing, student loans," or to dock the federal transfers to the states that help pay for similar programs on a local level. But, he insisted, "we have no choice but to make these tough decisions now." And yet—how odd—it seems that the decisions were never especially tough on those with the most to spare, the rich. And while students did without books, the purse was opened wide to defense contractors.

Reagan launched total war on labor unions. Flawed as they were, like any large structure that commands resources and some power, unions were the only organizations able to leverage the power of numbers against the power of money—that stood for the egalitarian coalition against Reagan's increasingly determined coalition of meat hogs. By ordering the dismissal of eleven thousand striking air traffic controllers in 1981—backed, as in the Gilded Age, by court orders and the permanent, legal blacklisting of strikers—Reagan set the example for private-sector employers and state governments. The result has been a labor market so punishing that wage earners are back to working twelve-hour shifts or several jobs, or have to resort to public welfare to make ends meet.

Reagan's flagship economic initiative was a sharp tilt in the tax burden. Billed as a cut, his Economic Recovery Tax Act did sharply reduce overall tax revenues to the government. But not everyone got the same relief. Taxes on corporations fell approximately by half, and on capital gains and estates similarly. In a trend that has gained attention recently, several top companies ended up paying no taxes at all, or even won rebates.

"Taking inflation and the large 1981 and 1982 increases in social security tax into account," write Thomas Ferguson and Joel Rogers, "over the 1982–84 period, taxes actually increased for all those making less than $30,000 a year. . . . For those making over $200,000 a year, however, the Reagan cuts brought an average reduction of . . . 15 percent." Thus was perpetrated, say two other analysts, "what may well have been the most accelerated upwards redistribution of income in the nation's history."

The outcome of these measures has been the collapse of the middle class in America.

What strikes me, reviewing this record and comparing it to what Reagan said, is his deceit. Reagan was called the Great Communicator, who could make complex ideas clear. It turns out he was just plying his old trade: acting.

When lambasting regulations, he stressed the hardship they "imposed on the shopkeeper, the farmer, the craftsman, professionals," not the banking, oil, chemical, or real estate magnates who would gain most from the deregulation he championed.

On taxes, "in point of fact," Reagan lied, "we're cutting taxes for people who pay taxes—the people earning between 5 thousand and 50 thousand dollars now pay 67 percent of all of the income tax. They'll receive 70 percent of the total cut."

Reagan pretended he would scrutinize the wealthy as well as welfare queens. He vowed to close loopholes: "We continue the review of where there are places where people are getting undeserved tax breaks," he assured a pool of press interviewers in December 1981. But during the final negotiations on the tax act, according to Ferguson and Rogers, a feeding frenzy tore the text full of new loopholes. Reagan himself, 1970s-era investigations revealed, had reduced his own tax payments, sometimes to zero, via undeserved breaks.

Most disturbing is the way he talked about the most egalitarian and widely prosperous four decades of the nation's history. Prior to his administration, his autobiography alleges, a system had reigned that "penalizes success and accomplishment . . . that discourages work, discourages productivity, discourages economic progress." Such a system, he hardly needed to add, "is wrong."

Politicians don't have a great reputation for truth telling. So here's what I find odd in all these distortions. I had thought that the entire country had shifted in 1980, that the national pendulum had swung in a more pro-business direction. Reagan was always invoking the views of the American people in support of his radical moves. "Your ideas," he assured Republican members of Congress, "are shared and supported by the majority of the American people." His cuts to spending on social programs were "a tremendous victory" for "all of the people of this country." Now "millions of Americans are renewing their faith in our political system," happy "for someone in Washington to listen and care."

But if Reagan was indeed that someone, if he was truly responding to public demand, then why not advertise what he was doing with fanfare? Why lie about it?

The truth is, a majority of Americans did not support Reagan's initiatives.

He admitted to those congressional Republicans that, when pollsters asked citizens to choose between tax cuts and balancing the budget, "the answer, of course, has been a balanced budget."

Just consider that for a moment. Faced with the abstract public good of a balanced federal budget or the tangible benefit of lower taxes, voters were putting the country's interests as they understood them ahead of their own.

They got neither. They got a spiraling federal deficit—much of it going toward a major military buildup, including those six-hundred-dollar toilet seats. And they had to send more of their hard-earned money to the IRS.

In their eye-opening book, *Right Turn,* Thomas Ferguson and Joel Rogers wade through public opinion polling from the 1970s and early 1980s. Far from encountering widespread frustration with regulations and fear for the enterprise system, they find the opposite. What was causing concern was the rising power of the largest businesses. In one 1979 poll, 60 percent of respondents favored a cap on corporate profits.

Amid maximum positive spin for Reagan's deregulatory push, support for current rules on worker safety, the minimum wage, water and air quality, and use of public lands *increased.* Nor did Ferguson and Rogers discover any drop in public approval of welfare, health coverage, education, or efforts to preserve the environment. In one 1980 poll the authors cite, less than a quarter of those surveyed responded that government spending in those areas was too high.

In other words, ordinary Americans did not swing. The rich did.

2

The Validation (1980s-1990s)

All means all. It is comfortable for Democrats to blame and Republicans to credit President Reagan for the 1980s transformations in governmental policy and public values. But leading lights of the Democratic Party and the businesses affiliated with them quickly embraced the new plutocratic ethos.

The point is not to compare the magnitude of the violations of public trust that went with this shift, or the intent. Americans will never agree on those subjective judgments. But we don't have to. We have to look—honestly—at the impact.

I sat transfixed at lunch with a colleague one day as she described a scene from her young adulthood. She and her fiancé and some friends, mostly graduates of Georgetown University and/or Harvard Law School, had moved to Washington, DC, "to change the world," she said. It was about 1986. The group would gather to play cards at one couple's house on Capitol Hill. My colleague can still hear the conversations: " 'We need to move the Democratic Party away from its anticorporatism,' " she remembers the chorus, " 'or we'll keep losing.' They were for privatizing government services," she told me. "They knew the money was on Wall Street, and they wanted to get it. They were devoid of any purpose except winning."

She described herself sitting on the margins of this conversation, raising an objection: "But if the price of winning is forsaking your principles, then what's the point? Politics isn't just another football game, where you blindly root for your team." The responses, as she remembers them, were like pats on the head: "There, there, you just don't understand."

Members of this group went far in the Democratic politics of the next decades. One is on the Supreme Court.

Scholars have documented how the Democratic Party—since FDR's day the self-appointed champion of ordinary Americans—began courting moneyed interests. President Carter previewed the pro–big business pivot with his tax and deregulation policies. After 1980, leading Democrats began calling their own New Deal legacy—still so popular with the great bulk of the American electorate—lazy, obsolete, and fiscally irresponsible. They wantonly stripped for Reagan's tax-cut orgy. They "deliberately sought out millionaires and other wealthy business figures to run as candidates." They set up checkout lines (at least figuratively) for corporate executives seeking to influence policy, and for committee chairmanships in Congress. Investment bankers, military contractors, and real estate magnates, including Donald Trump, gravitated toward this remodeled Democratic Party.

What these moves share is their obsessive focus on money—as opposed, for example, to votes. Many 1980 and 1982 margins were thin, dwarfed by the mass of eligible voters who had not cast ballots. Yet, while top Democrats courted business and tapped Wall Street for loans, they dawdled over get-out-the-vote drives. Inevitably, as Democrats spent more of their time wooing the wealthy, they tuned in to what the wealthy wanted—and had to offer.

Much of this tilt is credited to an organization called the Democratic Leadership Council. The DLC was founded in 1985 by governors and members of Congress and their key staffers—including some of my colleague's card-shark friends. One of its masterminds, then–House Democratic Caucus staff director Al From, wrote a book about it. Published in 2012, the pages are littered with tropes from those early days, repeated without a hint of irony.

The Democratic Party, From declares, had been defined by "special interest politics." He was not referring to large corporations and their lobbyists who write special clauses into draft legislation. He meant wage earners, women, and disadvantaged minorities. "Private

sector growth was and is the prerequisite to expanding opportunity."
So "more cooperative . . . relations between business and labor"
were needed.

He was anxious to keep "boll weevils" in the party. Those were
"conservative southern Democrats who would vote with President
Reagan on key budget and tax votes in 1981, giving the Republicans
de facto control of the House on important votes." This book's very
title, *The New Democrats and the Return to Power,* corroborates my
colleague's recollections. The objective, baldly stated, is power—
even won at the price of recasting the Democratic Party in the image
of members of Congress who were indistinguishable from Reagan
Republicans. "When a number of boll weevils . . . spoke in favor of
our [proposed] budget," From exults about a 1983 episode, "I knew
we were home free."

Power, then, to what end?

DLC staff operatives hailed largely from north of the Mason-
Dixon Line. But the politicians who waved the organization's flag
were southern Democrats—a group that had stuck with the party out
of sectionalist feeling tracing back to the Civil War. They included the
governors of Virginia and Florida, Chuck Robb and Lawton Chiles,
Georgia senator Sam Nunn, and Missouri congressman Dick Gephardt, as well as Bill Clinton and Al Gore, of Arkansas and Tennessee.

In his 2001 book, *Democracy Heading South,* political scientist
Augustus Cochran argues that American politics in general was
southernizing. "By the 1990s, Southerners, long excluded from
national leadership, dominated both the executive and legislative
branches of government as well as both parties."

Southern political culture was spreading too, writes Cochran.
The "maladies of the Solid South" that were spreading "included . . .
rampant corruption and policy making by deals . . . an appallingly
narrow electoral base . . . [and] a resulting tilt toward the elites, while
the have-not majority got taken for a ride."

The thesis is striking. But economist Thomas Ferguson follows
the money. "No one," he writes, "should be fooled. [The DLC]
was financed extensively from New York—not least by investment
houses—and by defense concerns and utilities."

———

Across the spectrum, in other words, elites were falling under the spell of money—and of those who had it—in a way unseen since the 1930s. The Midas disease, in remission for decades, was flaring up again.

Lavish glitz became the fashion in urban architecture. Reagan's friend Alfred Bloomingdale allied his store with the Metropolitan Museum for an exhibit/sales extravaganza exalting the brocaded shimmer of medieval Chinese aristocracy—and its rigid hierarchy. His inaugurations' unprecedented display bestowed the Gipper's blessing on ostentation.

In a subtler example, a 1980 move by investment bank Goldman Sachs helped spur the brain drain I observed as a college senior. The bank pioneered a novel recruitment strategy: a two-year analyst's position for top Ivy League graduates. Then, as now, many anxious students were finishing their college years without much sense of direction. Goldman beckoned. Other firms copied its approach. A feedback loop developed. Ivy League prestige validated the financial-services industry and, in turn, the prospect of a top-dollar Wall Street job making money from nothing was gilded.

While stressed-out overachievers began seeing the world of high finance as a default career option, movies like *Risky Business*—in which the apprentice criminal reaps every possible reward—were injecting big-money lifestyles into popular culture as the ultimate cool. For some young adults, clashing with the hippie norm of the 1970s seemed risqué. Thus was the plutocratic lifestyle, with its crystal eggs, conspicuous waste, and hollowness at the core, being validated by cultural trendsetters.

Reagan's deceit helped. By dressing the new selfishness in affable decency, by appealing to hard work and fair play, he held out a psychological dodge—a crutch. He invited people at the top to see themselves in the everyday heroes he celebrated in his first inaugural address: the ones

> going in and out of factory gates. [The ones who] produce enough food to feed all of us and then the world beyond. You meet heroes across a counter, and they're on both sides of that counter. There are entrepreneurs with faith in themselves and faith in an idea who create new jobs, new wealth and opportu-

nity. . . . [I say] "they" and "their" [but] I could say "you" and "your," because I'm addressing the heroes of whom I speak.

People like to think of themselves as heroes.

Reagan called all this "freedom." But among early humans, freedom—a fierce attachment to autonomy—went with egalitarianism, not with apelike hierarchy. Reagan flipped the pairing. He wrapped submission to a big-business dominator coalition in the bunting of freedom. "Reagan used the word more often than any president before or since," finds historian Eric Foner. That may have been his biggest lie.

Meanwhile, the Powell Memo's spawn of new think tanks and university professorships and media outlets reinforced this vision. Their spokesmen repeated Reagan's mantra that government was the problem with America, government was bad. The corollary was that business was good. Such a contention broke with decades of sharp-eyed wariness.

As significant as these efforts were, however—as effective as they were in transforming attitudes on everything from the role of government to the reality of climate change—the point here is about the other side. The other side climbed onto the bandwagon. When it came to admiring wealth and mocking egalitarianism, Democrats joined the chorus.

It is not as though these seismic changes were only playing out in the United States, however. The whole world was experiencing them. From Nigeria to Norway, regardless of GDP, geography, or government system, attitudes toward money and how it was made were molting.

A generation was passing. Everywhere, the disaster-survivor ethos was wearing off.

What paved the way for the return of global kleptocracy might therefore best be understood as another feedback loop. A brilliant and lavishly financed plan to wrench government policy and public thought away from disaster-survivor values was launched in the early 1970s. With the coming of a generation born in unparalleled safety from hardship, culture was drifting away from those values anyway— with elites across the political spectrum in the lead. The spread of this less egalitarian culture, in turn, allowed the plan to take root.

And part of the plan, closing the loop, was to take steps meant to accelerate and reinforce the cultural transformation.

The skipper who confirmed Reagan's coming about—the president who validated the new course—would be the first one born clear of the hardships the world had weathered in the first half of the twentieth century: Bill Clinton.

It is amusing to look back at pictures from his years as a Rhodes Scholar or at Yale. His abundant hair is messy; he's got a beard. Yale Law School was a different place in the early 1970s. Hippiedom was still foaming at the crest of the cultural wave.

Before long, Clinton cut his hair. Though he diverged from the most conservative on race and other issues, he was a southern Democrat. As cultural norms shifted in the 1980s, Clinton did too. He both shaped and was shaped by the Democratic Leadership Council.

He even wrote the preface to From's book. "When I was elected president in 1992, I knew I owed a great deal to the DLC and to Al From," it reads. Even appearing in 2012, when the scars from the 2008 panic were still fresh, Clinton's preface bubbles with self-congratulation. It revalidates all the DLC's 1990s buzzwords: "expand opportunity, not government," "economic growth is a prerequisite for expanding opportunity," "expand trade," "reduce crime." The main theme seems to be expansion—with little thought, even then, of costs or consequences.

Temperamentally, Clinton matched the DLC. Like the card sharks who helped birth it, he was obsessed with winning. Accounts of his life are freighted with his overpowering ambition, from his high-school electioneering to be Youth Senator for Arkansas, to running for Congress at twenty-seven, to abandoning policy positions or faithful henchmen if they might threaten his political future.

As the country slipped into its relapse of the Midas disease, the symptoms start appearing in his and his wife Hillary Rodham's biographies. As young adults, both seemed to disdain money, in their contrasting ways. Bill was lackadaisical: he "always worked but seemed to have little money," biographer David Maraniss found. "Travel aides remember how he would bum quarters from them on the road." Hillary worked for nonprofits and watched where early campaign contributions came from and where the money went. She seemed "prudent if not parsimonious."

But by the late 1970s, the couple's reflexes swiveled. Hillary went to work for the eminent Rose Law Firm, which serviced Arkansas's wealthiest and most powerful. She took up commodities trading. Bill, writes Maraniss, had never exactly been allergic to money. "When he could see a direct correlation between money and political success . . . he excelled at going after the cash." Soon the Democratic Leadership Council would highlight that correlation, giving Clinton a pretext to put his mind to making money.

The Little Rock the Clintons embraced beginning in 1977, when Bill was Arkansas attorney general, then governor, was "a setup for people with money," says Herbert Reid, an emeritus professor of politics with a deep understanding of dynamics in his native Arkansas. "Arkansas doesn't fund the political process," he explains, "doesn't pay state legislators. Short terms make for weak government structures. Officials don't have the wherewithal to resist big money."

That big money, says Reid, fell into two blocs. In Arkansas's northwest, it lay with timber interests, which clear-cut prime Appalachian forest, using migrant workers who lived in tattered camps called "ragtowns." And there was the agriculture and processed food giant Tyson Foods, and retailers like Walmart. In both, ambitions and business models were overhauled as younger men transformed family firms into expanding—soon multinational—conglomerates. Across the state, near its southern borders with Louisiana and Mississippi, select lawyers, bankers, and real estate magnates, many of them Rose clients, were buying up old plantations. They constituted "a second New South oligarchy," says Reid.

Leveraging their separate contacts, the Clinton pair wove a network that linked players from both blocs. When Bill ran for president in 1992, this network formed the core of his business coalition, along with the New York investment bankers who had bet on the DLC— including Roger Altman of Lehman Brothers and the Blackstone Group, and Goldman Sachs's Robert Rubin.

Clinton—as governor and president—knew how to reciprocate. His favor might come in the form of policies he championed, such as aggressive banking deregulation. It might be a custom-tailored tax break, like the Arkansas state incentives he bestowed on homegrown

Tyson Foods. Or a job that allowed the appointee to rewrite the rules to advantage his businesses. In such ways was a network bent on harnessing government power to personal enrichment cultivated.

By the time Clinton returned to private life in 2001, that objective—personal enrichment—had grown not just respectable, but preeminent. The man who once "always seemed to have little" began making money. Often the payoffs he reaped were camouflaged as speaking fees. Clinton could bring in a comfortable year's salary for forty minutes of platitudes. On the side, he might be leveraging influence or mediating deals.

Reid does not especially blame the Clintons for such practices. "A lot of the time," he says, "they were just the facilitators—or the functionaries—of a deeper trend." That trend was one of crystalizing kleptocracy, a return to the Gilded Age syndrome.

Oddly, given two hard-fought elections, the last-minute tidal wave of cash that helped propel a radical pro–big business majority into Congress in 1994, and bitter impeachment proceedings, Clinton's policies hammered much of the Reagan Revolution home.

Implicitly framing the poor as moochers, his welfare overhaul pitted different groups of ordinary or disadvantaged Americans against one another. It diverted attention away from the rich, who were paying less taxes while gaining more from government policies.

While his banking deregulation was incentivizing fraud, Clinton's war on crime led to the highest incarceration rate in the world, and the lasting second-class citizenship of those mostly poor and nonwhite former convicts upon release. Singling out petty burglary, drug offenses, and street violence, the push largely ignored white-collar wrongdoing. "But corporate crime and violence inflict far more damage on society than all street crime combined," wrote white-collar-crime expert Russell Mokhiber in 1996. He compared the estimated $4 billion that burglary and robbery cost the country to some $200 billion for fraud. Or the 24,000 homicides per year, as against 56,000 people who died from job-related causes such as black lung disease or accidents due to safety violations. How to count the tens of thousands of consumers who were hurt or killed in car accidents or by lung cancer, while auto giants lobbied against airbags and big tobacco fought warning labels? While Clinton's anticrime push was putting cohorts of street-level offenders behind bars, his

Justice Department hesitated to prosecute white-collar suspects. In retrospect, the memorable prosecutions—of Enron executives, for example—seem like splashy exceptions.

Domestically, the policy that still gives Clinton pride was deficit reduction—ever a rallying cry for big-money networks bent on reserving the power of the purse for themselves. Internationally, Clinton's stamp is on what has come to be called "globalization"—the lifting of curbs on the flow of money and goods across borders, including free-trade agreements such as NAFTA—and wholesale privatization in the former Soviet Union. Both of those were executed in ways that suited the networks, especially his own.

I am not arguing that there was no difference between Clinton and Reagan, or that all politicians are equal, so why vote. The point here is that Clinton's policies had the effect of validating approaches that had been seen as outlandish extremism just a few years earlier. He turned the radical project fomented by one coalition of meat hogs—to harness the government to its selfish purposes—into bipartisan orthodoxy.

This type of validation brings dangerous ideas into the mainstream. For Columbia Law professor Tim Wu, for example, "Bork won the culture war" because of two Harvard professors' validation of his radical remake of antitrust law. Faced with such elite consensus, everyday citizens, who are dismayed by the values and sense the heist, feel like exiles. Their sensible concerns ignored, their interests unrepresented, they despair of democratic government and opt out—or revolt.

And when practices that benefit kleptocratic networks are mainstreamed, those networks take it as an invitation to keep pushing. In a race with no finish line, their members can never be satisfied. Once one set of values and advantages has been normalized, they seek more. The 1994 Gingrich revolution can be seen in this light, as well as the bipartisan plunge into naked influence peddling since 1990, the breathtaking absence of prosecutions after the 2008 financial disaster, and, finally, amid the Trump administration's open marriage of public and private and criminal sectors in an astonishing replication of third-world kleptocracies, the astronomical handout to networked insiders delivered by coronavirus emergency measures on his watch.

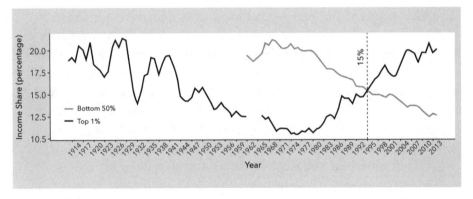

In 1995, for the first time post–World War II, the top 1 percent of earners took home the same share of the nation's income as the bottom
50 percent.

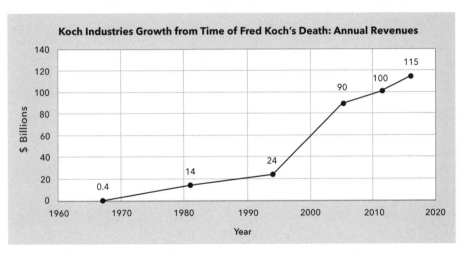

The Koch brothers' fortunes shot up beginning in 1995, in line with the rest
of the 1 percent. The launch of their massive injection of resources and
focus into their network and its political activities came quickly, in 1997.

Ordinary Americans get sacrificed: the twelve-hour factory shift
is the norm again where I live in West Virginia.* Even before 2020's

---

* This is in a state whose governor won office as a Democrat, though he had previously been a Republican, and then switched parties again as soon as he was elected.
Taking validation to an extreme, the state Democratic Party threw itself into his
campaign; its former head made large contributions to the re-election campaign

added burdens on many—and mass unemployment for others—
workers in industries from warehousing to video gaming were balk-
ing at the pressure to produce ever more, ever faster, the way their
forebears did in the Gilded Age. As for incomes, one more graph
tells the story. In 1995, the share of all salaries paid out in the United
States captured by the top 1 percent of earners equaled the share
taken home by the bottom half. The fates of these two segments of
the population have diverged ever since.

That same year, the Koch brothers' fortunes lifted off.

---

of the born and born-again Republican. For a blistering takedown of this propen-
sity, see Christopher Hegan, "Hoppy Is Wrong About Why Dems Are Losing,"
Charleston Gazette-Mail, January 24, 2020. Former New York City mayor Michael
Bloomberg represents a nationally renowned example of the same phenomenon—
a former Republican seeking to validate certain protections for wealth maximizers
under a Democratic Party label. See Anand Giridharadas, "The Billionaire Election:
Does the World Belong to Them or to Us?" *New York Times,* February 21, 2020.

3

Courting Calamity (1990s-)

For the rest of the world, the most consequential event of the decade was the collapse of the Soviet Union, in 1991. Overnight, entire government institutions and incalculably valuable assets that had been the collective property of everyone in that vast empire were Russia's alone. The stage was set for the wholesale transfer of those assets to private hands.

How to conjure the drama of those events? The Richter scale has not been invented that could measure that earthquake. An entity that just months before had controlled the destinies of millions of people, an existential threat to Western democracies, a well of resources and even inspiration for Africa and Latin America was no more. The implosion created a vortex that sucked vast energies in, then flung them outward, leaving no part of the world untouched.

These chaotic events helped launch the resurgence of kleptocracy around the world.

First, they unleashed a powerful, ruthless, and adaptive new type of network.

A black market had long existed in the Soviet Union, but in Stalin's day, smugglers or those who dared "misappropriate" state goods were outlaws. Many landed in the gulag, says Ilya Zaslavskiy, who was born during the last years of the Soviet Union and now investigates the Russian export of kleptocracy to the West. But, "as people stopped believing in this communism stuff"—as their faith and their fear faded—the black market turned grey. Clans of jail-hardened criminals forged alliances with managers of state-owned factories. Together they launched side hustles, trading on government goods and connections. In this way, Soviet public and criminal sectors began twining together.

The third strand of these emerging networks was a budding business sector: entrepreneurs who came of age as novel opportunities were opening up under the perestroika of those years. Many had traveled to the West and had learned how to open a bank account, how to pepper their sentences with the latest free-market jargon, and other such useful skills.

Composite networks like this "operate in, mediate, and blur different spheres—state and private, bureaucracy and market, legal and illegal," writes Janine Wedel, the anthropologist of elite networks who examined U.S. defense industry ties, who worked on and off in Poland from 1982 into the 1990s. Their "strength derives . . . from [their] ability to access the resources and advantages in one sphere for use in another."

Informal and dynamic as these organisms may be, they function not as collections of individuals, Wedel emphasizes, but as entities. "The individual must take the interests of the group into account when making choices about how to respond to new opportunities." The network, in other words—the whole body, not any one of its nine heads—makes the final decisions.

So was born the type of dynamic, multitalented, shape-shifting hydra that now sits atop kleptocracies the world over. The three strands I found entwined across public and private and criminal sectors from Honduras to Tunisia to Azerbaijan are here perfectly described.

The scene in post-Soviet capitals is brilliantly captured in Misha Glenny's *McMafia,* which charts the 1990s explosion in transnational organized crime. These once drab cities were conjured into places of "sudden energy and suppurating wealth" where "knockout prostitutes were . . . soliciting in public," where "the most exotic food and expensive wines were being piled high in the restaurants . . . [and] the casino lights dazzled at night."

Trafficking in everything from cigarettes and sex to stolen cars and caviar kept the chaos flush with cash. The violence was unheard-of too, as private security companies staffed by former murderers or weightlifters or KGB operatives enforced business contracts. It was as though the whole former Soviet bloc was mainlining the Midas disease and the ideology of "What the fuck" freedom in a single uncut dose. Glenny's conclusion is stark: "The collapse of the Communist superpower . . . is the single most important event promoting the exponential growth of organized crime around the world in the last two decades."

Classic organized crime is one lens through which to view the madness. Equally fateful was the wholesale transfer of Russian public property to a few individuals. After a phase of privatization open only to the *nomenklatura*—those with connections—came a voucher program. It was designed by U.S. advisors in league with members of President Boris Yeltsin's inner circle. The theory was that the faster enterprises passed into private hands, the sooner the economy would become efficient.

"As though privatization would work by magic," recalls kleptocracy analyst Ilya Zaslavskiy. He was twelve at the time and got his share of vouchers. "They were worth ten thousand rubles, more than the price of a car. But even with my child brain, I knew this whole thing was collapsing." Disobeying his stepfather's orders, Zaslavskiy snuck out and sold them on the street, for about a hundred dollars. "That was pretty good. Everyone else got nothing." The process, says Wedel, "encouraged the accumulation of vouchers in a few hands."

Then, starting in the mid-1990s, the most valuable commodities—gas and mining concerns—were sold off. Some insiders borrowed money from the state to use as the collateral they put up for these state assets, or got huge stakes in return for advances of cash *to* that same, now penniless, state—or for contributions to Yeltsin's re-election campaign. This is the period during which well-known oligarchs, such as Pyotr Aven, Leonid Blavatnik, Oleg Deripaska, Mikhail Fridman, Mikhail Khodorkovsky, and Viktor Vekselberg made their fortunes.

At the whiteboard brainstorming these initiatives were Western economists and development experts, led by a web that reached from Harvard University's Institute for International Development to Clinton's inner circle. Members of this mini integrated network included Lawrence Summers, who was moving up the ladder in Robert Rubin's Treasury Department, economist Jeffrey Sachs, and their protégés David Lipton and Andrei Shleifer. Through the Russian Privatization Center—a hybrid "nonprofit and nongovernmental" organization that was founded by a stroke of Yeltsin's pen,* of which Harvard University was a full member—this network shaped the privatization process and steered billions of dollars of Western assistance. Some members also used their insider positions to trade in privatized assets for themselves.

The whole thing was a lavishly funded laboratory experiment in the Reagan-era unfettered pro-business principles that the Clinton administration was validating. Harvard, with its liberal reputation, added to the validation. Simultaneously across Asia and Latin America, similar experiments were being launched.

Unfortunately, the grotesque virus that resulted did not stay sealed inside the post-Soviet laboratory.

It spread along the trading routes and among the elite circles that had long crisscrossed the fifteen states the USSR spawned. A single example helps illustrate how interconnected those circles remain today, despite the young countries' apparently separate political regimes. Emin Agalarov, the "Russian" rock star who helped usher Donald Trump's Miss Universe contest to Moscow in 2013 and organize the infamous June 2016 meeting between top Trump campaign officials and likely proxies for the Russian government, was born not in Russia, but in nearby Azerbaijan. He is its president's former son-in-law. In other words, Agalarov is actually a member of Azerbaijan's kleptocratic network, one of the most consolidated and tight-knit I have ever researched. But he's also part of Putin's. And Trump's.

Other former Soviet republics became nodes in the burgeoning transnational networks. Latvia and Moldova, for example, provided wholesale money-laundering services to corrupt former Soviet officials seeking to siphon cash to stable banks in the West. A more infamous example, since the impeachment of President Trump, is Ukraine. Corrupt officials from that key chunk of the former USSR

---

* What Nigerians call a GONGO: a Government Organized Non-Governmental Organization.

have linked into the networks of U.S. figures ranging from such Democrats as former vice president Joe Biden and former White House counsel Greg Craig to Republican political strategist Paul Manafort, or former Republican mayor of New York, and Trump personal lawyer, Rudy Giuliani.

The erstwhile Soviets best positioned to capitalize on the privatization bonanza were already internationalized outside the old USSR. In embassies, Zaslavskiy notes, they had executed wheat purchases for Moscow, or negotiated gas and pipeline deals, or worked for the KGB. They hired strategic communications consultants and lawyers. Thus did Western facilitators begin servicing the most powerful and unsavory post-communist networks.

Flaunting high-status Western connections and flush with cash, these networks spread the metastasizing Midas disease. Glenny, again, is priceless on their "exuberant standards of tastelessness." He describes a Soviet Union nostalgia party near Paris in 2004. "Skipping between the fountains of champagne and lines of coke" inside a historic château rented for the weekend, "women with miniskirts split to reveal their buttocks would writhe" to the music of Soviet-era anthems. The image is an updated version of those Gilded Age parties where cigarettes wrapped in large-denomination bills were languidly smoked.

Slathered on top of the excesses of the 1980s, this grotesque display of money—whose sources were hidden, usually criminal, and largely ignored—reinforced the new garish culture. These were fashions to emulate. And elites across the global south emulated. Interviewees in countries I have researched could always tell me when the problem got intolerable. They almost always pointed to the mid- to late 1990s.

In other words, if 1980 marks the transformation in attitudes toward money, the second phase in the rise of global kleptocracy was under way by about fifteen years later. The generation that took over from former colonies' independence-era rulers, I kept hearing, felt less bound to provide for the people—especially with communism discredited.

It's not that the communist ideology, as practiced, delivered. Yet even its false promises held elites to some standard. When I first visited Tunisia, for example, I was startled at the excellent condition of the roads—far better than the street outside my mother's house near Boston—and the upkeep of the public schools, even twenty-five years after the death of its first postcolonial ruler, the socialist Habib Bourguiba. Public infrastructure in the former Soviet republic of Uzbekistan contrasted starkly with neighboring Afghanistan's. "In the third world, where the Soviets were competing with the United States, they tried to offer something," suggests Zaslavskiy. "And local elites felt they had to make at least an effort."

"In virtually every country," echoes Nils Gilman, in an illuminating essay devoted to what he calls the "twin insurgencies" of globalized plutocracy and violent organized crime, "elites felt some duty to underwrite the well-being of the middle class." With the collapse of communism, "what died was . . . not just the [state-planned] economic system and authoritarian politics of the Soviet Union and its satellites. Cremated along with the corpse . . . was the civic-minded conception of development as the central responsibility of the state and allied elites."

Gilman touches on another way the Soviet implosion promoted the rise of kleptocracy. During the Cold War, people across the West lived in the shadow of an existential threat. That shared peril helped prolong the postdisaster solidarity left over from the catastrophes of the first half of the twentieth century. With yellow and black signs in every town pointing to the nearest fallout shelter, and schoolchildren's days disrupted not by active-shooter drills, which affect individual communities, but by drills for what to do in case of the shared disaster of nuclear war, Americans had something to unite around. Public service messages during popular 1950s radio programs like *Gunsmoke* called on listeners to compete by stepping up production—not just of goods, but "above all, of democracy."

But after 1991, with the enemy of four decades defeated and the generation forged in the actual disasters of the first half of the twentieth century aging out, there was no more calamity—either remembered or imagined—to draw people together. The solidarity born of shared sacrifice to address a great challenge was gone.

Compounding all this upheaval was the phenomenon now called globalization.

As Reagan's brand of freedom was promoted across international frontiers, doors were flung open for the accumulation of wealth. Western companies rushed to exploit lax environmental and labor standards in foreign countries. New revenue streams gushed.

And the revolution in new technologies, together with headlong financial deregulation, made it easy to whisk lucre out of sight. The attributes that made money the ultimate means of exchange—its units being alike, inconspicuous, and portable—reached their logical extreme in the 1990s. Money became an invisible electronic signal.

Whole new fields of Western business sprang up to help secure ill-gotten lucre: in bank accounts shielded by tight-lipped discretion, or in high-status property or investments in hedge funds. Even if that wealth did represent the sack of the economies of entire nations.

This is the context in which to understand Donald Trump's business operations, including his long-standing collaborations with Russians—and his personal style. The heart of his story is not a diabolical Vladimir Putin or today's Russia, per se. Nor is it just that most Western banks ceased offering Trump no-strings-attached loans in the early 1990s, after his many defaults. During those years, the collapse of the Soviet Union was propelling a shock wave of dirty money into Western safe havens and spawning a vast new demand for the vulgar display of riches. Those with the loot were anxious to spray it around and to convert it to real assets protected by law. Since it wasn't really theirs anyway, inflated prices for movie-set mansions did not pose a problem.

This is the market Trump's operation is built to serve.

Thus, along with everything else that was going global in the 1990s, the burgeoning kleptocratic networks were globalizing too. In my analyses of third-world countries and in this discussion of the United States, I have drilled down on networks within national boundaries. But that's the wrong way to look at all this. Picture instead an airline route map, with big dots at the hubs and lines arcing over land and sea. A network or set of them will be anchored

in Palm Beach or Washington, or Cairo. But like the business conglomerates and transnational criminal organizations woven into their
fabric, they arc over land and sea.

As these webs have spread out from their hubs—not just in Moscow and Baku, but Beijing, Dubai, Lagos, Riyadh, São Paulo, and
so on—they have implanted their brazen practices and their personnel in the West. Their members have bought property and media
outlets, invested in blue-chip companies and private funds, made
large donations to prestigious institutions, sent their children to top
universities, put former prime ministers and glittering celebrities
on their payrolls, and obtained citizenship. In this way, they have
woven themselves into our fabric—and our fabric has rewoven itself
around them. It is impossible to do business with them and keep the
thread of your operations or your personal life separate from theirs.

The Western individuals and institutions banking their money
have served as sales representatives, affixing the validating stamp of
their democracy-rule-of-law credentials and their personal prestige.
The examples are too numerous to count: from former New York
mayor Rudy Giuliani's work on behalf of a gold trader who pleaded
guilty to helping Turkish strongman Recep Tayyip Erdogan's network
circumvent U.S. sanctions against Iran, to the counsel such blue-chip
firms as McKinsey and Boston Consulting provided to the likes of
Isabel dos Santos, daughter of the former president of Angola, now
charged with money laundering and influence peddling, to former
British prime minister Tony Blair's lucrative services to Kazakh dictator Nursultan Nazarbayev, former German chancellor Gerhard
Schroeder's chairmanship of the boards of Russia's Nord Stream 2,
a subsidiary of Gazprom, and Rosneft, or named gifts by Russian
oligarchs to Oxford University and the Council on Foreign Relations,
or the board seats offered by other think tanks. Money, as that West
Virginia householder told me, is washing these kleptocrats' hands.
In turn, their Western ambassadors have been absorbing their ways.

Ilya Zaslavskiy sees in this phenomenon an existential threat to
the Western experiment in government by and for the people. "The
truth is," he observes, "the West has largely failed to export its democratic norms and is instead witnessing an increasingly coordinated
assault on its own value system."

Zaslavskiy did not choose that word, "assault," lightly. In his view, these developments cannot be chalked up to individual opportunism. Kleptocratic elites, he writes, "trade tips on going global with sophisticated tools of propaganda, cooptation, subversion, repression, and corruption." Bearing in mind anthropologist Janine Wedel's finding that the network is the locus of decision-making, we are witnessing the workings of a deliberate strategy. But the West is not only on the receiving end. American networks have been purposefully exporting these norms as well, injecting them south of the Rio Grande and across the Atlantic. The objective is to transform global norms.

This threat to democracy does not denounce liberty and egalitarianism. It claims to represent those values. For that reason, it may be the most dangerous menace they ever faced.

Forty years after the 1980 turning, the world today seems to be back on the course first charted in the Gilded Age. Bending and distorting economic and political systems to suit their purposes, globalized networks of kleptocratic elites compete in pursuit of wealth without limit. In the process, they are debasing or destroying priceless treasures and countless human lives.

In the Gilded Age, these ways led to a series of economic crises that struck every eight or ten years with a baleful regularity. The Panics of 1873, of 1882, 1896, 1907, and 1929—they tolled like a dirge, reverberating across industrialized economies.

Since 1980, for the same reasons, the same incessant knell has rung.

- The 1980s was rocked not only by the savings and loan crisis, but also the collapse of a flash market for junk bonds, which climaxed in the deepest one-day stock-market plunge since the Great Depression. In a frenzy of corporate raiding and leveraged buyouts, companies made obviously questionable bonds look sexy by offering dizzying interest rates. Nineteenth-century French scam artist Thérèse Humbert did something similar, promising above-market rates on notes she sold to finance her personal lifestyle.

- That same decade, the most far-flung criminal organization in history was putting down roots in seventy-three countries.

Incorporated in Luxemburg and the Cayman Islands, operating out of stylish headquarters in London, the Bank of Credit and Commerce International funneled financing for the Iran-Contra Affair, the Iran-Iraq War, arms deals between Israel and its Arab neighbors, drug cartels, and the CIA. Feeding this Frankenstein were the new globalized financial practices. By operating from different jurisdictions and exploiting the exotic corporate and banking structures and globalized trading patterns that were coming into vogue, it could dodge regulators. It also benefited from the image-laundering services of former Carter Office of Management and Budget chief Bert Lance, Arkansas financier and fossil fuel giant Jackson Stephens, a key Clinton backer, and a Rose Law Firm attorney representing Stephens's companies, Hillary Clinton. In simultaneous raids in seven countries in 1991, BCCI was finally shut down. But its majority owners—the ruling family of one of the United Arab Emirates—retained their glamorous prestige. As did the new financial practices.

· During that time, epidemic use of crack cocaine, sold by criminal conglomerates imitating the latest corporate management techniques, swept across American cities. The like had not been seen since the widespread descent into opium addiction in the Gilded Age.

· Six years later, amid worldwide promotion of the same banking practices that produced BCCI, came a cascade of financial meltdowns in Asia, the former Soviet Union, and Latin America. The linked crises touched off in 1997 crushed whole economies, saddled developing countries with billions of dollars in debt they could never repay, and toppled multiple governments. The United States was nearly swept up in the maelstrom, with the implosion of giant hedge fund Long-Term Capital Management.

The disaster's causes lay in currency trading and cross-border investing—both new to the globalized era. In combination, they were lethal. Foreign exchange speculators sold off great quantities of Thailand's currency, the baht, gambling that they could force down its value. Investors who had been lured by Thailand's high interest rates lost as the value of their holdings, measured in their home currencies, plunged with the plunging baht. Multiple Asian economies crashed. Next, the speculators aimed at the Russian ruble, with the same results. Then Brazil. From there the Panic of 1997–1998 sent shock waves across Latin America.

As the price of emergency loans, international financial institutions dosed victim economies with more of the same medicine—deregulation, privatization, and spending cuts. These were the crises that drew wheeling clouds of the vulture investors who are now prominent in the U.S. government.

· The turn of the millennium saw a classic Gilded Age–style panic: frenzied investment in an exciting new technology—not railroads or cinema, but dot-coms. Like their nineteenth-century predecessors, these start-ups followed a get-big-fast formula and spent lavishly on marketing to keep share prices rising. After all, the profits were to be made not on running the businesses, but on selling the shares. All the insiders had to do was keep mom-and-pop investors fooled long enough to make their killing and get out.

· The Enron scandal also began unfolding around 2000, amid rolling blackouts in California, where the company was scamming the electricity market. President George H. W. Bush and much of Congress had banked Enron campaign contributions. Texas senator Phil Gramm's wife, Wendy—a Koch network member—had been Bush's head of the Commodity Futures Trading Commission and blocked attempts to regulate trade in Enron's specialty, commodities derivatives. Then she took her well-paid seat on Enron's board.

· Eight years later came the Great Recession. And gaping income and wealth inequality, now back to Gilded Age levels. Take a second glance at the graphs on pp. 249 and 267.

· Corruption as commonly understood is back to Gilded Age levels too. Never since the scandal-ridden administration of Ulysses S. Grant has there been an executive branch as nakedly given over to self-dealing as that of Donald Trump. To describe even a few of the dynamics not yet mentioned would take pages.

They include, amid the administration's unprecedented top-level turnover, a striking number of cabinet-level officials who departed under a cloud: Alexander Acosta, Michael Flynn, Carl Icahn, Rick Perry, Scott Pruitt, and Ryan Zinke, for example.

Or, consider the doings of the Elaine Chao–Mitch McConnell couple. In itself that marriage violates the constitutional principle of separation of powers. From Chao's bids to use her position to promote her family's Beijing-linked shipping business to the nearly $80 million in Transportation Department grants she funneled to her husband's backers, to McConnell's actions to benefit the aluminum plant largely owned by Russian oligarchs who made millions of dollars of campaign contributions, such reflexes—and the obvious contempt for U.S. national security—would guide any infrastructure projects implemented under the couple's watch.

McConnell's autocratic control over the U.S. Senate is due, at least in part, to the tsunami of money that flooded into campaign chests he controlled in the final days of the 2016 election. At that time, betting was heavy that Trump would

Senate majority leader Mitch McConnell, immediately after the 51–49 Senate vote not to call witnesses in the impeachment trial of Donald Trump, January 31, 2020.

lose the presidential election. So Republican donors pulled out the stops to ensure that their Senate majority did not go down with him. Republican senators owe their political survival to Mitch McConnell at least as much as to Trump—or to their constituents.

Another fraught family pairing is Education Secretary Betsy DeVos and her brother, the mercenary Erik Prince. She joined the Trump administration to advance the goal of putting the sacred value of education into the hands and at the service of the rich. Prince's designs are equally ominous. After his infamous Blackwater private security company was expelled from Iraq for killing civilians and then imploded, he moved to the United Arab Emirates and founded a new company in the same line of work. Via interlocking boards, this Frontier Services Group is stapled to the parent company of Cambridge Analytica and its burner-entity offshoots, which provide private intelligence services and political dirty tricks to rulers of such countries as the UAE, Indonesia, Libya, and Somalia. Prince has pushed to privatize U.S. military and intelligence functions in similar ways.

But no family has mixed business interests with public office like the Trumps. The appointment of close family members who are also corporate executives to ill-defined but top-level White House jobs is a first in American history.

There are White House innovations director Jared Kushner's personal and financial entanglements with notoriously corrupt, even sadistic, leaders in Israel and across the Persian Gulf, a region covered by one of the Trump son-in-law's many official portfolios. "Every policy decision is examined for what it can do for him," a former Pentagon aide who frequently accompanied a secretary of defense to White House meetings confided to me. Kushner has established a back channel with the son-in-law of Turkish strongman Recep Tayyip Erdogan (who serves as finance minister in his father-in-law's government) and with a private-sector member of Erdogan's network (who is Trump's business partner). Kushner's friend the then–energy minister appears to have approved a massive scheme to evade international sanctions against Iran. At home, like the secretaries of commerce and treasury, Kushner has made a profit center out of gouging low-income renters, and accepted a miraculously timed $1.8 billion lease on his failing 666 Fifth Avenue skyscraper. He played an ill-defined role steering COVID 19 emergency resources.

His daughter Ivanka Trump has served as an inspiration to dictators around the world. A month after her father named her advisor to the president, Azerbaijan's potentate Ilham Aliyev one-upped him, appointing his wife vice president. A development official told me he had heard more than one African strongman celebrate Ivanka's job as a green light to arrange succession for their own children. That may be what the Trumps have in mind.

After her father's election, Ivanka received a series of invaluable patent protections in China, even though she declared her fashion brand closed. Her brothers Don Jr. and Eric repeatedly travel for business purposes accompanied by a phalanx of impressive taxpayer-funded attendants.

And then there is Trump himself. He is at once a symptom—a kind of apotheosis—of America's increasingly corrupt system, and an exaggeration of it so extreme as to seem like a grotesque aberration, like reality distorted by one of those curved fun-house mirrors. Trump's bald use of his office to patronize and promote his businesses—including raking in "kick-ups" from lower echelons, such as military contingents and subordinates who take detours to stay in his hotels, and at least one effort to award himself a giant federal contract—outstrips anything I have witnessed in a developing country. As does his penchant for surrounding himself with men entwined with foreign criminal networks, and his donlike demand for fealty. Even the emir of Kano, Nigeria, into whose presence I was ushered by a troupe of robed criers singing me into the room, would not stoop to demanding a round of flattery before launching a meeting. Trump has taken mafia government to heights unrivaled in this country's history.

His swiftness to trade U.S. policy concessions for personal advancement will be the most shameful legacy of his presidency. Indeed, the case at the heart of impeachment proceedings launched in 2019—of a shadow foreign policy channel that was leveraging the Ukrainian government for potentially damaging information on Democratic Party leadership—may be just one example among many. What quid pro quos characterize Trump's dealings with Saudi Arabia? With Turkey? What explains his consistent policy tilt in favor of Moscow, from pushing Russia's readmission to the Group of Seven countries, to cold-shouldering its most important regional counterweight, Ukraine, to abruptly abandoning Kurdish allies in Syria, leaving Moscow master of the field, to his insistent dismissal of repeated warnings about ongoing Kremlin efforts to suborn U.S. elections?

Trump and those in his orbit hardly hold a monopoly on corrupt doings, of course. Sitting near Bob Menendez on the Democratic benches of the U.S. Senate is his West Virginia colleague Joe Manchin. Not only was Manchin's daughter CEO of the Mylan pharmaceutical company, which tripled the price of the emergency anti-allergy injection device EpiPen on her watch, but his wife lobbied to get the device required in schools, and he likely voted on federal guidelines to that effect.

But Trump is president of the United States, and that is a public trust of a completely different order.

· Today's world is witnessing cascading catastrophes that were as yet unimaginable in the nineteenth century. They can be traced directly to the Midas disease. In its grip, we have destroyed forests, wetlands, marine ecosystems, and prairies— complex systems that are crucial for stabilizing the earth's temperature and water cycle. We have contaminated the air and water, often willfully. This damage, together with overpopulation, overdevelopment, industrial agriculture, and genetic engineering, has triggered a mass die-off of species like the one that occurred when an asteroid collided with the earth and wiped out the dinosaurs. Extinctions of this magnitude have only happened five other times in 4.5 billion years. The gone-forever or depleted life-forms also played their role in the planet's health. Add the wanton production and burning of fossil fuels that has rapidly changed earth's chemistry, and no wonder we are suffering a biblical onslaught of fires and floods.

Every one of these chapters contains countless shattered careers, wrecked lives, ruined landscapes—each a drama in and of itself. But it's the succession that raises the hair on my neck. This is the Gilded Age pattern, only worse. This is a crescendo of thunderclaps. And it seems hardly to shake us.

Consider the implications. Last time humanity was locked onto this course, it led to the collapse of the global economy and two world wars—and genocide, starvation, plague, and the detonation of nuclear bombs that wiped some 200,000 human beings off the earth and gave us the power to end our species.

What manner of calamity lies ahead of us now?

Breaking the Pattern

(Now)

When the many-headed Hydra was laying waste to the country around her bog at Lerna—raiding flocks and poisoning villages with her noxious breath—no hero could best her. So Herakles was summoned, for the second of his epic labors. Rousting the Hydra from her repair with a volley of fiery spears, he gripped his great club and began to pound off her heads. But it was no use. As soon as he severed one, two more would sprout. Finally, he called out to his charioteer for help. Young Iolaus sprang to the nearby woods and cut some resiny boughs. With these he improvised cautering brands and stood shoulder to shoulder with Herakles, searing each blood-spurting stump.

That those who do not learn from history are condemned to repeat it is by now a familiar saw. Observing our astonishing times, I have come to a parallel intuition about mythology. Because our society has turned its back on the storehouse of wisdom contained in our ancient sacred stories, we are condemned to live our myths in flesh and blood. So many of the exaggerated characters who walk our public stages seem to step directly from their pages, it is as though we have created them. This is why I keep coming back to mythology.

There is no magic formula, no step-by-step method for bringing the hydras that are laying waste to our societies under control. That's what people understandably call for when subjected to an analysis like this. Still, for those of us who don't choose to live in a community organized by and for the most prideful and wealthy among us, and

HERCVLES VNA CVM IOLAO HYDRAM OCCIDIT. 15 ʜB 45

Even Hercules could not kill the Hydra alone.

don't want to wait, overwhelmed, for the coming apocalypse, myths offer some guiding principles.

A first, unspoken, is this: the need to imagine what sort of society we do choose to live in. To dream it and sing it and teach it and revere the heroes who incarnate its values. A second is that bringing such a society forth will require herculean labors.

Our hydras must be accurately identified and located, and some of their heads must be cleaved off. Our species did not stay egalitarian for 180,000 years just naturally. As primates, we were naturally hierarchical. Egalitarianism was deliberate, avidly policed. The domineering, the grasping, the sneaky hoarders were punished, sometimes executed.

But our ancestors never leaped straight to that extreme. They chose from a range of sanctions, increasing their severity if hints failed to work.

A Nigerian friend once told me that an Islamic precept is not to punish a wrongdoer in a material he has in abundance. That is, a rich person should not be fined; it won't trouble him. The trick then is to discover what is dearer to today's kleptocrats than money—even in this era of full-blown Midas disease. Two such precious substances might be the prestige their money buys and the freedom—the "What the fuck" freedom to do anything they want with the people and the world around them.

For organizations to resist rewarding breachers of the public trust with deference and the next lofty job would be a start. For example, executives and HR departments should not offer the vice president of Enron a string of government jobs in the public-private international development and infrastructure industries after his company's debacle. That past should crop up in vetting and mark him as unsuitable. Employees in such organizations have every right to join forces with like-minded colleagues and object. A ratchet-up would be to expel violators like him from powerful jobs they currently hold if the wrongdoing continues or their contracts come up for renewal. The next notch would be to take their freedom—that is, to investigate, prosecute, and send them to jail. That option terrifies the dominator coalition. Why else would it have worked so hard for thirty years to eliminate it?

Today it seems as though no such wrongdoer is—or ever will be—called to account in this unmistakable way. And it is true: bringing our institutions to mete out such an unflinching punishment will require deep changes in law and enforcement priorities and resourcing. For, between 1987 and 2020—just as kleptocracy was spreading around the globe—the category of acts that counted as corruption under U.S. law was shrinking. White-collar criminal investigations became posturing for the upcoming bargaining session, instead of preludes to prosecution.

To end the impunity that now protects members of our kleptocratic networks, statutes will have to be drafted and passed and signed into law to bring the legal definition of corruption more in line with the common understanding of that crime. Alongside federal statutes, a systematic state-by-state review of prohibitions on bribery, gifts, and conflict of interest is needed. Citizens could rewrite these bans: make them clearer and stronger and advocate for the new versions. Staffs and budgets for public integrity detectives and prosecutors, federal and state, will have to grow. The reflex to seek fines and deferred prosecution, to avoid lengthy and complex criminal litigation, will have to be unlearned, by way of redesigned metrics, released to the public with fanfare, and career incentives that make going after perpetrators of major fraud and bribery a badge of honor. Regulatory agency enforcers, at the EPA, the FEC, even the IRS, and their state-level counterparts, need similar improvements. These professionals should be out chasing dangerous criminals, not pulling guard shifts for a pampered boss.

I wish some creatives would produce a great cop show devoted to some fictional Public Integrity Squad, rather than the usual fare of vice and murder. Citizens across the political divide should be asking candidates where they stand on corporate law enforcement as often as they do on gun rights. They might start calling for plans and drafting initiative petitions. Their kids should be dreaming of a job on the integrity beat.

For those working on sentencing reform: it is critical to distinguish—in the difficult dealing over mandatory minimums or eligibility for early release—between different types of nonviolent offenses, and to hold the line on leniency for the perpetrators of corporate crime and corruption. Given the consistent lowballing on sentences, mandatory minimums might make sense for these crimes.

But just cutting off a few heads won't curb these hydras. More heads will sprout. So, the Greek myth suggests a further principle. Even the mightiest of all heroes, Herakles, could not defeat the monster alone. It took him and his charioteer both, with their contrasting talents. The skills of each were needed.

This battle is the same. It calls for different approaches simultaneously. It calls on every one of us. It demands all of our often-unsuspected abilities and reflexes. There is something for each of us to do.

Those efforts may not even need to be organized into a single coordinated campaign. Perhaps multiple actions, tailored to local priorities and the hydra's local incarnations, can deliver death by a thousand cuts. That idea is an invitation to all of us to look around our neighborhoods. Whose land is a gas company trying to buy? Can we band together and demand better terms? Is the owner of the nearest charter school leasing the school building from her husband? Can we override our own impulse to pass over in silence the violations of the public trust that we witness?

A third principle comes not from ancient Greece, but from the

Farmers' Alliance. It is the importance of ideas, the need for independent analysis, developed and transmitted in a constant exchange with and among neighbors, and the need to teach it actively. Too much dogma, unquestioned across the political spectrum—such as that unlimited growth is a sign of health—serves to reinforce the business model of the kleptocrats, or to distract us from it. Much of that dogma was deliberately instilled to make us submissive, as the dominator coalition restructured our society.

How such a broad-based self-education campaign might unfold is a puzzle. I can't quite see us gathering on schoolhouse benches for the purpose. What new formats and means of communication might foster such an exchange today? Would in-person gatherings be helpful? Would they be possible? Could they serve to reinforce the crosscutting coalition? Could they be fun as well as educational? Or could COVID 19 innovations help? What about virtual meetings? A curated online resource bank? What form of leadership would be needed to pilot an experiment in mass civic education? Where would the money come from?

The curriculum might start with ethics. What values do we want our society to honor? What is the alternative to market-based morality? Rules must be devised to reinforce a different ethical vision. What about democracy? What does that word exactly mean? What must its substance consist of, concretely, to deliver on its promise?

Biologists and ethnographers and spiritual leaders could explore how we are woven inseparably into nature—not placed above it, free to subjugate it—and how social animals like humans function best not in bitter competition, but cooperatively.

What about a serious challenge to the dogma of growth, of economy of scale? In 1968, running for president in an election whose stakes were no less than "the national soul of the United States," as he put it, Robert F. Kennedy had this to say about the GDP:

> Our Gross National Product . . . if we judge the United States of America by that . . . counts air pollution and cigarette advertising, and ambulances to clear our highways of carnage. It counts special locks for our doors and the jails for the people who break them. It counts the destruction of the redwood and the loss of our natural wonder in chaotic sprawl.

It counts napalm and counts nuclear warheads and armored cars for the police to fight the riots in our cities. . . . Yet the gross national product does not allow for the health of our children, the quality of our education or the joy of their play. It does not include the beauty of our poetry or the strength of our marriages, the intelligence of our public debate or the integrity of our public officials. It measures neither our wit nor our courage, neither our wisdom nor our learning, neither our compassion nor our devotion to our country, it measures everything in short, except that which makes life worthwhile. And it can tell us everything about America except why we are proud that we are Americans.

Do we always need more? Are bigger businesses and cities always better? Do we need infinite population growth? Why? In order to sustain economic growth? I thought the economy was supposed to be in service to the health of people and their communities and landscapes. Since when is our very procreation placed in service to the god Economy? Let's take RFK's words to heart and design metrics to substitute for growth as a measure of a nation's or a business's vitality.

There will be no beating this monster unless we can see through its justifying verbiage. If such crucial matters as how the economic and legal systems work remain impenetrable to ordinary people, then ordinary people will keep losing. Obfuscation and complex language are the cloud of confusion this hydra hides in, like a squid in its ink. Our People's Curriculum could offer primers that cut to the heart of such plain concepts as the difference between investment and speculation, the actual process for making a law and what has to happen before it can be enforced, or identifying how and where and by whom decisions are made. Lessons could help us recognize deliberate complexity when it is being used on us and supply methods for disabling it. A library of crisp two- to four-page documents could anchor the resource bank.

The curriculum should cover principles and exercises for conducting the type of network analysis done in this book, including on a local level. Examples might be stored and kept constantly updated in the online resource bank.

Such weapons would place ordinary people on a more equal footing with the hydra and her ranks of experts. Thus armed, we could speak up: challenge media tropes, submit public comments, attend community meetings, visit our representatives' offices, steer conversations with friends in productive directions. With an eye to network dynamics, we could choose our targets strategically.

Such activities may not change outcomes immediately. But they will change the terms of the debate. And that is the prerequisite to a different reality.

The phenomenon we confront is the worldwide equivalent of a forest fire, of the Blitz. We must react accordingly—with that same impulsive solidarity. Or, to restate this idea in terms of the other metaphor that has threaded through these pages: the only way to defeat the tiny but powerful coalition of meat hogs that is imperiling our whole community is to join together in a far-reaching egalitarian coalition and confront them in unison.

That means noticing and resisting all the crafty attempts to pit us against one another, even if we don't especially care for that neighbor who's in the same fix as we are—or care for her views on gun rights or his professed religion. It means resisting the impulse to hang him out to dry and cut a separate deal. It means finding remedies that benefit all members of the coalition—and are seen to do so—not just a subgroup. It means adopting the egalitarian ethos in our own affairs. It means ceasing to make excuses for the meat hogs inside our own political or racial or gender or cultural in-group and demanding the same rigor from our own favorites as we do from the others.

That last one can feel disloyal, even suicidal. It runs counter to humans' strongest group-survival instincts—so threatened do many of us feel by those on the other sides of our various divides. Still, if we keep making up excuses for "our" meat hogs, they and their like will keep defeating us. Freeloaders would never be tolerated, whatever their political party or sexual orientation, in a flood or a group of shipwreck survivors. That is the mind-set we must attain.

Then what? What to do with our shared analysis and sense of urgency? What actions might each of us take that could actually hurt the hydra?

The first part of the answer is to say yet again: it will take every one of us. And that is not an impossible burden, it's a blessing. There is something for everyone to do. Some of us are gifted leaders; some play the accordion; some think like a platoon sergeant; some love to plan; some have great tech skills, a dash of guile, or love to ferret out information; some are just stubborn; some are strong; some weave beautiful garlands of flowers; some can read spreadsheets; some are hilarious; some take joy in group happenings; some stand on the sidelines, sensing dynamics that others may miss. Every one of our native aptitudes is priceless. No one is required to martyr himself or feel she must do it all. Let each of us just give of our talents and effort.

I say "accordion" in all seriousness. I have envied the cultural effervescence that illuminated the uprisings against the Gilded Age syndrome or the civil rights movement, finding it lacking today. But on September 19, 2019, I was blessed to attend the inaugural reading by the nation's twenty-third poet laureate, Joy Harjo. She is a Muscogee Creek Native American. In the 1830s, her people were driven out of what is now Alabama on the Trail of Tears. She plays the saxophone and the wooden flute and she got up there with two black guys on bass and guitar and a white guy on keys, and spoke and sang and stomped out her poetry in cream-colored cowboy boots. The hall was packed; there were overflow rooms and thousands listening online. With her final poem, "Bless This Land," she declared: *"Luminous forests, oceans, and rock cliff sold for the trash glut of gold, uranium, or oil bust rush yet there are new stories to be made, little ones coming up over the horizon."*

Harjo did this revolutionary thing under the great greened dome of the Library of Congress, next door to the Supreme Court, opposite the Capitol. She planted the banner of that ethos right up there on that Hill—right in the midst of them. It was a counterweight, the first I have felt in years. It was a note on a ram's horn, before the walls of Jericho.

Mass civic action is what it took in countries like Burkina Faso and Guatemala and South Korea and Ukraine to show leaders their ways were no longer acceptable. Drawing their mandate from the crowds in the streets week after week, justice professionals in those countries found the courage to investigate and prosecute top officials. I do not see the United States healing without mass mobilization of some sort. And it is under way. Led by West Virginia schoolteachers and bus drivers, and by Marriott hotel staff and Amazon warehousers, and medical personnel saving lives without enough protective gear, workers are building coalitions inside and outside of traditional unions and demanding better. Schoolchildren everywhere are shrugging off school and crying out to their elders, "The waters are rising and so are we."

But demonstrations can sometimes seem like a primal scream, lacking a clear objective. They start in some nondescript public place and end in another, and everyone disperses. Or, like Lebanon's, they may be sectarian. Only the already activated members of a specific subgroup of our fractured polity even know they're happening. The vast majority of Americans, too busy or turned off by the shouting, are left by the side of the road. And even at their most powerful and dramatic, protests cannot be the sole form of action. They burn time and energy, and they are blunt—like Herakles's club.

There are other and more flexible ways of disciplining our meat hogs. Criminal investigations and prosecutions are necessary, and many groups are bringing civil suits to challenge some of the wrongdoing considered here. But for now such actions are too rare. And under the best conditions they could not sanction enough, alone, to alter the incentive structure.

So why outsource 100 percent of society's capacity to hold its powerful members to account to a single, excessively formalistic institution (the selection of whose personnel has become a new battleground)? Thinking of punishment as a type of "propaganda by the deed"—designed to imprint on everyone's mind where the community draws the line between what's right, or OK, and what is intolerable—we might imagine other, more democratic "performances" to send those signals.

Social shaming, which has come into vogue of late, is a potentially dangerous practice. Too often, ostracism is inflicted not on the powerful but on the weak, the already marginalized, or on those who hold unpopular convictions but are not the authors of systemic harm. Too often people are shamed in ways that divide us from our natural allies. Too often, a group of shamers leaps straight to the severest sanction—some version of "Off with his head!"

Our hunter-gatherer ancestors never did that. They started with the minimum signal that matched the gravity of the misbehavior and had a chance of changing it. Most importantly, they gathered a broad consensus before meting out any penalty at all. Their example offers lessons.

One way to draw some lines in public is to vote with our money. If money is speech, then let's get talking. People have been doing so already. What would happen if most of us did?

The suggestions below are not always possible; many are more expensive than the alternatives. Some of us have no money to spare. But others do; we just don't think of our purchases in this way: as investments in a more humane economy. Instead, we put a few dollars in the church plate or send them to a nonprofit dealing with the results of the system we implicitly endorse.

These suggestions should support, not replace, policy demands; they would require field-testing. Our resource bank could include accounts of real-life experiments and suggested improvements.

With those cautions in mind, here are a few sample ideas.

What if we chose which bank to give our business to, as Wells Fargo customers did after the company fleeced millions of them by opening accounts and lines of credit they had not requested, then charging fees? If the tone of its 2019 advertising campaign was any indication, Wells Fargo got the message.

If we believe too-big-to-fail is a dangerous proposition, let's make banks smaller ourselves. Let's open accounts at community banks, instead of defaulting to the usual suspects. We could look at banks' record of making loans to local families and businesses and avoid ones that speculate in exotic financial instruments.

When choosing where to buy, let's try considering the hours companies make their employees work or what they throw in the nearby street or river. Let's find out whether they pay taxes to our communities and our nation. No one can do that in every situation. But if those criteria became our default preference, instead of what's cheapest or coolest or most convenient, how might our whole economic system change?

We could research how much money a corporation spends on lobbyists each year, how much it pays its CEO compared to its median worker, how big its campaign contributions are. Those are not charitable donations, they are bribes. What if we find out how many local businesses—and jobs—a large chain has destroyed by deliberately opening branches beside a homegrown alternative, in order to drive it under? That is not a neighborly practice, and we could refuse to reward it with our business.

In fact, what if we systematically patronized smaller, independent shops and manufacturers wherever they exist? If Mary Heaton Vorse brought one idea to life in her depictions of those man-dwarfing steel mills, it was this: giant size is dehumanizing, always. It makes us puny. It makes us interchangeable. It makes us no-account. And it delivers too much access to power.

The largest, most profitable, powerful, and destructive corporations are those connected to petroleum and its derivatives, wrenched from the guts of the earth. Wherever these corporations exist, they are at the center of kleptocracies. I do not see how we curb systemic corruption and help nurture the miraculous planet on which we were born without buying less of what these corporations are selling. That means gasoline, but also related fuels used for heating and cooling and flying airplanes. It means plastics, synthetic fabrics, most cosmetics. Just look at your shopping cart at the supermarket sometime. Look at the packaging. Consider the length of time you will enjoy one of those snacks. Is the trade-off worth it? If you're hosting a meeting or friends in your kitchen, do you have to make bottles of water available? Or can you provide a jug and glasses? I am not trying to guilt anyone. I am calling on all of us to notice, and adjust, a little.

We have accepted bigness as inevitable—even necessary—to modernity. But all it is necessary for is wealth maximization. It does not advance our survival or well-being or ability to face the future. Reducing the size of government is an admirable goal. The same principle should apply to businesses, which determine many more aspects of our daily life. What would happen if a whole crop of modern small enterprises run by people we could know personally crowded out today's giants? While insisting on it, must we wait around for antitrust enforcement? Or can we help make that happen ourselves?

What if those of us who are lucky enough to have a 401(k) account or a stock portfolio opted for impact investing instead of the default settings? What if we insisted our plans offered that choice?

Such actions are already working. On August 19, 2019, the Business Roundtable officially repudiated one of the core principles underpinning today's kleptocracy: the dictum that a corporation's purpose is to maximize shareholder value. CEOs of companies including Amazon, Bechtel, Boeing, Chevron, Citigroup, Coca-Cola, Comcast, the Ford Motor Company, Fox, and on down the alphabet to Xerox signed their names to a radically new "Statement on the Purpose of a Corporation." It commits them to deliver value to customers, first; to invest in employees, including by compensating them fairly and providing benefits, training, and education; to deal ethically with suppliers; to support surrounding communities; and, much later in the litany, to generate *long-term* value for shareholders. Maybe these CEOs don't mean it. Maybe they're just trying to stave off the pitchforks. Still, public pressure forced them to abandon a key ideology. That is a major victory. Now their pledge is in print. Go online. Look at the companies. Let's hold them to it.

If we are in a position to receive money from wealthy organizations or individuals, either as grants, purchase orders, dividends, or campaign contributions, or a new corporate headquarters or factory, let's consider the color of that money. That's what the prestigious National Portrait Gallery in London did with a prospective donation from the Sackler family in 2019. Patagonia, likewise, has refused new orders for personalized fleeces from big Wall Street banks or Silicon Valley giants. New York City residents decided they did not want an Amazon headquarters after all, and certainly not at the cost of $3 billion in corporate tax breaks. Universities that enjoyed the munificence of child molester Jeffrey Epstein were belatedly shamed into investigating themselves and donating equivalent sums to relevant charities. Their reputations are permanently tarnished. But the Council on Foreign Relations and the Democratic Congressional Campaign Committee have both unapologetically taken gifts from Russian oligarch Leonid Blavatnik. Media companies seek a corporate sponsorship, then insist that their coverage is unaffected. We've got lots of work left to do.

A similar scrutiny should go into choosing recipients for honors or awards.

If we are employees or members of such entities and don't call the shots, do we have to stay mum as we witness the poor choices? Or can we discuss an ill-advised donation or contract with our peers? If we discover a concerned consensus, let's challenge the decision together. Let's put our names to that letter of protest. Let's blow that whistle.

Many of us in such situations keep still by reflex. It seems politer, certainly safer. But is it? What is the worst that could happen: we get fired for raising questions? How would that look on our employers' records? Is today's job worth our personal integrity? Were we likely to stay in that job forever anyway?

Remember the General Motors workers who, in 2008, volunteered to reduce health benefits for retirees and wages for incoming hires to help their crippled company win a taxpayer-funded bailout. A decade later those workers heard their now profitable company announce massive layoffs. How fleeting are the gains we reap from the even deeper sacrifice of our irreplaceable principles? How lasting is the damage to ourselves, to our society?

Any of these actions will be less convenient—at a minimum—than doing nothing. Convenience is another default, admired as a good in itself, like growth. What if it is a drug? What if it is fooling us into placing it ahead of other values we treasure, the way opium tramples love? What if less convenience, even a little risk, adds pleasure?

The point here is to do something. Not just anything, not waste our time just blowing off steam. Let's all of us pick some part of our exploitative economy that especially galls us, consider our own assets and aptitudes, and change our behavior. Then let's consider how best to serve as a welcoming example, to help our friends and neighbors follow suit.

Sometimes requests I get to reel off a list of solutions frustrate me. I remember, in Kabul and in the Pentagon, working up detailed plans for addressing corruption in Afghanistan. One set of carefully thought through recommendations would be ignored, and I'd be asked for another. When I pointed out that the conditions were less favorable now, I'd get a retort: "OK, fine, it would have been better if we had done something then, but now is now; what do we do *now*?" And I'd come up with another plan. I started feeling like a magician, pulling rabbits out of a hat: "That's a nice rabbit, but don't you have a yellow one?" And I'd stick my hand in and find a yellow rabbit. "That's a nice yellow rabbit, but I really wanted one with floppy ears." After a while, there were no rabbits left in the hat:

the window of opportunity had closed. I realized no one had any intention of carrying out any of these plans. What they wanted was a formula showing that some version of what they were already doing would solve the problem. And it wouldn't.

There will be no defeating this hydra without changing our ways, without putting in effort—without traveling a little farther or making do with a product that isn't exactly what we thought we wanted, or getting it delivered in a week instead of a day, or taking time to consider our choices, or generating new ones, or, again and again, demanding better of our leaders. But I'm not talking martyrdom here.

So please: let's stop obsessing about what we might have to give up. What we're doing now is not bringing us joy. To make an effort, together, in pursuit of a shared, life-giving goal does not spell privation. Ask a disaster survivor. It is the opposite. The experience is exhilarating, a fond memory. It ushers new options in. Let's make it part of our everyday lives. Let's travel together and make an outing of it. Let's make this struggle a celebration.

The ideas above are aimed at the private-sector strands of our networks. The intent is to place the economy back in the service of life, instead of subordinating life to the economy. The steps are designed to refashion our free enterprise system into an engine that preserves and contributes to priceless values, instead of converting them to poisonous gold. I can hardly imagine a more exciting objective.

As for the public-sector strands of the networks, it's a bit harder for ordinary people to make an impact. How ironic. What else is democracy supposed to mean? But kleptocratic structures and practices have become a constant. "There's not one of them who doesn't do it," we tell ourselves. So we select candidates based on other criteria, or we opt out in disgust.

Limiting money in politics must be citizens' top priority. The power of campaign donations to determine political outcomes is the primary factor allowing kleptocratic networks to dominate us. As Thomas Ferguson put it, "Campaigning isn't free . . . either everyone pays a little to fund campaigns or a few pay for nearly everything—

and control the system." This is one problem on which just about all Americans agree.

Given the Supreme Court cases that culminated in *Citizens United,* it is impossible to address it directly via legislation. We should consider whether a single nine-justice panel is the best way to decide such weighty measures in a democracy. The Supreme Court's structure is not enshrined in the Constitution; it is a matter of law. Laws can be changed. A much larger court, expanded over time, would allow more cases to be heard by subpanels, as in federal courts of appeals. It would allow for more diversity, different perspectives— and ultimately better decisions.

In the meantime, what about a pledge that citizens of all stripes could use as a litmus test for every candidate? It would be something almost as simple as the 1980s' "No new taxes," but focused on ethical standards—first among them to end the legalized bribery that is the American way of financing political campaigns.

A candidate's refusal to participate would have to be sweeping and strict. A look-alike, such as "No corporate PAC money," won't do. It would have to amount to a vow not to accept any contributions above a certain limit. It would have to get at expenditures on the candidate's behalf by supposedly separate organizations, or from the candidate's personal wealth. It would have to include an iron-clad commitment to work to change the rules of campaign financing however doing so is constitutional.

Such a pledge would require policing: voting anyone who breaks it out of office, whatever his or her party. It would require voting against any elected official of any party who makes it easier to spend more money on political campaigns. We must put this priority first. During the civil war in Liberia in 2003—as in Spike Lee's 2015 movie *Chi-Raq*—women vowed not to have sex with their husbands till the fighting stopped. We must get that adamant.

Even without such a citizen-policed ethics pledge, voters should be adamant. Where candidates turn for the financial backing needed to run is the first piece of evidence at to the reality of their stated ideals. It should be the first question we ask, the first sieve to sort the choices.

A candidate's ethics pledge might add two or three more promises to this basic one.

Who can trust our elected officials to abide by voluntary norms? A whole range of standards for public office must be tightened and made enforceable, turned into hard-edged law, such as financial disclosures and release of tax returns for all officials and candidates for state or federal office (including judges); an end to the ability of the leader of one legislative chamber to refuse to bring bills passed by the other chamber up for vote; a change in the tax laws to curb the use of tax-free charitable organizations as a vehicle for political activities; a code of ethics for the Supreme Court.

Drafting such new statutes is a job for those among us with technical expertise. A number of nongovernmental organizations have been working hard on this agenda. Several examples have been floated by members of Congress or presidential candidates.

Those prototypes, and the effort and expertise that brought them forth, deserve our gratitude. But I would also welcome a more interactive process. Sometimes these good-governance experts forget the people on whose behalf, presumably, they are working. Their attitude can resemble that of the would-be dominators they are fighting: "Leave it to me; I know what's best for you." That is no way to run a democracy. That is no way to gather an egalitarian consensus. There is no technical expertise that is not improved by street smarts.

The people of Iceland tried a different way of modifying complex laws. Through a committee of citizens chosen by lot and an online consultation process, they revised their entire constitution after the 2008 economic crisis. So frightened was the country's kleptocratic network when the draft came out that the parliament, in the hydra's grip, changed the rules for passing constitutional provisions. Ultimately, the experiment failed, but it is an idea worth adapting.

In 2019, West Virginia gubernatorial candidate Stephen Smith hammered out his platform by way of a painstaking process of public engagement: town meetings in every county in the state; hundreds of conversations with individuals and small groups; an online suggestions form, and attention to stray ideas that came across the transom in emails or on folded scraps of paper; a specialized app to help capture and collate it all; a three-day writing retreat, during which campaign staffers assisted by a couple of dozen subject-matter experts converted the ideas to concrete platform planks, costing every one out so that all were paid for; and then, at a mini-convention, a vote on the whole platform by delegates from all the committees of supporters across the state.

Not only did this process result in a truly representative platform, it also gave West Virginia citizens a way to substantively engage with the political process. Telling Smith by a five to one margin that political corruption was their number one concern, they imagined numerous ways of curbing it: from creating a new corporate crime and corruption unit in the state police to enacting lifetime bans on public officials serving as lobbyists (let alone doing both jobs at once, as West Virginia's state house majority whip, Paul Espinosa, currently does).

In her 2014 book, *Corruption in America,* Fordham University law professor Zephyr Teachout provides a rule of thumb for any effort to improve legal restraints on corruption. It is far easier to prevent corrupt practices from taking root by way of absolute bans like that than to punish an act of corruption after the fact. Mincing definitions and improbable standards of proof make it hard to pin a sophisticated perpetrator down.

That explains the United States Constitution's hard-and-fast rule against accepting any item of value from a government official or his or her agent. The idea was a startling novelty when our founders dreamed it up, Teachout notes. It made U.S. envoys seem boorish in European royal courts. But the presumption behind it has been confirmed by countless social science experiments. When people receive gifts, no matter how innocent, they feel obligated and try to reciprocate. It is a lovely reflex in everyday life and has furthered community bonding and artistic vocation. But in politics, it leads to corruption. An outright ban on such gifts would protect officials from the unintended worst consequences of their best reflexes— and from the temptations that will inevitably be dangled before them.

A promise to work actively to enact such ethics legislation might fit on our nonpartisan candidates' pledge. Some officials, like Smith, have already staked out this ground, not just with slogans, but with focus and specific programs. Vote for them. Point your own representative to their example if you don't live in one of their districts. Demand that reforms include reinforced and expanded anticorruption laws at every level, and the material and moral resources to enforce them, and bans on receiving gifts from anyone while in office.

What about the unspoken gift of likely future contracts or employment?

Along with money in politics, that may be the key to the meat hogs' operating system: the ability to cycle network members back and forth between the private and public sectors. That is how they weave the two so closely together that government no longer represents the people. Rules on conflict of interest have become as narrow and technical as the definition of corruption—where they even exist. They do not stop former top officials from taking jobs in industries that they were just in charge of regulating, or keep top executives from taking over agencies that regulate the industries where they spent their lives. Private-sector network members now command whole swaths of our government.

We need rules that *do* criminalize some aspects of politics as it is practiced today.

I wonder if community discipline might also help here. How many politicians can you name who have not gone on the board of an industry they once oversaw? How many have not opened or joined a consulting firm where their role is to traffic in influence? How many don't run a hedge fund on the side, where they trade on the insider information gained from the consulting? How did this get to be standard practice? What sort of public dunce cap could we fashion to embarrass these people—even if they are members of our preferred party? How could we make them shrink from such practices, wincing at their disgracefulness?

To get at the sector where the strands of our network are most tightly woven together, what about an association lodged in a business school or an economics department somewhere aimed at supporting up-and-coming young economists who are devoted to the public interest? Through symposia and social events, publications, internships, and job placements, it could prepare a new generation of candidates for positions at the Federal Reserve and the Treasury Department, as well as at the regulatory agencies and on the staffs of relevant congressional committees and their state-level counterparts. Members could write short papers converting key economic and financial principles to plain English (items for the online resource bank) to help their fellow citizens gain the literacy needed to participate meaningfully in the political process.

Now that the coronavirus has demonstrated that we *do* need government, what about demanding higher taxes, as some are currently discussing—at least restoring the burden on the very highest earners to closer to what it was in the 1950s and 1960s? The candidates' pledge might include no voting for tax breaks for the top 1 percent of the income/wealth distribution, for capital gains, or for large corporations.

Communities could try local petitions, aimed at specific types of corporate activity that are especially harmful. What about raising the price of leases and severance fees for the extraction of mineral wealth from our collective understory? What about taxing huge companies' expenditures on lobbying activities? Or demanding a fixed schedule of damages owed when practices that violate health and safety and environmental rules harm people and landscapes, so the penalties can't just be negotiated in private among network members? Corporations, whose top stated goal has long been enriching their shareholders, have won their personhood. But they have avoided its responsibilities. Why let them get away with that?

Along with a simple nonpartisan candidates' pledge, we might focus some of our public advocacy on policies that would shrink kleptocrats' revenue streams, while repairing damage their practices have done.

· With a tax on securities trades, the burden of our collective needs would rest less cripplingly on useful work and instead serve to brake speculation.

· Alongside stiffer penalties when disaster strikes, we could ask for a pollution tax for industries that automatically soil their surroundings, such as chemical plants, paper mills, and fossil fuel production and transport. The proceeds could be earmarked to care for suffering people and landscapes. We could vote against any candidate who undermines environmental protections.

· With a dying planet posing more of a threat than any government or terrorist group, we could call for a new Civilian Conservation Corps to help heal it. The money is there: $50 or

$100 billion from the bloated defense budget would do it. Plus the pollution tax, plus revenues recovered from tax evaders. Physically demanding outdoor jobs—in inner cities and on the scarred flanks of mountains—could offer pride and a dignified salary. Uniforms and billboards on highways could celebrate this new cohort of patriots.

· The boost that agricultural subsidies offers farmers could be shifted to reward regenerative practices instead of the industrial ones, contemptuous of life, which currently reap the bulk of the money. That priority concerns all of us, not just Big Ag lobbyists and their indentured farmers.

Then, as with our purchasing power, we could focus our political activism on the local level, where the issues hit home and we know our neighbors and can join forces more easily. Who is your state senator? Who's running for judge? Who contributed to her campaign? When was the last time you went to a community consultation meeting? Who did you go with?

The point here, again, is to do something. But be judicious. Avoid activities that seem aimed more at waving some banner than achieving a goal. We all have limited time and energy and material resources. They are dwarfed by those on the other side. We must aim every investment for maximum impact. Consider the kleptocrats' needs, practices, and vulnerabilities. Consider your own gifts and passions. Then commit them toward an objective.

Above all else, we must get the money changers out of our temples. It is time to expel the Midas disease—money maximization—from our sacred spaces and return them to the public trust. That means our places of worship, of course. It means our schools and universities, and our health-care facilities, the provision of our fundamental necessities, such as water and electricity and garbage collection, our food, and our natural surroundings. We must resist efforts to privatize these crucial functions. That means charter schools. It means public infrastructure such as railroads and ports and broadband. It means the fighting of our wars.

Let us be adamant: money does *not* equal speech, that singularly human gift.

Let us also abstain from judging ourselves by the standard of money. If you seek a raise, or are considering switching jobs for a higher salary, if you get a voice in managers' compensation levels or are setting a revenue goal for the start-up you launched, examine the target number. What is it based on? Real needs? Or some abstract concept of what you think you're "worth," or what someone else in a comparable position is making? Those factors should not be ignored, but they should not be the only weights in the balance.

It is time to restore other values to primacy. That means honoring them, not just with words, but in ways that matter. For culture does not just happen. It must be nurtured. We do so by honoring people who build their lives around other priorities—ensuring they can earn a dignified living, even if we must pay more taxes ourselves to raise salaries for public servants. We do so by buying something hand-made or hand grown when we possibly can, instead of at Walmart, or spending our own time and money on beauty and its creators. We do so by reducing our tolerance for ugliness.

We reinforce better values by ceasing to assume that if someone is spectacularly rich, he must be smarter and more hardworking than the rest of us. Instead, we should view such people with suspicion. If there is one thing work on this book has taught me, it is this: it is impossible to become a billionaire without bending the rules. Most of the members of that class run their operations and live their lives in ways that injure our communities. Most are trying to rig the system even further. These are not upstanding citizens. They are parasites and freeloaders—however they try to justify themselves. We do not owe them deference.

We can do this. We are our society. We can make it reflect the beauty in us. We don't have to wait for the next devastating calamity that lies on the horizon to discover, in survival, that precious communion. We can find it now, in the battle to ward off that calamity. We can find that fierce joy.

In 1991, an archaeologist from Cambridge University named Eberhard Zangger published a paper on the prehistoric geology of the area near the ancient city of Argos, where a thumb of earth meets the three southernmost fingers of Greece. There, until recently, was a freshwater lagoon called Lake Lerna. This is the landscape where the wisdom of the Hydra's story lies.

Examining more than two hundred cores of the surrounding bedrock, Zangger made a discovery. That lagoon, he concluded, was formed in the Neolithic era, maybe around 8000 BC, when warming temperatures melted glaciers, raising the sea level worldwide. For the next four thousand years, as soil washed down the hillsides, the nearby coastline silted up and the silt compressed. A rock barrier formed between Lake Lerna and the sea. The lake was fed by many springs, but the water had no way to drain out. A vast marsh expanded its morass around the lake. People, it was said, would get sucked to its bottomless depths.

This was the Hydra's home.

Physical anthropologists examining Bronze Age remains around the now-dry lake have found evidence of malaria. Bones bear the markers of sickle-cell anemia, which provides resistance to the mosquito-borne infection. It was as though the very air around that boggy lake was pestilential, killing villagers who lived nearby and leaving the survivors weak and ill.

These facts may explain the myth of the Hydra. The villagers, Zangger suggests, struggled to stop up the springs that kept pouring their water out on the already waterlogged ground. But every time laborers got one sealed, others would well up somewhere else.

The Hydra, says science, was a swamp that could not be drained.

Wetlands are inconvenient to humans who want to use the land for their purposes. Often led by real estate developers colluding with corrupt politicians, we drain swamps to make way for the latest overpriced subdivision or luxury hotel complex, built on unsound ground. For the earth's purposes, however, wetlands are irreplaceable: a vital organ that serves as a filter and a buffer and incubates a glorious profusion of life.

Maybe it is time to reframe this metaphor. Let's revive our precious swamps and nurture them, and with them a human culture and politics that—unpolluted by money—are hospitable to life.

Acknowledgments

Culture is under attack in the United States. Its beleaguered guardians—those who create spaces where it can flourish, uphold its standards, defend its creators (sometimes even from themselves)—perform a heroic, irreplaceable, and often invisible service to our society. Victoria Wilson, of Alfred A. Knopf, is in their vanguard. It is a great privilege to work with her. It is our privilege as a people to have her in our midst, fighting for the best in us. My agent, Kathleen Anderson, is another of these ferocious protectors, gifted with a special kind of sight. She has shaped the course of my life, in sometimes dramatic ways.

This book has been a collective enterprise. Much of the thinking in it has been honed through an unflagging process of examination driven by the piercing insights and tenacious insistence of Kent Shreve. He has drawn my attention to key individuals and artifacts (*Risky Business,* for example) that perfectly exemplify the concepts I seek to convey. Several of the remedies in the Epilogue are his ideas. And he has constantly stressed the importance to democracy of precision and clarity in exposition. Sebastian Junger, my friend since before I can remember, pushed me to restructure this book when it was bogging down and aimed me at some of its fundamental tenets—egalitarianism in hunter-gatherer bands, for example, or the sometimes salutary effects of disaster. His work on a future television series, to be titled *The Radical Bureau,* inspired me to explore much of the material in Part IV, Chapter 1, "Fighting the Hydra: The Cities." When he showed up at my cabin in West Virginia in December 2018 and announced he was working on this early-twentieth-century period, my jaw dropped. I had just finished Part II, on the Gilded Age. Once again, we had found our separate ways to overlapping topics. Alan Huffman, also working on *The Radical Bureau* and a separate book on that story, helped with sources, as well as with information on a current political figure. Ever alight with the importance of this project, my longtime friend the preternaturally insightful Amir Soltani has helped keep my eyes on the horizon, the big picture. Lissa Lucas read the whole manuscript, mindful of touching the broadest possible audience. Former federal prosecutor Bruce Searby recommended the focus on the "honest services" cases discussed in the Prologue and in Part III, Chapter 8, "Colluders."

   In that connection, a word here of gratitude to Don Ayer, who features there. He was most generous with his time, not to mention incredibly helpful in tracking down old case materials and scanning and sending them. I feel a bit guilty for the light I shine on him, poor recompense for his openness. And I salute his activism in defense of the rule of law in the United States since his retirement. (See, for example: "Bill Barr Must Resign," *The Atlantic,* February 17, 2020.)

   I am grateful to the merry band of bloodhounds who helped with research: Gustavo Berrizbeitia, Susan Foster, Smriti Kumble, Steve O'Keefe, and David Wistocki. I sold them a bill of goods: initially I thought detailed mapping of the actual networks currently sharing power in the United States would be central to this book. The team did a lot of bushwhacking in those thickets. But then I realized that in a dynamic system, that degree of detail would soon be dated, and what readers needed more were the basic principles—so they would be equipped do the mapping themselves, in any situation. Even where specifics of the work are not recorded in these pages, however, the process was priceless in shaping their content. And, out on my own to write this book, I found welcome collegiality and intellectual inspiration in these friends' thoughtful fellowship. Apart from her membership in that band, former bookshop owner and literary publicist Sue Foster, my host on the Nigeria trips mentioned, has been far-seeing and energetic on how to get the word out, especially in Britain.

   Without Mustapher Hamza, Promise O. F. J. Airhumwude, and Esther Tewogbola, I would not have understood the first thing about Nigeria. I have been a faithless friend, losing touch with them. But I hold them in great tenderness, and am forever indebted for their generous welcome into their communities and their hearts.

Knopf's Marc Jaffee shepherded the details—and there are more of those than you can imagine—to include crouching, catcher's mitt up, in his Brooklyn apartment during coronavirus lockdown to field the two-inch-thick manuscript that carried all my penciled corrections and additions.

My sisters, again . . . there are no words. And, ever, my Sainted Mother, with her bottomless appetite for versions of this, as sausage meat and then sausage. Above all, for the irreplaceable security of her confidence.

Doo: You did one piece of corruption work, for the Bosnian government. And here I am still stuck on it. *And* I wrote my first brief! How I ache for the chance to talk about all this with you.

Notes

PROLOGUE: DISMISSING CORRUPTION

3 They were there for: 579 U.S. _____ (2016).

3 A woman in a pale blue sundress: *The Daily Signal,* "Pro-Lifers React to Supreme Court's Abortion Ruling," June 27, 2016 (https://www.youtube .com/watch?v=Ic9CDhN0vCM).

4 Williams's company had formulated: See John Reid Blackwell, "Anatomy of Anatabloc: Supplement Tied to Probe Spawns Supporters and Lawsuits," *Richmond Times-Dispatch,* July 21, 2013.

4 "The Governor says it's okay": *McDonnell v. United States,* 579 U.S. _____ (2016), p. 4.

5 All three judges: For the facts of the case and prior decisions, see *McDonnell v. United States* and *United States v. McDonnell,* 792 F.3d 478 (2015), https:// www.ca4.uscourts.gov/Opinions/Published/154019.P.pdf.

6 The link between corruption and violent extremism: Sarah Chayes, *Thieves of State: Why Corruption Threatens Global Security* (New York: W. W. Norton, 2015).

6 Since then, I've watched outraged: For analysis of some of these uprisings, see Sarah Chayes, "Fighting the Hydra: Lessons from Worldwide Protests Against Corruption," Carnegie Endowment for International Peace, April 12, 2018.

7 On June 27, 2016: See Sarah Chayes, "When Corruption Is the Operating System: The Case of Honduras," Carnegie Endowment for International Peace, May 30, 2017.

7 It says a public official: 18 U.S.C. 201 (b) (2). Verb tenses have been changed to fit the grammar of the sentence here.

7 "The issue in this case": *McDonnell v. United States* 579 U.S. _____ (2016), p. 13.

8 The way he leaned on: *McDonnell v. United States* 579 U.S. _____ (2016), pp. 14–22.

8 Thus did the unanimous Supreme Court: *McDonnell's* narrow focus on the meaning of "official act" helps to explain House Intelligence Committee chairman Adam Schiff's repetition of those words during Trump's impeachment proceedings, and their inclusion in the first Article of Impeachment. The decision not to explicitly charge Trump with bribery—which is enumerated as a sample high crime or misdemeanor in the U.S. Constitution—was largely due to the narrow post-*McDonnell* scope of the statutory crime, according to a member of the Judiciary Committee, interviewed on March 16, 2020. But the use of the words "official act" in Article 1 make implicit reference to the crime of bribery.

9 If the *McDonnell* decision stood: *McDonnell v. United States* 579 U.S. ____ (2016), p. 22.

9 "People think you shouldn't criminalize": Telephone interview, August 27, 2019.

10 Because politicians get away: "Analysis of the Last Supreme Court Decisions of the Term," *The Diane Rehm Show,* National Public Radio (WAMU), June 27, 2016. *The Diane Rehm Show* went off the air on December 23, 2016, and was replaced by a weekly podcast, *Diane Rehm: On My Mind.*

11 The splashy convictions: Sheldon Silver, a two-decade holder of the New York State Assembly speaker's gavel—making him arguably the most powerful state official—steered state grants and other services to a doctor who was referring patients to Silver's law firm. Silver told two real estate developers to use another firm, in return for favorable legislation and tax abatements. He banked fees from both firms for each referral. See *United States v. Silver,* 16-1615 (2d Cir., 2017), and Benjamin Weiser, "Sheldon Silver's 2015 Corruption Conviction Is Overturned," *New York Times,* July 13, 2017. New York State Senate majority leader Dean Skelos was convicted of using his office to pressure three different companies to hire his son as a consultant: see *United States v. Skelos et al.,* 16-1618 (2d Cir., 2017), and Emily Saul and Kirstan Conley, "Dean Skelos' Corruption Conviction Overturned," *New York Post,* September 26, 2019. Both men were retried. Silver was convicted in district court a second time on May 11, 2018, and sentenced to seven years in prison plus three on supervised release: United States Department of Justice, U.S. Attorney's Office, Southern District of New York, "Former New York State Assembly Speaker Sheldon Silver Sentenced to 7 Years in Prison," press release, July 27, 2018. Skelos, also reconvicted, was sentenced to three years and three months in jail: United States Department of Justice, U.S. Attorney's Office, Southern District of New York, "Dean Skelos, Former New York State Senate Leader, Sentenced to 51 Months, Son Adam Skelos Sentenced to 4 Years in Manhattan Federal Court," press release, October 24, 2018.

11 And the top Democrat: *United States v. Robert Menendez and Salomon Melgen,* "Indictment," April 1, 2015.

12 A grateful Menendez: *United States of America v. Robert Menendez,* 15 F.3d 3459 (3d Cir., 2016), https://caselaw.findlaw.com/us-3rd-circuit/1744003

.html; see also *United States v. Robert Menendez and Salomon Melgen,* "Indictment," April 1, 2015.

12 But all this failed to convince: NJTV News Staff, "Judge Declares Mistrial in Menendez Bribery Case," NJTV, November 16, 2017; U.S. District Court, District of New Jersey, case 2:15-cr-00155 WHW, "United States' Motion to Dismiss Superseding Indictment," filed January 31, 2018, https://www.courthousenews.com/wp-content/uploads/2018/01/menendez.pdf; Max Greenwood, "DOJ Files Motion to Dismiss Menendez Indictment," *The Hill,* January 31, 2018.

12 The thought of how Democratic Party leaders: Expressions of disappointment from Democratic Party sympathizers were relegated to the margins. See, for example, Alex Pareene, "Sticking with Menendez Was Stupid, Pointless, and Damaging," *Splinter,* June 8, 2018.

12 With this curt confirmation: It is Shakespeare, from *The Tempest:* "Full fathom five thy father lies / Of his bones are coral made / Those are pearls that were his eyes / Nothing of him that doth fade / But doth suffer a sea change / Into something rich and strange / Sea nymphs hourly ring his knell / Ding dong / Hark now I hear them—ding dong bell."

12 In a 2018 article: Amie Ely, "What *McDonnell v. United States* Means for State Corruption Prosecutors, Part I: *McDonnell,* Its State Progeny, and How to *McDonnell*-Proof Your State Corruption Case," *NAGTRI Journal* 3, no. 2 (May 2018).

13 "*McDonnell* means prosecutors' job": Telephone interview, June 17, 2018.

13 "They've made it so only": Interview, July 31, 2018.

13 According to the U.S. Sentencing Commission: United States Sentencing Commission, "Quick Facts: Bribery Offenses," no date.

13 "An overall change": Telephone interview, June 5, 2018. Perhaps the most extreme example of the *McDonnell* logic was the argument made by Alan Dershowitz when representing President Trump at his impeachment trial in the Senate. A quid pro quo (the essence of bribery) could not be impeachable, Dershowitz maintained, if the official involved believed that the item of value he was receiving in return for the official act he performed would benefit the national interest as well as himself. And, he added, "every public official that I know thinks that his election is in the public interest." (For a synopsis of Dershowitz's argument and the ensuing controversy, see William Cummings, "Trump Lawyer Dershowitz Argues President Can't Be Impeached for an Act He Thinks Will Help His Reelection," *USA Today,* January 30, 2020.) On the legal side, the post-*McDonnell* narrowing of the concept of corruption took another step two weeks before Dershowitz made his assertion. On May 7, 2020, the Supreme Court unanimously overturned convictions in the notorious "Bridgegate" case. In 2013, aides to then–New Jersey governor Chris Christie ordered two of three lanes on the busiest bridge in the world to be shut, causing traffic chaos for four days. The admitted objective was to punish the mayor of the town on the New Jersey end of the bridge for failing to endorse Governor Christie's re-election bid. But a phony traffic study was commis-

sioned to provide public cover. One defendant pleaded guilty; two others were convicted of fraud, conspiracy, and other charges. When one of them appealed, the Third Circuit Court of Appeals upheld her conviction (United States Court of Appeals for the Third Circuit, "Opinion, *U.S. v. William E. Baroni, Jr.,* 17-1817, and *U.S. v. Bridget Anne Kelly,* 17-1818," November 27, 2018). Federal prosecutors argued to the Supreme Court that New Jersey citizens were defrauded of the public moneys used in the operation. The defense argued that if the official's conviction was upheld, that would "allow any federal, state, or local official to be indicted based on nothing more than the (ubiquitous) allegation that she lied in claiming to act in the public interest" (Supreme Court of the United States, Bridget Anne Kelly v. United States, "Petition for a Writ of Certiorari," February 19, 2019). January 14, 2020, oral arguments before the Supreme Court are available at https://www.oyez.org/cases/2019/18-1059. McDonnell, together with U.K. peer Conrad Black, who was convicted in the United States of felony fraud and pardoned by President Donald Trump, submitted an amicus curiae brief in support of Christie aide Kelly. Supreme Court of the United States, *Bridget Anne Kelly v. United States of America,* 18-1059, "Brief for *Amici Curiae* Lord Conrad Black and Former Governor Robert F. McDonnell in Support of Petitioner."

14 "There is no doubt that this case": *McDonnell v. United States,* p. 28.

14 "No word is innocent": Kent Shreve, originator of "precision-based language style" as a weapon in the fight for democracy.

16 exactly the type of systemic corruption: Ashley Kirzinger et al., "Kaiser Health Tracking Poll—Late Summer 2018: The Election, Pre-Existing Conditions, and Surprises on Medical Bills," Kaiser Family Foundation, September 5, 2018. The year 2018 was the first time Kaiser even included corruption on its list of topics, and though it came in first, the word is still not used in the headline announcing the poll results. See also Suffolk University, "Poll: Non-Voters Cite 'Corrupt System' as Reason for Opting Out," press release, April 23, 2018.

I. MONEY
1. Midas

21 When it comes to corruption: I am often asked whether money is not corruptly amassed for the sake of gaining power. While that has certainly been the case in human history, it is this book's contention that today, at this particular juncture, the equation is almost always reversed: power is being amassed for the purpose of maximizing wealth. For wealth, not public office, is the primary marker of social status. For a contrary view, see Zephyr Teachout, *Break 'Em Up: Recovering Our Freedom from Big Ag, Big Tech, and Big Money* (New York: All Points Books, 2020). In a sickening number of cases, the "currency" extorted in corrupt exchanges is not cash but services, in particular sex. This is a critically important component of any wider understanding of corruption.

22 "Money washes hands": Door-to-door interviews, Riverside Drive, St. Marys, West Virginia, August 20, 2018.

22 "Whenever [myth] . . . has been dismissed": Joseph Campbell, *The Mythic Dimension: Selected Essays, 1959–1987* (New York: The Joseph Campbell Foundation and HarperCollins, 1997), p. 27.

23 "If you pray to Olokun": Interview, Benin City, Nigeria, July 19, 2015.

24 "Don't you know?": Interview with Promise Igbinoba and Gladys Osabor, Benin City, Nigeria, July 22, 2015.

24 A complicated god: He is known in Greek as Dionysus, or as Bacchus in Latin. That Latin name may derive from an Anatolian deity, Baki. (See George Hanfmann, *Sardis from Prehistoric to Roman Times* [Cambridge, MA: Harvard University Press, 1983], p. 5.) That etymology would align with the god's association with this particular region of the Greco-Roman world, the setting for this story intertwining inebriation and the lust for wealth.

24 "joyful festival . . . twice": Ovid, *Metamorphoses* 11:85ff. I have used two translations here: Brookes More's flowery one (Boston: Cornhill, 1922) and Rolf Humphries's annotated version (Bloomington: Indiana University Press, 1955) for the final "No food relieves his hunger" quote.

25 According to the great Greek historian: Herodotus has Midas as the first of all the "barbarians known to us" to have dedicated an offering to Delphi. Robert Strassler, ed., *Herodotus: The Histories* (New York: Anchor, 2007), p. 10, I:1:14.

25 He probably died: Susanne Berndt-Ersöz, "The Chronology and Historical Context of Midas," *Historia: Zeitschrift für alte Geschichte* 57, no. 1 (2008): 1–37. In fact, Berndt-Ersöz finds there are likely to have been three or even four Midases—the name was probably a royal one, or even a title. Like a surgeon untangling tendons of a severed hand, Berndt-Ersöz teases apart separate events that have been put down to a single individual.

25 To this day: For a good review of the latest numismatic analyses, see François Velde, "On the Origin of Specie," The Federal Reserve Bank of Chicago, February 2012. Velde emphasizes that the proportion of gold to silver and copper in these early coins varied dramatically, as did, therefore, their intrinsic value. See also David Schaps, *The Invention of Coinage and the Monetization of Ancient Greece,* ch. 7, "The First Coins" (Ann Arbor: University of Michigan Press, 2004), pp. 93–110; Jacques Melitz, "A Model of the Beginnings of Coinage in Antiquity," École Nationale de la Statistique et de l'Administration Économique, 2016. Felix Martin has a thoughtful discussion in *Money: The Unauthorized Biography—From Coinage to Cryptocurrencies,* ch. 3, "The Aegean Invention of Economic Value" (New York: Vintage, 2015), pp. 51–66.

27 But it's close enough: The only classicist I have read who makes the explicit connection is Richard Seaford. See *Money and the Early Greek Mind* (Cambridge, UK: Cambridge University Press, 2004), p. 151.

27 To the east, in Mesopotamia: Ingots may have been stamped to indicate their provenance or purity. Schaps, *The Invention of Coinage,* pp. 90–91.

27 Greece, less developed: Ibid., pp. 83–88. See also John Kroll, "Observations on the Monetary Instruments of Pre-coinage Greece," in Miriam S. Balmuth, ed., *Hacksilber to Coinage: New Insights into the History of the Near East and Greece, Numismatic Studies* 21 (2004): 77–91.

27 "The ancient, regular": Seaford, *Money and the Early Greek Mind,* p. 41.

28 And their symbolic worth: In his brilliant examination of the trickster motif in myth and folktale, *Trickster Makes This World: Mischief, Myth and Art* (New York: Farrar, Straus and Giroux, 1998), pp. 32–33 and 58–59, Lewis Hyde teases out another connection between Greek sacrifice and the birth of the human capacity to create and understand symbols—that is, markers that serve as stand-ins for a meaning, the way money symbolically represents a specific material value. He uses the "Homeric Hymn to Hermes," by the poet Hesiod, who lived in the seventh century BC. In that sacred story, Hermes, a baby immortal spurned by the rest of the gods, stole cattle belonging to his half brother, the shining sun god, Apollo. Hermes slaughtered two of the beasts. After skewering the "richly marbled meat" and roasting it and dividing it up into twelve equal portions, one for each of the gods, he stowed all of the sacrificial meat in the rafters of a barn—"a token" (or symbol) of his theft. Hyde reads this episode as a mythological explanation of the origins of the human capacity for symbolic thought. Perhaps not coincidentally, the end of Hesiod's productive life coincides with the dawn of money, that ultimate symbol.

28 For Seaford: Seaford, *Money and the Early Greek Mind,* p. 45; see also pp. 48–52.

28 "communality and equality": Ibid., p. 107. See also Martin, *Money,* pp. 58–59.

28 The practice reaches far: As I might have expected if I stopped to think about it, given all the cognates from different cultures, preserved in figurative expressions in English: "sharing salt," for example, or "breaking bread" together. For a far-flung example, see Lars Levi Laestadius and Juha Pentikainen, eds., *Fragments of Lappish Mythology* (Beaverton, ON: Aspasia Books, 1997; written around 1840), pp. 148–52, in which Sami reindeer sacrifice is carefully described, including the sharing by all participants in a meal of the meat. Only the organs, bones, and a morsel from each limb were reserved for the god to which the sacrifice was dedicated.

29 "a similar sense of social pressure": Barry Lopez, *Of Wolves and Men* (New York: Scribner, 1978), pp. 89–90.

29 No matter which individual: Christopher Boehm, *Moral Origins: The Evolution of Virtue, Altruism, and Shame* (New York: Basic Books, 2012), pp. 137–40. In *The Dictator's Handbook: Why Bad Behavior Is Almost Always Good Politics* (Philadelphia: Public Affairs, 2011), authors Bruce Buena de Mesquita and Alistair Smith argue that this tactic is typical of modern human oligarchies and plutocracies: a coalition of dominators cements alliances by direct transfer of spoils to allies. Together they dominate the subordinate majority.

30 "Foragers use social control": Christopher Boehm, *Hierarchy in the Forest: The Evolution of Egalitarian Behavior* (Cambridge, MA: Harvard University Press, 1999), p. 67. The brief quotes reproduced here do not do his fascinating argument justice. Punishment can be severe, up to execution. Boehm cites a Paleolithic cave painting of a prone figure with eleven arrows in its back, surrounded by other figures, as possibly depicting an execution. Primatologist Richard Wrangham makes an allied argument, with far more focus on this

ability, thanks to language, to plan and apply violence. Richard Wrangham, *The Goodness Paradox: The Strange Relationship Between Virtue and Violence in Human Evolution* (New York: Pantheon, 2019).

30 Apart from killing someone: Boehm, *Moral Origins,* pp. 137–44; Boehm, *Hierarchy in the Forest,* pp. 191–92, on change of diet and meat-sharing; Boehm, *Moral Origins,* pp. 195–204, for the punishment of bullies who hog more than their share of meat, though the earlier book, *Hierarchy in the Forest,* is probably the clearest exposition. Note that the most prized virtues included the humility to downplay one's exploits and generosity. Boehm also looked at how the punishments were decided on and meted out. Two important points emerge. One is that the band would almost always work to reach consensus before members showed their displeasure with anyone's behavior. The other is that a graduated range of sanctions was used, including ridicule, open criticism, disobeying would-be alpha characters who try to boss people around, ostracism, exclusion from the band, and execution. Boehm, *Hierarchy in the Forest,* pp. 72–84, 112–22. On consensus and the "coalition of subordinates," see pp. 159–62, and Boehm, *Moral Origins,* pp. 49–75, 179–213, 239–67.

30 It remained the pillar: Culturally modern *Homo sapiens* are usually estimated to have emerged approximately 200,000 years ago, and the spread of agriculture, which favored the revival of more apelike hierarchies, around 15,000 years ago. I am conservatively subtracting 20,000 years for that modern period.

30 Indeed it did: Seaford, *Money and the Early Greek Mind,* pp. 9, 90–92, 111, 151. Note that the Old Testament law "An eye for an eye, a tooth for a tooth" represents an analogous evenhanded approach to punishment, unique to the tribes of Israel. The point is that an eye is worth no more or less than an eye, no matter whose it is, nobleman or commoner. Neighboring kingdoms, by contrast, calibrated punishments to the rank of those involved in the crime. In the antebellum United States, assault or murder were crimes if committed against white people but not if the victims were black. Discrepancies in enforcement persist to this day. Another point to make here: hunter-gatherer and many "primitive" tribal societies are in fact democratic. The Greeks hardly invented the idea. Their innovation was to apply a formal, democratic mode of governance to a complex, sedentary society.

31 So completely did it disappear: Muslims had never stopped using money and developed a further sophisticated stand-in that soon made the Templars and Italian bankers rich: letters of credit, or checks. The towering eighth-century Arabic author Abu Uthman Amr Ibn Bahr al-Jahiz wrote a book about it, *Avarice and the Avaricious,* spoofing misers who hoarded money. It was the Crusaders who brought money back to Europe from Islamic countries, sparking the first postclassical stirrings of democracy of the thirteenth century. For an excellent examination of the widespread and significant effects of the use of money and bills of exchange even in the thirteenth century, see Peter Spufford, *Money and Its Use in Medieval Europe* (Cambridge, UK: Cambridge University Press, 1988). See also Martin, *Money,* pp. 84–85, on the disappearance of money along with the Roman Empire; p. 89, on the slow remonetization of

Europe beginning in the thirteenth century; and p. 91, on money framed as a public good, not a sovereign prerogative, around 1360.

31 "For the first time": Jack Weatherford, *Indian Givers: How Native Americans Transformed the World* (New York: Broadway Books, 2010), p. 17.

31 As in ancient Greece: Velde, "The Origin of Specie," p. 5.

31 "The new coins": Weatherford, *Indian Givers,* p. 19. See also his *The History of Money* (New York: Three Rivers, 1997), p. 107.

31 It was during this same: See, for example, Wim Blockmans, *L'Histoire Parlementaire dans les Pays-Bas et la Belgique, XIIème—XVIIème Siècles,* in *Las Cortes de Castilla y Leon, 1188–1988: Actas de la tercera etapa del Congreso Científico sobre la historia de las Cortes de Castilla y Leon, del 26 a 30 de septiembre de 1988* (Valladolid, Spain, 1995), vol. 2, pp. 172–92; Peter Arnade, *Beggars, Iconoclasts, and Civic Patriots: The Political Culture of the Dutch Revolt* (Ithaca, NY: Cornell University Press, 2008), pp. 1, 5–8. Compare the early Italian merchant city-state republics, most notably Venice.

31 Nobles and wealthy merchants: Anonymous, "Political Education" (published 1582), in Martin van Gelderen, ed., *The Dutch Revolt* (Cambridge, UK: Cambridge University Press, 1993), p. 184.

32 They turned an insult: Solange Deyon and Alain Lottin, *Les "Casseurs" de l'Été 1566* (Paris: Hachette, 1981), pp. 24–25.

32 The future United States: Adam Winkler, *We the Corporations: How American Businesses Won Their Civil Rights* (New York: Liveright, 2018), pp. 6–31.

32 But so did the pecuniary interests: Marc Egnal, *A Mighty Empire: The Origins of the American Revolution* (Ithaca, NY: Cornell University Press, 1988; new preface, 2010). The preface to the later edition helpfully reviews scholarly developments since the 1988 publication. See also Robert H. Patton, *Patriot Pirates* (New York: Vintage, 2008), and Phillip Mossman, *Money of the American Colonies and Confederation* (New York: American Numismatic Society, 1999; digital version, 2016), pp. 2–3.

32 Meanwhile, a burgeoning religious ideology: Chris Lehmann, *The Money Cult: Capitalism, Christianity, and the Unmaking of the American Dream* (Brooklyn, NY: Melville House, 2016), pp. 59–60.

32 The colonies, forced to buy: Weatherford, *The History of Money,* p. 132; Mossman, *The Money of the American Colonies,* pp. 4–9, 18–20, 67–77. Mossman is more nuanced on the severity of the shortages than Weatherford, but the effects remain. Benjamin Franklin favored the paper money innovation: "A Modest Enquiry into the Nature and Necessity of a Paper-Currency," Philadelphia, April 3, 1729, Founders Online, National Archives. On the democratizing influence of paper money, see Jeffrey Winters, "Wealth Defense and the Complicity of Liberal Democracy," in Jack Knight and Melissa Schwartzberg, eds., *Wealth* (New York: New York University Press, 2017), pp. 181–82.

32 "Paper Money, Paper Money": Quoted from "Attack on Paper Money Laws" in Eric Foner, ed., *Paine: Collected Writings* (New York: Library Classics, 1955), p. 364. See also Benjamin Franklin, "Of the Paper Money of America," 1780?, Founders Online, National Archives. For the early postindependence

period, see also Gordon Wood, *The Radicalism of the American Revolution* (New York: Vintage, 1993), p. 339.

32 "Americans," sums up historian: Gordon Wood, *The Radicalism of the American Revolution,* p. 325.

32 Commerce and the quest: Ibid., pp. 336, 338.

33 Still, a great paradox: The Greeks were distressed by this paradox. Tyrants, they found, were "the paramount men of money." Seaford, *Money and the Early Greek Mind,* p. 1308. See also Joseph Campbell, *The Hero with a Thousand Faces* (Novato, CA: New World Library, 2008), pp. 11–12.

2. Jesus

34 "And Jesus went up": John 2:13–15. I have used the most recent version to be written down, from the Gospel of John, rather than those in the three earlier Gospels because it is the most vivid and detailed. The translation throughout is from the Revised Standard Version (*The New Oxford Annotated Bible*).

34 Nearly three-quarters: The Pew Research Center, Religious Landscape Survey, "Attendance at religious services," 2014. See also Frank Newport, "Church Leaders and Declining Religious Service Attendance," Gallup, September 7, 2018, which puts the total of those reporting once-a-week and once-a-month attendance at about 50 percent.

36 At length, Macgill: Quotes from a recorded conversation with Revs. Marsha Bell, Caroline Kelly, Martha Macgill, and Laura Underwood, Emmanuel Episcopal Church, Cumberland, Maryland, September 20, 2018.

36 But no other would do: His words made me think of another Greek myth: of Minos, legendary king of Crete. Vying for the throne of that storied kingdom, he begged Poseidon, god of the sea, for some sign to show he was the rightful claimant. Poseidon sent a snow-white bull plunging through the foaming waves to shore. But there was one condition: at his crowning, Minos had to offer the bull in sacrifice back to the god. Once king, Minos could not bring himself to do it. He found a white bull within his own herds and substituted the earthly beast for the god-sent one at the solemn ritual. Poseidon knew the difference. Furious, he caused the king's wife to fall in love with his immortal gift bull. Their unnatural coupling begot a terrible monster, the Minotaur. At length, Poseidon—also known as Earth-shaker—sent a great tremor that threw the vast palace of Minos at Knossos to the ground, and with it the whole Cretan civilization.

37 Some small farmers: The same problem led to an analogous uprising in western Massachusetts after the American Revolution. It was called Shays' Rebellion and is credited with spurring the organization of the Constitutional Convention—in part to curb the wealth-equalizing tendencies of some state administrations. Wealthy creditors who had lent to individuals, and to state governments for the cost of the war, were demanding repayment not in plentiful paper money but in coin. The states in turn raised taxes to meet the obligations. Small farmers, many of them Revolutionary War veterans who had gone unpaid for their military service, saw their land seized to cover their taxes and

other debts and attacked the courts where judgments were pronounced. See, for instance, Jeffrey Winters, "Wealth Defense and the Complicity of Liberal Democracy," in Jack Knight and Melissa Schwartzberg, eds., *Wealth* (New York: New York University Press, 2017), pp. 182–84.

37 For those without, the monetary obligation: Interview, Slanesville, West Virginia, November 7, 2018.

37 "a project of unparalleled size": Lee Levine, *Jerusalem: Portrait of a City in the Second Temple Period, 638 BCE–70 CE* (Philadelphia: Jewish Publication Society, 2002), p. 219.

37 There were rows of towering pillars: Ibid., p. 232.

37 "On entering the Temple": Joachim Jeremias, F. H. Cave, and C. H. Cave, trans., *Jerusalem in the Time of Jesus: An Investigation into Economic and Social Conditions in the Time of Jesus* (Philadelphia: Fortress Press, 1969), p. 23.

38 I thought of the signature gold trim: "Inside Donald and Melania Trump's Manhattan Apartment Mansion," *iDesignArch,* no date; "Trump Tower's 5-Star Bathroom," *The Travel Channel,* no date. For the gold curtains selected when the Trumps redecorated the White House, see Lindsay Matthews, "Every Single Change the Trumps Have Made to the White House," *Marie Claire,* January 18, 2018. In Yanukovych's case, the bathroom fixtures were not plate but solid gold. Vivienne Walt, "Inside Yanukovych's Opulent Private Mansion," *Fortune,* March 8, 2014.

38 "Owners of capital": Jeremias, *Jerusalem in the Time of Jesus,* p. 28.

38 "An important function": Levine, *Jerusalem: Portrait,* p. 236.

38 "In Jerusalem sat the customs officials": Jeremias, *Jerusalem in the Time of Jesus,* pp. 55–56.

38 They had to go through: Levine, *Jerusalem: Portrait,* p. 236.

38 No wonder the priestly aristocracy: Jeremias, *Jerusalem in the Time of Jesus,* p. 98.

39 When he roared: Mark 11:18.

39 It was only after: Mark 11:18; Luke 19:47–48.

39 If that is so: All quotes are from a recorded evening conversation at the Emmanuel Episcopal Church, Cumberland, Maryland, September 20, 2018. I have made slight grammatical edits to the spoken words.

40 What gets defiled: Modern examinations of this topic are plentiful. Among the best are Lewis Hyde, *The Gift: Creativity and the Artist in the Modern World* (New York: Vintage, 1979); Michael Sandel, *What Money Can't Buy: The Moral Limits of Markets* (London: Penguin, 2012); and the work of Philip Tetlock.

40 Spurred perhaps by the twin revolutions: Athenian tragedy, Seaford points out, "was the first genre to be created in the brave new world of the widespread use of coined money." Seaford, *Money and the Early Greek Mind,* p. 147.

41 In recent memory: Much of the following argument is drawn from Seaford, *Money and the Early Greek Mind.*

42 Those values included excellence: The best discussion of these themes is, re-

markably, a novel, by Mary Renault, about the hero Theseus: *The King Must Die* (New York: Vintage, 1988).

42 Money tends to bring: Wendell Berry makes the same point in *Life Is a Miracle* (Berkeley, CA: Counterpoint Press, 2001), pp. 41–42: "There is a kind of egalitarianism which holds that any two things equal in price are equal in value—forest = field = parking lot if the price is right." Hunter-gatherer egalitarianism values each person's distinct contributions. Money-based egalitarianism tends to rub out the distinctions and reduces everyone to his or her monetary value.

42 "Not for nothing, Wealth": Theogenes, *Theognis,* lines 523–24, in Douglas Gerber, ed. and trans., *Greek Elegiac Poetry, from the Seventh to the Fifth Centuries BC* (Cambridge, MA: Harvard University Press, 1999), p. 249.

42 This "universal value," applauded: See *Nicomachean Ethics* 1133b16–18: "Money, then, acting as a measure, makes goods commensurate and equates them; for neither would there have been association if there were not exchange, nor exchange if there were not equality, nor equality if there were not commensurability; Now in truth it is impossible that things differing so much should become commensurate . . . [but] it is [money] that makes all things commensurate, since all things are measured by money." (W. D. Ross translation, available online: http://classics.mit.edu/Aristotle/nicomachaen.html.) In *Wealth,* by Aristophanes, born about 450 BC, Wealth is depicted as an aged, doddering god, wearing smelly rags and blind. Asked how he lost his sight, he accused the chief god, Zeus. "I used to threaten him when I was young that I'd only visit the mortals who were honorable, wise and virtuous. So he went and plucked my eyes out so that I couldn't see who's who." Aristophanes, *Wealth,* trans. George Theodoridis, Bacchicstage website, 2008, line 87. See also below, Chapter 3, "Aristotle," p. 45. For discussion of the parallel effect in early America, see Gordon Wood, *The Radicalism of the American Revolution* (New York: Vintage, 1993), pp. 340–46.

42 "He bent down": Nathaniel Hawthorne, *The Golden Touch Told to the Children* (Boston: Houghton Mifflin, date unknown; first published 1851), p. 21, https://archive.org/details/goldentouchtoldt00hawt/page/n11.

43 "It plunders cities": Sophocles, *Antigone,* trans. Robert Bagg (New York: Harper Perennial, 2004), p. 27 (lines 327–31).

3. Aristotle

44 In *Politics,* the philosopher tries to distinguish: Aristotle, *Politics,* trans. T. Sinclair, rev. T. Saunders (London: Penguin, 1981), p. 79, I:viii 1256b26.

45 And here's the crucial difference: Ibid., I:ix, 1257b24–25.

45 "No one can ever get enough": Aristophanes, *Wealth,* trans. George Theodoridis, Bacchicstage website, 2008, lines 185–98. Solon—or an aphorism attributed to Solon—also warned about this trait: "Of wealth no limit lies revealed to men, since those of us who now have the greatest livelihood show twice as much zeal" to rake in more. Solon, from Stobaeus, *Anthology,* in Douglas Gerber, ed. and trans., *Greek Elegiac Poetry from the Seventh to the*

Fifth Centuries BC (Cambridge, MA: Harvard University Press, 1999), p. 133; see also p. 207. On this whole issue, see Richard Seaford, *Money and the Early Greek Mind* (Cambridge, UK: Cambridge University Press, 2004), pp. 165–69.

45 I met with another group: Quotes from a taped civic conversation I guided about the meaning of money and the "rigged system," hosted in Lexington, Kentucky, by the Livelihoods Knowledge Exchange Network (LiKEN), October 5, 2018.

45 It was titled, in all seriousness: Steve Jones, *No Off Season: The Constant Pursuit of More. A Playbook for Achieving More in Business and Life* (Charleston, SC: ForbesBooks, 2018). Note that Allied Universal, of which Jones is CEO, has settled a number of complaints over a different kind of corruption: a climate of rape and sexual harassment at JFK Airport in New York. See one complaint here: http://www.ecbalaw.com/wp-content/uploads/2018/05/Powell.2017.12 .05-First-Amended-Complaint-dkt-22-00312324x9CCC2.pdf. For an in-depth treatment, listen to "LaDonna," *This American Life,* May 25, 2018.

A striking example of the cultural shift described here at work in one individual is what associates have described as the transformation of former New York City mayor Rudy Giuliani. Although it lagged the bulk of U.S. culture by about two decades, the change was complete. Learning once he left the mayor's office a few months after 9/11 that the fame he had gained during that crisis could garner him as much as $1 million to make a speech, he became transfixed by the objective of making money. See Josh Dawsey et al., "Inside Giuliani's Dual Roles: Power-Broker-for-Hire and Shadow Foreign Policy Adviser," *Washington Post,* December 8, 2019. See also the Netflix series *Dirty Money.*

46 "In my last year": Sam Polk, "For the Love of Money," *New York Times,* January 18, 2014.

46 "Nothing else after all": Theogenes, *Theognis,* lines 699–718, in Douglas Gerber, ed. and trans., *Greek Elegiac Poetry from the Seventh to the Fifth Centuries,* pp. 276–79.

46 "If you're penniless": Interview, January 15, 2018, quote taken from my notes.

47 A village elder: These reflections are drawn from a series of interviews in the Nigerian capital, Abuja, the northern city of Kano, and villages in Edo state, around Benin City and Igarra, November 10–29, 2014. I launched the conversations with two questions: (1) What are the qualities of a good person? (2) Has the meaning of money changed in your lifetime? Quotes taken from my notes. It was hard to choose from among the profusion of very similar, often poetic answers.

47 When I asked: Interviews, Oslo, June 7, 2018; quote taken from my notes.

48 After the Reformation: See Simon Schama, *The Embarrassment of Riches: An Interpretation of Dutch Culture in the Golden Age* (New York: Knopf, 1987).

48 That idea, that God signaled: See Chris Lehmann, *The Money Cult: Capitalism, Christianity, and the Unmaking of the American Dream* (Brooklyn, NY: Melville House, 2016).

48 "When I was growing up in the forties": Lexington, Kentucky, conversation hosted by LiKEN, October 5, 2018.

49 The 1983 youth flick *Risky Business:* I owe much of this analysis to Kent Shreeve, who has written an unpublished monograph highlighting it as marking the moment when culture pivoted, and examining the subliminal messages the movie conveys via a freeze-frame analysis.

50 For a whole generation: The trend in American literature was similar. In "Fictions of Acquisition," Josephine Hendin describes the "youthcult fiction" of the 1980s as one in which "character is entirely the product of acts of appropriation indistinguishable from buying," including the "serial purchase" of drugs and prostitutes. In Nicolaus Mills, ed., *Culture in an Age of Money: The Legacy of the 1980s in America* (Chicago: Ivan R. Dee, 1990), pp. 216–33.

50 The graduating class: Bob Greene, "A $100 Million Idea: Use Greed for Good," *Chicago Tribune,* December 15, 1986.

50 Between 1977 and 1987: Robert Reich, "A Culture of Paper Tigers," in Mills, ed., *Culture in an Age of Money,* p. 97.

51 Starting in those same years: In their book *13 Bankers*—one of the best accounts I've read of the 2008 Great Recession—economists Simon Johnson and James Kwak showed just how disproportionate the rewards have been to the sector. On page 115 is an unforgettable graph, displaying the average profits of banks compared to the private sector as a whole. From 1948 until about 1982, you can hardly pick the lines apart without a magnifying glass. Then, around 1982—just when my classmates were about to graduate and get their first jobs—the banks' line takes off: suddenly it is Everest, climbing from peak to peak. The line for the rest of business seems to plod across a plain.

51 They tell us if: Sister Simone Campbell, the spokeswoman for the Nuns on the Bus, told interviewer Krista Tippett she asked a CEO if he couldn't get by on $10 million. "It's not about the money," she said he replied. "We're very competitive, and we want to win. Money just happens to be the current measure of winning." *On Being with Krista Tippett,* "Simone Campbell: How to Be Spiritually Bold," June 11, 2015.

53 Participants who had seen: Kathleen Vohs et al., "The Psychological Consequences of Money," *Science* 314 (November 17, 2006): 1154–56; Kathleen Vohs et al., "Merely Activating the Concept of Money Changes Personal and Interpersonal Behavior," *Current Directions in Psychological Science* 17, no. 3 (2008): 208–12; Xinyue Zhou et al., "The Symbolic Power of Money," *Psychological Science* 20, no. 6 (2009): 700–706. Money has the same tendency to isolate the rich, making them unable to trust almost anyone. See Brooke Harrington, *Capital Without Borders: Wealth Managers and the One Percent* (Cambridge, MA: Harvard University Press, 2016).

54 Multiple experiments: See, for instance, Daniel Kahneman and Angus Deaton, "High Income Improves Evaluation of Life but Not Emotional Well-being," *Proceedings of the National Academy of Sciences* 107, no. 38 (September 21, 2010): 16489–93; Andrew Jebb et al., "Happiness, Income Satiation, and Turning Points Around the World," *Nature Human Behaviour* 2 (2018): 32–38; Lora Park et al., "It's All About the Money (For Some): Consequences of Financially

Contingent Self-Worth," *Personality and Social Psychology Bulletin* 43, no. 5 (February 2017): 601–22.

54 Economic growth has become: In unforgettable words at the United Nations Climate Summit on September 23, 2019, teenaged environmental activist Greta Thunberg took aim at this conceit: "We are at the beginning of a mass extinction, and all you can talk about is money and fairytales of eternal economic growth. How *dare* you?"

II. CRAZY MONEY
1. Europe

60 "was just the same as presenting him": Mark Twain and Charles Warner, *The Gilded Age: A Tale of Today* (New York: The Modern Library, 2006), Ch. XXXIII: Society in Washington—The Antiques, The Parvenus, and the Middle Aristocracy, p. 244.

60 The modern job was initially budgeted: Dan Barry, "Courthouse That Tweed Built Seeks to Shed Notorious Past," *New York Times,* December 12, 2000.

60 And in 1984, O'Riley's descendant: See Part III, "The Hydra," Chapter 3, "Powers Wielded: The Purse," pp. 134–45.

60 "So honored" were those authors: See Part III, "The Hydra," Chapter 6, "Bowing to the Money Changers," pp. 159–72.

61 A dozen years later: Yalman Onaran and Sonali Basak, "Key 2008 Financial Crisis Players Are Back for Coronavirus," Bloomberg, April 3, 2020; "Representative Richard Neal on Coronavirus Response," Getting to the Point, April 13, 2020.

61 Flush with cash, Twain's O'Riley: Twain and Warner, *The Gilded Age,* p. 244.

61 Those names are usually: See "Towers of Secrecy," the *New York Times*'s excellent 2015 investigation. In part 1, "Stream of Foreign Wealth Flows to Elite New York Real Estate," February 7, Louise Story and Stephanie Saul write, "Many Time Warner buyers have taken even greater steps, beyond using LLCs, to keep their names out of sight." "On many deeds, the line for the buyer's signature is blank, is illegible, or is signed by a lawyer or other representative. Phone numbers are registered under lawyers' names; the owner's line on renovation permits is signed by Time Warner staff members; tax statements are addressed to the LLCs." See also Transparency International U.K., "Corruption on Your Doorstep: How Corrupt Capital Is Used to Buy Property in the U.K.," March 2015.

61 Another former New York mayor: Michael Howard Saul, "Bloomberg Wants Every Billionaire on Earth to Live in New York City," *Wall Street Journal,* September 20, 2013.

62 They used their official positions: See, for instance, Charles Kindleberger, *Historical Economics: Art or Science?* (Berkeley: University of California Press, 1990), pp. 310–23. See also Special Correspondent, "Vienna's Fair," *New York Times,* May 24, 1873.

62 "So many and doubtful": "The Vienna Panic," *New York Times,* June 12, 1873, p. 4. On the previous page of that day's paper is an advertisement for investment bonds for the Northern Pacific Railroad, posted by Jay Cooke & Co. Three months and four days later, the Vienna Panic of the editorial would bring both those ventures down.

62 "The panic," reported: "Vienna's Fair," *New York Times,* May 24, 1873. See also "Excitement on the Vienna Bourse—The Exhibition—The Archduke Charles Disgusted," May 10, 1873.

62 Just a year before, Americans: "The King of Frauds: How the Crédit Mobilier Bought Its Way Through Congress," *New York Sun,* September 4, 1872, https://chroniclingamerica.loc.gov.

62 had created a shell company: To perform the work on the ground in Nebraska and Utah Territory, Union Pacific had contracted the Crédit Mobilier of America, an "independent" construction company. But the boards of directors of the two corporations were one and the same. The only purpose of Crédit Mobilier was to submit bills to Union Pacific, which paid them and then displayed its perfectly auditable receipts to Congress as justification for ongoing appropriations. The conspirators vastly inflated the bills they were charging themselves and pocketed the difference between the bloated reimbursements and the actual outlays. To further dissuade Congress from reviewing the land grants and loan guarantees it had accorded the Union Pacific, or from investigating its operations or from taking up regulation of the railroads in the public interest, Massachusetts representative Oaks ("Hoax") Ames had sold company stock at a markdown to his colleagues on both sides of the aisle. This basic methodology was common to several of the Pacific railroad companies. Richard White, "Information, Markets, and Corruption: Transcontinental Railroads in the Gilded Age," *Journal of American History* 90, no. 1 (June 2003): 19–43, esp. p. 37.

63 Railroad companies still racing: See, for instance, Scott Reynolds Nelson, *A Nation of Deadbeats: An Uncommon History of America's Financial Disasters* (New York: Knopf, 2012), pp. 165–66, and for the Panic of 1873 and resulting depression in general, pp. 161–79; "The Real Great Depression: The Depression of 1929 Is the Wrong Model for the Current Economic Crisis," *Chronicle Review,* October 17, 2008, https://www3.nd.edu/~druccio/documents/TheRealGreatDepression-ChronicleReview.pdf.

63 "For a moment": Elisha Benjamin Andrews, *The United States in Our Own Times: A History from Reconstruction to Expansion* (New York: Scribner, 1895), p. 257, and pp. 95ff. for the Union Pacific/Crédit Mobilier scandal. See also "The Panic: Excitement in Wall St.—Suspension of Jay Cooke & Co.," *New York Times,* September 19, 1873; "More Failures Yesterday: The Scene in Wall Street—List of Suspensions—the Government to Buy $10,000,000 of Bonds Today," *New York Times,* September 20, 1873.

63 It was a time of pitched battles: See, for instance, "Business in the Country: Virginia—Distressing Effects of the Panic on Industry," *New York Times,*

November 5, 1873; Robert Justin Goldstein, *Political Repression in Modern America, from 1870 to the Present* (Cambridge, MA: Schenkman, 1978), pp. 27–34. "Defeat of the Communists" headlined the conservative *New York Times* about a huge rally in the city: "The Mass Meeting and Parade Broken Up—Encounter Between the Mob and Police—Arrest of Rioters . . . ," January 14, 1874. On the first opioid epidemic, see Andrew Sullivan, "The Poison We Pick," *New York,* February 2018.

64 "epidemic desire to become": Max Wirth, *Geschichte der Handelskrisen,* 1874 (rev. ed. 1890), quoted in Kindleberger, *Historical Economics,* p. 315.

64 "A whole aristocracy": Quoted in Janine Verdes, "La Presse devant le krach d'une banque catholique: l'Union Générale," *Archives de sociologie des religions* 19 (1965): 137.

65 In one, an impoverished noblewoman: Émile Zola, *L'Argent,* ed. Henri Mitterand (Paris: Éditions Gallimard, 1972), pp. 175–79.

65 "What's the use of slaving": Ibid., p. 151. For history and analysis of the Union Générale scandal, see Jean Bouvier, *Le Krach de l'Union Générale* (Paris: Presses Universitaires de France, 1960). See also Frederick Brown, *For the Soul of France: Culture Wars in the Age of Dreyfus* (New York: Anchor, 2011), pp. 59–80.

65 "had sold himself": Zola, *L'Argent,* p. 289.

65 But a canal without locks: See Bernard Meunier, *L'Homme oublié du canal de Panama: Adolphe Godin de Lépinay* (Paris: CNRS Éditions, 2018).

65 "The Panama Canal Company": Brown, *For the Soul of France,* p. 162. For a complete account of this debacle, see pp. 155–74. See also Pierre-Cyrille Hautcoeur, ed., *Le Marché Financier Français au XIXᵉ Siècle,* chs. 10–12 (Paris: Publications de la Sorbonne, 2007), pp. 357–437.

66 It was the spellbinding biography: Hilary Spurling, *La Grande Thérèse, l'escroquerie du siècle* (Paris: Éditions Allia, 2003), is the version I read, a translation into French. The English original is *La Grande Thérèse: The Greatest Swindle of the Century* (London: Profile Books, 1999).

67 The magazine finally concluded: Dan Alexander, "The Case of Wilbur Ross' Phantom $2 Billion," *Forbes,* December 12, 2017.

68 The real number: Bob Garfield, "Trump's Financial House of Cards," *On the Media,* May 10, 2019. See also *CBS This Morning,* "In lawsuit deposition, Trump repeatedly called out for exaggerating wealth," May 23, 2016. According to his former lawyer-fixer Michael Cohen, Trump also inflated his net worth in filings to insurance companies and a bid to secure a loan to buy the Buffalo Bills. Such mischaracterizations in such contexts, if proven, would amount to criminal fraud. "Testimony of Michael D. Cohen, Committee on Oversight and Government Reform, U.S. House of Representatives," p. 11, and for questions by members of the committee, Jerry Zremski, "Trump Inflated Net Worth by $4 Billion in Bid to Buy Bills," *Buffalo News,* February 27, 2019.

68 While a handful of perpetrators: U.S. authorities were similarly lax. Despite the eruption of outrage that the Union Pacific scandal unleashed, for example, the congressional and criminal investigations yielded nothing more than censures

for two U.S. representatives and Colfax's removal from the vice presidential slot on President Ulysses Grant's re-election ticket.

68 In the same way that millions: Verdes, "La Presse devant le krach," p. 137.

69 It had stakes in: Ibid., p. 130; Rondo Cameron and V. I. Bovykin, eds., *International Banking, 1870–1914* (Oxford, UK: Oxford University Press, 1991), pp. 74ff.; United States Department of Justice, "Deutsche Bank Agrees to Pay $7.2 Billion for Misleading Investors in Its Sale of Residential Mortgage-Backed Securities: Deutsche Bank's Conduct Contributed to the 2008 Financial Crisis," press release, January 17, 2017; "Donald Trump Sues Deutsche Bank and Capital One: A Once Chummy Relationship Goes Sour," *The Economist,* May 2, 2019. Like Goldman Sachs, Deutsche Bank is a multi-recidivist. See David Enrich, "The Money Behind Trump's Money," *New York Times Magazine,* February 4, 2020.

69 Junius Morgan and his son: See, for instance, Nomi Prins, *All the Presidents' Bankers: The Hidden Alliances That Drive American Power* (New York: Nation Books, 2014), pp. 4–5, 42; Ron Chernow, *The House of Morgan* (New York: Grove Press, 1990), pp. 10ff., 21–28.

69 Once the money was moved: Sarah Chayes, "When Corruption Is the Operating System: The Case of Honduras," Carnegie Endowment for International Peace, May 30, 2017, pp. 21–22, 35–37. A related issue is concern over secrecy provisions in cities' deals to attract major businesses such as Amazon. See, for instance, Martin Austermuhle, "Public Money Private Records: Parts of the Amazon Deal Concern Critics," WAMU, November 14, 2018. Members of Transparency International Finland confided similar worries to me about public infrastructure projects in Helsinki in 2016; see Martijn van den Hurk et al., "National Varieties of Public-Private Partnerships (PPPs)," *Journal of Comparative Policy Analysis: Research and Practice* 18, no. 1 (2016): 1–20.

69 They are not designed: See James Robinson and Ragnar Torvik, "White Elephants," *Journal of Public Economics* 89, nos. 2–3 (February 2005).

69 "Utilities tried to build": Tony Bartelme, "Power Failure: How Utilities Across the U.S. Changed the Rules to Make Big Bets with Your Money," *Post and Courier,* December 10, 2017.

70 When l'Union Générale bank: Gabriel Terrail, pseudonym Mermeix, *Les Antisémites en France: Notice sur un fait contemporain* (Paris: E. Dentu, 1892), p. 27.

70 "In the disaster that cost": Quoted in Brown, *For the Soul of France,* p. 171.

2. The United States

71 For example, Jim Fisk: Edward Renehan, *Dark Genius of Wall Street: The Misunderstood Life of Jay Gould, King of Robber Barons* (New York: Basic Books, 2005), p. 107.

71 One of John Pierpont: H. W. Brands, *American Colossus: The Triumph of Capitalism, 1865–1900* (New York: Anchor, 2011), pp. 3–4; John Frank, "Recapturing War Profits—A Civil War Experience," *Wisconsin Law Review* (March 1947): 216–17; United States War Department, "Report of the Commission

on Ordnance and Ordnance Stores," July 17, 1862 (Washington, DC: U.S. Government Printing Office, 1862), pp. 465ff.

72 And in their frightened grip: "Modern Tactics," in John Thompson, ed., *The Southern Literary Messenger* 26–27 (January–June 1858): 11.

72 "those that grow": Quoted in Christopher Munden, "Jay Cooke: Banks, Railroads, and the Panic of 1873," *Pennsylvania Legacies* 11, no. 1 (May 2011): 5. See also Christopher Faille, "Jay Cooke, Salmon Chase, and the Booming Civil War Bond Market," *Forbes,* May 19, 2011.

73 In particular, Cooke hawked: Richard White, "Information, Markets, and Corruption: Transcontinental Railroads in the Gilded Age," *Journal of American History* 90, no. 1 (2003): 26–27. See also Matthew Josephson, *Robber Barons* (San Diego: Harcourt, 1934; 1962 paperback cited), pp. 53–58.

74 Indeed, they were far more dangerous: White, "Information, Markets, and Corruption," p. 38; Gaye LeBaron, "Widow's Santa Rosa Trial Revealed Much About Money, Politics," *Press Democrat,* August 12, 2012.

75 He wished, he said, to draw: Abraham Lincoln, "First Annual Message," December 3, 1861.

75 Then these moguls unleashed: See, for instance, Josephson, *Robber Barons,* p. 338.

76 Once, police officers were ambushed: See Sarah Chayes, *The Punishment of Virtue: Inside Afghanistan After the Taliban* (New York: Penguin Press, 2006).

76 But, as former steamboat man: Josephson, *Robber Barons,* pp. 121–48, 208–9, also pp. 424–42 for later episodes with J. P. Morgan, John D. Rockefeller, et al.; Brands, *American Colossus,* pp. 25–29, 35–42.

77 It was a somewhat later: "The Phoebus Cartel," *Throughline* podcast, National Public Radio, March 28, 2019.

77 Before long came: Josephson, *Robber Barons,* p. 258. See also pp. 112, 162, 280–89, 381–403, 424–32. Brands, *American Colossus,* pp. 598–603.

78 Woodrow Wilson was: Nomi Prins, *All the Presidents' Bankers: The Hidden Alliances That Drive American Power* (New York: Nation Books, 2014), pp. 14–15, 40–43.

78 "The masters of business": Josephson, *Robber Barons*, p. 347. See also, for example, Brands, *American Colossus,* p. 521, on Grover Cleveland's attorney general, Richard Olney, who maintained his private practice representing railroads while in office.

78 "They do it via coalitions": Telephone interview, October 30, 2018. See also Richard Wrangham, *The Goodness Paradox: The Strange Relationship Between Virtue and Violence in Human Evolution* (New York: Pantheon, 2019). His focus differs from Boehm's, stressing violence instead of hierarchy.

79 "the army of the Nation": *In re Debs,* 158 U.S. 564 (1895), https://supreme.justia.com/cases/federal/us/158/564/.

79 "conspiracies to control": *United States v. E. C. Knight Co.,* 156 U.S. 1 (1895). An earlier case, *Wabash v. Illinois,* 118 U.S. 557 (1886), which made it impossible for states to regulate railroads under the Commerce Clause of the Constitution, prompted passage of the Interstate Commerce Act.

79 "Gatling gun on paper": Quoted in Jeremey Brecher, *Strike!* (San Francisco: Straight Arrow Books, 1972), p. 85.

79 Thanks largely to: Adam Winkler, *We the Corporations: How American Businesses Won Their Civil Rights* (New York: Liveright, 2018), pp. 113–58.

80 "The offices of our great corporations": Charles Francis Adams, Jr., and Henry Adams, *Chapters of Erie* (New York: Henry Holt, 1886), p. 95.

80 "The acquisition of wealth": Ibid. For the empty, dissatisfied lives of the Gilded Age barons, see Josephson, *Robber Barons,* pp. 335–38; on collecting art they did not understand or care for, including Pierpont Morgan wondering who Vermeer was, see pp. 341–45. For today's version, see Kenny Schachter, "Where in the World Is 'Salvator Mundi,'" *Artnet News,* June 10, 2019. It reports that a painting of Christ attributed to Leonardo or his studio that sold for more than $400 million in 2017 hangs aboard the yacht of Mohammed bin Salman, who rules over one of the most conservative Muslim countries on earth. Kim Kavin wrote about the annoyance of protecting such masterpieces from sun and wind and salt for Virgin Island Sailing; Kim Kavin, "Protecting a Yacht's Artwork," Virgin Island Sailing website.

80 Their obsession was stoked: Adams and Adams, *Chapters of Erie,* p. 95.

81 And still, writes historian Matthew Josephson: Josephson, *Robber Barons,* p. 315.

3. The Late-Born Baron

82 At his birth, his father: Laurence Leamer, *The Kennedy Men: 1901–1963* (New York: William Morrow, 2001), pp. 4–5.

82 While the Boston Machine: Doris Kearns Goodwin, *The Fitzgeralds and the Kennedys: An American Saga* (New York: Simon and Schuster, 1987), pp. 117–20, 133–42, 147–58; Seymour Hersh, *The Dark Side of Camelot* (New York: Little, Brown, 1997), pp. 35–43.

83 Standing in for her austere mother: David Nasaw, *The Patriarch: The Remarkable Life and Turbulent Times of Joseph P. Kennedy* (New York: Penguin Press, 2012), p. 28.

83 The razor-thin election: Hersh, *The Dark Side of Camelot,* pp. 36–38; "Contested-Election Case: *Peter F. Tague v. John F. Fitzgerald,* from the Tenth Congressional District of Massachusetts," Government Printing Office, 1919, https://archive.org/details/contestedelectio00tagu/page/n3. Note that it seems from the proceedings that Tague engaged in similar practices.

83 At twenty-five, Kennedy boasted: "The Man: Joseph P. Kennedy," *Fortune,* September 1937.

84 "The turn of the century": Goodwin, *Fitzgeralds and Kennedys,* p. 235.

84 That reality survived: Demonstrating the bipartisan nature of the financiers' network, two of the bankers singled out in the report, Jacob Schiff and Paul Warburg, supported Woodrow Wilson in the 1912 election, despite his outwardly anti–money trust campaign. Nomi Prins, *All the Presidents' Bankers: The Hidden Alliances That Drive American Power* (New York: Nation Books, 2014), p. 28.

84 At twenty-five, Kennedy staved off: Goodwin, *Fitzgeralds and Kennedys,* pp. 253–55; Richard Whalen, *Founding Father: The Story of Joseph P. Kennedy* (New York: New American Library, 1964), p. 42, which quotes a former *Boston Post* editor saying the paper covered Kennedy "almost the way we covered City Hospital and the courts"; also "Joe Kennedy: Power Plays and Speculation," *Fortune,* January 1963.

84 Still, the title of bank president: Nasaw, *The Patriarch,* p. 32.

84 He aggressively pursued: Trawling for such information was one of the reasons big bankers joined or put their people on the boards of directors of large corporations whose stocks they were trading, a feature of the "money trust."

84 He tried to divine: Goodwin, *Fitzgeralds and Kennedys,* pp. 296–300, 322–48, 369–80; Nasaw, *Patriarch,* pp. 65–104; Whalen, *Founding Father,* pp. 52–70, 75–99.

85 "I know of nothing fundamentally wrong": Quoted in Whalen, *Founding Father,* p. 103. See also James Arnold, "Wall Street Crash: The Perils of Punditry," *BBC News Online,* October 27, 2004.

85 But Kennedy broke: Whalen, *Founding Father,* pp. 100–105; Goodwin, *Fitzgeralds and Kennedys,* p. 420.

85 He methodically decided: Whalen, *Founding Father,* pp. 106–9; Goodwin, *Fitzgeralds and Kennedys,* p. 420; Leamer, *The Kennedy Men,* p. 69.

86 It is highly doubtful: President Donald Trump's grandfather Friedrich Trump, for example, did, choosing crime as his principal business model. The family fortune has its roots in the bar and brothel Friedrich established in the Canadian northwest in the last years of the nineteenth century, during the Klondike Gold Rush. Natalie Obiko Pearson, "Trump's Family Fortune Originated in a Canadian Gold-Rush Brothel," Bloomberg, October 26, 2016. See also McKay Coppins, "The Heir," *The Atlantic,* October 2019; Andrea Bernstein, *American Oligarchs: The Kushners, the Trumps, and the Marriage of Money and Power* (New York: W. W. Norton, 2020).

86 Marshaling votes: Hersh, *The Dark Side of Camelot,* pp. 35–38, 53–54, 102–20. See also Leamer, *The Kennedy Men,* pp. 38–39. Daniel Okrent's exhaustively researched *Last Call: The Rise and Fall of Prohibition* (New York: Scribner, 2010), pp. 368–71, refutes the bootlegging allegations. Tina Sinatra confirmed to *60 Minutes* that her father was the go-between passing Joe Kennedy's electioneering request to Sam Giancana. "Tina Sinatra: Mob Ties Aided JFK," CBS News, October 5, 2000.

86 "If an Irishman": Whalen, *Founding Father,* p. 44.

87 "With all his growing success": Summering in a Protestant enclave on Boston's South Shore, on that occasion, his application for membership at the Cohasset Golf Club was denied. Goodwin, *Fitzgeralds and Kennedys,* p. 325.

87 After World War II: Whalen, *Founding Father,* pp. 391, 202. In the 1930s, Kennedy had called for the equivalent of peerages or other marks of social distinction to be bestowed on public officials.

88 Stung by the silence that emanated: Goodwin, *Fitzgeralds and Kennedys,* pp. 436–38. On Kennedy sensing the shift in society's respect from big busi-

ness to government, see pp. 427–28: "In the next generation," she quotes him telling a friend, "the people who run the government will be the biggest people in America." Nasaw, *Patriarch,* pp. 185–91; Whalen, *Founding Father,* pp. 130–31.

88 He appointed one of the affected: Jeremey Brecher, *Strike!* (San Francisco: Straight Arrow Books, 1972), pp. 84ff.; Scott Reynolds Nelson, *A Nation of Deadbeats: An Uncommon History of America's Financial Disasters* (New York: Knopf, 2012), p. 193.

88 It was Olney who promoted: Robert Justin Goldstein, *Political Repression in Modern America, from 1870 to the Present* (Cambridge, MA: Schenkman, 1978), pp. 54–55; Jerry Cooper, *The Army and Civil Disorder: Federal Military Intervention in Labor Disputes, 1877–1900* (Westport, CT: Greenwood, 1980), pp. 102–4.

88 He cultivated: Goodwin, *Fitzgeralds and Kennedys,* pp. 441–44; Hersh, *Camelot,* pp. 46–47, 62, 65; Leamer, *The Kennedy Men,* p. 72; Whalen, *Founding Father,* pp. 135–36.

89 To the consternation: Goodwin, *Fitzgeralds and Kennedys,* pp. 446–50; Nasaw, *Patriarch,* pp. 206–13; Whalen, *Founding Father,* pp. 138–41.

89 And yet, far from protecting: Goodwin, *Fitzgeralds and Kennedys,* pp. 447–55; Whalen, *Founding Father,* pp. 141, 150–54.

90 Kennedy also recoiled: Goodwin, *Fitzgeralds and Kennedys,* p. 551; Whalen, *Founding Father,* p. 234.

90 Even "Nazism": Goodwin, *Fitzgeralds and Kennedys,* p. 551; see also Hersh, *Camelot,* pp. 69–70, which recounts Kennedy's leaking information about a plot to kill Hitler to the U.S. press, because, according to U.K. Foreign Office files, he feared the death of Hitler would leave Europe open to Soviet communism.

90 In the spring of 1939: Hersh, *Camelot,* pp. 63–65, 68; Leamer, *The Kennedy Men,* pp. 114–17; Nasaw, *Patriarch,* pp. 200–203. For the long pro-Nazi letter his son Joe Jr. sent him, and his approval, see Goodwin, *Fitzgeralds and Kennedys,* p. 572.

90 Before long, Kennedy was backstabbing: Nasaw, *Patriarch,* pp. 187–89.

91 When Churchill became prime minister: see Goodwin, *Fitzgeralds and Kennedys,* p. 598.

III. THE HYDRA
1. "Eight Mortal Heads"

95 In the swamps of Lerna: Quotations from the authors Pseudo-Apollodorus, Quintus Smyrnaeus, Ovid, and Ptolemy Hephaestion. The best easily accessible anthology of the ancient sources on the Hydra is at the Theoi Project's Hydra Lernaia page.

96 "There is no terrorist organization": Hydra, Marvel website.

97 Using techniques: John Padgett and Christopher Ansell, "Robust Action and the Rise of the Medicis, 1400–1434," *American Journal of Sociology* 98, no. 6 (May 1993): 1259–1319.

98 For the United States: Jane Mayer, *Dark Money: The Hidden History of the Billionaires Behind the Rise of the Radical Right* (New York: Doubleday, 2016), pp. 16–24, 469–70, gives a good snapshot of core members of the Koch network as of 2010. See also the UnKoch My Campus website for Koch donations to universities. Nancy MacLean, in *Democracy in Chains* (New York: Viking, 2017), narrates the development of the network's ideology and its aim of permanently returning the United States to the legal framework of the Gilded Age, ultimately by revising the Constitution. For early views, see Kevin Bogardus, "Koch's Low Profile Belies Political Power," Center for Public Integrity, July 15, 2004, updated 2014; Patrick Young et al., "Koch Industries, Inc., Strategic Corporate Research Report," Cornell University School of Labor and Industrial Relations, June 2006.

99 The result, boasts an operative: Mayer, *Dark Money,* p. 6.

99 "common cause": Telephone interview, August 4, 2018.

99 MacLean puts it this way: Telephone interview, December 29, 2018. See also a startling biography of Justice Clarence Thomas by Corey Robin, *The Enigma of Clarence Thomas* (New York: Metropolitan Books, 2019), which suggests a strange intersection with this Koch philosophy. Just as the Kochs believe democracy can't work for the superrich, because the bulk of the population does not share their objectives, Thomas, according to this reading, believes democracy can never work for African Americans, because the bulk of the population is too racist. The solution, in both views, is wealth-maximization in order to impose the minority's will.

99 The aim, writes MacLean: MacLean, *Democracy in Chains,* p. xxxii.

99 "They want to imbue kids": My source's perceptions are corroborated by such outside reporting as Christina Wilkie and Joy Resmovits, "Koch High: How the Koch Brothers Are Buying Their Way into the Minds of Public School Students," *HuffPost,* December 6, 2017; Hank Stephenson, "Controversial Course with Links to Koch Network Won't Be Offered in TUSD Schools This Year," *Arizona Daily Star,* July 11, 2018.

99 But thirty-three states have applied: Robert Natelson, "Counting to Two Thirds: How Close Are We to a Convention for Proposing Amendments to the Constitution?" *Federalist Society Review* 19 (May 9, 2018): 50–60. See also Jamiles Lartey, "Conservatives Call for Constitutional Intervention Last Seen 230 Years Ago," *The Guardian,* August 11, 2018.

100 Thanks to the work: See, for example, the UnKoch My Campus website and kochdocs.org, as well as two more recent books: Daniel Schulman, *Sons of Wichita: How the Koch Brothers Became America's Most Powerful and Private Dynasty* (New York: Grand Central, 2015), and Christopher Leonard, *Kochland: The Secret History of Koch Industries and Corporate Power in America* (New York: Simon and Schuster, 2019). Note that Charles Koch's brother David died in 2019. They operated in tandem for decades, but Charles was the dominant partner. For simplicity's sake I am referring to him.

100 Interweaving with it: The 2016 work by economist Thomas Ferguson and colleagues highlights the importance of this apparently more mainstream strand

in the network. Findings indicate "that the largest American corporations supported Tea Party . . . candidates and organizations . . . at much higher rates than . . . exceptionally ideological individual entrepreneurs." The authors add, "If the center is not holding in American society—and it rather plainly is not—America's largest companies are as implicated as anyone else; indeed, perhaps more so." A way to understand this phenomenon is that Chamber leadership companies provided much of the money, while Koch-led entities provided the ideology and strategy. See Thomas Ferguson, Paul Jorgensen, and Jie Chen, "How Money Drives US Congressional Elections," Institute for New Economic Thinking, working paper no. 48, August 1, 2016, pp. 22–25.

100 The personal relationships: When I ran this network construct past Ferguson for comment, he responded, "That's just close enough to right to be misleading." The bulk of Ferguson's work in economics emphasizes what he calls "investor blocs." Still, the corporations he highlights are few and big enough that their top officers represent a fairly interconnected group. He is now also calling for a network analysis of the Koch empire. See also G. Willian Domhoff, *Who Rules America: The Triumph of the Corporate Rich* (New York: McGraw-Hill, 2014). Domhoff uses the language of class to describe this phenomenon. Stefania Vitali, James Glattfelder, and Stefano Battiston, "The Network of Global Corporate Control," *PLOS ONE* 6, no. 10 (October 26, 2011): 1–6, crunches global megadata to identify a core of 147 companies that control nearly two-fifths of the combined revenue of some 43,000 multinational corporations. This core, they found, is densely interconnected: "¾ of the ownership of firms in the core remains in the hands of firms in the core itself. . . . This means that network control is much more unequally distributed than wealth"—on the order of ten times more unequally, the authors find.

100 On the advisory board: Albright Stonebridge Group, About Us: Thomas Donohue; Sheryl Gay Stolberg, "Pugnacious Builder of the Business Lobby," *New York Times,* June 1, 2013.

100 Elliott is known for buying up: See, for instance, Sheelah Kolhatkar, "Paul Singer, Doomsday Investor," *New Yorker,* August 20, 2018.

101 APR promotes itself: See, for instance, International Mining, "Mobile Turnkey Power Offers Flexibility in Face of African Hydropower Problems," February 12, 2016; on who profits from mineral extraction in Africa, see Tom Burgis, *The Looting Machine: Warlords, Oligarchs, Corporations, Smugglers, and the Theft of Africa's Wealth* (New York: Public Affairs, 2016).

101 The list includes trading violations: U.S. Department of Justice, Office of Public Affairs, "Goldman Sachs Agrees to Pay More Than $5 Billion in Connection with Its Sale of Residential Mortgage Backed Securities," press release, April 11, 2016. See also Good Jobs First, Violations Tracker Parent Company Summary: Goldman Sachs. JPMorgan Chase has a similar record of repeat offenses. See Pam Martens and Russ Martens, "JPMorgan Chase Is Under Fourth Criminal Probe After Pleading Guilty to Three Prior Felony Counts," *Wall Street on Parade,* February 6, 2020.

101 Yet Mnuchin was proud: United States Senate, Finance Committee, "Treasury

Secretary Designee Steven Mnuchin Confirmation Hearing Statement," January 19, 2017.

102 More recently, Goldman: See Alexander Cockburn, "The Malaysian Job," *Harper's Magazine,* May 2020.

102 On a historical network map: Nomi Prins, *All the Presidents' Bankers: The Hidden Alliances That Drive American Power* (New York: Nation Books, 2014), pp. 117–18, 202–3, 322, 366, 369ff., 403–7. Prins points out that Goldman started out in 1928 as a shady little investment house, deep in pre-crash speculation. Like Joseph P. Kennedy but more successfully, its founder, Sidney Weinberg, sought to launder his image by supporting Franklin D. Roosevelt. Sources tracing the Goldman–U.S. government links are legion. See, for instance, David Floyd, "26 Goldman Sachs Alumni Who Run the World," Investopedia, April 18, 2017; Niv Sultan, "The Revolving Door Always Spins for Goldman Sachs—by Design," Center for Responsive Politics, OpenSecrets .org, March 23, 2017. ProPublica's database Trump Town reveals how much further into the U.S. government the connections go. However, the findings understate the phenomenon by dividing Goldman up into several subentities and neglecting former employees who did not leave Goldman directly, such as Steven Mnuchin.

102 A *New York Times* portrait: Robin Pogrebin, "At 80, Mnuchin Remains a Passionate Promoter of Postwar Art," *New York Times,* October 25, 2013.

103 Warehouses in Geneva: See, for instance, Georgina Adam, *The Dark Side of the Boom* (London: Lund Humphries, 2017), pp. 131–39.

103 A set has sold: Christie's, Artists/Makers/Artists, Donald Judd.

103 When he opened his gallery: Carol Vogel, "A Cézanne Moves to Los Angeles," The Art Market, *New York Times,* November 13, 1992.

103 His first wife was a director: See photo on p. 48 of "Solomon R. Guggenheim Foundation, Annual Report, 2015," http://www.sismus.org/museums/report /USA/Guggenheim/SRGM0506.pdf.

104 That method is Joe Kennedy's old favorite: Adam, *The Dark Side of the Boom,* p. 142.

104 "Trustees know ahead of time": Maureen Mullarkey, "Painting Money: The Ugly Business of Contemporary Art," *Crisis Magazine,* September 1, 2006.

104 Mnuchin's 2019 financial disclosure: The entries, both referring to a 1978 painting called "Untitled III," are listed separately. In Mnuchin's 2017 financial disclosure, one of these interests was listed as worth less than $1 million. United States Office of Government Ethics, "Executive Branch Personnel Public Financial Disclosure Report (OGE Form 278e), Steven Mnuchin, 2019," https://assets.documentcloud.org/documents/6157799/Mnuchin -Steven-Annual-2019.pdf.

104 Thus does the Midas disease: For a further discussion of the impact of such uses of the art market on culture and aesthetic values, listen to the radio show *1A,* "Paintbrushes and Deep Pockets: The State of the Art World," National Public Radio, June 12, 2019.

104 Alongside Soros: Damian Paletta and Dan Fitzpatrick, "Soros, Dell Join Flowers in Purchase of IndyMac," *Wall Street Journal,* January 3, 2009.

104 With its name changed: Peter Dreier, "Steve Mnuchin, Meet Rose Gudiel," *HuffPost,* October 3, 2011; Consent Order: OneWest Bank Before the Office of Thrift Supervision, April 13, 2011. Mnuchin is also affiliated with Russian oligarch Leonid Blavatnik, a private-sector member of Vladimir Putin's kleptocratic network, along with such sanctioned oligarchs as Viktor Vekselberg and Oleg Deripaska. Blavatnik may have been an initial investor in Mnuchin's Hollywood production and financing venture RatPac–Dune Entertainment, and he bought out another partner as Mnuchin was divesting his shares to take over at Treasury. Mnuchin and Blavatnik rub shoulders as supporters of the Appeal of Conscience Foundation, a public charity that has raised questions among human rights activists for bestowing awards on known rights violators. See Connie Bruck, "The Billionaire's Playlist: How an Oligarch Got into the American Music Business," *New Yorker,* January 12, 2014; Ilya Zaslavskiy, "Why Comrade Sir Leonid (Len) Blavatnik Is a Putin Oligarch, and Why Hudson Institute, Harvard, Oxford and Other Entities Should Not Accept His Tainted Money," *Underminers,* February 13, 2019. Senate majority leader Mitch McConnell is also woven into this network of Putin-linked oligarchs: see Part III, "The Hydra," Chapter 5, "Powers Sabotaged," pp. 146–58. On the decision by the Department of the Treasury to lift sanctions on an oligarch close to Blavatnik, see Morgan Chalfant and Olivia Beaver, "Democrats Are Zeroing In on Treasury's Mnuchin," *The Hill,* February 1, 2019. Mnuchin's holdings are almost indescribably complex. Assisting with research for this book, David Wistocki developed a partial map of his holdings, https://www.mindmeister.com/1122917758?t=EY1lCyiwXA.

104 The heads of private equity: Those with the capital to invest are in a position to exploit the fear and desperation surrounding a bankruptcy or a series of bankruptcies to extract highly advantageous terms—from governments as well as the private sellers. Private equity funds can shield the identities of all but a very few owners, so they are magnets for questionable money. Able to wield that type of capital, as well as that of government-backed pension funds, they obtain breaks on normal legal obligations to staff, customers, and communities under bankruptcy protection or purchase agreements and typically impute debt they take on to buy the troubled company to that company, not themselves. While the public assumes the risk in these ways, the purchasers pocket generous management fees, whatever the ultimate fate of the purchased companies. For a summary, see Nomi Prins, "The Truth About Private Equity: Politicians Need It, Taxpayers Fund It," *Daily Beast,* July 13, 2017.

105 Trump confidant Tom Barrack: Shawn Tully, "I'm Tom Barrack and I'm Getting Out," *Fortune,* October 31, 2005; Yoji Cole, "Thomas Barrack, Jr.: The LA Real Estate Titan Keeps Riding Waves," *CSQ,* March 2013; Aaron Glantz, "After the Bubble Burst," *Reveal,* June 20, 2017, and *Homewreckers* (New York: HarperCollins, 2019); Stacy Kravitz, "Asia's Woes Inspire Colony Capi-

tal to Invest $2 Billion in the Region," *Wall Street Journal,* August 26, 1998; Nanette Byrnes, "Tom Barrack's Search for Life After Resolution Trust," Bloomberg, May 6, 1996.

105 Since then, tens of thousands: For an excellent investigation of this epidemic, listen to Brooke Gladstone, "The Scarlet E," *On the Media,* WNYC Studios, June 7, 14, 22, and 28, 2019.

105 In 2010, Colony sold: Bradley Hope and Tom Wright, "Stolen Emails Show Ties Between UAE Envoy and 1MDB Fund's Central Figure," *Wall Street Journal,* August 1, 2017; Squawk Box, "Real Estate Investor Tom Barrack: Commercial Mortgages Could Be on the Brink of Collapse," CNBC, March 25, 2020; Benjamin Wallace, "Monetizing the Celebrity Meltdown," *New York,* November 24, 2010.

105 Commerce Secretary Wilbur Ross: Leslie Norton, "Ross Redux," *Wall Street Journal,* October 5, 1998; Makoto Kajiwara, "Trump's Commerce Secretary Pick Is a Familiar Face in Asia," *Nikkei Asian Review,* December 15, 2016.

106 and the three overlapped at Kirkland & Ellis: See also Cockburn, "The Malaysian Job."

106 Trump filled Kennedy's seat: There is some speculation as to whether Kennedy's resignation was contingent on the appointment of Kavanaugh. In any case, it is clear Kennedy lobbied hard for his hand-picked successor, highly unusual behavior for a Supreme Court justice. See, for instance, Christopher Cadelago, Nancy Cook, and Andrew Restuccia, "Private Meeting with Kennedy Helped Trump Get to 'Yes' on Kavanaugh," *Politico,* July 9, 2018. On Deutsche Bank and Justin Kennedy's employment, see David Enrich, "The Money Behind Trump's Money," *New York Times Magazine,* February 4, 2020.

106 Anne Gorsuch had to resign: See, for instance, Philip Shabecoff, "House Charges Head of E.P.A. with Contempt," *New York Times,* December 17, 1982.

106 He kept raping children: The best source on the Epstein case is the early and in-depth reporting by Julie Brown for the *Miami Herald.* The most complete series, entitled "Perversion of Justice," was published in November and December 2018. It includes three parts: "A Sex Pyramid Scheme," "Undermining the Case," and "Another Kind of Justice," and other resources. Lefkowitz has remained a white-collar defense attorney at Kirkland & Ellis almost throughout his career. A Federalist Society member and Koch-linked grant recipient, he is a school voucher activist whose clients include numerous unnamed hedge funds and Teva Pharmaceutical Industries, which settled with the state of Oklahoma in 2019, in the context of the opioid epidemic. He worked with Kavanaugh in the George W. Bush White House.

107 U.S. District Judge Richard Berman: Berman was bound to dismiss the case, upon Epstein's death, but opened his court to the victims before doing so.

107 But not till Maria travels: On that residence—built near Epstein benefactor L Brands' Les Wexner's home—see Robert Fitrakis, "Wexner's Royal Connection," *Columbus Alive,* January 25, 2001.

108 "There are different kinds": For the *New York Times* audio, listen to Michael Barbaro, host, "The First Women to Report Jeffrey Epstein," *The Daily*, August 26, 2019. Additional details and images in Rachel Corbett and Ben Davis, "Jeffrey Epstein Accuser Maria Farmer Says the New York Academy of Art Helped Enable the Disgraced Financier," *Artnet News*, August 26, 2019.

108 She makes it through: *Today*, "Jeffrey Epstein accuser shares story of rape for 1st time," NBC News, July 10, 2019.

108 A 2003 portrait: Jaquelyn M. Scharnick, "Mogul Donor Gives Harvard More Than Money: Reclusive Investor Epstein Forges Intellectual and Financial Connections with University," *Harvard Crimson*, May 1, 2003.

108 This self-gratifying logic: Harvard's website for the program, called the Program on Evolutionary Dynamics, is laconic. See also Harvard University, Mind, Brain, Behavior: Interfaculty Initiative, which is equally silent about Epstein's long-standing seat on its advisory board.

109 The New York literary scene: Kate Darling, "Jeffrey Epstein's Influence in the Science World Is a Symptom of Larger Problems," *The Guardian*, August 27, 2019. While past connections to Epstein have caused some researchers and institutions anguish, Harvard is not among them. See Molly McCafferty and Aiden Ryan, "Billionaire and Convicted Sex Offender Epstein Boasts Deep, Longstanding Ties to Harvard," *Harvard Crimson*, December 3, 2018. See also Max Larkin, "Accused Sex Trafficker Epstein Supported Many Boston-Area Causes—Several at Harvard," WBUR, July 10, 2019. Not until September 2019 did Harvard announce that it was redirecting unspent funds received from Epstein to charities supporting sex-trafficking victims. See Lawrence S. Bacow, "A Message to the Community Regarding Jeffrey Epstein," open letter published on www.harvard.edu, September 12, 2019.

109 A devastating 2019 *New Yorker* magazine portrait: Connie Bruck, "Alan Dershowitz, Devil's Advocate," *New Yorker*, July 29, 2019.

109 It's not just Harvard: MIT's relationship was at least as problematic. See Ronan Farrow, "How an Elite University Research Center Concealed Its Relationship with Jeffrey Epstein," *New Yorker*, September 6, 2019; Tiffany Hsu, David Yaffe-Bellany, and Marc Tracy, "Jeffrey Epstein Gave $850,000 to M.I.T. and Administrators Knew," *New York Times*, January 10, 2020.

109 Epstein's highest-profile public-sector contacts: A glance at the way Epstein conducted himself in the Virgin Islands reveals a familiar pattern. On one side, cultivated friendships with public officials, employment and contracts for their relatives, campaign contributions and other gifts. On the other side, a see-no-evil attitude toward practices ranging from persistent and egregious environmental crimes to tax evasion to clear indications of child molesting. Steve Eder, "Epstein's Island, 'Little St. Jeff's': A Hideaway Where Money Bought Influence," *New York Times*, August 28, 2019. A more sensationalized—and exclusively Democratic Party focused—network analysis, entitled "Jeffrey Epstein's St. Thomas Network, Comms, and an Elite School," is available at a site connected with various conspiracy theories, *Corey's Digs*, August 9, 2019. Many of the connections are tenuous, and the choice of individuals to feature is

patently selective. Still, this is a fruitful type of investigation. And the Clintons' connections with Epstein make some of the conspiracy theories seem a bit less fanciful now than they may have in the past.

109 Both outsized figures loudly distanced: Angel Ureña, press secretary to Bill Clinton, tweet, July 8, 2019 (https://twitter.com/angelurena, scroll down to July 8)—and note the lawyerly precision of the statement; Donald Trump, press availability, video posted by Ian Schwartz, "Trump 'Not a Fan' of Jeffrey Epstein; 'Feel Very Badly' for Alex Acosta," Real Clear Politics, July 9, 2019.

109 Their statements are false: Maria Farmer recalled to the *New York Times* that Trump looked at her suggestively, but that Epstein told him she wasn't for him. See Barbaro, "The First Women to Report Jeffrey Epstein." Virginia Roberts Giuffre, who states she was recruited from Mar-a-Lago, recalls hearing Maxwell claim she joined Clinton and Epstein in a helicopter ride to the Virgin Islands. She recalls seeing Trump with Epstein but not seeing him having sex with any of the girls who served Epstein. See U.S. District Court, Southern District of New York, "*Virginia Giuffre v. Ghislaine Maxwell,* Plaintiffs' Response to Defendant's Motion for Summary Judgement," August 9, 2019, p. 56; Adam Klasfeld, "Clinton, Trump Emerge in Unsealed Epstein Evidence," *Courthouse News,* August 9, 2019.

110 Former Soviet republics have been: In 2000, I researched and wrote a draft article for the *New York Times Magazine* about sex trafficking from Moldova into France, for which I crossed from Vlorë, Albania, to Brindisi, Italy, in a rubber dinghy with half a dozen trafficked women and a cargo of drugs. The article was not published. For fashion as a cover, see Sarah Chayes, *Thieves of State: Why Corruption Threatens Global Security* (New York: W. W. Norton, 2015), p. 109, and Agence France-Presse, "Scandale Epstein: Le Français Jean-Luc Brunel, un chasseur de mannequins au coeur des accusations," *Le Point,* August 16, 2019. Sarah Jacobs, "2 Models Who Worked for Trump's Controversial Agency Tell What It Was Like for Them," *Business Insider,* February 14, 2017.

110 Trump and Epstein fell out: Trump outbid Epstein for the mansion, and though he called Epstein the day after the auction, it does not appear the two spoke again. See Beth Reinhard, Rosalind Helderman, and Marc Fisher, "Donald Trump and Jeffrey Epstein Partied Together. Then an Oceanfront Palm Beach Mansion Came Between Them," *Washington Post,* July 31, 2019; Andrew Prokop, "Jeffrey Epstein's Connections to Donald Trump and Bill Clinton, Explained," *Vox,* August 10, 2019; Ken Silverstein, "The Salacious Ammo Even Donald Trump Won't Use in a Fight Against Hillary Clinton," *Vice,* January 29, 2016.

110 Charged with weaving: On Rybolovlev, see, for instance, John Bowden, "Russian Oligarch Who Bought Mansion from Trump Detained and Questioned on Corruption Charges: Report," *The Hill,* November 6, 2018; Ilya Zaslavskiy, "Monaco's Minister of Justice Implicated by Kremlin's Autocrat," Free Russia Foundation, no date; Gérard Davet and Fabrice Lhomme, "Le milliardaire russe Dmitri Rybolovlev au centre d'un 'Monacogate,'" *Le Monde,* Septem-

ber 14, 2017; *Der Spiegel* staff, "A Russian Billionaire's Monaco Fiefdom," *Spiegel Online,* November 16, 2018.

110 Fundraisers and several: On Epstein's White House visits, see Emily Shugerman and Suzi Parker, "Jeffrey Epstein Visited Clinton White House Multiple Times in Early '90s," *Daily Beast,* July 24, 2019, updated August 19, 2019. See also Gabriel Sherman, " 'It's Going to Be Staggering, the Amount of Names': As the Jeffrey Epstein Case Grows More Grotesque, Manhattan and DC Brace for Impact," *Vanity Fair,* July 17, 2019. Dershowitz credits Forester de Rothschild with introducing him to Epstein in 1996. Forester switched her political allegiance to support Senator John McCain when Obama beat Hillary Clinton for the Democratic nomination. For Prosperi, see Leon Fooksman, "Embezzler Gets House Arrest," *South Florida Sun-Sentinel,* March 3, 2001. Epstein seems to have lent his lawyer to Prosperi; see Julia La Roche, Aarthi Swaminathan, and Calder McHugh, "Jeffrey Epstein's lawyers deeply involved in his business dealings for decades, documents show," Yahoo Finance, August 13, 2019; Jonathan Peterson and Lisa Getter, "Clinton Pardons Raise Questions of Timing, Motive," *Los Angeles Times,* January 28, 2001.

110 Then there are Clinton's rides: Angel Ureña tweet, July 8, 2019.

110 But by my reading: A printed version of the logs is available at https://archive.org/stream/EpsteinFlightLogsLolitaExpress/Epstein%20Flight%20Logs-%20Lolita%20Express_djvu.txt. Because everything in the landscape-format table is printed in a single column, it can be difficult to distinguish which passengers are linked to which flight. A scan of the handwritten version is available at https://www.documentcloud.org/documents/1507315-epstein-flight-manifests.html. It is sometimes illegible. My reckoning is based on cross-checking the two. Secret Service appear to accompany Clinton on every flight, and his controversial aide and Clinton Foundation mastermind Douglas Band on most.

110 Even without adding: On the Clinton Foundation, see Bethany McLean, "The Power of Philanthropy," *Fortune,* September 18, 2006; Peter Schweizer, *Clinton Cash: The Untold Story of How and Why Foreign Governments and Businesses Helped Make Bill and Hillary Rich* (New York: HarperCollins, 2015), especially pp. 81–93. Note that the Clintons' challenges to this obviously partisan book undermine little of its evidence and none for this section; a draft memo Band sent to John Podesta in response to Chelsea Clinton's accusations that he was using the foundation for personal enrichment was part of the 2016 WikiLeaks dumps of internal emails from Democratic Party operatives. It details significant irregular behavior within the nonprofit. It is available at https://wikileaks.org/podesta-emails/emailid/32240. See also Anand Giridharadas, *Winners Take All: The Elite Charade of Changing the World* (New York: Knopf, 2019), especially pp. 200–210, and on Clinton's attitude more generally, pp. 236–44.

111 It—and the lower-profile Trump Foundation: Supreme Court of the State of New York, County of New York, "The People of the State of New York, by

Barbara D. Underwood, Attorney General of the State of New York v. Donald J. Trump et al., Verified Petition," June 14, 2018. The Trump Foundation was dissolved in December 2018.

111 Overshadowed by his sex trafficking: On the origins of Epstein's fortune, see, for instance, Matt Stieb, "How Jeffrey Epstein Made His Money: Four Wild Theories," *New York,* July 9, 2019.

111 "I thought Jeffrey was": Marc Fisher and Jonathan O'Connell, "Final Evasion: For Thirty Years, Prosecutors and Victims Tried to Hold Jeffrey Epstein to Account. At Every Turn, He Slipped Away," *Washington Post,* August 19, 2019.

111 But when a network: For a discussion of the relative effectiveness of loose networks (in this case social-media friends and followers) and more structured, hierarchical organizations pursuing an explicit goal, see Malcom Gladwell, "Why the Revolution Won't Be Tweeted," *New Yorker,* September 27, 2010. With social media revolutions breaking out all over the world a few months after publication of this article, Gladwell may have been a bit chagrined. But his point about the lack of depth and staying power was borne out.

2. Powers Wielded: The Scales

113 In Nigeria, the education system: See Sarah Chayes, "Nigeria's Boko Haram Isn't Just About Western Education," *Washington Post,* May 16, 2014.

115 The administration of justice: Adjudicating quarrels is an important function of alpha males in chimpanzee communities. See Frans de Waal, *Good Natured: The Origins of Right and Wrong in Humans and Other Animals* (Cambridge, MA: Harvard University Press, 1999).

115 He was king in name only: Charles I, *His Majesties Answer to the XIX Propositions of Both Houses of Parliament* (London: Robert Barker, 1642). See also Geoffrey Robertson, *The Tyrannicide Brief* (New York: Pantheon, 2005).

115 It was the first step: In a series of conversations in southern Nigeria, villagers told me about the "idols" whose justice was absolute, falling upon rich and poor, powerful and unconnected alike. An evangelical pastor drew a sharp contrast between the fearful, rumbling "thunder god," who delivered justice, and Jesus and his mercy, which allowed for corrupt government courts. In this Christian pastor's view, Nigeria's breathtaking levels of corruption were due to the absence of the impartial and strict justice of the old gods. See Sarah Chayes, "Thunder God: Values, Corruption, and Nigeria's Election," *World Politics Review,* April 28, 2015.

115 "the President a Kind": William Maclay, diary entry, September 26, 1789, in Maeva Marcus, ed., *Documentary History of the Supreme Court of the United States, 1789–1800,* vol. 4, *Organizing the Federal Judiciary, Legislation and Commentaries* (New York: Columbia University Press, 1992), pp. 518–19. Note, Maclay was using the phrase sarcastically, to describe the positions of those he was arguing against, such as John Adams.

116 Presidents Thomas Jefferson and Bill Clinton: Akhil Amar and Neal Katyal, "Executive Privileges and Immunities: The Richard Nixon and Bill Clinton

Cases," *Harvard Law Review* 108 (1995): 701–26. See also Fred Barbash, "Pop Quiz: Can a President Be Indicted?" *Washington Post,* February 1, 1998.

116 Having helped investigate Clinton: Brett Kavanaugh, "Separation of Powers During the Forty-Fourth Presidency and Beyond," *Minnesota Law Review* 19 (2009): 1454–86; Bill Barr, "Memorandum, to Deputy Attorney General Rod Rosenstein, Assistant Attorney General Steve Engel, Re: Mueller's 'Obstruction' Theory," June 8, 2018. See especially pp. 9ff.

116 He took office just as: Eliana Johnson, "The Real Reason Bill Barr Is Defending Trump: The Attorney General Didn't Want to Serve Donald Trump. But He Did Want to Fight for a Theory of Presidential Power," *Politico,* May 1, 2019; Neil Kinkopf, "The Barr Memo and the Imperial Presidency," American Constitution Society, January 17, 2017. See also Matthew Whitaker, "Mueller's Investigation of Trump Is Going Too Far," CNN.com, November 7, 2018.

116 Current Justice Department policy holds: U.S. Department of Justice, "A Sitting President's Amenability to Indictment and Criminal Prosecution," Memorandum Opinion for the Attorney General, October 16, 2000 (https://www .justice.gov/sites/default/files/olc/opinions/2000/10/31/op-olc-v024-p0222_0 .pdf).

116 If any revelation emerged: See Sarah Chayes, "This Is How Kleptocracies Work," *The Atlantic,* February 23, 2020. A more detailed exposition can be found in Chayes, *Thieves of State: Why Corruption Threatens Global Security* (New York: W. W. Norton, 2015), pp. 52–64, 135–44, 154–55.

116 When the 2008 nonprosecution deal: In 2011, Acosta sent a letter explaining his 2008 actions to the *Daily Beast,* emphasizing the adversarial nature of his interactions with defense team—which is cast as an intimidating and unfamiliar group of men. "What followed [his office's initial presentation of a plea deal offer]," he wrote, "was a year-long assault on the prosecution and the prosecutors. I use the word assault intentionally, as the defense in this case was more aggressive than any which I, or the prosecutors in my office, had previously encountered." He detailed tactics he alleges the "army of legal superstars" employed, including investigating prosecutors to find pretexts to disqualify them. The text is available in Conchita Sarnoff and Lee Aitken, "Jeffrey Epstein: How the Hedge Fund Mogul Pedophile Got Off Easy," *Daily Beast,* March 25, 2011, updated August 19, 2019. The thirty-seven-minute-long press conference Acosta held on July 10, 2019, can be viewed at https://www.youtube .com/watch?v=omWJfjTtB34. See also Julie Brown, "Perversion of Justice," part 2, "Undermining the Case," *Miami Herald,* November 2018.

117 When Acosta announced his resignation: Laura Ingraham, host, "Former Epstein Attorney Ken Starr Says Alex Acosta Played Tough in 2008," *Fox News,* July 12, 2019.

117 It was his father: Epstein was hired in the spring of 1974, after Barr had announced he was stepping down as Dalton's headmaster, reportedly because of a conflict with the board of trustees over his educational approach, but before Barr actually left the school in the summer. The previous year (a decade before Margaret Atwood's *The Handmaid's Tale*), Barr Sr. published a bizarre science

fiction novel featuring juvenile sexual slavery and eugenics. Epstein reportedly expressed a desire to launch a personal eugenics program, using his New Mexico ranch as a site to inseminate as many women as possible. Donald Barr's successor as Dalton headmaster was forced out more than two decades later amid accusations of sexual exploitation of minors. See Intelligencer staff, "Come Back Mr. Barr," *New York,* no visible date, available at https://grondamorin .com/2019/07/09/story-of-ag-barrs-dad-as-headmaster-who-ran-school-with -discipline-and-authoritarian-rule/; Thomas Volscho, "Jeffrey Epstein Dodged Questions About Sex with His Dalton Prep-School Students," *Daily Beast,* July 12, 2019, updated August 19, 2019; Becky Ferreira, "Epstein Truthers Are Obsessed by a Sci-Fi Book About Child Sex Slavery Written by Bill Barr's Dad," *Vox,* August 16, 2019; James Stewart, Matthew Goldstein, and Jessica Silver-Greenberg, "Jeffrey Epstein Hoped to Seed Human Race with His DNA," *New York Times,* July 31, 2019; Elisabeth Bumiller, "Headmaster at Dalton Resigns Under Pressure," *New York Times,* March 13, 1997.

117 including asking a judge: United States District Court for the District of Columbia, "Government's Supplemental and Amended Sentencing Memorandum," Case number 18-cr-18-ABJ, February 11, 2020, available at https:// assets.documentcloud.org/documents/6774092/New-Stone-Sentencing -Memo-Post-Tweet.pdf. The move caused a firestorm among nonpartisan rule-of-law professionals, including the resignation of all four leading prosecutors on the case, and an open letter from more than one thousand former Justice Department employees calling for Barr's resignation.

117 At a breakfast in Kathmandu: This was part of a series of events organized by George Varughese, then of the Asia Foundation, to apply my analysis of kleptocratic networks to Nepal. Varughese moved on to the Niti Foundation, which published a report growing out of the work: "Nepal's Kleptocratic Network— Mapping Corruption and Impunity," Niti Foundation, May 22, 2019.

118 So, pushing laws through parliament: Amr Hamzawy, "Legislating Authoritarianism: Egypt's New Era of Repression," Carnegie Endowment for International Peace, 2017.

118 Almost every stage: Information on Nigeria is from a discussion with lawyers Tajudeen Funsho, Kemaludeen Yahya Said, and Aminu Sani Gadanya, in Kano, Nigeria, July 15, 2015, among other discussions. On legal fees as disguised bribes, see Thomas Ferguson, Jie Chen, and Paul Jorgensen, "Fifty Shades of Green: High Finance, Political Money, and the U.S. Congress," The Roosevelt Institute, May 2, 2017.

119 That's what a lot of: See, for instance, the entry for "Military" on Wikia.org (consulted March 8, 2020). This appears to be a duplicate of the Wikipedia entry I consulted when writing this book, in 2019. That entry has since been changed to remove the moderate aura.

119 Sharing this model with: While plenty of everyday Americans have joined, this was no grassroots movement, investigators crunching internal documents and funding data have found, but rather, a Koch network operation. Amanda Fallin et al., " 'To Quarterback Behind the Scenes, Third-Party Efforts': The

Tobacco Industry and the Tea Party," *Tobacco Control,* February 2013; Jeff Nesbit, *Poison Tea: How Big Oil and Big Tobacco Invented the Tea Party and Captured the GOP* (New York: Thomas Dunne, 2016). The evidence on the tobacco industry's decades of duplicity is incontrovertible. See, for instance, Clive Bates and Andy Rowell, "The Truth About the Tobacco Industry . . . in Its Own Words," University of California at San Francisco, Center for Tobacco Control, Research, and Education, 2004. For details on the 1998 Master Settlement Agreement between the five largest tobacco companies and the attorneys general of forty-eight states and the District of Columbia and five U.S. territories, see the website maintained by the Mitchell Hamlin Law School's Public Health Law Center: https://publichealthlawcenter.org/topics /tobacco-control/tobacco-control-litigation/master-settlement-agreement.

119 Just months before his appointment: Lewis Powell, "Confidential Memorandum, to: Eugene Snydor, Chairman, Education Committee, U.S. Chamber of Commerce," August 23, 1971. See also Adam Winkler, *We the Corporations: How American Businesses Won Their Civil Rights* (New York: Liveright, 2018), ch. 9, "The Corporations' Justice," pp. 279–324.

120 "Outsmarted and undermanned": Steven Teles, *The Rise of the Conservative Legal Movement* (Princeton, NJ: Princeton University Press, 2008), p. 1.

120 Harvard University, roiled: See especially Jane Mayer, *Dark Money: The Hidden History of the Billionaires Behind the Rise of the Radical Right* (New York: Doubleday, 2016), pp. 130ff.

120 For years, often in luxurious settings: On hostility to the public interest, see Mayer, *Dark Money,* p. 123. On these views at George Mason University Law School (renamed in 2016 the Antonin Scalia Law School), see UnKoch My Campus, "Donor Intent of the Koch Network: Leveraging Universities for Self-Interested Policy Change," December 2018, p. 7. On the seminars, see Chris Young et al., "Corporations, Pro-Business NonProfits Foot Bill for Judicial Seminars," Center for Public Integrity, March 28, 2013, updated; Sheldon Whitehouse, *Captured: The Corporate Infiltration of American Democracy* (New York: The New Press, 2017), pp. 72–75.

120 Yale's chapter, enthuses a post: P. R., "Yale Federalist Society: Lawyering Up Right," Yale Law School website, April 8, 2015.

121 The weaving of this subnetwork: Literature on the Federalist Society is now— now that the damage is done—voluminous. For example: Amanda Hollis-Brusky, *Ideas with Consequences: The Federalist Society and the Conservative Counterrevolution* (Oxford, UK: Oxford University Press, 2015); Michael Kruse, "The Weekend at Yale That Changed American Politics," *Politico,* September/October 2018; Sheldon Whitehouse, Richard Blumenthal, and Mazie Hirono, "Brief of *Amici Curiae*" in *Seila Law LLC v. Consumer Financial Protection Bureau,* U.S. Supreme Court, No. 19-7, January 22, 2020, pp. 15ff.; Lydia Wheeler, "Meet the Powerful Group Behind Trump's Judicial Nominations," *The Hill,* November 16, 2017; Tod Lindberg, "One of a Kind: Why the Success of the Federalist Society Is Unlikely to Be Replicated," *Weekly Standard,* July 23, 2018, updated. On money flows, see Anna Massoglia, "Trump

Judicial Adviser's Dark Money Network Hides Supreme Court Spending,"
Center for Responsive Politics, OpenSecrets.org, January 2, 2020.

121 More—and younger—jurists: Telephone interview, March 16, 2020. Russell
Wheeler, "Trump Has Reshaped the Judiciary, but Not as Much as You Might
Think," Brookings Institution, August 27, 2018; David Lat, "A Look Inside
the Conservative Judge-Making Machine: When It Comes to Transforming the
Federal Judiciary, What Is the Secret to the Republicans' Success?" *Above the
Law,* November 16, 2018; on changing the venerable blue slip policy whereby
senators could block a nominee from their home state, see David Hawkings,
"GOP Slips Past Another Senate Custom, and Democrats Turn Blue," *Roll
Call,* May 30, 2018; Emily Cadei and Kate Irby, "Trump Defies California Sena-
tors with 9th Circuit Judge Nominations," *Sacramento Bee,* October 11, 2018;
Barry McMillion, "The Blue Slip Process for U.S. Circuit and District Court
Nominations, Frequently Asked Questions," Congressional Research Service,
October 2, 2017. On March 11, 2020, Judge James Dannenberg sent a scath-
ing letter to Chief Justice Roberts resigning his membership in the Supreme
Court bar, saying that his majority has "cynically undermined basic freedoms
by hypocritically weaponizing others," so as to, among other things, "elevate
the grossest forms of political bribery beyond the ability of the federal government or states to rationally regulate it. . . . There is nothing 'conservative'
about this trend. This is radical 'legal activism' at its worst." Text available in
Dahlia Lithwick, "Former Judge Resigns from the Supreme Court Bar," *Slate,*
March 13, 2020. On April 3, 2020, Trump named Federalist Society member
and former Kavanaugh clerk, thirty-seven-year-old Justin Winter—rated "not
qualified" by the American Bar Association—to the powerful U.S. Court of
Appeals for the DC Circuit. See Seung Min Kim, "Trump Taps Former Kava-
naugh Clerk to Fill Vacancy on Powerful D.C. Appeals Court," *Washington
Post,* April 3, 2020. While much has been written about the acceleration of this
process during the Trump administration, I was unable to find a tabulation of
Federalist Society members appointed to state and federal benches over time.
See Rebecca Ruiz et al., "A Conservative Agenda Unleashed on the Federal
Courts," *New York Times,* March 16, 2020.

121 No president until Trump: Alan Smith, "Trump Is Going Through an 'Ex-
tremely Unusual Process' of Picking U.S. Attorneys—and It Has Ethics
Experts Bewildered," *Business Insider,* October 21, 2017. One of those interviewees, whom Trump passed over, was appointed by a vote of some forty
New York judges to be U.S. attorney for the Southern District of New York.
Benjamin Weiser, "With No Nomination from Trump, Judges Choose U.S.
Attorney for Manhattan," *New York Times,* April 25, 2018. Trump appointed
and the Senate confirmed another in September 2017, to serve in the District
of Columbia, which is not represented in the Senate. As in the case of federal
judges, senators are traditionally empowered to block U.S. attorney appointments to their states.

122 It is such clauses: The cases include *Rent-A-Center, West, Inc. v. Jackson,* 561
U.S. 63 (2010); *AT&T Mobility LLC v. Concepcion,* 563 U.S. 333 (2011);

Walmart Stores, Inc. v. Dukes, et al., 564 U.S. 338 (2011); *Am. Express Co. v. Italian Colors Rest.,* 570 U.S. ____ (2013); *DIRECTV, Inc. v. Imburgia,* 577 U.S. ____ (2015). See the *New York Times*'s excellent three-part investigation, "Beware the Fine Print," including Jessica Silver-Greenberg and Robert Gebeloff, "Stacking the Deck of Justice," October 31, 2015; Jessica Silver-Greenberg and Michael Corkery, "In Arbitration, a 'Privatization of the Justice System,'" November 1, 2015; Michael Corkery and Jessica Silver-Greenberg, "In Religious Arbitration, Scripture Is the Rule of Law," November 2, 2015.

122 This series of cases: Whitehouse, *Captured,* p. 65.

122 The first petition: The FDIC and Consumer Financial Protection Bureau later ordered Discover to pay some $200 million to three million customers for deceptive banking practices almost identical to Wells Fargo's later offenses. Consumer Financial Protection Bureau, "Federal Deposit Insurance Corporation and Consumer Financial Protection Bureau Order Discover to Pay $200 Million Consumer Refund for Deceptive Marketing," news release, September 24, 2012.

123 In Washington, that temple: Office of the Curator, Supreme Court of the United States, "Figures of Justice," information sheet.

123 The hydra has already seized: See Lee Epstein, William Landes, and Richard Posner, "How Business Fares in the Supreme Court," *Minnesota Law Review* 97 (2013): 1431–72. They point out that "liberal" justices follow the trend. See also the Constitutional Accountability Center's study of the Chamber's record before the Roberts court, "Corporations and the Supreme Court," https://www.theusconstitution.org/series/chamber-study/, and Whitehouse, *Captured,* pp. 77–80.

3. Powers Wielded: The Pen and the Mace

125 It was subtitled: Karl Rove, "The GOP Targets State Legislatures: He Who Controls Redistricting Can Control Congress," *Wall Street Journal,* updated March 4, 2010.

125 "107 seats in 16 states": Ibid.

126 "the most strategic": David Daley, *Ratf**ked: Why Your Vote Doesn't Count* (New York: Liveright, 2017), p. xviii.

126 On June 27, 2019: *Rucho, et al. v. Common Cause, et al.,* U.S. 18-422 (October 2018), https://www.supremecourt.gov/opinions/18pdf/18-422_9oll.pdf.

126 "a variety of social, economic": Lilliana Mason, *Uncivil Agreement: How Politics Became Our Identity* (Chicago: University of Chicago Press, 2018), pp. 19–20.

126 "seek comfort in increasingly": Ibid., p. 41.

127 "435 sets of lines": Daley, *Ratf**ked,* p. xxiii.

127 Whatever color manipulation: See, for instance, Lake Research Partners and WPA Intelligence memorandum dated September 11, 2017, on a poll on partisan redistricting they conducted, https://campaignlegal.org/sites/default/files/memo.CLCPartisanRedistricting.FINAL_.2.09082017%20%28002%29.pdf.

127 They have to: The same principle applies to the power of the scales, in places where judges are elected. Big money dominates dozens of races for state judgeships. Eighty-five percent of U.S. court cases are heard in state courts.

127 This state of affairs: Thomas Ferguson, Paul Jorgensen, and Jie Chen, "How Money Drives US Congressional Elections," Institute for New Economic Thinking, working paper no. 48, August 1, 2016, p. 4. Note that there are always exceptions, sometimes spectacular, such as former New York mayor Michael Bloomberg's withdrawal from the 2020 Democratic primary contest, after spending approximately half a billion dollars on advertising and then doing poorly on Super Tuesday, March 3, 2020. But this research looks at total trends, over time, in congressional elections.

127 Using data from the IRS: Ibid., p. 7.

128 For every race but one: Ibid., pp. 15ff., figures 2 and 3. See also the updated paper: Thomas Ferguson, Paul Jorgensen, and Jie Chen, "How Money Drives US Congressional Elections: Linear Models of Money and Outcomes," *Structural Change and Economic Dynamics,* September 20, 2019.

128 As part of this work: Thomas Ferguson, Jie Chen, and Paul Jorgensen, "Fifty Shades of Green: High Finance, Political Money, and the U.S. Congress," Roosevelt Institute, May 2017, pp. 12ff.

128 Banks, for example, may provide: Ahmed Tahoun and Florin Vasvari, "Political Lending," Institute for New Economic Thinking, working paper no. 47, August 2016. In 2008, a cash-strapped Mitch McConnell turned to one of his donors—his banker at Branch Banking and Trust, in Louisville, Kentucky. The establishment agreed to remortgage his house, converting the original $250,000 personal note to $1.2 million in the name of his re-election campaign—that is, extending a loan of more than a million dollars to an institutional third party, on a private residence worth about a quarter of that. A scan of the mortgage, from records of the Louisville courthouse, is in my possession.

128 about a third of members: This actually represents a reduction compared with previous decades and especially centuries. See Nick Robinson, "The Decline of the Lawyer Politician," *Buffalo Law Review* 65, no. 4 (August 2017): 657–737. On Senator Bob Corker's prolific stock trading while in office, see Matt Taibbi, "Bob Corker Facing Ethics Questions? What a Surprise," *Rolling Stone,* December 22, 2017.

128 Elections boil down to: Ferguson et al., "Industrial Structure and Party Competition in an Age of Hunger Games," Institute for New Economic Thinking, working paper no. 66, January 2018, p. 23.

128 In Honduras, a group of villagers: Interviews in Monte Copado, Honduras, July 23, 2016.

128 Native North Americans: Nick Estes, cofounder of Red Nation and professor of American studies at the University of New Mexico, interviewed in "Standing Rock and the History of Indigenous Resistance in the United States," *Backstory,* September 6, 2019.

128 Another map that circulated: Philip Kearney, "United States of Apathy," Philip

Kearney Cartography, April 20, 2018. "Disaffection" might have been a better word than "apathy."

130 Women, much of the workforce: Elizabeth Gurley Flynn, *The Rebel Girl: An Autobiography, My First Life* (New York: International Publishers, 1973), p. 132.

130 The mace was employed: U.S. House of Representatives, "The Strike at Lawrence, Mass.: Hearings Before the Committee on Rules, March 2–7, 1912" (Washington, DC: Government Printing Office, 1912), p. 343.

130 In February, troopers: Flynn, *Rebel Girl,* p. 138.

130 An avalanche of telegrams: U.S. House of Representatives, "The Strike at Lawrence, Mass.," p. 12.

130 The congressional Strike Commission: United States Strike Commission, "Report on the Chicago Strike of June–July, 1894" (Washington, DC: Government Printing Office, 1895), p. xliv. See also Robert Goldstein, *Political Repression in Modern America, from 1870 to the Present* (Cambridge, MA: Schenkman, 1978), especially pp. 1–102. From about 1873 till passage of the Wagner Act in 1937, writes Goldstein, "American labor suffered governmental repression that was probably as severe or more severe than that suffered by any labor movement in any other Western industrialized democracy" (p. 3).

130 "We are American citizens": *New York Times,* May 25, 1894.

130 "the governmental apparatus": Goldstein, *Political Repression,* p. 4. See also Jeremy Brecher, *Strike!* (San Francisco: Straight Arrow Books, 1972).

130 Two decades later: See James Green, *The Devil Is Here in These Hills: West Virginia's Coal Miners and Their Battle for Freedom* (New York: Grove Press, 2015), and the website of the West Virginia Mine Wars Museum. A moving novel about the events is Denise Giardina, *Storming Heaven* (New York: Ivy Books, 1988).

131 Arrested under vagrancy laws: Douglas Blackmon, *Slavery by Another Name: The Re-Enslavement of Black Americans from the Civil War to World War II* (New York: Anchor, 2008), p. 1.

131 Blackmon found records detailing: Ibid., p. 52.

131 When gangs of such mostly black: See Karin Shapiro, *A New South Rebellion: The Battle Against Convict Labor in the Tennessee Coalfields, 1871–1896* (Chapel Hill: University of North Carolina Press, 2017). A period folk song bears witness: "The corruption of Buchanan / Brought the convicts here / Just to please the rich man / And take the miner's share. / The miners acted manly / When they turned the convicts loose." In Archie Green, *Only a Coalminer: Studies in Recorded Coalmining Songs* (Chicago: University of Illinois Press, 1972).

131 During the epic 1892 Homestead strike: Brecher, *Strike!,* p. 58.

131 Court injunctions applying: On injunctions, see, among many others, Edwin Witte, "Early American Labor Cases," *Yale Law Journal* 35, no. 7 (1926): 825–37; Felix Frankfurter and Nathan Green, *The Labor Injunction* (New York: MacMillan, 1930). One—issued under conspiracy law, rather than the

Sherman Antitrust Act—is cited in *American Steel Foundries v. Tri-City Trades Council* 257 U.S. 184 (1921): "Defendants were 'perpetually restrained and enjoined from . . . interfering by persuasion, violence or threats of violence, in any manner with any person desiring to be employed by said American Steel Foundries . . . and from inducing or attempting to compel or induce by persuasion, threats, intimidation, force or violence or putting in fear or suggestions of danger any of the employees of the American Steel Foundries or persons seeking employment with it so as to cause them to refuse to perform any of their duties.'" The Strike Commission report, "Report on the Chicago Strike of June–July, 1894" (Washington, DC: Government Printing Office, 1895), pp. 361–62, records union members booing the reading of one such injunction. The *Chicago Tribune* judged that the object of such injunctions during the 1894 Pullman Strike was precisely to "lay the foundations for calling out the United States troops." *Chicago Times,* July 3, 1894, quoted in Brecher, *Strike!,* p. 85. Under the fifteen-year-old Posse Comitatus Act, the U.S. Army could not be deployed domestically to execute the law without congressional authorization. Congress did so authorize, after the strike was broken up, making the deployment legal after the fact. Other sources include: Ralph Winter, "Labor Injunctions and Judge-Made Labor Law: The Contemporary Role of Norris-LaGuardia," *Yale Law Journal* 70, no. 1 (1960): 70–102; Missouri Bureau of Labor Statistics, *The Use of Injunctions in Labor Disputes* (Jefferson City: Tribune Publishing Company, 1886), https://archive.org/stream/official historyo00miss/officialhistoryo00miss_djvu.txt.

131 "No president deemed it wise": Jerry Cooper, *The Army and Civil Disorder: Federal Military Intervention in Labor Disputes, 1877–1900* (Westport, CT: Greenwood Press, 1980), p. 17.

131 Today, these Gilded Age practices: See Sarah Chayes, *Thieves of State: Why Corruption Threatens Global Security* (New York: W. W. Norton, 2015), ch. 9, "The Post-Soviet Kleptocratic Autocracy," pp. 101–18. As recently as 2019, soldiers and police exercised force in Hong Kong, Iraq, and Lebanon, among other countries.

132 Yet, here and now, sheriffs' deputies: Thomas Dressler, "How Many Law Enforcement Agencies Does It Take to Subdue a Peaceful Protest," ACLU, November 30, 2016.

132 North Dakota proceeded to pass: North Dakota Senate Bill 2302, January 3, 2017. According to the International Center for Not-for-Profit Law, more than a dozen states have enacted laws protecting pipelines and other "critical infrastructure" from peaceful protests, by expanding the definition and punishment of "unauthorized entry" or trespass. ICNL, US Protest Law Tracker. One such law passed in West Virginia, theater of the 1921 Mine Wars, on March 7, 2020. See also the American Legislative Exchange Council's model Critical Infrastructure Protection Act.

132 In a similar pipeline fight: Aleen Brown and Will Parrish, "Recent Arrests Under New Anti-Protest Law Spotlight Risks That Off-Duty Cops Pose to Pipeline Opponents," *The Intercept,* August 22, 2018.

4. Powers Wielded: The Purse

133 At the time, defense spending: It is impossible to estimate Nigerian defense expenditures, because the budget is classified. Numerous press reports at the time cited the $6 billion figure. For a careful examination of the numbers in 2017, as well as the nature and implications of ongoing corruption in the Nigerian military, see Eva Anderson and Matthew Page, "Weaponising Transparency: Defence Procurement Reform as a Counterterrorism Strategy in Nigeria," Transparency International, 2017.

133 "Commanders see": "'Why We Could Not Defeat Boko Haram'—Army Commander Writes a Powerful Letter to President Jonathan," *Sahara Reporters,* December 15, 2014.

134 Or, perhaps, "simply ignorant": See, for instance, United States Department of Justice, U.S. Attorney's Office, Southern District of California, "Former U.S. Navy Captain Pleads Guilty . . . in Sweeping U.S. Navy Corruption and Fraud Probe," news release, November 13, 2018. For an overview, see "Glenn Defense Marine Asia and the U.S. 7th Fleet (the 'Fat Leonard' Scandal)," World Peace Foundation. See also Special Inspector General for Iraq Reconstruction, *Learning from Iraq,* March 2013, p. 7, for criminal indictments, prosecutions, and convictions and sums recovered during that war, and specific cases in boxes throughout.

134 In Washington, that same day: Called the "LOGCAP Contract," it is available at https://www.documentcloud.org/documents/239358-logcap.html. For discussion of how such "undefinitized" task orders were abused, see Defense Contract Audit Agency, "Memorandum for Department of the Army, Headquarters, U.S. Army Field Support Command, Subject: Payments of Allowable Costs Before Definitization, LOGCAP Contract DAAA-09-02-D-00007," August 16, 2004 (available at http://pogoarchives.org/m/cp/cp-DCAAHalliburton-040816 .pdf). For questions raised for congressional consideration, see Valerie Grasso, "Defense Contracting in Iraq: Issues and Options for Congress," Congressional Research Service, January 26, 2007. For a roundup of questionable Halliburton practices as of 2006, see CorpWatch et al., "Hurricane Halliburton: Conflict, Climate Change, and Catastrophe," May 2006. The documentation on contract abuses in Iraq and Afghanistan is voluminous, with an emphasis on "learning lessons" that is almost plaintive. See the reports of the Special Inspectors General for Iraq and Afghanistan Reconstruction, respectively. Reports from the Special Inspector General for Iraq Reconstruction can be found at https://www.globalsecurity.org/military/library/report/sigir/index .html. SIGAR's reports can be found at https://www.sigar.mil/. For an overview on both Afghanistan and Iraq, see Commission on Wartime Contracting, "Transforming Wartime Contracting: Controlling Costs, Reducing Risks," Final Report to Congress, August 2011. For just one of the False Claims Act suits DynCorp had to answer to, see U.S. Department of Justice, Office of Public Affairs, "U.S. Files Suit Against DynCorp International," press release, July 19, 2016.

135 Also $74,165: See, for instance, Jack Smith, "$37 Screws, a $7,622 Coffee Maker,, $640 Toilet Seats: Suppliers to Our Military Just Won't Be Oversold," *Los Angeles Times,* July 30, 1987.

136 In December 1985: *St. Louis Post-Dispatch,* "Arms Costs: A Wasteland?," December 15, 1985, and "Pentagon's Suspension Proceedings Against Major Defense Contractors/1985," December 20, 1985.

136 Some of the stories are collected: Dina Rasor, ed., *More Bucks, Less Bang: How the Pentagon Buys Ineffective Weapons* (Washington, DC: Fund for Constitutional Government, 1983). For an example from the Afghanistan and Iraq wars, see Robert Bauman and Dina Rasor, *Shattered Minds: How the Pentagon Fails Our Troops with Faulty Helmets* (Washington, DC: Potomac Books, 2019).

136 But shortly after taking: "Remarks by President Clinton Announcing the Initiative to Streamline Government," March 3, 1993.

136 With the stated goal: On Clinton's "Reinventing Government" in general, see Donald Kettl, "After the Reforms," Brookings Institution, April 1, 1998.

136 Now, she says, the situation: Telephone interview, January 11, 2019. Today, spare parts prices don't have to be listed at all. 2018 guidance allows numbers to be fudged if the program in question is classified. Charles Clark, "Accounting Board Sides with Secrecy Hawks on Classified Defense Spending," *Government Executive,* August 28, 2018. And one problem encountered by anyone who has worked in the Pentagon is overclassification.

136 For fiscal year 2020: Joe Gould, "Pentagon Finally Gets Its 2020 Budget from Congress," *Defense News,* December 19, 2019; Mark Cancian, "U.S. Military Forces in FY 2020: The Strategic and Budget Context," Center for Strategic and International Studies, September 30, 2019.

137 That's what the State Department pays: The Security Assistance Monitor collects and organizes the difficult to find data on security aid. Its dashboard, "A citizen's guide to U.S. security and defense assistance," allows users to search by country and by program.

137 On those contracts: Terminology quoted from the 2001 LOGCAP contract and U.S. Department of Defense, "Selected Acquisition Report: F-35 Lightning II Joint Strike Fighter Program, as of FY 2018 President's Budget," December 2016, p. 76.

138 In other words, the U.S. government: The top five contractors gain approximately one-third of defense contracts. See Federal Procurement Data System, "Top 100 Contractors Report." The largely unwanted $1.5 trillion F-35 fighter jet program is the most egregious current example of defective weapons whose failings are concealed. See, for instance, Dan Grazier, "The Next F-35 Headache Is Here," *National Interest,* December 9, 2018.

138 "Service contractors are": Interview January 9, 2019. See this graph of expenditures on contract labor versus DoD civilian and military personnel, which a whistle-blower made available to the Project on Government Oversight (POGO): https://pogoblog.typepad.com/.a/6a00d8341c68bf53ef0167624a8 e5c970b-800wi. Note that POGO is a successor to Rasor's Project on Defense

Procurement. I am a member of its board of directors. POGO has found that the U.S. government pays nearly double market rates for private contractors in civilian as well as security-related positions. See Paul Chassy and Scott Amey, "Bad Business: Billions of Taxpayer Dollars Wasted on Hiring Contractors," Project on Government Oversight, September 13, 2011; Scott Amey, "DoD Contractors Cost Nearly 3 Times More Than DoD Civilians," Project on Government Oversight, November 30, 2012. For 2012 Senate hearings on the topic, see "Contractors: How Much Are They Costing the Government?" U.S. Senate Committee on Homeland Security, Subcommittee on Contracting Oversight, March 29, 2012. On the relationship between campaign contributions, staff exchanges between DoD and contractors, and contract awards, see Scott Amey, "The Politics of Contracting," Project on Government Oversight, June 29, 2004. On intelligence contractors, see also Janine Wedel, *Unaccountable: How the Establishment Corrupted Our Finances, Freedom, and Politics, and Created an Outsider Class* (New York: Pegasus, 2014), pp. 150–58. Note that with the wars in Afghanistan and Iraq largely wound down, procurement expenditures are on the rise again. See, for instance, Andrew Cockburn, "Like a Ball of Fire," *London Review of Books* 42, no. 5 (March 5, 2020).

138   In 2014—like those: The U.S. Department of Justice has fined multiple defense contractors for fraudulent labor charges. MPRI's "ghost soldier" violation is detailed in U.S. Department of Justice, Office of Public Affairs, "MPRI Inc. Agrees to Pay $3.2 Million for False Labor Charges on Contract to Support Army in Afghanistan," press release, February 12, 2014. Here is a Boeing example: U.S. Department of Justice, Office of Public Affairs, "Boeing Pays $23 Million to Resolve False Claims Act Allegations," press release, October 10, 2014. The government's complaint in the underlying case details the various scams, from p. 15: "United States District Court for the Southern District of Texas, San Antonio Division, "Plaintiffs' *Qui Tam* Complaint Pursuant to the Federal False Claims Act," filed October 29, 2007 (under seal), available at http://s3.amazonaws.com/fcmd/documents/documents/000/003/289/original/Boeing_-_Craddock_COMPLAINT.pdf?1428692973. For an example from a narco-terrorism program, see U.S. Department of Defense, Inspector General, "Northrop Grumman Improperly Charged Labor for the Counter Narco-terrorism Technology Program," May 13, 2014. Even where fraud is not constituted, roughly 50 percent of contracts go to profit and overhead, though 70–80 percent of the contracted work is done inside government buildings using government equipment. Therefore, taxpayers are paying overhead costs twice. And note that unlike soldiers, civilian labor can walk off the job or commit atrocities, making it just as unreliable under fire, at times, as a shoddy tank. See "FY 2011 Contract Services Inventory," chart used in the 2012 Senate Homeland Security Committee hearing, available at https://www.hsgac.senate.gov/imo/media/doc/Chart%20used%20by%20McCaskill%20during%203.29.12%20hearing.pdf. Another way that private defense companies have evolved is to market equipment aggressively to foreign countries. See, for the most recent figures, Paul McLeary, "US Arms Sales Overseas Skyrocketed

33% in 2018," Breaking Defense, October 9, 2018. Persian Gulf governments have been massive buyers—with severe impacts on U.S. foreign policy. See Jodi Vittori, "A Mutual Extortion Racket: The Military Industrial Complex and US Foreign Policy—the Cases of Saudi Arabia & UAE," Transparency International Defense & Security Program, December 2019.

138 In the words of: "Congress: Why the Biggest Watchdog Seldom Barks," *St. Louis Post-Dispatch,* December 21, 1985.

139 "It is a relationship that is based": See the 2001 LOGCAP Contract, https://www.documentcloud.org/documents/239358-logcap.html, p. 2.

139 But I'm not sure: As Janine Wedel put it in *Unaccountable:* "It's almost as if the door has disappeared completely," p. 151.

139 Combing through years of records: Mandy Smithburger, "Brass Parachutes: The Problem of the Pentagon Revolving Door," Project on Government Oversight, November 5, 2018. In "From the Pentagon to the Private Sector: In Large Numbers, and with Few Rules, Retiring Generals Are Taking Lucrative Defense-Firm Jobs," *Boston Globe* reporter Bryan Bender charts the steep rise in retired top brass working for defense contractors since 1992. *Boston Globe,* December 26, 2010. See also Wedel, *Unaccountable,* pp. 158–65. Wedel maintains her own Pentagon revolving-door database.

139 President Obama quickly waived: Barack Obama, "Executive Order: Ethics Commitments by Executive Branch Appointees," The White House, Executive Orders, January 21, 2009; The White House, President Barack Obama, "Ethics Pledges and Waivers." See also Robert Cusick, "Annual Report Pursuant to Executive Order 13490," Office of Government Ethics, March 31, 2010.

140 Former Lockheed vice president: Lockheed has committed the most misconduct of any federal government contractor, including a dozen instances— ranging from overbilling to violating federal elections law to violating the Arms Export Control Act—while Comey was vice president and general counsel. Federal Contractor Misconduct Database, "Lockheed Martin." And see Francine McKenna, "James Comey and KPMG: Isn't It Ironic," *Forbes,* May 31, 2013.

140 Under President Trump, at least: "General Dynamics Names Gen. Mattis to Its Board," UPI, August 9, 2013. https://www.gd.com/news/press-releases/2013/08/general-dynamics-elects-james-n-mattis-board-directors. Mattis received a congressional waiver of the law banning officers from taking civilian leadership posts in the Pentagon unless they have been out of uniform for seven years or more.

140 former Boeing vice president Patrick Shanahan: United States Department of Defense, "Ellen Lord: Under Secretary of Defense for Acquisition and Sustainment," https://dod.defense.gov/About/Biographies/Biography-View/Article/1281505/ellen-m-lord/.

140 French economist Thomas Piketty: Thomas Piketty, *Capital in the Twenty-First Century* (Cambridge, MA: Harvard University Press, 2017), pp. 168–73. For the former Soviet Union see below, Part V, Chapter 2, "Courting Calamity," pp. 269–75.

140 Few countries on earth: Read "Bless This Land," by U.S. poet laureate Joy
     Harjo, in her collection *An American Sunrise* (New York: Norton, 2019),
     pp. 106–8. Or better, listen to the inaugural reading at https://www.youtube
     .com/watch?v=HiIJFRXxa3o.

140 George Washington, for example: Stanley Elkins and Eric McKitrick, *The Age
     of Federalism: The Early American Republic, 1788–1800* (Oxford, UK: Oxford
     University Press, 1996), p. 36.

141 rare earth metals: Wyoming Mining Association, "Rare Earths."

141 A 1976 law shifted: See the Report to the President and the Congress, by the
     Public Land Law Review Commission, established 1964, "One Third of the
     Nation's Land," and U.S. Department of the Interior, Bureau of Land Manage-
     ment, "The Federal Land Policy and Management Act of 1976, as Amended,"
     October 2001.

141 Art left on timeless: Jim Mimiaga, "Mesa Verde Reports Increase in Vandalism,
     Graffiti," *The Journal* (Colorado), July 30, 2017.

142 People and groups now familiar: Johanna Wald and Elizabeth Temkin, "The
     Sagebrush Rebellion: The West Against Itself—Again," *UCLA Journal of Envi-
     ronmental Law and Policy* 2, no. 2 (1982): 187–207; Lyndsey Gilpin, "How
     an East Coast Think Tank Is Fueling the Land Transfer Movement," *High
     Country News,* February 26, 2016. For the perspective of members of the
     rebellion, who have served as public officials and lobbyists for energy and
     mining interests, see David Leroy and Roy Eiguren, "State Takeover of Federal
     Lands—the 'Sagebrush Rebellion,'" *Rangelands* 2, no. 6 (December 1980):
     229–31.

142 The "rebellion" flamed up again: Back as far as the mid-1990s, Charles and/
     or David Koch have been on the periphery of the Sagebrush Rebellion, with
     links to such allied organizations as the Western States Coalition and Defend-
     ers of Property Rights. David Koch is listed as a member of WSC in the
     February 1996 issue of *People for the West,* https://www.documentcloud.org
     /documents/1659501-pftwnews0015-001.html. In its July/August 1997 issue,
     Property Rights Reporter thanks the Charles Koch Charitable Foundation for
     funding four interns, enabling Defenders of Property Rights to "help train
     the next generation of lawyers in the importance of property rights," https://
     www.documentcloud.org/documents/1349939-defendersofpr00719.html. In
     2005, Koch Industries bought Georgia Pacific, a paper products corporation,
     adding an appetite for cheap lumber to other reasons for coveting public land.
     Most recently, Koch entities delivered their largest grant ever to a university in
     the western United States to Utah State University, for the Center for Growth
     and Opportunity, which overlaps with the private (Koch-funded) Strata Policy.
     The work of both entities is devoted to challenging federal land protections.
     See Ryan Beam and Samantha Parsons, "Insidious Gift: How the Koch Foun-
     dation's $25 Million Donation to Utah State University Aims to Dismantle
     Protections for America's Public Lands," Center for Biological Diversity and
     UnKoch My Campus, October 2018. For the linked Strata think tank, see
     https://strata.org/pdf/2017/ar-2016.pdf.

142 It required the secretary of the interior: H.R. 621: Disposal of Excess Federal Lands Act of 2017.

142 Another is to accelerate: U.S. Department of the Interior, Bureau of Land Management, "Updating Oil and Gas Leasing Reform—Land Use Planning and Lease Parcel Reviews," instruction memorandum, January 31, 2018.

142 "There is a rush to offer": Telephone interview, January 23, 2019. See also Hannah Nordhaus, "Battle for the American West: The New Push to Cut Back Protected Land Is Fueling a Dispute Rooted in Our History and Culture," *National Geographic,* November 2018. For a careful study on similar cut-rate deals on leases for coal mining, see Tom Sanzillo, "The Great Giveaway: An Analysis of the Costly Failure of Federal Coal Leasing in the Powder River Basin," Institute for Energy Economics and Financial Analysis, June 2012.

143 American citizens lost: Taxpayers for Common Sense, "Taxpayers Lose in Noncompetitive Montana Lease Sale," November 27, 2018.

143 The World Wildlife Fund: Ove Hoegh-Goldberg et al., "Reviving the Ocean Economy: The Case for Action," World Wildlife Fund, 2015.

143 Deliberately, like the Sagebrush vandals: Valerie Volcovici, "Drillers Snap Up Federal Leases Near Utah's Wilderness Monuments," Reuters, March 20, 2018. In fact, though leases on all forty-three parcels put up for auction did sell, the low sales prices (as low as two dollars per acre) suggest there was not "strong industry demand" in the region, as the article purports.

143 Not only where the bones: See Keith Basso's remarkable book *Wisdom Sits in Places: Landscape and Language Among the Western Apache* (Albuquerque: University of New Mexico Press, 1996).

143 Among clauses on how many: United States House of Representative, H.R. 5, "Adopting Rules for the One Hundred Fifteenth Congress."

143 In the absence of much other: Material on privatization of public services at the federal, state, and local levels is voluminous. For a pathway into it, see the work of In the Public Interest: https://www.inthepublicinterest.org/. Multitrillion-dollar coronavirus packages provided unprecedented opportunities for wielding the power of the purse. See, for instance, Richard Henderson and Robin Wigglesworth, "Fed's Big Boost for BlackRock Raises Eyebrows on Wall Street," *Financial Times,* March 27, 2020; Alan Rappeport and Jeanna Smialek, "How Powell and Mnuchin Became the Duo in Charge of Saving the Economy," *New York Times,* March 31, 2020; Sarah Chayes, "Look Out, Corruption Ahead," *The Atlantic,* April 17, 2020.

5. Powers Sabotaged

144 bills flooded Congress: Martin Nie and Patrick Kelly, "State and Local Control of Federal Lands: New Developments in the Transfer of Federal Lands Movement," *Ecology Law Currents* 45 (2018): 187–99.

144 In a September 2018 memorandum: Secretary of the Interior, "State Fish and Wildlife Management Authority on Department of the Interior Lands and Waters," memorandum to heads of bureaus and offices, September 10, 2018.

145 "Now someone has ginned up": The rule in question was published in the *Federal Register* on January 23, 2020 (https://www.epa.gov/sites/production /files/2020-01/documents/navigable_waters_protection_rule_prepbulication .pdf). See Annie Snider, "Trump Erodes Water Protections: 6 Things to Know," *Politico,* January 23, 2020. The method used was to change the definition of "navigable waters," which are protected under the Clean Water Act—as per the definition mincing described later in this section. The Koch-funded Reason Institute supports similar devolution to the states for meat inspection. See Baylen Linnekin, "It's Time to Put Our Federal Meat Inspection Law Out to Pasture," *Reason,* May 19, 2018. In 2009, the state of California obtained a waiver of Clean Air Act provisions, provided the standards it substituted were *stricter* than federal guidelines. Now that same EPA is fighting California in court to prevent it from enforcing its state-level provisions. In August 2019, the Department of Justice launched an antitrust investigation against four automakers that have chosen to abide by California's standards—presumably to oblige them to pollute more than they find to be in their economic interest. See U.S. Environmental Protection Agency, "Proposed California Waiver Withdrawal," fact sheet, no date; David Shepardson, "U.S. Launches Antitrust Probe into California Automaker Agreement," Reuters, September 6, 2019.

145 Even before the coronavirus pandemic: Susan Bodine, "COVID-19 Implications for EPA's Enforcement and Compliance Assurance Program," EPA Memorandum, March 26, 2020.

146 At the Department of Agriculture: Isaac Arnsdorf, "Chicken Farmers Thought Trump Was Going to Help Them. His Administration Did the Opposite," *West Virginia Gazette and Mail,* June 5, 2019. See also Deena Shanker, "Farmers' Beef with Trump over 'Big Meat,'" Bloomberg, April 21, 2017.

146 A December 2018 study: Leif Fredrickson et al., "A Sheep in the Closet: The Erosion of Enforcement at the EPA," Environmental Data and Governance Initiative, November 2018, updated May 2019, tracks civil actions. Criminal referrals are also sharply down: Ellen Knickmeyer, "E.P.A. Criminal Action Against Polluters Hits 30-Year Low," Associated Press, January 15, 2019.

146 and is doing so: Nadja Popovich et al., "83 Environmental Rules Being Rolled Back Under Trump," *New York Times,* updated June 7, 2019.

146 For the purposes of required: For examples among countless others, see The President of the United States, "Promoting Energy Independence and Economic Growth," Executive Order 13783, March 28, 2017. The OMB guidance this executive order reinstates, written in 2003 (without benefit of the next fifteen years of global research and increasingly advanced computer modeling), allows for carbon to be considered as having no social cost. Following the executive order above, an EPA impact analysis of several proposed regulatory changes uses an estimate of the social cost of carbon at either one dollar or eight dollars per ton, in contrast to the approximately fifty dollars per ton that had to be put into these calculations prior to this executive order. See United States Environmental Protection Agency, "Regulatory Impact Analysis for the Proposed Emission Guidelines for Greenhouse Gas Emissions from Existing

Electric Utility Generating Units . . . ," August 2018, p. 4–4. By using low cost estimates, regulatory rollbacks are made to seem more economically beneficial on balance than they are. The December 2018 draft of new guidelines on the definition of ambient air: U.S. Environmental Protection Agency, "Revised Policy on Exclusions from 'Ambient Air,'" draft, November 2018. See also, on safety levels for the chemical TCE, which damages the ability of hearts to form in fetuses, Elizabeth Shogren et al., "The Tell-Tale Hearts," *Reveal,* February 29, 2020.

147   I interviewed a European Union functionary: See Sarah Chayes, "When Corruption Is the Operating System: The Case of Honduras," Carnegie Endowment for International Peace, May 30, 2017.

148   An across-the-board federal hiring freeze: Louis Jacobson, "No Sign of a Revived Hiring Freeze for Now," *Politifact,* January 23, 2018, quoting Budget Director Mick Mulvaney in April 2017. But the high vacancy rate almost adds up to a de facto freeze. See Charles Clark, "Vacancy Rate for Top Agency Jobs Continues to Set Records," *Government Executive,* August 1, 2018.

149   In spring 2020: American Foreign Service Association, "Tracker: Current U.S. Ambassadors"; *Washington Post* and Partnership for Public Service, "Tracking How Many Key Positions Trump Has Filled So Far," database; Ryan Goodman and Danielle Shulkin, "Timeline of the Cornonavirus Pandemic and U.S. Response," Just Security, April 16, 2020.

149   The very first provision: U.S. House of Representatives, H.R. 6, "Adopting the Rules of the House of Representatives for the One Hundred Fourth Congress," January 5, 1995.

150   Today, the number of staff: Bill Pascrell, "Why Is Congress So Dumb?" *Washington Post,* January 11, 2019. See also Paul Glastris and Haley Sweetland Edwards, "The Big Lobotomy," *Washington Monthly,* June/July/August 2014, and this February 27, 2020, open letter to the U.S. Senate, signed by seventy former colleagues: https://www.washingtonpost.com/opinions /former-us-senators-the-senate-is-failing-to-perform-its-constitutional -duties/2020/02/25/b9bdd22a-5743-11ea-9000-f3cffee23036_story.html.

150   Fumed a former staff lead: Interview, January 31, 2019.

150   A new college graduate: Interview, January 28, 2020.

151   Democrats also copied the internal pay-to-play: Economist Thomas Ferguson calls it "a Sears Catalogue." See "Big Money, Mass Media, and Polarized Politics," in William Crotty, ed., *Polarized Politics: The Impact of Divisiveness in the US Political System* (Boulder: Lynne Rienner, 2014), p. 96. Also see Russ Choma, "DCCC Leads NRCC on Strength of Member Dues," Open Secrets, February 24, 2015. On February 12, 2020, I also discussed with a former candidate her own experience with the DCCC, which dismissed her proven ability to mobilize supporters, and withheld assistance due to a perceived inability to attract big donors.

151   In *Money in the House:* Marian Currinder, *Money in the House* (Boulder, CO: Westview Press, 2009), p. 37. See her discussion of the implications on pp. 36–40. Lobbyists might welcome a similarly clear price list. An analyst on

the Joint Staff, who uses sophisticated modeling to advise the Department of Defense on force structure, told me on February 1, 2020, that a lobbyist had told him the holy grail in his industry would be an algorithm that could calculate the amount of money that would have to be delivered to elected officials in order to secure a given desired outcome.

151 Starved of funds: In late 2019, for example, the EPA resurrected a proposed measure that would restrict the use of peer-reviewed scientific and medical research in devising public health regulations, unless all the "underlying data"—including confidential medical records—is available for scrutiny. See "Strengthening Transparency in Regulatory Science," supplemental notice of proposed rulemaking, Environmental Protection Agency, no date but likely fall 2019, available at https://int.nyt.com/data/documenthelper/6438-epa-science -rule/0056cd3a5a080415e713/optimized/full.pdf#page=1. See also "SAB [Science Advisory Board] Consideration of the Scientific and Technical Basis of EPA's Proposed Rule Titled Strengthening Transparency in Regulatory Science," draft report to the EPA, October 16, 2019, available at https://yosemite .epa.gov/sab/sabproduct.nsf/ea5d9a9b55cc319285256cbd005a472e/8a4da bc3b78f4106852584e100541a03!OpenDocument; Goodman and Shulkin, "Timeline of the Coronavirus Pandemic."

151 Even the leadership of the nation's numerous: Ellen Nakashima et al., "Senior Intelligence Official Told Lawmakers That Russia Wants to See Trump Reelected," *Washington Post,* February 21, 2020.

152 It permitted debate: This rule may have its roots in a more consensus-oriented approach to government. It held during the Constitutional Convention. The notion was, at some point, after lengthy debate, the majority would give enough ground to allow the minority to accept the provision, and it would do so, its lingering reservations subsiding. This is how democratic decisions are made at the village level in Afghanistan, for example.

153 For years, bipartisan measures: Note that it would be my preference to reserve that money for its original purpose: restoring denuded and contaminated forests and hillsides to health. While wealthy mining executives and other creditors are made whole in bankruptcy settlements, mineworkers are placed in competition with the landscapes around them. On pensions, part of a historic 1946 settlement with the employers and the U.S. government that ended the last of the often bloody conflicts in the coalfields, see, for instance, United Mine Workers of America, "The Promise of 1946," UMWA website; Lesley Clark, "Coal Miners Appeal to McConnell to Back a Rescue of Their Pensions," McClatchy, May 8, 2019; Tracie Mauriello, "Retired Coal Miners Seek Congress's Help to Preserve Their Pensions," *Pittsburgh Post-Gazette,* June 12, 2019; Editorial Staff, "Are McConnell, Congress Friends of Coal Mining Communities? We're About to Find Out," *Lexington Herald-Leader,* no date, but likely August 2019; Editorial Staff, "Now to Save Coalminers' Pensions," *Lexington Herald-Leader,* no date, but likely August 2019. On the RECLAIM Act, see Greg Stotelmyer, "Grassroots Petition to McConnell: Get Moving on RECLAIM Act," Kentucky Council of Churches, December 6, 2016. The bill's

current status can be found at https://www.congress.gov/bill/116th-congress/house-bill/2156/all-info.

153 McConnell—a senator from coal-rich Kentucky: McConnell abruptly reversed his long-standing position when a Democrat won the Kentucky governor's race in November 2019. See, for instance, Rebecca Rainey, "Congress Rushes to Save Miners' Pensions but Ignores Larger Retirement Crisis," *Politico,* December 26, 2019.

153 McConnell countered: Naomi Jagoda, "Miners Union Pleads with Senators for Pension Fix," *The Hill,* March 1, 2016. One explanation for the real reason behind the stonewalling has been that the pensions in question are those guaranteed to United Mineworkers of America members, and McConnell is opposed to unions. A more venal explanation suggests that the only major mine operator still contributing to the fund is Murray Energy, and a rival, Alliance Resources and its CEO Joe Craft and his wife, Kelly, are close allies of McConnell.

153 That appointee, who took office: Hartogensis, a dot-com millionaire, has a background in private equity, including energy and real estate, and no experience with manufacturing industries or pension plans. Pension Benefit Guaranty Corporation, "Gordon Hartogensis Sworn in as PBGC Director," press release, May 16, 2019; Michael Katz, "Senate Confirms Gordon Hartogensis as Director of PBGC," *Plansponsor,* May 6, 2019; Madison Alder, "McConnell Brother-in-Law Gets Pension Agency Nomination Hearing," Bloomberg Law, September 21, 2018.

153 But no such plant existed: "$4M Abandoned Mine Lands Pilot Grant Announced for EastPark Industrial Park," *Lane Report,* October 17, 2018; Morgan Watkins, "Braidy Industries Must Raise $300M in 4 Months or Risk Losing $100M from Russian Company," *Louisville Courier Journal,* July 16, 2019; Simon Shuster and Vera Bergengruen, "A Kremlin-Linked Firm Invested Millions in Kentucky. Were They After More Than Money?" *Time,* August 13, 2019.

153 While McConnell was working: Aikin Gump, "Brendan M. Dunn, Former McConnell Policy Advisor, to Join Akin Gump," press release, May 21, 2018; Open Secrets, "Lobbyists Representing Braidy Industries, 2019."

154 Within nine months: U.S. Department of the Treasury, "Treasury Designates Russian Oligarchs, Officials, and Entities in Response to Worldwide Malign Activity," press release, April 6, 2018; U.S. Department of the Treasury, "OFAC Delists En+, Rusal, and EuroSibEnergo," press release, January 27, 2019.

154 McConnell vaunted his party's tough line: Mitch McConnell, floor speech, in "Disapproving the President's Proposal to Take an Action Relating to the Application of Certain Sanctions with Respect to the Russian Federation—Motion to Proceed," *Congressional Record,* January 15, 2019, p. S201; Kenneth Vogel, "Republicans Break Ranks over Move to Lift Sanctions on Russian Oligarch's Firms," *New York Times,* January 15, 2019; Patricia Zengerie, "Bid to Keep U.S. Sanctions on Russia's Rusal Fails in Senate," Reuters, January 16, 2019.

154 Three months later, Rusal announced: Joe Deaux, "With Sanctions Lifted, Rusal to Invest in U.S. Aluminum Mill," Bloomberg, April 14, 2019; Shuster and Bergengruen, "A Kremlin-Linked Firm," August 13, 2019.

154 One of Rusal's top shareholders: Jake Rudnitsky, "Tangled Rusal Ownership Thwarts Easy End to Sanctions: Quick Take," Bloomberg, April 25, 2018.

154 Blavatnik has spent around $7 million: Blavatnik was questioned during the special prosecutor's probe into Russian interference in the 2016 election. See John Santucci et al., "EXCLUSIVE: Special Counsel Probing Donations with Foreign Connections to Trump Inauguration," ABC News, May 11, 2018. He escapes close scrutiny largely because of his acquisition of U.S. and U.K. citizenship and his donations to such institutions as the Council on Foreign Relations and select political causes. Ruth May, "How Putin's Oligarchs Funneled Millions into GOP Campaigns," *Dallas Morning News,* December 15, 2017. See also Open Secrets, "Donor Lookup: Blavatnik," Center for Responsive Politics, no date; Open Secrets, "Access Industries, Profile for 2018 Election Cycle," Center for Responsive Politics, no date; Open Secrets, "Ai Altep, Donor Detail," Center for Responsive Politics, no date; Max de Haldevang, "Major GOP Donor Len Blavatnik Had Business Ties to a Russian Official," *Quartz,* January 22, 2019.

154 Another major (21 percent) shareholder: Via Rusal's parent company EN+, the originally sanctioned entity. Polina Devitt and Arshad Mohammed, "Questions Linger over Deripaska's Rusal Influence After U.S. Deal," Reuters, February 4, 2019; on VTB, see Carrie Levine, "How a Sanctioned Russian Bank Wooed Washington," Center for Public Integrity and Public Radio International, December 18, 2018.

154 Since 2015, VTB: "VTB in Talks with Chinese Companies over Potential EN+ Investment," *Financial Times,* September 8, 2019; VTB, "VTB to Increase Financing of Russian-Chinese Trade," press release, August 5, 2015.

154 In October of that year: Lee Hong Liang, "China, Taiwan Banks Extend Shipbuilding Loan to US Firm," *Seatrade Maritime News,* October 22, 2015. Chao is standing fifth from the left in the photo.

155 These are the Chaos: Michela Tindera, "A $59 Million Will Sheds Light on Shipping Fortune Connected to Elaine Chao and Mitch McConnell," *Forbes,* June 10, 2019; American Oversight, "Elaine Chao Calendars Reveal New Links to Family's Company, Including Private Photo Sessions," June 10, 2019; Michael Forsythe et al., "A 'Bridge' to China, and Her Family's Business, in the Trump Cabinet," *New York Times,* June 2, 2019.

155 Along with her stint on the board: As per her personal website: https://www.angelachao.org/.

155 In 2016, the Bank of China: James Marson and Andrey Ostroukh, "Gazprom Secures $2.17 Billion Loan from Bank of China," *Wall Street Journal,* March 3, 2016. Many Gazprom entities and executives are also under U.S. Treasury sanctions: Risk Advisory, "Russia Sanctions List," accessed April 17, 2019.

155 It has a partnership: VTB, "VTB to Expand Financing Trade Contracts with Bank of China," press release, March 30, 2016.

155 So, to recap: For a portrait of McConnell, further corroborating many of these details and adding more, see Jane Mayer, "How Mitch McConnell Became Trump's Enabler-in-Chief," *New Yorker,* April 20, 2020.

6. Bowing to the Money Changers

157 That event caused more people: There is some debate as to how much the Great Recession pushed up the number of suicides, but the rough consensus seems to be around five thousand. See, for instance, Aaron Reeves et al., "Economic Suicides in the Great Recession in Europe and North America," *British Journal of Psychiatry* 205, no. 3 (September 2014): 246–47, and, for an opposing view, see Harper and Bruckner, "Did the Great Recession Increase Suicides in the USA? Evidence from an Interrupted Time-Series Analysis," *Annals of Epidemiology* 27, no. 7 (July 2017): 409–14. Financial Crisis Inquiry Commission, "Financial Crisis Inquiry Report" (Washington, DC: Government Printing Office, January 2011), p. xvii.

157 The cofounder of a California: Financial Crisis Inquiry Commission (FCIC), "Report," p. 9.

157 In 2000, Cleveland's county treasurer: Ibid., p. 10.

157 State attorneys general battled: Several states passed laws that tightened requirements on mortgage lending. Wachovia sued Michigan. The Office of the Comptroller of the Currency joined Wachovia, against forty-nine states' attorneys general, who supported their Michigan colleague. The states lost in the Supreme Court by a 5–3 vote—in April 2007. *Watters v. Wachovia Bank, N.A.,* 550 U.S. 1 (2007).

158 By law and by willful inaction: William Black, *The Best Way to Rob a Bank Is to Own One* (Austin: University of Texas Press, 2013), pp. 32–38; George Akerlof and Paul Romer, "Looting: The Economic Underworld of Bankruptcy for Profit," in *Explorations in Pragmatic Economics: Selected Papers of George Akerlof (and Coauthors)* (Oxford, UK: Oxford University Press, 2005), pp. 248–52.

159 Alongside such moves: Speaking to savings bank executives in November 1982, shortly after signing the Garn–St. Germain Depository Institutions Act, President Reagan called the legislation "the Emancipation Proclamation for America's savings institutions." Ronald Reagan, "Remarks at the Annual Convention of the United States League of Savings Associations," New Orleans, November 16, 1982.

159 The lines branching out: Kitty Calavita, Henry Pontell, and Robert Tillman, *Big Money Crime: Fraud and Politics in the Savings and Loan Crisis* (Berkeley: University of California Press, 1997), p. 92. "Evidence suggests that political corruption was at the very heart of the thrift scandal," the authors begin their chapter "The Political Connection," which spells out these networked links, as well as what they call "implicit bribery."

159 "Higher deposit insurance": Telephone interview, August 11, 2015.

160 The details of the thefts: Akerlof and Romer, "Looting," pp. 243, 252–53;

Calavita et al., *Big Money Crime,* pp. 39–41, 47–85; Black, *The Best Way to Rob a Bank,* pp. 44, 47–52.

161 Just like their assets: See Calavita et al., *Big Money Crime,* pp. 156–68, for data on the extremely low risk of criminal prosecution even for identified suspects, and the lenient sentences that convicted fraudsters received.

161 The result that got them: Akerlof and Romer, "Looting," p. 239. See also Calavita et al., *Big Money Crime,* p. 63.

162 Already concerned and now nauseated: Black, *The Best Way to Rob a Bank,* pp. 44–45.

162 "When there was a spike": More recently, mechanics, especially at Southwest Airlines, described management directives not to report safety issues and complained about outsourcing maintenance to jurisdictions not covered by FAA rules. See CBS News, "Airline Mechanics Feel Pressured to Overlook Potential Safety Problems: 'Accident Waiting to Happen,' " February 4, 2019. The type of coziness that characterizes relations between the Pentagon and defense contractors has spread to the FAA's relationship with Boeing. See Natalie Kitroeff and David Gelles, "Before Deadly Crashes, Boeing Pushed for Law That Undercut Oversight," *New York Times,* October 27, 2019. See also Connor Raso, "Boeing Crisis Illustrates Risks of Delegated Regulatory Authority," Brookings, December 18, 2019, and House Committee on Transportation and Infrastructure, Democratic Staff, "The Boeing 737 Max Aircraft: Costs, Consequences and Lessons from Its Design, Development, and Certification," report of preliminary investigative findings, March 2020.

163 Three white-collar criminologists: Calavita et al., *Big Money Crime,* p. 42.

163 A comparison between S&Ls: Akerlof and Romer, "Looting," pp. 253–57.

164 Whereas, complex as they were: Federal Crisis Inquiry Commission, "Report," pp. 47–48.

164 Federal Reserve chairman Alan Greenspan: On Greenspan's unwillingness to use the regulatory authority provided under the 1994 reform, see Raymond Natter, "Home Ownership Equity Protection Act," a note to the American Bar Association. Natter served on the Senate Banking Committee when the law was passed, then at the Office of the Comptroller of the Currency; Richard Spillenkothen, director of banking supervision and regulation at the Federal Reserve Board until 2006, provided a detailed submission on supervisory deficiencies to the Financial Crisis Inquiry Commission: "Notes on the Performance of Prudential Supervision in the Years Preceding the Financial Crisis by a Former Director of Banking Supervision and Regulation at the Federal Reserve Board (1991–2006), May 31, 2010," available on the Stanford Law School's online archive of documents pertaining to the Financial Crisis Inquiry Commission, fcic.law.stanford.edu. For Greenspan on fraud, see Manuel Roig-Franzia, "Brooksley Born, the Cassandra of the Derivatives Crisis," *Washington Post,* May 26, 2009.

164 Now banks were legally allowed: Permission for automated underwriting is published in rule #1210, Semiannual Regulatory Agenda, part IX, Department

of Housing and Urban Development, "Single Family Mortgage Insurance: Direct Endorsement for Automated Underwriting," *Federal Register* 63, no. 80 (April 27, 1998): 22063.

164 Even so, "liar's loans": See statement by Steven Krystofiak, president, Mortgage Brokers Association for Responsible Lending, to the Federal Reserve Board, in August 2006: https://www.federalreserve.gov/secrs/2006/august/20060801 /op-1253/op-1253_3_1.pdf.

164 One argument for gutting: The 1998 merger of Travelers and Citigroup, illegal under Glass-Steagall, helped force repeal of the law. Nomi Prins, *All the Presidents' Bankers: The Hidden Alliances That Drive American Power* (New York: Nation Books, 2014), pp. 381–82.

164 "We were heavy into prosecuting": Telephone interview, July 19, 2019. See also Federal Bureau of Investigation, Office of the Inspector General, *The External Effects of the Federal Bureau of Investigation's Reprioritization Efforts,* ch. 3, "FBI Resource and Casework Analysis," September 2005; Robert Mueller, "The FBI Transformation Since 2001," testimony before the House Appropriations Subcommittee on Science, etc., September 14, 2006.

165 Either they were exceptionally dim-witted: Recent social science research, examining why humans—gifted with our unique intelligence—so often cling to false ideas, suggests an alternative explanation. *The Misinformation Age: How False Beliefs Spread,* by Cailin O'Connor and James Weatherall (New Haven, CT: Yale University Press, 2018) deliberately focuses on a community that prides itself on its rigorous training to draw impartial conclusions on the basis of evidence alone: scientists. The book charts how correct scientific theories backed by clear evidence—such as fewer deaths of women in childbirth when doctors washed their hands—have nevertheless been rejected by a stubborn consensus of scientists. Even today, the book argues, theories gain followers via trust relationships more than independent analysis of data. Applied to the Treasury and Fed officials of the 1990s and 2000s, that finding raises a further question: Who constituted these officials' community of trust? Public servants motivated by the people's interests? Or individuals addicted to maximizing wealth? See also Gene Marks, "21 Percent of CEOs Are Psychopaths. Only 21 Percent?" *Washington Post,* September 16, 2016.

166 The U.S. government chose: In 1907, with yet another panic on, depositors mobbed savings and loans across New York, clamoring to withdraw their money. Big bankers, corralled by J. P. Morgan, coughed up tens of millions of dollars to bail out the Trust Company of America. (See Prins, *All the Presidents' Bankers,* pp. 8–12.) There is evidence that their successors eight decades later *hoped* the S&L damage would be so huge that only the federal government could cover it, and that they worked to make their wish come true (Calavita et al., *Big Money Crime,* p. 98). They succeeded. And so a trend was launched.

166 "Given the amount of risk": Telephone interview, March 21, 2019.

167 "They kept nodding": Telephone interview, August 7, 2018. See also Jeff Connaughton, *The Payoff: Why Wall Street Always Wins* (Westport, CT: Prospecta, 2012), pp. 65–74.

167 "We were picking off": Interview, July 19, 2019; Black, *The Best Way to Rob a Bank,* p. 286. Holder pioneered the idea that when considering prosecution of large corporations, "the risk of harm to the public" and "substantial consequences to a corporation's officers, directors, employees, and shareholders, many of whom may . . . have played no role in the criminal conduct," may be taken into consideration (Eric Holder, "Bringing Criminal Charges Against Corporations," memorandum to component heads and U.S. attorneys, June 16, 1999). He wrote this directive as deputy attorney general in the Clinton administration, in 1999. After the demise of the Arthur Andersen accounting firm in the wake of the Enron scandal in 2002, costing thousands of employees their jobs, the principle gained traction. It was the embryo of "too big to fail." Holder also expanded the use of "deferred prosecution agreements," whereby Justice Department lawyers negotiate with corporate general counsels the size of a fine their companies can pay to avoid prosecution altogether. His Obama administration Criminal Division chief, Lanny Breuer, shared his philosophy (and history representing banks at Covington and Burling). See, among other accounts, Jesse Eisinger, *The Chickenshit Club: Why the Justice Department Fails to Prosecute Executives* (New York: Simon and Schuster, 2017). See also Patrick Radden Keefe, "Why Corrupt Bankers Avoid Jail: Prosecution of White-Collar Crime Is at a Twenty-Year Low," *New Yorker,* July 31, 2017—which, however, neglects the network connections.

168 Trump's private equity blowflies: The most detailed examination of this phenomenon within the real estate sector is Aaron Glantz, *Homewreckers: How a Gang of Wall Street Kingpins, Hedge Fund Magnates, Crooked Banks and Vulture Capitalists Suckered Millions Out of Their Homes and Demolished the American Dream* (New York: HarperCollins, 2019).

168 Commerce Secretary Wilbur Ross: See, for instance, Choe Sang-Hun and Claudia Deutsch, "Mixed Record Marked Mine Owner's Seoul Ventures," *New York Times,* January 6, 2006, which uses the fatal accident at the Sago coal mine in West Virginia as a peg to examine Ross, who owned International Coal Group, Sago's owner; Makoto Kajiwara, "Trump's Commerce Secretary Pick Is a Familiar Face in Asia," *Nikkei Asian Review,* December 15, 2016; Tim Sharrock, "Labour-Korea: Backlash over US Role in Strike-Breaking," Inter Press Service, April 20, 1999; Philip Eade, "Wilbur Ross, Senior Managing Director, Rothschild, New York," Euromoney website, December 1, 1998.

168 The company was repeatedly sued: Louise Story, "Investors Stalk the Wounded of Wall St.," *New York Times,* April 4, 2008. For a lawsuit, see, for instance, "*State of Texas v. American Home Mortgage Servicing, Inc.,* Plaintiff's Original Petition," District Court of El Paso County, Texas, case number 2010-3307, available at http://stopforeclosurefraud.com/wp-content/uploads/2010/09/TEXAS-v.-AMERICAN-HOME-MORTGAGE-SERVICING-INC.pdf.

168 In 2011, Ross got: Donal O'Donovan, "How Two Billionaires Made Huge Killing on Bol Shares," *The Independent,* March 5, 2014. The sale (to Deutsche Bank) discussed here came before the sudden announcement of unexpected losses, leading to charges that the value of Bank of Ireland had been artificially

inflated. See John McDonnell, partner, PricewaterhouseCoopers, "Testimony before the Joint Committee on Banking Crisis," May 20, 2015.

168 In 2006, treasury-secretary-to-be: On Dune and the S&L bailout asset management company, called the Resolution Trust Corporation, see, for instance, Gary Shorter, "The Resolution Trust Corporation: Historical Analysis," Congressional Research Service, September 26, 2008, p. 3.

169 There, "the ethical and moral tombstones": Calavita et al., *Big Money Crime,* pp. 110–17. Barrack's "tombstone" quote is from Yoji Cole, "Thomas Barrack, Jr.: The LA Real Estate Titan Keeps Riding Waves," *CSQ,* March 2013. Nathan Vardi, "The Bass Billionaires," *Forbes,* March 1, 2016, lists Barrack side by side with Steven Mnuchin's college roommate and longtime business partner Edward Lampert.

169 In the Great Recession: Alejandro Laslo, "Colony Capital Buys 970 Foreclosed Homes for $176 Million," *Los Angeles Times,* November 2, 2012. See also "The Scarlet E," *On the Media,* and evictionlab.org. On the whole post–Great Recession business model, see also Francesca Mari, "A $60 Billion Housing Grab by Wall Street," *New York Times Magazine,* March 5, 2020.

169 Amid the 2020 coronavirus pandemic: See, for instance, Herbert Lash, "Mortgage Securities Rebound as Fed Starts Buying," Reuters, March 30, 2020.

169 Private equity funds also specialize: Charles H. Ferguson, *Predator Nation: Corporate Criminals, Political Corruption, and the Hijacking of America* (New York: Crown Business, 2012), pp. 233–38; Julia Horowitz, "Here's What Could Really Sink the Global Economy: $19 Trillion in Risky Corporate Debt," *CNN Business,* March 14, 2020. *Predator Nation* is another must-read on the Great Recession.

170 Called the Consumer Financial Protection Bureau: Nicholas Confessore, "Make America Pay Again: Mick Mulvaney's Master Class in Destroying a Bureaucracy from Within," *New York Times Magazine,* April 16, 2019. See also, in general, Keefe, "Why Corrupt Bankers Avoid Jail." The Supreme Court case is *Seila Law LLC v. Consumer Financial Protection Bureau.* For the latest action on the case, underlying documents, and commentary, see *SCOTUSblog,* "Seila Law LLC v. Consumer Financial Protection Bureau."

170 Then came coronavirus: Yalman Onaran and Sonali Basak, "Key 2008 Financial Crisis Players Are Back for Coronavirus," Bloomberg, April 3, 2020; Sarah Chayes, "Look Out, Corruption Ahead," *The Atlantic,* April 17, 2020.

170 It may even be the victim: Black, *The Best Way to Rob a Bank,* p. 272.

7. Tactics and Countermoves

171 "Restoring itself by its own destruction": The first quote is from Seneca, *Medea,* 700ff., the next two are from Ovid, *Metamorphoses,* 9:69ff. Both are available at https://www.theoi.com/Ther/DrakonHydra.html#Haides.

172 But less than two years later: Lauren Carasik, "Guatemala's Slow-Motion Coup Rolls Onward," *Foreign Policy,* January 26, 2019. In 2019, Guatemala's con-

stitutional court barred the popular attorney general who had allied with the CICIG and conducted many of the prosecutions, Thelma Aldana, from running to replace Morales. Sonia Perez D. and Peter Orsi, "Court Ruling Puts Vote, Anti-Graft Fight in Doubt," Associated Press, May 16, 2019.

172 In an examination: Sarah Chayes, "Fighting the Hydra: Lessons from Worldwide Protests Against Corruption," Carnegie Endowment for International Peace, April 12, 2018.

173 People would no longer: Renewed protests in the fall of 2019 took up the chant again. See Mersiha Gadzo, " 'All of Them,' Lebanon Protesters Dig In After Nasrallah's Speech," Al Jazeera, October 25, 2019.

173 In *Uncivil Agreement:* Lilliana Mason, *Uncivil Agreement: How Politics Became Our Identity* (Chicago: University of Chicago Press, 2018), pp. 1–2, describing Muzafer Sherif et al., *The Robbers Cave Experiment: Intergroup Conflict and Cooperation* (Middletown, CT: Wesleyan University Press, 1988).

174 In Beirut in 2015: Chayes, "Fighting the Hydra."

174 "Those with intense conservative": Mason, *Uncivil Agreement,* p. 21.

175 They are manipulating us: Meanwhile, kleptocratic networks actively work to weave themselves across these same identity divides. For a recent striking example, see Kevin Sullivan, "Anthony Scaramucci Was Fired from the Trump White House After 11 Days. Now, He's Convening A-listers for Bipartisan Healing," *Washington Post,* May 10, 2019, about a Las Vegas investment conference Scaramucci ran, whose participants included Ben Carson, Chris Christie, Nikki Haley, Valerie Jarrett, John Kelly, William McRaven, David Petraeus, Susan Rice, Lynn Forester de Rothschild, Jeff Sessions, and Carlyle Group chairman David Rubenstein together with at least a thousand private equity investors.

177 He writes of an Aboriginal boy: Joseph Campbell, *Primitive Mythology* (New York: Penguin, 1991), p. 93.

177 Screening allegories: Ibid., p. 97.

177 "In its most extravagant form": Anne-Marie Bouttiaux, "Les Initiés: Entre conformisme et marginalisation—la fabrique des 'sages,' " in Christine Falgayrettes-Leveau et al., eds., *Initiés Bassin du Congo* (Paris: Musée Dapper, 2013), pp. 27–28.

178 By the same token: *On the Media,* "A Tell-All Memoir and an NDA," WNYC, January 30, 2019.

178 If money is speech: Even the Supreme Court's opinion in *Citizens United,* which established the equivalency between money spent on speech and speech itself, states, "The Government may not by these means deprive the public of the right and privilege to determine for itself what speech and speakers are worthy of consideration." *Citizens United v. Federal Election Commission,* 08-205, January 21, 2010, p. 24. However, a new Supreme Court case, *Americans for Prosperity Foundation v. Becerra,* is challenging California's right to require nonprofit organizations that make contributions to political campaigns to identify donors to the state. See *SCOTUSblog* for actions in the case to date

and accompanying documents. The long list of briefs by outside experts to help the justices' deliberation (amici curiae) is instructive as to the importance attributed to this case.

178 Defense Department budget numbers: Charles Clark, "Accounting Board Sides with Secrecy Hawks on Classified Defense Spending," *Government Executive,* August 28, 2018.

179 "I was as secretive": Frank Vanderlip, in Frank Vanderlip and Boyden Sparkes, *From Farm Boy to Financier,* quoted in Nomi Prins, *All the Presidents' Bankers: The Hidden Alliances That Drive American Power* (New York: Nation Books, 2014), p. 22.

179 "Audio technicians planted": Jane Mayer, *Dark Money: The Hidden History of the Billionaires Behind the Rise of the Radical Right* (New York: Doubleday, 2016), pp. 12–13.

179 The philosophy can be summed up: Ibid., p. 342. UnKoch My Campus, "Donor Intent of the Koch Network." Historian Clayton Coppin titled the chronicle of Koch political operations that Bill Koch commissioned him to write during a family feud "Stealth." https://static1.squarespace.com/static /5400da69e4b0cb1fd47c9077/t/5c181cfd562fa7e5dc228ecf/1545084159707 /Donor+Intent+of+the+Koch+Network.pdf, p. 16. See excerpts from Coppin's work at https://ia600705.us.archive.org/3/items/Stealth2003Excerpt /Stealth%202003%20Excerpt.pdf. Note pp. 56–57. Jane Mayer's first *New Yorker* exposé on Charles Koch and his brother David, in 2010, was titled "Covert Operations."

179 "They can generate an unlimited number": Telephone interview, August 4, 2018. For corroboration of this former insider's insight, see, on entities focused on the justice sector, Anna Massoglia, "Trump Judicial Adviser's 'Dark Money' Network Hides Supreme Court Spending," Center for Responsive Politics, OpenSecrets.org, January 2, 2020.

179 So effective has the Koch entities' secretiveness: Mayer, *Dark Money,* p. 317.

180 and the Tea Party: See Jeff Nesbit: *Poison Tea: How Big Oil and Big Tobacco Invented the Tea Party and Captured the GOP* (New York: Thomas Dunne, 2016).

180 In a 1997 speech: Charles G. Koch, *Creating a Science of Liberty* (Fairfax, VA: Institute for Humane Studies, George Mason University, 1997). See also, on Justice Clarence Thomas, Corey Robin, *The Enigma of Clarence Thomas* (New York: Metropolitan Books, 2019).

180 Initiation rites: Joseph Campbell, *Primitive Mythology* (New York: Penguin, 1991), p. 99.

181 According to a court filing: All quotes are from the filing *Commonwealth of Massachusetts v. Purdue Pharma et al.,* First Amended Complaint and Jury Demand, in Massachusetts Superior Court 1884-cv-01808 (BLS2). See also Patrick Radden Keefe, "The Family That Built an Empire of Pain," *New Yorker,* October 23, 2017. The last time the United States witnessed an opioid epidemic of these proportions was in the 1870s, at the beginning of the Gilded Age. For a thoughtful consideration of the crisis, see Andrew Sullivan, "The

Poison We Pick," *New York,* February 2018. By mid-2019, at least forty-five states and hundreds of city or county governments had filed suits against one or more of the Sacklers and/or Purdue Pharma and other opioid manufacturers. A single broad agreement, similar to that reached with the tobacco industry, may result. Eric Heisig, "Settlement Talks Begin in Cleveland Between Drug Companies and Governments over Opioid Epidemic," Cleveland.com, February 1, 2018. Geoff Mulvihill and Mark Gillispie, "Lawyers Pause Plan to Divide Any National Opioid Settlement," Associated Press, June 25, 2019.

182 In War, West Virginia: Rebecca Klein, "Teachers Are First Responders to the Opioid Crisis," *Hechinger Report,* November 3, 2018; Lydia Nuzum, "Opioid Epidemic Touches Youngest West Virginians," *Charleston Gazette-Mail,* October 18, 2015.

182 In smaller towns: Dave Davies, host, "Tales of Corporate Painkiller Pushing: 'The Death Rates Just Soared,'" interview with Scott Higham, *Fresh Air,* August 22, 2019.

182 And they were not alone: In April 2020, Cardinal Health and McKesson, along with three other health-care supply companies, received an emergency Department of Justice waiver of antitrust regulations so they could collaborate to address the COVID-19 crisis. Makan Delrahim, Letter re "Business Review Request Pursuant to COVID-19 Expedited Procedure," U.S. Department of Justice, April 4, 2020.

183 This generation of Sacklers: See this assessment, quoted in the *New York Times,* that "Arthur invented the wheel of pharmaceutical advertising." Philip H. Dougherty, "Advertising; Generic Drugs and Agencies," *New York Times,* September 12, 1985. On Valium, see Nicholas E. Calcaterra and James C. Barrow, "Classics in Chemical Neuroscience: Diazepam (Valium)," *ACS Chemical Neuroscience* 5, no. 4 (April 16, 2014): 253–60. See also Keefe, "Empire of Pain."

183 Court filings in that saga: Cristin Kearns et al., "Sugar Industry and Coronary Heart Disease Research: A Historical Analysis of Internal Industry Documents," *JAMA Internal Medicine* 176, no. 11 (November 1, 2016).

183 Prosecutors identified: *United States et al. v. Philip Morris,* opinion of the United States District Court for the District of Columbia, 1:99-cv-02496-PLF, August 17, 2006; Clive Bates and Andy Rowell, "The Truth About the Tobacco Industry . . . in Its Own Words," University of California at San Francisco, Center for Tobacco Control, Research, and Education, 2004.

183 "When public opinion": Naomi Klein, *This Changes Everything* (London: Penguin Random House, 2015), p. 35.

184 The next year, the then current: Rebroadcast as part of Joe Palka, "The Changes in Science and Technology over the Last Four Decades," *Morning Edition,* National Public Radio, November 6, 2019.

184 It is now clear: See, among other sources, Steve Coll, *Private Empire: ExxonMobil and American Power* (New York: Penguin, 2013); Massachusetts Supreme Judicial Court, "*Exxon Mobil Corporation v. Attorney General,*" April 13, 2018. It and other oil companies have practiced similar deception regarding the

benefits of plastic recycling. Watch, for instance, *Frontline* and NPR, "Plastic Wars," March 31, 2020.

184 The objective, according to one: Robert O'Harrow, "A Two-Decade Crusade by Conservative Charities Fueled Trump's Exit from Paris Climate Accord," *Washington Post,* September 5, 2017. See also Robert Brulle, "Institutionalizing Delay: Foundation Funding and the Creation of the U.S. Climate Change Counter-movement Organizations," *Climatic Change,* December 21, 2013; Justin Farrell, Kathryn McConnell, and Robert Brulle, "Evidence-Based Strategies to Combat Scientific Misinformation," *Nature Climate Change* 9 (2019): 191–95. On the Heartland Institute's efforts to disrupt the consensus on climate in Europe, see CORRECTIV and Frontal21, "The Heartland Lobby," February 11, 2020.

184 That building bathes: Beginning with the high-profile move by the National Portrait Gallery in London in the spring of 2019, some recipients have begun rejecting or returning Sackler donations. See Nadeem Badshah and Joanna Walters, "National Portrait Gallery Drops £1m. Grant from Sackler Family," *The Guardian,* March 19, 2019. But see Christopher Rowland, "The Other Sacklers: Inside a Widow's Campaign to Protect Her Husband's Name from the Opioid Addiction Epidemic," *Washington Post,* November 27, 2019.

184 "People tend to accept": Quoted in Clayton Coppin, "Stealth: The History of Charles Koch's Political Activities, Part One," unpublished ms., 2003, p. 65.

185 Wilbur Ross: Dan Zak, "Don't Sleep on Wilbur Ross," *Washington Post,* September 30, 2019.

185 There is intimidation: See, for instance, Will Parrish and Sam Levin, " 'Treating Protest as Terrorism': US Plans Crackdown on Keystone XL Activists," *The Guardian,* September 20, 2018; Decca Muldowney, "A Short History of Threats Received by Donald Trump's Opponents," ProPublica, April 20, 2018.

185 They prefer to use: The tactic has become so widespread that it has gained an acronym, SLAPP (Strategic Lawsuit Against Public Participation). See George Pring, "SLAPPs: Strategic Lawsuits Against Public Participation," *Pace Environmental Law Review* 7, no. 1 (Fall 1989): 3–21; Penelope Canan, "The SLAPP from a Sociological Perspective," *Pace Environmental Law Review* 7, no. 1 (Fall 1989): 23–32. A task force has taken shape to counter SLAPPs. See Charles Denson, "Fighting Back Against SLAPP Suits," Civil Liberties Defense Center, November 1, 2018. On President Trump's use of SLAPPs, see Joshua A. Geltzer and Neal K. Katyal, "The True Danger of the Trump Campaign's Defamation Lawsuits," *The Atlantic,* March 11, 2020. Like almost all the other structures and operating principles in this book, this tactic is global. When I decided to work on and in Honduras, I paused to consider potential physical dangers. The place is infamous for its murder rate, and Afghanistan had taught me what excellent cover such apparently chaotic violence can provide for the occasional assassination. What I did not anticipate were the defamation proceedings that the top Honduran bank, Banco Ficohsa, would launch against my employer, the Carnegie Endowment for International Peace, in three different countries. The cases were entirely spurious; the only

one that made it to court was tossed out by a Belgian judge. Carnegie never hesitated in defending my work. I was frequently reminded, however, about how much the effort was costing.

185 "Lawsuits," as Ian MacDougall noted: Ian MacDougall, "Empty Suits: Defamation Law and the Price of Dissent," *Harper's Magazine,* March 2018. Sometimes network members in government participate in the intimidation, as in a series of actions by the House Committee on Energy and Mineral Resources against the Project on Government Oversight (POGO) after the group won a lawsuit against ExxonMobil for underpaying royalties. (See, for instance, U.S. House of Representatives, proceedings for October 27, 2000, "Privileges of the House in the Matter of Refusals to Comply with Subpoenas Issued by Committee on Resources," *Congressional Record,* October 27, 2000; background summarized in Richard Prince and Esther Cassidy, "Oil-Financed Congress Members Target Public-Interest Group," The Center for Public Integrity, June 14, 2000 (updated May 19, 2014).

186 Perhaps the most gut-wrenching example: Scott Higham and Lenny Bernstein, "The Drug Industry's Triumph over the DEA," *Washington Post,* October 15, 2014, and *60 Minutes,* "The Whistleblower," CBS News, October 15, 2017. In a final, cynical act of deception, pharmaceutical companies have sought to confuse the public by blaming the epidemic on lax government enforcement (see, for instance, John Gray, "DEA Had the Full Opioid Data, Not the Pharmaceutical Wholesale Distributors," *USA Today,* August 12, 2019) without acknowledging the lengths to which they themselves went in order to ensure that lax enforcement, both by suborning DEA officials and lobbying relentlessly for passage of a 2016 law that changed the standard of proof for DEA suspension orders and inserted other procedural roadblocks. The continuing political influence of this industry—across the party divide—was demonstrated in 2019, when, despite the universal outcry about Pharma's role in the opioid crisis and price-gouging, it won billions in tax breaks and rebuffed efforts to curb surprise billing or put downward pressure on prescription prices. See Jeff Stein and Yasmeen Abutaleb, "Congress Showers Health Care Industry with Multibillion-Dollar Victory After Wagging Finger at It for Much of 2019," *Washington Post,* December 20, 2019.

8. Colluders

187 Craig took that account: See Franklin Foer, "Paul Manafort, American Hustler," *The Atlantic,* March 2018. For a broader spectrum of the types of enablers who service foreign kleptocrats, see Michael Forsythe et al., "How U.S. Firms Helped Africa's Richest Woman Exploit Her Country's Wealth," *New York Times,* January 19, 2020.

187 whose daughter Craig pushed his firm to hire: Sharon LaFraniere, "Trial of High-Powered Lawyer Gregory Craig Exposes Seamy Side of Washington's Elite," *New York Times,* August 26, 2019. His acquittal in September 2019 of lying to federal investigators changes none of these facts.

188 Economist Thomas Piketty: Thomas Piketty, *Capital in the Twenty-First Cen-*

tury, trans. Arthur Goldhammer (Cambridge, MA: Harvard University Press, 2017), p. 330.

189 Under the terms of these laws: 18 U.S. Code §1341 and 1343.

189 It was, in the words of: Charles Fried et al., *"Charles J. McNally, petitioner v. United States of America; James E. Gray, petitioner v. United States of America:* Brief for the United States," March 1987, p. 22.

189 "The words 'to defraud' ": *McNally v. United States* 483 U.S. 350 (1987), p. 1.

190 Justice John Paul Stevens: Ibid., pp. 374, 366.

190 "It was a meat-axe": All quotes from an interview, April 28, 2018.

190 "For the purposes of this chapter": 18 USC 1346.

190 Skilling made Enron: Bethany McLean and Peter Elkind, *The Smartest Guys in the Room: The Amazing Rise and Scandalous Fall of Enron* (New York: Penguin Portfolio, 2003), pp. 28, 27.

191 Enron took the lead: In "A Culture of Paper Tigers," in Nicolaus Mills, ed., *Culture in an Age of Money* (Chicago: Ivan R. Dee, 1990), pp. 99–105, Richard Reich charts "how thoroughly the culture of the new American paper entrepreneur came to dominate the American economy of the 1980s," a culture in which "the historic relationship between product and paper has been turned upside down."

191 "Construing the honest-services statute": *Skilling v. United States,* 561 U.S. 358 (2010), p. 2. In the more famous decision decided that year—*Citizens United v. Federal Election Commission*—the court had also reduced a host of important issues to the sole crime of bribery. Corrupting a public official by way of campaign contributions, that opinion ruled, "would be covered by bribery laws." *Citizens United v. Federal Election Commission* 538 U.S. 310 (2010), pp. 43, 41. Five years earlier, the Supreme Court had decided, again unanimously, that jury instructions in the case against Enron's accountant, Arthur Andersen, had encountered one of those vagueness shoals and overturned his conviction for corruptly ordering employees to shred masses of potentially incriminating documents. 544 U.S. 696 (2005).

192 "Heritage was huge": All quotes from a recorded interview, June 4, 2018.

193 Cofounded by Senate majority leader: Ann Pearson, "Unlimited and Undisclosed: The Religious Right's Crusade to Deregulate Political Spending," Common Cause, February 2015. See also The Bridge Project, "Florida Man Buys State: Koch Impacts in the Sunshine State: The James Madison Institute Has Very Deep Ties to the Koch Network," April 1, 2015; Jane Mayer, *Dark Money: The Hidden Histories of the Billionaires Behind the Rise of the Radical Right* (New York: Doubleday, 2016), pp. 288–90. According to the "Officers and Directors" page on its website, consulted in spring 2020, the three corporate officers are also the only three members of the board of directors. Each worked only one hour per week, according to its 2018 tax filing, available from ProPublica's online Nonprofit Explorer.

193 "Honest services fraud": An October 2018 episode of the podcast *Decarceration Nation* suggests as much. In it, Koch Industries general counsel Mark Holder describes a case against Koch for environmental crimes at a Corpus

Christie oil refinery as the origin of Charles Koch's interest in criminal justice reform. Holder neglected to mention that Koch industries had pleaded guilty to covering up the violations: U.S. Department of Justice, "Koch Pleads Guilty to Covering Up Environmental Violations at Texas Oil Refinery," press release, April 9, 2001.

194 The signatories: Supreme Court of the United States, "Brief of Former Federal Officials as *Amici Curiae* in Support of Petitioner," November 16, 2015. On Davis, see Seth Hettena, "Michael Cohen, Lanny Davis and the Russian Mafia," *Rolling Stone,* August 28, 2018. In the 2020 case seeking to apply *McDonnell* to staff members of former New Jersey governor Chris Christie convicted for their role in the "Bridgegate" scandal, McDonnell and U.K. Peer Conrad Black, convicted in the United States of felony fraud and pardoned by President Donald Trump, submitted a joint amicus brief in support of the petitioner. Supreme Court of the United States, *Bridget Anne Kelly v. United States of America,* No. 18-1059, "Brief for *Amici Curiae* Lord Conrad Black and Former Governor Robert F. McDonnell in Support of Petitioner."

195 "I don't know how successful": Recorded interview, May 2, 2018.

195 "Fair warning": Lawrence Robbins et al., "*Jeffrey K. Skilling, Petitioner v. United States of America, Respondent,* Brief of the Chamber of Commerce of the United States of America as *Amicus Curiae* in Support of Petitioner," December 2009, p. 4.

195 It means power-mad prosecutors: Timothy Sandefur et al., "*Jeffrey K. Skilling, Petitioner, v. United States of America, Respondent,* Brief Amicus Curiae of Pacific Legal Foundation and Cato Institute in Support of Neither Party," December 2009, p. 6.

196 That grasp may not be based: Mary Oliver, "Winter Hours," in *Upstream* (New York: Penguin Press, 2016), p. 153.

197 So Ayer applied himself: Just as Trump counsel Alan Dershowitz tried to do during the impeachment trial, and as lawyers for Chris Christie aide Bridget Anne Kelly did in the Bridgegate case.

197 About the same percentage: See, for instance, Steven Kull et al., "Americans Evaluate Campaign Finance Reform: A Survey of Voters Nationwide," Voice of the People and Program for Public Consultation, University of Maryland School of Public Policy, May 2018, https://www.documentcloud.org /documents/4455238-campaignfinancereport.html.

197 I thought about the half: And yet, the court assured us in *Citizens,* "the appearance of influence or access" for big donors "will not cause the electorate to lose faith in our democracy." *Citizens United v. Federal Election Commission* 558 U.S. (2010), p. 44.

197 Who doesn't moon over: Emily Schmall, "Beyonce! Hillary! India Revels in a Very Big Wedding," Associated Press, December 12, 2018; Morgan Halberg, "The Obamas Reached Peak Vacation on This Yacht: Barack Obama Shall Now Be Known as the Ultimate Instagram Husband," *Observer,* April 19, 2017. More recently, Amazon CEO Jeff Bezos joined former Goldman Sachs CEO Lloyd Blankfein and supermodel Karlie Kloss and David Geffen on his

yacht, reinforcing the *Risky Business* ethos whereby great rewards—of size, sex, and infinite wealth—are mixed with brazen criminality. Hillary Hoffower, "Jeff Bezos Partied on Billionaire David Geffen's $590 Million Superyacht in the Balearics—Here's a Look at the Yacht, Which Has Hosted Everyone from Oprah Winfrey to Barack Obama," *Business Insider,* August 7, 2019.

IV. IT THROVE ON WOUNDS
1. Fighting the Hydra: The Cities

201 "The strike swept through": Mary Heaton Vorse, *Men and Steel* (New York: Boni and Liveright, 1920), p. 57. Available at: https://archive.org/details /mensteel00vors/page/57.

202 She described the open-hearth furnaces: Ibid., p. 21.

202 The strikers, she wrote: Ibid., p. 58.

202 Her account details methods: See also Robert Justin Goldstein, *Political Repression in Modern America* (Cambridge, MA: Schenkman, 1978), pp. 3–4. Note that Vorse's observations are corroborated broadly for the whole period in Jeremy Brecher, *Strike!* (San Francisco: Straight Arrow Press, 1971), and in Goldstein, pp. 3–59.

202 "The stories of beatings": Vorse, *Men and Steel,* p. 67. According to Goldstein, "Twenty-five thousand men chosen, paid by and armed by the major steel corporations were deputized." Goldstein, *Political Repression,* p. 13. Goldstein also provides multiple examples of shootings during other strikes of this period, p. 15.

202 "Each man gutted": Vorse, *Men and Steel,* p. 167.

204 "Man is puny": Ibid., p. 42.

204 "The mill gates open up": Ibid., p. 29.

204 "The mass of workers heaved": Ibid., p. 48.

204 "The toilers": Reprinted in Terrence Powderly, *Thirty Years of Labor: 1859– 1889* (New York: Excelsior, 1889), p. 117.

205 The intent "to elevate": Amalgamated Association of the Iron and Steel Workers of the United States, "Declaration of Principles," reprinted in Carroll Wright, "The Amalgamated Association of Iron and Steel Workers," *Quarterly Journal of Economics* 7, no. 4 (July 1893): 420.

205 "We want to feel": Quoted in James Green, *Death in the Haymarket: A Story of Chicago, the First Labor Movement and the Bombing That Divided Gilded Age America* (New York: Anchor, 2007), p. 153. See also Lucy Parsons, *Lucy Parsons: Freedom, Equality, and Solidarity, Writings and Speeches, 1878–1937,* ed. Gale Ahrens (Chicago: Charles Kerr, 2003), p. 35, on a few hours of healthful labor a day procuring everything one would need—therefore (she presumes) causing people to disdain wealth.

205 The Knights' 1878 platform: Reprinted in Powderly, *Thirty Years of Labor,* pp. 116–17.

206 Resolutions urged: Vorse, *Men and Steel,* p. 93.

206 Objective thirteen: Reprinted in Powderly, *Thirty Years of Labor,* p. 119.

206 hundreds of Slovaks: Vorse, *Men and Steel,* p. 76.

206 amateur theater groups: Green, *Death in the Haymarket,* pp. 61–63.

206 a few dozen men rolling cigars: Samuel Gompers, *Seventy Years in Life and Labor* (New York: Dutton, 1925), reprinted in Janette Greenwood, *The Gilded Age: A History in Documents* (Oxford, UK: Oxford University Press), p. 56.

207 "Nothing like this had ever happened": Green, *Death in the Haymarket,* pp. 146, 163.

208 Until Lucy Parsons's death: "For [former slave owners] are not even actuated by the moneyed interest they had in you in former years," she writes in 1886. "The overseer's whip is now fully supplanted by the lash of hunger! And the auction block by the chain gang and convict's cell." From "The Negro: Let Him Leave Politics to the Politicians and Prayers to the Preacher," first published in *The Alarm,* April 3, 1886. In Lucy Parsons, *Lucy Parsons,* p. 55.

209 "Such concentrated power": Lucy Parsons, "The Principles of Anarchism," pamphlet, ca. 1905, in Lucy Parsons, *Lucy Parsons,* p. 29.

209 "We can judge from experience": Parsons, "Principles," pp. 32–33.

209 "When once free from the restrictions": Emma Goldman and Johann Most, "Anarchy Defended by Anarchists," *Metropolitan Magazine* 4, no. 3 (October 1896).

210 Lined up by the maws: Alexander Berkman (the man who tried to kill Carnegie henchman Henry Clay Frick), *Prison Memoirs of an Anarchist,* ch. 3, "The Spirit of Pittsburgh" (New York: Mother Earth Press, 1912).

210 "So we have crossed": Marie Ganz, with Nat Ferber, *Rebels: Into Anarchy— and Out Again* (New York: Dodd, Mead, 1920), p. 4. See also Vorse, *Men and Steel,* pp. 183–84.

210 In a study of anarchism: Kenyon Zimmer, "The Whole World Is Our Country: Immigration and Anarchism in the United States, 1885–1940" (PhD diss., University of Pittsburgh, Department of History, 2010), pp. 47, 63.

210 Performance art, writes Zimmer: Ibid., p. 69.

211 Yom Kippur balls: Ibid., pp. 74–75, 100ff.

212 "This world," writes Zimmer: Ibid., p. 101.

212 Lucy Parsons avowed: Lucy Parsons, "I Am an Anarchist," *Kansas City Journal,* December 21, 1886.

212 In "the voice of dynamite": Quoted in Green, *Death in the Haymarket,* p. 141. See also Parsons's 1886 recommendation to African Americans that they resort to "deeds of revenge" for the outrages they were suffering. "For the torch of the incendiary . . . cannot be wrested from you." Parsons, *Lucy Parsons,* p. 56. Also "What Anarchy Means," *The Advance and Labor Leaf,* March 12, 1887, in Parsons, *Lucy Parsons,* p. 61.

212 They strewed grotesque images: All of these descriptions are from Beverly Gage, *The Day Wall Street Exploded* (Oxford, UK: Oxford University Press, 2009), pp. 31–36.

212 On July 23, 1892: See Berkman, *Prison Memoirs.*

213 Police infiltration: Associated Press, "Charges Inciting of Red Outrages," "Death Threat Here Laid to Burns Man in Spy's Testimony," and "Gave False

Scent in Wall St. Plot," in *New York Times,* February 13, 14, and 15, 1923. My thanks for this reference to Alan Huffman, who is writing a book on the birth of the "Radical Bureau," precursor to the FBI, in this chaos, and to Sebastian Junger and Barbara Hammond for the steer on this material in general, including Emma Goldman and especially Mary Heaton Vorse. For a modern example of such politically significant entrapment, see Krissy Clark, "30 Years Ago, George H. W. Bush Held Up a Baggie of Crack on Live TV. Where'd He Get It?" *Marketplace,* March 21, 2019.

213 German-born Johann Most: Johann Most, "Action as Propaganda," *Freiheit,* July 25, 1885.

214 And that is just what happened: See Sarah Chayes, "A Mullah Dies and War Comes Knocking," *Washington Post,* November 19, 2007.

214 Some of the motivations: Quoted in Sarah Chayes, *Thieves of State: Why Corruption Threatens Global Security* (New York: W. W. Norton, 2015), p. 183.

2. Fighting the Hydra: The Countryside

218 As one correspondent put it: H., "Some Sensible Talk from a Sensible Man," letter to the editor, *Progressive Farmer,* August 18, 1882, p. 2, available at https://chroniclingamerica.loc.gov.

218 The merchants insisted: Michael Schwartz, *Radical Protest and Social Structure: The Southern Farmers' Alliance and Cotton Tenancy, 1880–1890* (Chicago: University of Chicago Press, 1976), pp. 68–70. A modern equivalent is industrial poultry farming, whereby farm families raise chickens for mega-corporations, which determine every aspect of the process. See Isaac Arnsdorf, "Chicken Farmers Thought Trump Was Going to Help Them. His Administration Did the Opposite," *West Virginia Gazette and Mail,* June 5, 2019; Zephyr Teachout, *Break 'Em Up: Recovering Our Freedom from Big Ag, Big Tech, and Big Money* (New York: All Points Books, 2020), pp. 17–24.

219 A fictional exchange: William Attaway, *Blood on the Forge* (New York: New York Review Books, 2005; originally published 1941), p. 31.

219 By underweighing and undervaluing: Lawrence Goodwyn, *The Populist Moment: A Short History of the Agrarian Revolt in America* (Oxford, UK: Oxford University Press, 1978), p. 22.

219 African Americans had the unspeakable worst: For a discussion of these factors, see Schwartz, *Radical Protest,* p. 10.

219 "Once a farmer had signed": Goodwyn, *Populist Moment,* pp. 22–23. See also the careful and detailed discussion of this system in Schwartz, *Radical Protest,* pp. 34–39, and, for his comparison to slavery, p. 70: the lienholder "had a captive labor force (the debtors), so he could cut their supplies to subsistence level with some assurance that he would not lose his workers. . . . He could also increase his yield by close supervision of his laborers and the emphasis on cash crops which he knew he could sell. All the advantages of 'economy of scale' were applied and all the production decisions were made in favor of the planter-merchant. It is not surprising that the largest Alabama landlord, who controlled 30,000 acres in the 1880s, announced that he 'has no use for a

nigger [*sic*] who pays out.' He wanted tenants who would remain in debt and therefore be vulnerable to maximum exploitation. . . . Merchants and landlords literally refused food for the family unless the debtor's work met their standards."

220 It began in 1877: Robert McMath, *American Populism: A Social History, 1877– 1898* (New York: Hill and Wang, 1992), p. 6.

220 But the objective: Goodwyn, *Populist Moment,* p. 25.

220 They avidly studied: Charles Postel, *The Populist Vision* (Oxford, UK: Oxford University Press, 2007), pp. 45–67.

220 Alliance leaders developed: Ibid., p. 64.

220 or questions they themselves submitted: "Questions for Discussion in Farmers' Clubs," *The Progressive Farmer,* May 12, 1886, p. 4, available at https://chroni clingamerica.loc.gov/lccn/sn92073049/1886-05-12/ed-1/seq-4/.

221 "small stories of personal tragedy": See Goodwyn, *Populist Moment,* pp. 45 (especially for the radicalizing effect of the traveling lecturers and this quote), 56–69.

221 "Education may not at first appear": Postel, *Populist Vision,* p. 48.

221 "It extended to frequent": Goodwyn, *Populist Moment,* pp. 34–35. For accounts of such open-air meetings, complete with Alliance-friendly bands and speakers' stands "beautifully decorated with wreaths and festoons of cedar and ornamented with varieties of the different products of the garden and field, with lovely flowers scattered here and there lending added beauty to the scene," see Jimplicute, "Grand Alliance Pic-Nic of Davidson County Farmers' Alliance at Thomasville Baptist Orphanage, Aug. 7th, 1891," *The Progressive Farmer,* August 25, 1891, available at https://chroniclingamerica.loc.gov. This front page includes several accounts of other gatherings. The article below the picture (reproduced on p. 222) titled "The Blue and the Grey" declares that with chattel slavery gone, sectionalism should go the same way. It makes the slogan on a figurative Alliance banner read "Equal Rights to All and Special Favors to None." Of course, that handshake was paid for with the redoubled oppression of African Americans.

222 In a region where most: This evolution was neither automatic nor immediate, however, and may have been largely imposed by Alliance members who were landholders, with tenants of their own. At the Alliance's 1888 national convention, it resolved that "it is detrimental to both white and colored to allow conditions to exist that force our colored farmers to sell their products for less, and pay more for supplies than the markets justify." Quoted in Schwartz, *Radical Protest,* pp. 98–99.

222 On the white side of the line: Ibid., p. 97.

223 Gut loyalties to the parties: Goodwyn, *Populist Moment,* pp. 99 (where the issue of race is startlingly omitted), 113, 151–52.

223 "All are fighting unsupported": H., "Some Sensible Talk."

223 Its first battle: Goodwyn, *Populist Moment,* pp. 74–77; Postel, *Populist Vision,* pp. 105, 117–21; Schwartz, *Radical Protest,* pp. 213–24.

224 It saved Alliance members: Schwartz, *Radical Protest,* p. 218.

224 In Texas, local merchants: Ibid., pp. 228–29.

224 As Alliance president Charles Macune: Quoted in Goodwyn, *Populist Moment*, p. 77.

224 That summer, the Alliance adopted: "Grand Alliance: By a Vote of 92 to 75 a Series of . . . Political Resolutions Are . . . Adopted at Cleburne" [some words lost in digitization], *Fort Worth Daily Gazette*, August 8, 1886, p. 5, available at https://chroniclingamerica.loc.gov.

225 Agriculture was thus: L. L. Polk, "Agricultural Depression: Its Causes—the Remedy," speech before the Senate Committee on Agriculture and Forestry, April 22, 1890. See also Postel, *Populist Vision*, pp. 150–53.

225 The Alliance called for: "Grand Alliance," *Fort Worth Daily Gazette.*

225 A revolutionary "sub-treasury" plan: John Hicks, "Birth of the Populist Party," *Minnesota History*, September 1928, p. 224; Samuel Porter, "The National Farmers' Alliance Convention of 1890 and Its 'Ocala Demands,'" *Florida Historical Quarterly* 28, no. 3 (January 1950); Senate testimony, Charles Macune, L. L. Polk, 1890; notice in the *Congressional Record—Senate,* for May 2, 1890: "Mr BERRY presented a petition of the Farmers' Alliance of Clark County, Arkansas, praying for the passage of House bill 7162, providing for the deposit of agricultural products in Government warehouses," *Congressional Record— Senate,* May 2, 1890, p. 4111; Polk, "Agricultural Depression."

226 Not surprisingly, individual: For the North Carolina example as representative, see Schwartz, *Radical Protest,* pp. 266–69. See also Goodwyn, *Populist Moment,* pp. 127ff.

226 "We have witnessed": "National People's Party Platform," Omaha, Nebraska, July 4, 1892.

226 Apart from the sectional divide: Goodwyn, *Populist Moment,* pp. 177–78.

226 Such a threat did this groundswell represent: At such rare moments of real democratic power, argues Thomas Ferguson in *Golden Rule: The Investment Theory of Party Competition and the Logic of Money-Driven Political Systems* (Chicago: University of Chicago Press, 1995), p. 48, "the political atmosphere heats up enormously. As whole sections of the population begin investing massively in political action, elites become terrified and counterorganize on a stupendous scale. The volume—and acrimony—of political debate and discussion increase . . . and invariably, elites begin discussing antidemocratic policy measures and more than usually exalt order and discipline as social goods."

226 Those means included: Goodwyn, *Populist Moment,* p. 193.

226 Barriers to voting: Ferguson, *Golden Rule,* pp. 72–73.

227 Press aligned with one party: Postel, *Populist Vision,* p. 275.

227 And, especially in 1896: Goodwyn, *Populist Moment,* p. 281. Thomas Ferguson, *Golden Rule,* p. 77, discusses the importance of the silver mining companies' resources in dominating the Democratic Party and co-opting the Populists.

228 "The money changers have fled": Franklin Delano Roosevelt, "First Inaugural Address," March 4, 1933.

3. "It Had Needed a War"

229 "a nation of gloriously happy people": Charles Fritz, "Disasters and Mental Health: Therapeutic Principles Drawn from Disaster Studies," University of Delaware Disaster Research Center, 1996, p. 4.

230 "The country forgot": Ibid., p. 31.

230 "chefs, cooks, bartenders": David Leftwich, "People Needed to Be Fed. They Fed Them," *Houston Chronicle,* five-part series, beginning October 2, 2017.

230 There are the citizen first responders: Federal Emergency Management Agency, "Louisiana Cajun Navy Rescues Thousands, Inspires Many More," press release, August 24, 2018.

230 When Superstorm Sandy deluged: Katy Waldman, "The Science of Disaster: Where Was All the Chaos, Looting and Mass-Panic During Hurricane Sandy?" *Slate,* November 6, 2012.

230 Numerous recent studies: See, for instance, Christopher Peterson and Martin Seligman, "Character Strengths Before and After September 11," *Psychological Science,* July 1, 2003; Jacob Binu et al., "Disaster Mythology and Fact: Hurricane Katrina and Social Attachment," *Public Health Report* 123, no. 5 (September–October 2008).

231 Boiled down, the basic principle: Sebastian Junger, *Tribe* (New York: Hachette, 2016), p. 44. See also Fritz, "Disasters and Mental Health," p. 10.

231 Houston food writer: David Leftwich, "A Hundred Bowls of Pho and 2,000 Sandwiches," *Houston Chronicle,* October 3, 2017.

231 Solnit quotes a survivor: Charles Sedgwick, quoted in Rebecca Solnit, *A Paradise Built in Hell* (New York: Penguin Books, 2009), p. 31.

231 "You walked on that boat": Quoted in Solnit, *Paradise,* p. 209.

231 "emergent community develops": Fritz, "Disasters and Mental Health," pp. 30, 28.

231 He quotes a 1958 study: Harry Moore, *Tornadoes over Texas* (Austin: University of Texas Press, 1958), p. 313, quoted in Fritz, "Disasters and Mental Health," p. 31.

232 As a report on a 1955 flood: S. Z. Klausner and H. V. Kinkaid, "Social Problems of Sheltering Flood Victims," Columbia University Bureau of Applied Social Research, 1956, p. 58, quoted in Fritz, "Disasters and Mental Health," p. 32.

232 Or, in this elegant framing: Ignazio Silone, quoted in Fritz, "Disasters and Mental Health," p. 59. Of course, this proves not to be quite true. Every natural disaster, including an earthquake, is in part a man-made one, in that those living in the most poorly constructed or exposed buildings suffer most. Corruption always worsens the effects of natural disasters and epidemics, by gutting regulatory and health agencies, or finding profit in ignoring safety and zoning provisions for a fee or a favor. In the coronavirus epidemic, the death toll in poor communities, especially of color, was steeply disproportionate. As Solnit explores, and a recent study of FEMA buyouts of damaged properties corroborates, the underprivileged also typically suffer the most from poorly conceived

recovery efforts. Robert Benincasa, "Search the Thousands of Disaster Buyouts FEMA Didn't Want You to See," National Public Radio, March 5, 2019.

232 Those afflicted feel: Fritz, "Disasters and Mental Health," p. 58.

232 But those conditions: Mary Heaton Vorse, *Men and Steel* (New York: Boni and Liveright, 1920), pp. 112–13, discusses the contrasting perceptions: "Silence ebbed up around the strikers in a stealthy smothering tide. People outside thought the strike was broken. . . . News didn't get out. . . . The fight of these men still on strike didn't exist." Her next section is titled "What Everybody Knew": "Before the strike began every one in America knew two things about the steelworkers. One was they were rich. Fabulously rich. They got fifty dollars a day. They all lived in steam-heated cottages with hot and cold running water. The papers said so." A similar disparity may explain why regions that are subject to hardship conditions as a feature of everyday life—such as Norway and other Scandinavian countries—tend to display higher levels of social solidarity than their more comfortable neighbors.

233 "For the first time in history": Timothy Winegard, *The First World Oil War* (Toronto: University of Toronto Press, 2016), p. 7.

233 Arno Mayer calls out: Arno J. Mayer, "Domestic Causes of the First World War," in Leonard Krieger and Fritz Stern, eds., *The Responsibility of Power: Historical Essays in Honor of Hajo Holborn* (New York: Doubleday, 1967). See also Laurence Lafore, *The Long Fuse: An Interpretation of the Origins of World War I* (Long Grove, IL: Waveland Press, 1997, reissued from 1971 original), p. 114, which argues that Bismarck and later chancellors "invoked patriotism and the glory of the army in order to induce voters to vote for . . . parties that were prepared to preserve the . . . existing social order."

234 Lyon became: All of this information is from primary documents reproduced in René Raffin, ed., *14–18, du Front à l'Arrière: Notre Région dans la Guerre* (Lyon: *Le Progrès,* 2014).

236 World War I veteran: All interviews from Chicago History Museum, "Studs Terkel: Conversations with America, Hard Times," available at http://studs terkel.matrix.msu.edu/htimes.php.

237 Disaster "provides": Fritz, "Disasters and Mental Health," p. 56.

237 "If paradise . . . arises in hell": Solnit, *Paradise,* p. 7.

237 At such times, wrote W. E. Hocking: W. E. Hocking, "The Nature of Morale," *American Journal of Sociology* 47 (1941): 316.

238 As William Sansom wrote: William Sansom, *Westminster in War* (London: Faber and Faber, 1947), p. 12, quoted in Richard Titmuss, *Problems of Social Policy* (London: HM Stationers' Office, 1950), p. 350. See also Titmuss's own comment on p. 508: "The mood of the people changed and, in sympathetic response, values changed as well."

238 "As he saw it": Goodwin, *The Fitzgeralds and the Kennedys: An American Saga* (New York: Simon and Schuster, 1987), p. 268.

239 He accused his friends: Ibid., p. 272.

239 He was "increasingly disturbed": Ibid., p. 281.

239 It was, according to another: Richard Whalen, *The Founding Father: The Story of Joseph P. Kennedy* (New York: New American Library, 1964), p. 49.

239 He awarded himself the contract: Ibid., p. 49. Seymour Hersh, in *The Dark Side of Camelot* (New York: Little Brown, 1997), pp. 45–46, says documents collected during the House Elections Committee investigation of Honey Fitz's fraudulent 1918 election indicate that the real stake in the election was a corrupt attempt to purchase land next to the plant, slated for a federal housing development.

240 While lamenting in letters: Goodwin, *Fitzgeralds and Kennedys,* pp. 280–83.

240 Two battleships: Whalen, *Founding Father,* p. 49. Roosevelt, much of whose close circle was also in uniform, and who lost a brother, twice asked President Woodrow Wilson for permission to resign and enlist. In the summer of 1918, he visited the sailors and troops and installations in Europe and experienced some of the war's realities.

240 While his neighbors were savaged: Goodwin, *Fitzgeralds and Kennedys,* pp. 422–24.

240 And yet in 1932: Ferguson, *Golden Rule: The Investment Theory of Party Competition and the Logic of Money-Driven Political Systems* (Chicago: University of Chicago Press, 1995), p. 147.

240 It is as though Kennedy sensed: See Goodwin, *Fitzgeralds and Kennedys,* p. 325, for his experience of that reality as early as 1922, and pp. 427–28, on his statement that in the next generation, "the people who run the government"— not business—would be "the biggest people in America." See Whalen, *Founding Father,* p. 202, for an account of a speech before the American Society of Newspaper Editors, in which Kennedy discoursed on the "honor and prestige" attaching to comparatively poorly paying public office in Britain (due to knighthoods) and judgeship in the United States.

241 "A mere builder": Franklin D. Roosevelt, "Commonwealth Club Address," September 23, 1932.

241 In a ploy favored by: Goodwin, *Fitzgeralds and Kennedys,* pp. 439–40; Whalen, *Founding Father,* p. 132.

242 Bathed in her exhaustive reading: Goodwin, *Fitzgeralds and Kennedys,* p. 551.

242 Maybe he understood that: It is not as though Kennedy was alone in cleaving to the Gilded Age past. In reviewing these details, I am struck by how close the United States came to looking like Germany, had men like him been in charge. When, against Roosevelt's orders, he set up that meeting with Goering's right-hand man about a possible loan of gold, the emissary of like-minded captains of such U.S. businesses as General Motors, Standard Oil, and the Chase Manhattan Bank was at the table. Leadership, in other words, matters decisively in how societies react to successive disasters (Goodwin, *Fitzgeralds and Kennedys,* p. 572).

V. THE PATTERN
1. The Turning (1980s)

247 **Expanding ideas of citizenship:** While independence movements did bring an end to colonialism during this period, Washington actively and repeatedly thwarted democratic stirrings abroad and reinforced dictators considered friendly. This approach helped bring on the Vietnam War, and helped create conditions for mass atrocities and violent ideological backlashes against oppressive governments, from Iran to Latin America. It helped make the exodus of millions, unable to live under the resulting political and economic conditions, inevitable.

247 **An intoxication with anything:** The costs to the land, the water, and human health are only now being fully measured. For a thoughtful consideration of these developments, see Wendell Berry, *The Unsettling of America: Culture and Agriculture* (San Francisco: Sierra Club Books, 1977), among many of his writings. For statistics on farm numbers and acreage, see United States Department of Agriculture, Economic Research Service, "Farming and Farm Income."

248 **On the contrary, it is as though:** See, for instance, Robert Frank, *Luxury Fever: Weighing the Cost of Excess* (Princeton, NJ: Princeton University Press, 2010), p. 15.

248 **If some are familiar:** Americans still vastly underestimate the magnitude of inequality in the United States. Gretchen Gavett, "CEOs Get Paid Too Much According to Pretty Much Everyone in the World," *Harvard Business Review,* September 13, 2014.

248 **From the end of World War II:** See Colin Gordon, "Growing Apart: A Political History of American Inequality," the introduction published under the same title in *Journal of American History* 102, no. 2 (September 2015): 500–504. See also Inequality.org, "Income Inequality in the United States." Note that much of the historical information is based on painstaking extrapolation from scattered data points. Solid income information comes from the IRS, but only goes back to the 1950s. For another calculation of growing income inequality since 1970, after taxes and transfers in this case, see Emmanuel Saez and Gabriel Zucman, *The Triumph of Injustice: How the Rich Dodge Taxes and How to Make Them Pay* (New York: W. W. Norton, 2019). They derive closer to a 30 percent increase since 1970 for the bottom 50 percent, compared to a threefold and fivefold increase, after taxes and transfers, for the top 1 percent and 0.1 percent, respectively. Their findings—with some new presentations based on the same data—are summarized by Greg Sargent, "The Massive Triumph of the Rich, Illustrated by Stunning New Data," *Washington Post,* December 9, 2019.

248 **By 2018, bosses were taking home:** See also AFL-CIO, "Executive Paywatch" for the S&P 500; for a different calculation, using the top 350 companies, see Lawrence Mishel and Jessica Schieder, "CEO Compensation Surged in 2017," Economic Policy Institute, August 16, 2018. Another way to consider this

equity is to compare the paychecks of similarly skilled professions: poachers and game wardens. During the postwar period, federal regulators—career civil servants at the helm of the SEC or the Food and Drug Administration, for example—could expect to earn salaries that approximated those of the corporate executives they were regulating. The graph below plots maximum federal salaries against the top segment of the private sector. (Federal salary levels are set by Congress and executive order. New classifications created over time explain the disjunct blue lines.) Please note that the Y axis is *logarithmic.* If the income numbers were plotted as steady dollars, it would be impossible to fit the graph on a single page. The important point here is that the growth in incomes of the top 1 percent vastly outstrips that of their presumed regulators from 1994 on. Graph by Gustavo Berrizbeitia. Source for federal pay scales: Office of Personnel Management, data tables from 1949 to 2014 in "Pay and Leave." For top 1 percent: Thomas Piketty et al., "Distributional National Accounts: Methods and Estimates for the United States," *Quarterly Journal of Economics* 133, no. 2 (May 2018): 553–609.

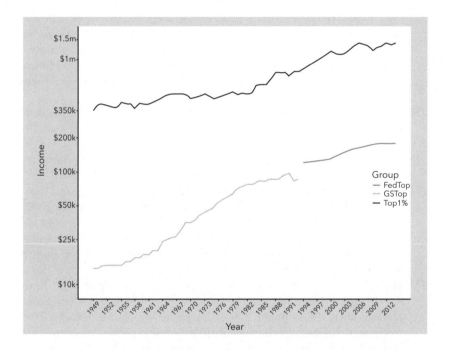

248 Companies, especially banks: Source: Federal Reserve Bank of St. Louis, from its time-series data for U.S. bank failures, 1934–2017. Here is a graph depicting all business failures since the middle of the nineteenth century. Note that the data set ends in 1997 but still shows a Depression-era jump, followed by a sharp post–World War II dip, then marked increase after 1980.

Graph by Gustavo Berrizbeitia. Source: Richard Sutch et al., "Table Ch408–413: Business Incorporations and Failures—Number and Liabilities: 1857–1998," in *Historical Statistics of the United States Millennial Edition Online,* http://hsus.cambridge.org/SeriesCh293-415.

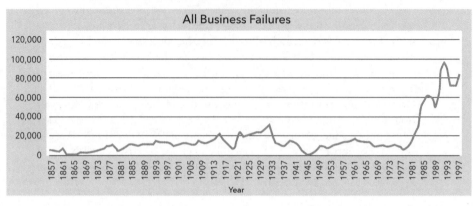

250 "In my opinion": General Omar Bradley, House of Representatives, Subcommittee for Special Investigations, Committee on Armed Services, "Employment of Retired Military and Civilian Personnel by Defense Industries," hearings, July 21, 1959. See also Janine Wedel, *Unaccountable: How the Establishment Corrupted Our Finances, Freedom, and Politics, and Created an Outsider Class* (New York: Pegasus, 2014), p. 159.

250 Sometimes they were regarded: See, for instance, Ginia Bellafante, "The Rich Didn't Always Need $238 Million Penthouses," *New York Times,* January 26, 2019.

250 "No thoughtful person can question": Lewis Powell, "Attack on American Free Enterprise System," confidential memorandum, August 23, 1971.

251 That decade, families started: Thomas Darkin, "Credit Cards: Use and Consumer Attitudes, 1970–2000," *Federal Reserve Bulletin,* September 2000. Another one of those unanimous Supreme Court decisions, *Marquette National Bank of Minneapolis v. First of Omaha Service Corp.,* decided in 1979, boosted the liftoff by allowing nationally chartered banks to issue credit cards at interest rates set by their home states.

251 His administration, like those: Thomas Ferguson and Joel Rogers, *Right Turn: The Decline of Democrats and the Future of American Politics* (New York: Hill and Wang, 1987), pp. 67, 100–102, especially graph p. 101, and p. 109; Augustus B. Cochran III, *Democracy Heading South: National Politics in the Shadow of Dixie* (Lawrence: University Press of Kansas, 2001), p. 94. This reality lent itself to later emphasis. By the end of the 1980s, according to Thomas Edsall, the impression many were left with was that the federal government "in the 1960s and 1970s promoted . . . policies intended to shift income from the working- and lower-middle class to the nonworking welfare poor." Thomas Byrne Edsall, "Clinton's Revolution," *New York Review of Books,* November 5, 1992, p. 7.

251 To shatter it, he contended: Robert Bork, *The Antitrust Paradox: A Policy at War with Itself* (New York: Free Press, 1978), summarized in United States Senate, "The Nomination of Robert Bork to Be Associate Justice of the Supreme Court of the United States," testimony by Charles Brown (Washington, DC: Government Printing Office, 1989), p. 3437. This testimony was only delivered on the twelfth and last day of the hearings, which focused on Bork's views on race.

251 This idea, an irreplaceable ingredient: George Priest, "Bork's Strategy and the Influence of the Chicago School on Modern Antitrust Law," *Journal of Law and Economics* 57, no. S3 (August 2014).

252 By the late 1980s, it had become: See Tim Wu, *The Curse of Bigness: Antitrust in the New Gilded Age* (New York: Columbia Global Reports, 2018), pp. 86–92, 102–10.

252 Entrepreneurs and laborers appear: See Reagan's first inaugural address: "We hear much of special interest groups. Well, our concern must be for a special interest group that has been too long neglected. It knows no sectional boundaries or ethnic and racial divisions, and it crosses political party lines. It is made up of men and women who raise our food, patrol our streets, man our mines and factories, teach our children, keep our homes, and heal us when we're sick—professionals, industrialists, shopkeepers, clerks, cabbies, and truck drivers." Ronald Reagan, "Inaugural Address," January 20, 1981.

252 "The freedom to take a risk": Ronald Reagan, "Remarks at a White House Reception for Representatives of the Business Community," September 15, 1981.

253 "The unique blend of individual opportunity": Ronald Reagan, "Proclamation 4866—American Enterprise Day," October 2, 1981.

253 To get a better idea: See Howard Kohn and Lowell Bergman, "Ronald Reagan's Millions: Inside the Candidate's Closet Cabinet and the Movie Studio Land Deal That Made Him Rich," *Rolling Stone,* August 26, 1976, for earlier network ties and the significant overlap between private- and public-sector players in Reagan's gubernatorial administration.

254 He helped solidify: Steven Teles, *The Rise of the Conservative Legal Movement* (Princeton, NJ: Princeton University Press, 2008); Glen Elsasser, "Federalist Society Grows into Conservative Big Shot," *Chicago Tribune,* January 11, 1987; Niskanen Center, "How the Federalist Society Changed the Supreme Court Vetting Process," August 1, 2018; Michael Kruse, "The Weekend at Yale That Changed American Politics," *Politico,* September–October 2018. Meese was joined in nurturing the Federalist Society by Robert Bork and Antonin Scalia, among others.

254 Measures requiring corporations to show: Ronald Reagan, "Address Before a Joint Session of the Congress on the Program for Economic Recovery," February 18, 1981.

254 Toxic waste enforcement: Ferguson and Rogers, *Right Turn,* pp. 131–32.

254 Apart from the savings and loan anomaly: Brandon Garrett, *Too Big to Jail: How Prosecutors Compromise with Corporations* (Cambridge, MA: Harvard University Press, 2014); Jesse Eisinger, *The Chickenshit Club: Why the Justice Department Fails to Prosecute Executives* (New York: Simon and Schuster,

2017), pp. 89–90ff. For later developments, see Patrick Radden Keefe, "Making Insider Trading Legal," *New Yorker,* October 27, 2015.

254 Reagan sounded sympathetic: Ronald Reagan, "Remarks on the Program for Economic Recovery at a White House Reception for Republican Members of the House of Representatives," June 23, 1981.

255 And while students did without: One of Reagan's Republican predecessors urged the opposite ordering of national priorities. In a speech dubbed "Cross of Iron"—in reference to Populist-Democratic presidential candidate William Jennings Bryan's Cross of Gold speech—Eisenhower said, "The cost of one modern heavy bomber is this: a modern brick school in more than 30 cities. It is two electric power plants, each serving a town of 60,000 population, it is two fine, fully equipped hospitals. It is some concrete pavement. We pay for a single fighter with a half-million bushels of wheat. We pay for a single destroyer with new homes that could have housed more than 8,000 people. . . . This is not a way of life at all . . . it is humanity hanging from a cross of iron." Dwight D. Eisenhower, "Address to the American Society of Newspaper Editors," April 16, 1953.

255 The result has been a labor market: Only in 2018 and 2019, with strikes by fast-food and hospitality workers, teachers, autoworkers, and warehousers gaining widespread sympathy, as well as broad-based campaigns for higher minimum wages, did labor organizing begin recovering from the blows of the Reagan era.

255 "Taking inflation": Ferguson and Rogers, *Right Turn,* p. 123. See also Cochran, *Democracy Heading South,* pp. 96–99.

255 Thus was perpetrated: Thomas and Mary Edsall, *Chain Reaction: The Impact of Race, Rights, and Taxes on American Politics* (New York: W. W. Norton, 1992), quoted in Cochran, *Democracy Heading South,* p. 99.

256 It turns out he was just plying: See the more diplomatic assessment in Eric Foner, *The Story of American Freedom* (New York: W. W. Norton, 1998), p. 320.

256 When lambasting regulations: Ronald Reagan, "Address Before a Joint Session of Congress on the Program for Economic Recovery," February 18, 1981.

256 On taxes, "in point of fact": Ronald Reagan, "Remarks on the Program for Economic Recovery at a White House Reception for Republican Members of the House of Representatives," June 23, 1981.

256 He vowed to close loopholes: Ronald Reagan, "Interview with the President," December 23, 1981, https://www.presidency.ucsb.edu/documents/interview-with-the-president.

256 But during the final negotiations: Ferguson and Rogers, *Right Turn,* pp. 122–23.

256 Reagan himself: Kohn and Bergman, "Ronald Reagan's Millions."

256 Prior to his administration: Ronald Reagan, *An American Life* (New York: Simon and Schuster, reprint, 2011), p, 232. See also Reagan's first inaugural address, in which he suggests that he is inheriting a government that rides on citizens' backs, smothers opportunity, and stifles productivity. Reagan, "Inaugural Address," January 20, 1981, https://www.reaganfoundation.org/media/128614/inaguration.pdf.

256 "Your ideas," he assured: Reagan, "Remarks on the Program for Economic Recovery at a White House Reception for Republican Members of the House of Representatives."

256 His cuts to spending on social programs: Reagan, "Remarks on the Program for Economic Recovery at a White House Reception for Business and Government Leaders," June 11, 1981, https://www.presidency.ucsb.edu/documents/remarks-the-program-for-economic-recovery-white-house-reception-for-business-and.

257 He admitted to those congressional Republicans: Ronald Reagan, "Address to a Joint Session of Congress on Economic Recovery," April 28, 1981, https://www.americanrhetoric.com/speeches/ronaldreagan1981jointsession.htm.

257 In their eye-opening book: Ferguson and Rogers, *Right Turn,* pp. 13–19. See also Benjamin Page and Robert Shapiro, *The Rational Public: Fifty Years of Trends in American Policy Preferences* (Chicago: University of Chicago Press, 1992), pp. 37–66, 117–47.

2. The Validation (1980s–1990s)

259 Members of this group: These recollections were discussed several times in 2018; quotes from my notes. My colleague asked to remain anonymous, so as to protect the identities of some individuals at these gatherings.

259 President Carter previewed: Cochran, *Democracy Heading South: National Politics in the Shadow of Dixie* (Lawrence: University Press of Kansas, 2001), p. 94; Thomas Ferguson and Joel Rogers, *Right Turn: The Decline of the Democrats and the Future of American Politics* (New York: Hill and Wang, 1987), pp. 106–11.

259 They wantonly stripped: Ward Sinclair and Richard Lyons, "Reagan Triumphant on Tax-Cut Bill," *Washington Post,* July 30, 1981.

259 "deliberately sought out millionaires": Ferguson and Rogers, *Right Turn,* p. 144.

259 They set up checkout lines: Ibid., p. 145.

259 Yet, while top Democrats courted: Ibid., p. 143. See also Ibram X. Kendi, "The Other Swing Voter," *The Atlantic,* January 7, 2020. Kendi refracts the contemporary version of this ongoing Democratic Party phenomenon almost exclusively through the lens of race. But it plays out across the board.

259 "special interest politics": Al From, with Alice McKeon, *The New Democrats and the Return to Power* (New York: Palgrave MacMillan, 2013), p. 39.

259 "Private sector growth was and is": Ibid., pp. 38–39. See also Cochran, *Democracy Heading South,* pp. 110–11.

260 "conservative southern Democrats": From *The New Democrats,* pp. 33, 41.

260 "By the 1990s, Southerners": Cochran, *Democracy Heading South,* p. 11.

260 The "maladies of the Solid South": Ibid., p. 174.

260 "No one," he writes: Thomas Ferguson, *Golden Rule: The Investment Theory of Party Competition and the Logic of Money-Driven Political Systems* (Chicago: University of Chicago Press, 1995), p. 295.

261 Lavish glitz became the fashion: Ross Miller, "Putting on the Glitz: Architec-

ture After Postmodernism," in Nicolaus Mills, ed., *Culture in an Age of Money* (Chicago: Ivan R. Dee, 1990), pp. 47–65.

261 His inaugurations' unprecedented display: See Mills's introduction to Mills, ed., *Culture in an Age of Money,* pp. 16–18; Deborah Silverman, "China, Bloomie's, and the Met," in Mills, ed., *Culture in an Age of Money,* pp. 175–200.

261 The bank pioneered: See Karen Ho, *Liquidated: An Ethnography of Wall Street* (Durham, NC: Duke University Press, 2007), and Michael Lewis, *Liar's Poker* (New York: Norton, 2010). For recent confirmations of the same trend, see Amy Blinder, "Why Are Harvard Grads Still Flocking to Wall Street?" *Washington Monthly,* September/October 2014; William Morris, "Harvard's Wall St. Problem," *Harvard Crimson,* February 17, 2016. A 2018 conversation with Yale undergraduates revealed that even after the 2008 stock-market crash, and despite all the evidence of repeated fraud, money laundering, and other malfeasance, Goldman Sachs is still considered a "prestige" destination for Yale graduates. In 2018, finance and consulting captured nearly a third of Yale graduating seniors, with similar or higher numbers at Harvard, Princeton, and Stanford. See, for instance, Tyler Foggatt, "Six Months After Receiving Their Diplomas, Members of the Yale Class of 2014 Are Now Full-Fledged Alumni," *Yale Daily News,* n.d.; Yale University, Office of Career Strategy, "First Destination Report: Class of 2018." Note that the deeper students are in debt, the more vulnerable they are to such recruitment. The resulting Ivy-League-to-financial-services pipeline is somewhat analogous to the Nigerian school-system-to-civil-service (and attendant corruption) pipeline that helped inspire the Boko Haram extremist movement.

261 Thus was the plutocratic lifestyle: See, for example, David Callahan, *The Cheating Culture: Why More Americans Are Doing Wrong to Get Ahead* (New York: Harcourt, 2004), pp. 106, 114–20; Elizabeth Olson, "Americans Have No Clue Just How Much More CEOs Make," *Fortune,* October 13, 2014.

261 "going in and out of factory gates": Reagan, "Inaugural Address," January 20, 1981, https://www.reaganfoundation.org/media/128614/inaguration.pdf. See also New York governor Andrew Cuomo, quoted in Mills's introduction to Mills., ed., *Culture in an Age of Money,* p. 19: "Reagan made the denial of compassion respectable. He justified it by saying . . . that poor people were somehow better off without government help in the first place."

262 But among early humans: On the value of personal autonomy and its connection to meat sharing and the sharing of political power, see Christopher Boehm, *Hierarchy in the Forest: The Evolution of Egalitarian Behavior* (Cambridge, MA: Harvard University Press, 1999), p. 67.

262 "Reagan used the word more often": Eric Foner, *The Story of American Freedom* (New York: Norton, 1998), pp. 320–21.

262 Democrats joined the chorus: Joe Biden is another example. See Tim Murphy, "House of Cards," *Mother Jones,* November/December 2019.

263 It is amusing to look back: See, for instance, "The Story Behind 1971 New Haven Photos of Bill and Hillary Clinton," *New Haven Register,* August 6, 2016. David Maraniss, in *First in His Class: The Biography of Bill Clinton* (New

York: Touchstone, 1996), gives a colorful sense of the atmosphere at Yale. See especially chapter 13, "Law and Politics at Yale," pp. 225–45. Yale was "not only elite and distinguished but also experimental and adaptable to the free-form culture of the era. . . . Grades had been all but eliminated before Clinton arrived, replaced by a more egalitarian pass-fail system. . . . The year before Clinton enrolled, a troop of long-haired, tie-dyed, Frisbee-playing students set up tents and an inflated air trampoline in the Quadrangle, which they said they had liberated, and lived there for weeks" (pp. 226, 237).

263 It revalidates all: From, *The New Democrats,* p. x.

263 Accounts of his life are freighted: Maraniss, *First in His Class,* pp. 14, 124, 296, 348, 367, 415, 418. On abandoning policy positions for business, see also Thomas Edsall, "Clinton's Revolution," *New York Review of Books,* November 5, 1992. As governor of Arkansas, "Clinton has assiduously avoided making enemies among the state's most powerful interests," including weakening promised environmental protections "in order to avoid the anger of local industry and agribusiness" (p. 11).

264 She seemed "prudent": Maraniss, *First in His Class,* pp. 368–69. "She often warned him away from taking what she considered tainted money from lobbyists." In one incident corroborated by "several . . . campaign aides," Hillary stopped Bill from accepting $15,000 from dairy interests that would have been used to buy votes in his 1974 congressional bid. Ibid., p. 336.

264 "When he could see a direct correlation": Ibid., p. 368.

264 Soon the Democratic Leadership Council: Ibid., pp. 418, 454, and my interviews with the friend of several young acolytes.

264 The Little Rock the Clintons embraced: Interview, Lexington, Kentucky, October 5, 2018.

264 In both, ambitions and business models: Tyson's own self-portrait corroborates this analysis. See Tysonfoods.com, "Our History."

264 along with the New York investment bankers: Nomi Prins, *All the Presidents' Bankers: The Hidden Alliances That Drive American Power* (New York: Nation Books, 2014), pp. 366ff.; Ferguson, *Golden Rule,* pp. 297–98.

265 Oddly, given two hard-fought elections: Ferguson, *Golden Rule,* pp. 359–75. This was the Gingrich class that set about dismantling that independent branch of government, Congress.

265 While his banking deregulation was incentivizing: See Prison Policy Initiative, "States of Incarceration: The Global Context 2018," June 2018; Michelle Alexander, *The New Jim Crow: Mass Incarceration in the Age of Colorblindness,* 10th anniversary ed. (New York: The New Press, 2020).

265 "But corporate crime and violence": Russell Mokhiber, "Underworld, U.S.A.," *In These Times,* April 1, 1996, p. 14.

265 While Clinton's anticrime push: Jesse Eisinger, *The Chickenshit Club: Why the Justice Department Fails to Prosecute Executives* (New York: Simon and Schuster, 2017), pp. 93–101; Brandon Garrett, *Too Big to Jail: How Prosecutors Compromise with Corporations* (Cambridge, MA: Harvard University Press, 2014).

266 Both of those were executed: Walmart, for example, launched its international division in 1993, and a handful of Robert Rubin's protégés gained an almost exclusive lock on USAID funding for privatization operations in the collapsing Soviet Union. See also Prins, *All the Presidents' Bankers,* p. 371, on the cross-border derivatives deals banks were eager to begin devising—which contributed to the global financial meltdown of 1997–1998. See below, Part V, "The Pattern," Chapter 3, "Courting Calamity," pp. 273–88.

266 For Columbia Law professor Tim Wu: Tim Wu, *The Curse of Bigness: Antitrust in the New Gilded Age* (New York: Columbia Global Reports, 2018), p. 105.

268 workers in industries: See, for instance, Terry Miller, "Amazon Worker: Why I'm Taking Action," *Labor Notes,* July 16, 2019; Joshua Johnson, host, "Game Mode: Work Hard, Play Hard," *1A,* July 17, 2019.

268 That same year, the Koch brothers' fortunes: Sources for the data points, in chronological order: "Koch Industries, Inc.—Company Profile, Information, Business Description, History, Background Information on Koch Industries, Inc.," *Reference for Business;* Koch Industries, Inc., "Summary of Koch Industries History," as submitted to the Securities and Exchange Commission (https://www.sec.gov/Archives/edgar/data/41077/000119312505225697/dex993.htm); "Koch Industries, Inc., Company Profile, Information, Business Description, . . ."; Leslie Wayne, "Pulling the Wraps Off Koch Industries," *New York Times,* November 20, 1994; "Koch Has Grown Quickly, Quietly," Koch Newsroom, March 23, 1997; "The Largest Private Companies: #1 Koch Industries," *Forbes,* November 9, 2006; "The Largest Private Companies: #2 Koch Industries," *Forbes,* November 16, 2011; Andrea Murphy, "America's Largest Private Companies 2015," *Forbes,* October 28, 2015.

3. Courting Calamity (1990s-)

269 Overnight, entire government institutions: See Julie Nelson and Irina Kuzes, *Radical Reform in Yeltsin's Russia: What Went Wrong?* (New York: Sharpe, 1995).

269 Many landed in the gulag: For a discussion of the values hatched in the gulag, see Ilya Zaslavskiy, "How Non-State Actors Export Kleptocratic Norms to the West," Hudson Institute, September 2017, pp. 5–9.

269 "as people stopped believing": Telephone interview, May 15, 2019.

270 In this way, Soviet public and criminal: In the late 1980s under new rules for state-owned enterprises, their operations were effectively legalized. See the careful analysis in Ilona Karpanos, "The Political Economy of Organised Crime in Russia: The State, Market and Criminality in the USSR and Post-Soviet Russia" (PhD diss., City University, London, October 2017).

270 Composite networks like this: Janine Wedel, "Corruption and Organized Crime in Post-Communist States: New Ways of Manifesting Old Patterns," *Trends in Organized Crime* 7, no. 1 (2001): 17. See also Misha Glenny *McMafia: A Journey Through the Global Criminal Underworld* (New York: Vintage, 2009), p. 70, quoting Jon Winer, a former official at the State Department's

Bureau of International Law Enforcement and Narcotics Affairs. He describes "seamless webs . . . between criminals on one side and political and bureaucratic elites on the other. Out of these seamless webs has emerged a triangle of crime, business and politics [that is] extremely strong and resilient." See also Alexander Cooley and John Heathershaw, *Dictators Without Borders: Power and Money in Central Asia* (New Haven, CT: Yale University Press, 2017), p. 11: Central Asia "is characterized by the blurring of politics and economics and public and private sectors to the extent that the boundary between them is completely absent." A very similar dynamic was under way in China at the same time. See Minxin Pei, *China's Crony Capitalism: The Dynamics of Regime Decay* (Cambridge, MA: Harvard University Press, 2016).

270 These once drab cities: Glenny, *McMafia,* p. 52.

271 The violence was unheard-of too: Ibid., pp. 14, 54–55, 59–64.

271 Glenny's conclusion is stark: Ibid., p. 52.

272 "nonprofit and nongovernmental" organization: Janine Wedel, "Corruption and Organized Crime in Post-Communist States: New Ways of Manifesting Old Patterns," *Trends in Organized Crime* 7, no. 1 (2001): 20.

272 Some members also used: See Janine Wedel, "The Harvard Boys Do Russia," *The Nation,* May 14, 1998; Janine Wedel, "Tainted Transactions: Harvard, the Chubais Clan and Russia's Ruin," *National Interest,* Spring 2000. The story is told in detail in her *Collision and Collusion: The Strange Case of Western Aid to Eastern Europe* (New York: St. Martin's Griffin, 2001), pp. 123–74. For the legal fallout, see *United States v. President and Fellows of Harvard College,* 323 F. Supp. 2d 151 (2004), materials available at https://www.courtlistener.com/opinion/2492903/united-states-v-president-and-fellows-of-harvard-college/.

272 In other words, Agalarov: The Aliyevs and their children own eleven banks, dominating the country's financial sector, and several massive conglomerates, which translate government appropriations and authority into vast riches. For a detailed examination of these transnational post-Soviet networks in a Central Asian context, see Cooley and Heathershaw, *Dictators Without Borders.* See also Sarah Chayes, "The Structure of Corruption: A Systemic Analysis Using Eurasian Cases," Carnegie Endowment for International Peace, June 30, 2016; Global Anti-Corruption Consortium, "The Azerbaijani Laundromat," September 4, 2017, and other reporting by the Organized Crime and Corruption Reporting Project; and Global Witness, "Azerbaijan Anonymous," December 6, 2013.

273 In embassies, Zaslavskiy notes: For a special focus on the KGB, see Karen Dawisha, *Putin's Kleptocracy: Who Owns Russia* (New York: Simon and Schuster, 2014), pp. 13–36.

273 Glenny, again, is priceless: Glenny, *McMafia,* p. 66.

273 The image is an updated version: Just years before, in 1989, a seventieth birthday party for *Forbes* magazine's Malcom Forbes in Morocco cost $2 million. Like the guests at the USSR nostalgia party, his celebrants were whisked there in chartered jets. An honor guard of three hundred Berber horsemen con-

ducted them to the festivities, where they consumed 216 magnums of champagne. Nicolaus Mills's introduction to Nicolaus Mills, ed., *Culture in an Age of Money* (Chicago: Ivan R. Dee, 1990), p. 20.

273   These were fashions: The examples of fawning coverage are too numerous to list. See, for instance, Phoebe Eaton, "How Much Is That in Rubles," *New York,* September 10, 2004.

274   "In virtually every country": Nils Gilman, "The Twin Insurgency: The Postmodern State Is Under Siege from Plutocrats and Criminals Who Unknowingly Compound Each Other's Insidiousness," *American Interest,* June 15, 2014. Note that I see these two groups as less separate than Gilman does, and less "unknowing" in their collaboration.

274   Public service messages: CBS, *Gunsmoke,* "The Kentucky Tolmans," August 9, 1952, available at https://www.oldtimeradiodownloads.com/western/gunsmoke/the-kentucky-tolmans-1952-08-09, minute 28:15.

276   Tony Blair's lucrative services: Robert Mendick, "Tony Blair's £5m Deal to Advise Kazakh Dictator," *The Telegraph,* April 26, 2016.

276   former German chancellor Gerhard Schroeder's chairmanship: Olesya Astakhova, "Russia's Rosneft Elects Former German Chancellor Schroeder as Chairman," Reuters, September 29, 2017.

276   "The truth is": Zaslavskiy, "How Non-State Actors Export," p. 2. See also Franklin Foer, "Russian-Style Kleptocracy Is Infiltrating America," *The Atlantic,* March 2019.

277   American networks have been purposefully exporting: Investigative journalist Lee Fang traces the development of what has come to be called the Atlas Network—which spearheads much of this work in Latin America—through a process like the one Lewis Powell's 1971 memo called for. Founded by a U.K. native who moved to the United States, and sharing inspiration with such U.S. organizations as the Heritage Foundation and the Cato Institute, the Atlas Economic Research Foundation set out in 1981 to spawn spin-off think tanks around the world. In four years, it was present in seventeen countries. The network of nonprofits has pulled in millions from the same sources that have lavished cash on the Koch galaxy of entities. Donors include foundations and blue-chip corporations. Koch funds themselves funnel money to Atlas groups, as has the U.S. government, in the form of grants to help build democracy, of all ironies. Atlas affiliates spearheaded the drive for the impeachment of Brazilian president Dilma Rousseff and gained the presidency of Argentina. Lee Fang, "Sphere of Influence: How American Libertarians Are Remaking Latin American Politics," *The Intercept,* August 9, 2017. A linked group helped Honduran president Juan Orlando Hernandez experiment with radical free-enterprise zones where national sovereignty would be suspended, allowing corporations to make their own rules. Fergus Hodgson, "Honduras: Free Marketeers Dominate ZEDEs Leadership," *Panama Post,* February 19, 2014.

277   That same decade: BCCI also got involved, and lost heavily, in commodities and financial futures trading, using depositors' money for its bets. John Kerry and Hank Brown, "The BCCI Affair," A Report to the Committee on Foreign

Relations, United States Senate, December 1992. Indeed, for several years, U.S. regulators and the Department of Justice, and their U.K. counterparts, dragged their feet and even actively hampered investigations into BCCI's doings. As a Rose attorney, Hillary Clinton helped BCCI in its quest to obtain ownership of a U.S. bank. Key actors in the drama included Carter Office of Management and Budget director Bert Lance, Democratic Party consiglieri Clark Clifford, and Republicans Robert Mueller and William Barr. The governor of the Bank of England was called to testify before Parliament, a first in U.K. history. It was work by the district attorney for New York—a state-level office—as well as investigative reporting that finally prompted criminal pursuit. See also Jonathan Beaty and S. C. Gwynne, *Outlaw Bank: A Wild Ride into the Secret Heart of BCCI* (New York: Beard, 2004).

278 Six years later: Among the copious sources are Paul Krugman, *The Return of Depression Economics* (New York: W. W. Norton, 1999); Dick Nanto, "The 1997–98 Asian Financial Crisis," Congressional Research Service, February 6, 1998; Vladimir Popov, "Currency Crises in Russia and Other Transition Economies," paper, October 2001. *The Economist*'s applause for the 1997 Nobel Prize award to Robert Merton and Myron Scholes, for the supposedly foolproof mathematical formula that was the basis of LTCM's business model— less than a year before the company began collapsing—is amusing. See "The Right Option," *The Economist,* October 16, 1997.

279 The Enron scandal also: See Bethany McLean and Peter Elkind, *The Smartest Guys in the Room: The Amazing Rise and Scandalous Fall of Enron* (New York: Penguin Portfolio, 2003). Note that the Enron ethos was handed down as a family legacy. The author of the spectacular twenty-first-century scam that may most closely resemble the doings of nineteenth-century Thérèse Humbert, and the founder of the bogus blood-screening company Theranos, which at its peak was valued at some $9 billion, is the daughter of former Enron VP (for due diligence) Christian Rasmus Holmes IV. After his stint at Enron, he held a string of government and private-sector positions that inserted him into the lucrative world of privatizing international development: director of the U.S. Trade and Development Agency, which focuses on energy and infrastructure, global water coordinator for the U.S. Agency for International Development, acting director of U.S. Office of Foreign Disaster Assistance, etc. Nick Bolton, "Exclusive: How Elizabeth Holmes's House of Cards Came Tumbling Down," *Vanity Fair,* September 6, 2015; The Webb Schools, "Christian R. Holmes IV, '64"; USAID Alumni Association, "Conversation with Chris Holmes."

279 To describe even a few of the dynamics: Below the officials mentioned, the overlap between private industry and agencies that regulate the same industries is unheard of. See, for example, OpenSecrets.org, "Lobbyists in (and out of) the Trump Administration," Center for Responsive Politics.

280 From Chao's bids to use: Michael Forsythe et al., "A 'Bridge to China,' and Her Family's Business in the Trump Cabinet," *New York Times,* June 2, 2019; Tucker Doherty and Tanya Snyder, "Chao Created Special Path for McConnell's Favored Projects," *Politico,* June 10, 2019. On McConnell's potential

reciprocal favors: Lee Fang, "McConnell's Freighted Ties to a Shadowy Shipping Company," *The Nation,* October 30, 2014; News Staff, "Top Three Priorities for Incoming Transportation Secretary Elaine Chao," *Government Technology,* December 22, 2016. See also Part III, "The Hydra," Chapter 5, "Powers Sabotaged," pp. 146–58.

281 Republican senators owe: On the last-minute flow of campaign contributions, see Thomas Ferguson et al., "How Money Drives US Congressional Elections: Linear Models of Money and Outcomes," *Structural Change and Economic Dynamics,* September 20, 2019. See also Jane Mayer, "How Mitch McConnell Became Trump's Enabler-in-Chief," *New Yorker,* April 20, 2020.

281 Another fraught family pairing: See Part III, "The Hydra," Chapter 5, "Powers Sabotaged," pp. 153–55, on market-based morality in secondary schools; Leslie Kaplan and William Owings, "Betsy DeVos's Education Reform Agenda: What Principals—and Their Publics—Need to Know," *National Association of Secondary School Principals Bulletin,* April 10, 2018; and on education more generally, see Diane Ravitch, *Slaying Goliath: The Passionate Resistance to Privatization and the Fight to Save America's Public Schools* (New York: Knopf, 2020). For a sample of reporting on Prince and Frontier's activities and connections to SCL—changed in 2018 to Auspex International, the parent company of Cambridge Analytica and its successor Emerdata—and the intelligence-focused Amyntor, as well as former Interior secretary Ryan Zinke's indirect link to Amyntor via an investment in Whitefish, Montana–based Proof Research, which shares at least one board member with Amyntor, see Antony Loewenstein, "Peace in Afghanistan? Maybe, but a Minerals Rush Is Already Underway," *The Nation,* January 30, 2019; Reuters, "Erik Prince Company to Build Training Center in China's Xinjiang" (the province where native Uighurs are suffering mass arrest and re-education), January 31, 2019; "Cambridge Analytica Links to Erik Prince, Blackwater Founder," Associated Press, March 21, 2018; for corporate documents, see DeSmogBlog, "Cambridge Analytica," no date; Katie McQuater, "Former Cambridge Analytica Director Opens New Political Consultancy," *Research Live,* July 17, 2018. On Cambridge Analytica generally, see Karim Amer and Jehane Noujaim, *The Great Hack,* Netflix, January 26, 2019; "Interior Secretary Ryan Zinke Held On to Undisclosed Shares in Gun Company," *Mother Jones,* January 22, 2018; Matthew Cole and Jeremy Scahill, "White House Weighing Plans for Private Spies to Counter 'Deep State' Enemies," *The Intercept,* December 4, 2017. See also Ken Silverstein, "How *The Intercept* Got Played by the Military-Industrial Complex," part 2, *Washington Babylon,* December 18, 2017. On Prince's domestic activities, see Mark Mazzetti and Adam Goldman, "Erik Prince Recruits Ex-Spies to Help Infiltrate Liberal Groups," *New York Times,* March 7, 2020.

281 The appointment of close family members: The appointment of Jared Kushner and Ivanka Trump appears to violate federal anti-nepotism laws. See Citizens for Ethics and Responsibility in Washington, "Nepotism and Conflicts of Interest—Jared Kushner and Ivanka Trump," no date.

281　There are White House innovations director: Julian Borger, "A Tale of Two Houses: How Jared Kushner Fuelled the Trump-Saudi Love-in," *The Guardian,* October 16, 2018; Erin Banco, "Embassy Staffers Say Jared Kushner Shut Them Out of Saudi Meetings," *Daily Beast,* March 7, 2019; Ryan Grim, "The UAE's Powerful Ambassador Is Still Hobnobbing in Washington After Jamal Khashoggi's Murder," *The Intercept,* October 23, 2018; Ryan Grim and Akbar Shahid Ahmed, "His Town," *HuffPost,* no date. The investigative radio program *Reveal* notes that Barrack's Colony Capital sold l'Hermitage Hotel to Malaysian 1MDB alleged co-conspirator Jho Low in 2010, on the advice of UAE ambassador Oteiba, and then bought Jared Kushner's debt in the same amount. "Checking into Trump's Washington Hotel," *Reveal,* April 7, 2018. See also Bradley Hope and Tom Wright, "Stolen Emails Show Ties Between U.A.E. Envoy and 1MDB Fund's Central Figure," *Wall Street Journal,* August 1, 2017. On Qatar, which is opposed to Saudi Arabia and the UAE in a local standoff, see Bess Levin, "Qatar Shocked, Shocked to Learn It Accidentally Bailed Out Jared Kushner," *Vanity Fair,* February 12, 2019; Daniel Estrin, "Trump Son-in-Law's Ties to Israel Raise Questions of Bias," *Times of Israel,* March 25, 2017. For some of the potential ramifications, see Reem Shamseddine and Katie Paul, "U.S., Saudi Firms Sign Tens of Billions of Dollars of Deals as Trump Visits," Reuters, May 20, 2017; Doug Bandow, "U.S. Support Has Fueled, Not Moderated the Yemen War," *National Interest,* May 19, 2019; Staff, "Netanyahu on US Embassy Relocation in May: 'A Great Day for Israel,' " *Times of Israel,* February 23, 2018. On China, see Adam Entous and Evan Osnos, "Soft Target: China's Suspect Courtship with Jared Kushner," *New Yorker,* January 29, 2018. On Turkey, see *U.S. v Turkiye Halk Bankasi,* U.S. District Court, Southern District of New York, Superseding Indictment, October 15, 2019, p. 33. Erdogan and his son-in-law are referred to as "the then–Prime Minister of Turkey" and "a relative of the then–Prime Minister of Turkey who later held multiple cabinet positions"; David Kirkpatrick and Eric Lipton, "Behind Trump's Dealings with Turkey: Sons-in-Law Married to Power," *New York Times,* November 12, 2019. See also Tim Miller, "Trump's Turkey Corruption Is Way Worse Than You Realize," *The Bulwark,* November 26, 2019. The point is not necessarily that specific policies resulted from personal conflicts of interest, but, at least as important, that U.S. citizens cannot trust that they do not. On Kushner as slumlord, see Doug Donovan, "Maryland Attorney General Investigating Kushner-Owned Properties," *Baltimore Sun,* October 30, 2017; "Slumlord Millionaire," *Dirty Money,* Season 2, Netflix, March 11, 2020. On vulture investors capitalizing on 2008 and becoming serial foreclosers and evicters, see Aaron Glantz, *Homewreckers: How a Gang of Wall Street Kingpins, Hedge Fund Magnates, Crooked Banks and Vulture Capitalists Suckered Millions Out of Their Homes and Demolished the American Dream* (New York: HarperCollins, 2019).

282　That may be what the Trumps: "Once Trump appointed his daughter, his son-in-law," he told me, "everything was destroyed. It was a huge gift to leaders in my zone. They're all trying to organize succession to their kids. The United

States was known for that separation between business and the public sector. Now you have this guy double-hatted, that guy double-hatted" (interview, June 5, 2018). On Ivanka's ambitions, see, for instance, Helaine Olen, "Ivanka Trump Wants Power, and Laughing at Her Expense Won't Stop Her," *Washington Post,* July 1, 2019.

282 He is at once a symptom: This thought is well stated by Greg Sargent, in "Elizabeth Warren Just Tore Apart a Billionaire. Why Not Trump?" *Washington Post,* February 20, 2020.

282 As does his penchant: Examples include Rudy Giuliani, Paul Manafort, Roger Stone, and the lesser-known Richard Grenell, ambassador to Germany and acting director of National Intelligence. Previously, he represented the government of Nigerian president Goodluck Jonathan, which siphoned off approximately a billion dollars per month of the country's oil revenues before the money reached the federal treasury, and Vladimir Plahotniuc, the boss of Moldova's kleptocratic network, who helped turn that country into a giant laundromat for questionable Russian cash and helped move a billion dollars (approximately 10 percent of Moldova's GDP) into secret bank accounts offshore. See Emma Brown et al.'s poorly headlined article: "Richard Grenell's Paid Consulting Included Work for U.S. Nonprofit Funded Mostly by Hungary," *Washington Post,* February 27, 2020; on Nigeria, see Aaron Sayne et al., "Inside NNPC Oil Sales: A Case for Reform in Nigeria," Natural Resource Governance Institute, August 2015. On Moldova, see reporting by the Organized Crime and Corruption Reporting Project, available at https://www.occrp.org/en/component /tags/tag/moldova, and see Sarah Chayes, "The Structure of Corruption: A Systemic Analysis Using Eurasian Cases," Carnegie Endowment for International Peace, June 30, 2016.

283 What quid pro quos: For a good roundup, listen to "The Family Business: Trump Inc.," WNYC, September 18, 2019.

283 Not only was Manchin's daughter: Jayne O'Donnell, "EpiPens Had High-Level Help Getting into Schools," *USA Today,* September 21, 2016. As of this writing, it appears that Manchin's daughter Heather Bresch will retire when Pfizer's generic division merges with Mylan, rescheduled for the end of 2020. See Max Nilsen, "Pfizer-Mylan Generic Giant Solves Two Problems with One Deal," Bloomberg, July 29, 2019. On Mnuchin's vote, see H.R. 2094, 113th Congress, "School Access to Emergency Epinephrine Act," voice vote with all votes recorded as "yes" at http://maplight.org/data /passthrough/#legacyurl=http://classic.maplight.org/us-congress/bill/113-hr -2094/2452770/total-contributions. Mylan, a major contributor to Manchin, is also invested in coal, for tax-break purposes, and sells medications for the respiratory ailments caused by breathing its smoke and dust. Michael Erman, "Drugmaker Mylan Gets Boost from Unlikely Source: Coal," Reuters, June 21, 2017. See also Emily Atkin, "A Major Asthma Drugmaker Has Been Quietly Investing in Coal on the Side," *New Republic* (no date, 2017).

EPILOGUE: BREAKING THE PATTERN (NOW)

285 So many of the exaggerated characters: The reading that sent me in this direction was Joseph Campbell's discussion of the Cretan tyrant Minos, and his
archetype: "The figure of the tyrant-monster is known to the mythologies, folk
traditions, legends, and even nightmares of the world; and his characteristics
are everywhere essentially the same. He is the hoarder of the general benefit.
He is the monster avid for the greedy rights of 'my and mine.' The havoc
wrought by him is . . . universal throughout his domain. . . . The inflated ego
of the tyrant is a curse to himself and his world—no matter how his affairs may
seem to prosper. Self-terrorized, fear-haunted, alert at every hand to meet and
battle back . . . anticipated aggressions . . . which are primarily the reflections
of the uncontrollable impulses to acquisition within himself, the giant of self-
achieved independence is the world's messenger of disaster, even though, in
his mind, he may entertain himself with humane intentions." *The Hero with a
Thousand Faces* (Novato, CA: New World Library, 2008), p. 12.

287 a systematic state-by-state review: A partial review—of the definition of "conflict of interest" and of gift statutes as applied to legislators—is available from
the National Conference of State Legislatures website, under "Conflict of
Interest Definitions" and "Legislator Gift Restrictions." Citizens might examine the texts, see what other public officials are covered, and examine their
state's history of enforcement. The Center for Public Integrity generated a
rather basic enforcement benchmark: Yue Qiu, Chris Zubak-Skees, and Erik
Lincoln, "How Does Your State Rank for Integrity?" Center for Public Integrity, updated February 2, 2018.

288 Is the owner of the nearest: See Diane Ravitch, *Slaying Goliath: The Passionate
Resistance to Privatization and the Fight to Save America's Public Schools* (New
York: Knopf, 2020), pp. 144–45. And see the investigations on In the Public
Interest's website.

289 In 1968, running for president: Robert F. Kennedy, "Remarks at the University
of Kansas, March 18, 1968," available on the John F. Kennedy Library and
Museum website.

290 Such weapons would place: In his 2009 article "How Wall Street Is Using
the Bailout to Stage a Revolution" (*Rolling Stone,* April 2, 2009), Matt Taibbi
wrote: "By creating an urgent crisis that can only be solved by those fluent in
a language too complex for ordinary people to understand, the Wall Street
crowd has turned the vast majority of Americans into nonparticipants in their
own political future. There is a reason it used to be a crime in the Confederate
states to teach a slave to read: Literacy is power."

292 With her final poem: Joy Harjo, "Bless This Land," *American Sunrise* (New
York: W. W. Norton, 2019), pp. 106–8. Watch the whole performance at
https://www.youtube.com/watch?v=HiIJFRXxa3o.

293 Schoolchildren everywhere: Sign from the Students' Climate Strike, Portland,
Oregon, September 21, 2019.

294 If the tone of its 2019 advertising campaign: A "Wells Fargo Stories" page

has been added to the company website. It features joyful faces of Americans of all walks, and subheadings titled "Volunteering and Giving" and "Diversity and Inclusion." A nationwide advertising campaign made the company sound more like a humanitarian development organization than a bank. These moves came well before the Office of the Comptroller of the Currency took the unprecedented step, on January 24, 2020, of fining several top executives and barring them from the financial services industry. The bank was responding to consumer pressure.

295 What would happen if a whole crop: See Tim Wu, "The Life and Death of the Local Hardware Store," *New York Times,* November 22, 2019.

296 It commits them to deliver: "Statement on the Purpose of a Corporation," Business Roundtable, August 19, 2019.

296 Patagonia, likewise, has refused: Kim Bhasin, "Patagonia Is Cracking Down on Making Logo Vests for Wall Street Banks and Tech Startups," *Time,* April 3, 2019.

298 What they wanted was a formula: On a show dedicated to science, the investigative news radio program *Reveal* interviewed former chemical industry lobbyist and more recently former EPA principal deputy assistant administrator Mandy Gunasekara, who identified helping take the United States out of the Paris Climate Accord and reversing the 2015 Clean Power Plan as her proudest achievements at EPA. When host Al Letson noted that the impacts of climate change are all around us, and asked, "What can we do?" she replied, "You're not going to like this answer, but it's doing what we're doing now." Al Letson, host, "Scuttling Science," *Reveal,* September 14, 2019, minute 46:33.

298 As Thomas Ferguson put it: Thomas Ferguson et al., "Big Money—Not Political Tribalism—Drives U.S. Elections," Institute for New Economic Thinking, October 31, 2018.

299 Given the Supreme Court cases: See Jacob Hale Russell, "The Supreme Court Doesn't Need 9 Justices, It Needs 27," *Time,* July 16, 2018.

300 Several examples have been: See, for instance, H.R. 1, the "For the People Act," which passed in the House of Representatives on August 8, 2019; Elizabeth Warren's Anti-Corruption and Public Integrity Act; Rohit Chopra and Julie Margetta Morgan, "Unstacking the Deck: A New Agenda to Tame Corruption in Washington," Roosevelt Institute, May 2, 2018. For a set of basic principles, applicable to any country, see U4, "International Good Practice in Anti-corruption Legislation," 2010.

300 In 2019, West Virginia gubernatorial candidate: David Dayen, "The People's Platform Rises in West Virginia," *American Prospect,* December 30, 2019, and email exchanges with West Virginia Can't Wait staff, January 2020.

302 How could we make them: I am grateful here again to Kent Shreeve. See also Sarah Chayes, "Hunter Biden's Perfectly Legal, Socially Acceptable Corruption," *The Atlantic,* September 27, 2019.

306 Examining more than two hundred cores: Eberhard Zangger, "Prehistoric Coastal Environments in Greece: The Vanished Landscape of Dimini Bay and Lake Lerna," *Journal of Field Archaeology* 18, no. 1 (Spring 1991): 1–15.

Index

Page numbers in *italics* refer to illustrations.

abortion, 3, 121
accountability, 287
Achilles, 41, 42
Acosta, Alexander, 106, 116–17, 280, 341*n*
Adams, Charles Francis, 79–80
Adams, John, 32
Afghanistan, 5–6, 7, 10, 76, 101, 116, 135, 147–49, 166, 177, 213–14, 274, 297, 368*n*
  elections in, 124–25
  networks in, 96–97, 100
  opium economy in, 218–19
Africa, 7, 101, 269
African Americans, 207, 237, 332*n*
  farmers, 219–20, 222, *222,* 223
  former slaves, 75, 79, 118, 131
  Populists and, *222*
  re-enslavement of, 131
Agalarov, Emin, 110, 272
agriculture, 78, 218, 225, 247, 264, 304
  see also farmers
Agriculture, Department of, 146
Ahearn, Jennifer, 195
airplane crashes, 162, 164, 361*n*
air traffic controllers, 255
Akerlof, George, 161
Akselberg, Øistein, 47

Albright, Madeleine, 61, 100–101
Albright Capital Management, 101
Albright Stonebridge Group, 100
Alexander, Ryan, 142
Algeria, 114
Aliyev, Ilham, 110, 282, 389*n*
Alliance for Justice, 121
al-Qaeda, 215
Altman, Roger, 165, 264
aluminum, 153–55
Amalgamated Association of Iron and Steel Workers, 205
Amazon, 296, 327*n*
American colonies, 32
American Enterprise Day, 252–53
American Home Mortgage Servicing, Inc., 168
American Legislative Exchange Council, 142, 180, 253
American Revolution, 32, 319*n*
Americans for Prosperity, 119
Americans for Prosperity Foundation v. Becerra, 365*n*
American Steel Foundries, 348*n*
Ames, Oaks, 325*n*
Amey, Scott, 138
Amway, 98
anarchists, 206, 207, *207,* 209–16, 223, 227, 228

Andijan Massacre, 131
Andrews, Elisha, 63
Angola, 276
Ansell, Christopher, 97
antitrust laws, 79, 131, 251, 266
Appeal of Conscience Foundation,
    335n
APR Energy, 101
Arab Spring, 6
Araoz, Jennifer, 108
L'Argent (Zola), 64–65
Argentina, 390n
Arghandab, 135
Aristophanes, 45–46, 321n
Aristotle, 42, 44–45, 54, 55
Arkansas, 263, 264
Army, U.S., 88, 131, 132, 348n
  contracts with, 134–35
Army and Civil Disorder, The (Cooper),
    131
art, 80, 102–4, 103, 329n
Arthur Andersen, 363n, 370n
AT&T, 127
Athens, 30, 42
Atiya, Abd al-Rahman, 215
Atlas Economic Research Foundation,
    390n
Australian Aborigines, 177, 183
Austria, 61–63, 70
Aven, Pyotr, 271
Ayer, Don, 188–90, 195–97
Azar, Alex, 105–6
Azerbaijan, 272, 282

Bailout (Barofsky), 166
Balkan Wars, 134
Banco Ficohsa, 368n
banking and financial services, 39, 51,
    61, 63, 64, 69, 83–84, 85, 87, 97, 102,
    104, 149, 157–70, 178–79, 185, 220,
    225, 294, 330n
  failures of, 249
  Ivy League schools and, 261
  Jerusalem Temple and, 38–39
  lifting of restraints on, 254
  political campaigns and, 128
  private equity firms, 104, 168, 169,
    335n

profits of banks compared to private
    sector, 323n
savings and loan institutions, 158–65,
    168–70, 191, 254, 277
  see also Wall Street
Bank of China, 155
Bank of Credit and Commerce
    International (BCCI), 278, 390–91n
Bank of Cyprus, 168
Bank of Ireland, 168
bankruptcy for profit, 161, 170
Barofsky, Neil, 166
Barr, Donald, 117, 341n
Barr, William, 116, 117, 391n
Barrack, Tom, 105, 169
Bartelme, Tony, 69
Beirut, 6, 173–75
Bell, Marsha, 36
Belle Époque, 64–68
Ben Ali, Zine el-Abedine, 115
Berkman, Alexander, 212–13
Berman, Richard, 107
Bernstein, Dorothy, 236
Berry, Wendell, 321n
Bethlehem Steel, 239, 240
Bible, 34, 55
  Jesus in, see Jesus
Biden, Joe, 273
bin Laden, Usama, 135
Black, Conrad, 371n
Black, William, 159, 161–63
Blackmon, Douglas, 131
Blackstone Group, 264
Blackwater, 281
Blair, Tony, 276
Blavatnik, Leonid, 154, 271, 296, 335n,
    359n
Blodget, Samuel, 32
Blood on the Forge (Attaway), 219
Bloomberg, Michael, 61, 268n, 346n
Bloomingdale, Alfred, 253–54, 261
Bochet, Gilbert, 177
Boehm, Christopher, 28–30, 78, 122,
    175, 316n
Boeing, 140, 150–51, 361n
Boko Haram, 6, 113–14, 133–34
bonds, see stocks and bonds
Bonus Army, 236

Bookbinder, Noah, 192–96
Bopp, James, 193
Bork, Robert, 120, 251–52, 266
Boston Consulting, 276
Boston Post, 84
Bourguiba, Habib, 274
Bouttiaux, Anne-Marie, 177–78
Bowes, Gregory, 101
Bradley, Omar, 250
Branch Banking and Trust, 346*n*
Brassfield, Shoshana, 40
Brazil, 172, 279, 390*n*
Breuer, Lanny, 363*n*
Brexit, 5
Breyer, Jim, 155
bribery, 21, 39, 62, 118, 192, 193, 226,
    250, 287, 294
  convictions for, 13
  McDonnell decision and, 7, 8, 14, 15
  Menendez case and, 12
  Trump impeachment and, 312*n,* 313*n*
  "Bridgegate" scandal, 313–14*n,* 371*n*
Brockman, John, 109
Brown, Frederick, 65–66
Brown, Julie, 117
Brunel, Jean-Luc, 110
Bryan, William Jennings, 213*n,* 227,
    384*n*
Bureau of Land Management (BLM),
    106, 148, 253
Burford, Anne Gorsuch, 106, 253
Burford, Robert, 106, 253
Burkina Faso, 172, 292
Bush, George H. W., 106, 121, 194, 279
Bush, George W., 102, 117, 121, 146,
    166, 167
business failures, 381*n*
Business Roundtable, 295–96

Cajun Navy, 230
California, 254
Cambodia, 7
Cambridge Analytica, 281
campaign contributions, 127–28, 178
Campbell, Joseph, 22, 177, 211, 395*n*
Campbell, Sister Simone, 323*n*
Cantor, Eric, 192
capacity building, 147

capital, labor and, 75
capitalism, 166
Capmark Financial Group, 168–69
Cardinal Health, 185
Carnegie, Andrew, 71, 75, 77, 87, 185,
    213
Carnegie Endowment for International
    Peace, 188, 368*n*
Carnegie Steel Company, 131, 213
Carter, Jimmy, 251, 259, 278
casinos, 168
Cato Institute, 192, 195, 390*n*
Cause of Action Institute, 98
Centers for Disease Control and
    Prevention, 149, 151
Central America, 7, 147, 149
CEOs, 100, 196, 296
  compensation for, 248, *249,* 380*n*
Chaffetz, Jason, 142, 144
Chamberlain, Neville, 89, 90
Chao, Angela, 155
Chao, Elaine, 154, 155, 280
Chamber of Commerce, U.S., 100, 101,
    127, 142, 192, 195, 333*n*
  Powell's memo to, 119–20, 122, 184,
    250, 252–53, 262
Charles I, King, 115, 116
Chase, Salmon, 72, 78
Chen, Jie, 127–28
Cheney, Dick, 134, 135
Chicago, Ill., 206–8
  Haymarket Square rally in, 131, 208,
    208, 212, 224
Chiles, Lawton, 260
China, 154–56, 280, 282
China Eximbank, 154
China Shipbuilding Industry
    Corporation (CSIC), 154–55
China State Shipbuilding Corporation
    (CSSC), 155
Chi-Raq (Lee), 299
Christ, *see* Jesus
*Christ Driving the Money Changers from
    the Temple* (Rembrandt), *35*
Christie, Chris, 313*n,* 365*n,* 371*n*
Churchill, Winston, 91
Church of Christ, 36
CIA, 178, 278

Citi, 122
cities, 201–16
Citizens for Responsibility and Ethics in Washington (CREW), 194–95
Citizens United, 180, 192–93
Citizens United v. Federal Election Commission, 179–80, 197, 299, 365*n*, 370*n*
Civilian Conservation Corps, 303
Civil War, 71–75, 207, 220, 222–23, 235, 260
Clean Air Act, 355*n*
Clean Water Act, 145, 355*n*
climate change, 183–84, 262, 396*n*
Clinton, Bill, 102, 105, 109, 116, 117, 136, 163–64, 194, 260, 263–66, 271, 272, 278, 339*n*, 363*n*, 387*n*
  deregulation and, 163–64, 264–65
  Epstein and, 109–11, 338*n*
  war on crime, 265–66
Clinton, Chelsea, 339*n*
Clinton, Hillary Rodham, 194, 263–65, 278, 338*n*, 339*n*, 387*n*, 390*n*
  emails of, 178
  Honduras and, 194
  in presidential election of 2016, 5, 129
Clinton Foundation, 15–16, 110–11
coalitions, 78, 96, 116, 122, 175
coal mines and miners, 153, 168, 357*n*
cocaine, 167, 278
Cochran, Augustus, 260
Cohen, Michael, 194
Cohen, Steven, 100
coins, 25–27, *26*, 30, 31, 38, 41, 55, 63
Cold War, 250, 274
Colfax, Schuyler, 62
colonialism, 32, 233, 380*n*
Colony Capital, 105, 169
Columbia Trust, 84
Comey, James, 140, 352*n*
Commonwealth Club, 240–41
communism, 238, 250, 273–74
  red scares, 208, *208*, 216
community, 13, 21, 27–28, 36–37, 52–53, 73, 83, 121, 209, 212, 230, 231, 232
Competitive Enterprise Institute, 184

Congress, U.S., 125, 138, 149, 151–52, 156, 256–57
  districts for, 125–27
  elections for, 125–29
  staff for, 149–51
  see also House of Representatives, U.S.; Senate, U.S.
Constitution, U.S., 99, 112, 144–45, 149, 152, 299, 312*n*
  Commerce Clause of, 99, 328*n*
  Fourteenth Amendment to, 79, 118
  gifts prohibited by, 301
Constitutional Convention, 319*n*, 357*n*
Consumer Financial Protection Bureau, 122, 149, 170, 345*n*
Consumer Product Safety Commission, 254
contract law, 121–23
Cooke, Henry, 73, 78
Cooke, Jay, 63, 72–75, *73*, 78, 102, 220
Cooper, Jerry, 131
cooperatives, 5, 125, 207, 209, 223, 224
Coors, Joseph, 142, 253
Coors Brewing Company, 98
coronavirus (COVID-19) pandemic, 61, 105, 145, 169, 170, 178, 230, 235, 266, 282, 289, 303, 367*n*, 377*n*
corporations, 79, 100, 118–21, 254, 294–96, 303
corruption:
  American understanding of, 21–22
  bribery, *see* bribery
  definitions of, 21
  developing-world kleptocracy, 69, 73, 98, 113–15
  downplaying of, 14, 15
  legal definition of, 287
  networks of, *see* networks
  significance of, 14
  in U.S., 7, 10, 13, 16, 21–22
Corruption in America (Teachout), 301
Corzine, Jon, 102
Council on Foreign Relations, 276, 296
countryside, 217–28
  see also farmers
courts, 115–23, 152
COVID-19, *see* coronavirus pandemic
crack cocaine, 278

Craft, Joe and Kelly, 358*n*
Craig, Gregory, 187–88, 194, 273
Crédit Mobilier of America, 62, 325*n*
Crete, 319*n*
crime, 11, 14, 30, 43, 50, 59, 71, 76,
    85–86, 102, 113, 123, 146, 158, 163,
    164, 167, 170, 191, 192, 196, 230,
    250, 270, 282, 288, 301
  criminal masterminds, 49, 74, 111
  nonviolent offenses, 193, 288
  organized, 86, 97, 171, 270–71, 274,
    277
  sentencing for, 193, 288
  white-collar, 10, 158, 159–62, 190, 193,
    254, 265–66, 287
Crimea, 154
cronyism, 140, 254
Curée, La (Zola), 64
Currinder, Marian, 151

Daily Beast, 341*n*
Daley, David, 125–26
Dalton School, 117, 341*n*
Dannenberg, James, 344*n*
Dark Money (Mayer), 98, 120, 179
Dark Side of Camelot, The (Hersh), 86
Dart, Justin, 254
Davis, Lanny, 194
Day, Henry Mason, 241
deception (as a tactic), 181–85
Defense Department, U.S. (DoD), 140,
    143, 150, 178, 250
defense spending, defense industry:
  business connections in, 138–40, *139*
  contracts and contractors, 138, 139,
    143, 255, 351*n*
  in Nigeria, 133–34, 137, 138, 349*n*
  in U.S., 136–38
de Kooning, Willem, 104
democracy, 30–33, 40, 42, 115, 122, 274,
    276–77, 289, 317*n*, 332*n*
  American, 32, 74, 99, 228
  business threats to, 251
  government force and, 130, 132
Democracy Heading South (Cochran),
    260
Democracy in Chains (MacLean), 98,
    120

Democratic Congressional Campaign
    Committee, 296
Democratic Leadership Council (DLC),
    259, 260, 263, 264
Democratic Party, Democrats, 11, 12,
    88, 101, 125–26, 150, 151, 166, 213*n*,
    258–60, 262, 267*n*, 283, 339*n*
  Populists and, 226, 227
  southern, 260, 263
  Wall Street and, 258, 259
Depository Institutions Deregulation
    and Monetary Control Act, 159
Depression, Great, 63, 85, 233–34, 236,
    240, 242, 277
deregulation, 159, 251, 259, 275
Deripaska, Oleg, 271, 335*n*
Dershowitz, Alan, 106, 108, 109, 313*n*,
    339*n*, 371*n*
Deutsche Bank, 69, 106, 168, 363*n*
developing-world kleptocracy, 69, 73,
    98, 113–15
DeVos, Betsy, 193, 281
Diane Rehm Show, The, 7, 9, 10
Dionysus, 24–26, 315*n*
disasters, 236–38
  natural, 230–32, 377*n*
  values and, 229–32, 236–38, 262
Discover Bank, 122, 345*n*
Dodd-Frank Wall Street Reform and
    Consumer Protection Act, 167
Dominican Republic, 12
Donohue, Thomas, 100
dos Santos, Isabel, 276
dot-coms, 279
Douglas, Michael, 50
Drew, Daniel, 76
Drug Enforcement Administration
    (DEA), 186, 369*n*
drugs:
  cocaine, 167, 278
  enforcement, 10, 164, 193, 265
  metaphor, 186, 297
  opioid epidemic, 182–83, 186, 218–19,
    278, 336*n*, 366*n*, 369*n*
  traffickers in, 85, 278
Dune Capital Management, 104, 168
Dunn, Brendan, 153–54
Dutch Republic, 48

earthquakes, 231, 232, 377n
Economic Recovery Tax Act, 255
Economic Stabilization Act, 167n
economy, 141, 156, 169
  financial crisis of 2008, 46, 60–61, 85,
    101, 104, 157–58, 167n, 170, 266
  GDP, 54, 163, 262
  Great Depression, 63, 85, 233–34, 236,
    240, 242, 277
  Great Recession, 69, 158, 166, 168,
    169, 279, 360n
  growth in, 54, 163, 248, 289–90
  Panic of 1873, 63–64, 72, 73, 130, 158,
    220, 277
  post–World War II, 248
  series of crises in, 277
Eddy, Debby, 45
Edsall, Thomas, 382n, 384n, 387n
education, 47, 81, 99, 119, 120, 143,
    147, 186, 221, 227, 257, 281, 289, 296
egalitarianism, 30, 31, 36, 39, 52, 78, 91,
    115, 151, 175, 212, 215–16, 222, 231,
    232, 234, 251, 256, 262, 277, 286,
    291, 300, 321n
Egypt, 11, 48, 70, 118, 137, 171
Eiffel, Gustave, 65
Eisenhower, Dwight D., 384n
elections in Afghanistan, 124–25
elections in U.S., 125–29, 153
  campaign contributions and, 127–28,
    178
  congressional, 125–29
  cost of, 127–28
  FEC and, 127, 148
  foreign interference in, 153, 359n
  litmus test for candidates in, 299
  Populist Party and, 226–27
  presidential, of 2016, 5, 15–16, 128–29,
    153
Electoral College, 128–29
electrum, 26, 26
elites and elitism, 180, 196, 232
Elliott Management, 100–101
Ely, Amie, 12–13
Emmanuel Episcopal Church, 35, 39
Energy Transfer, 132
Engels, Friedrich, 207
England, 235

Enron, 190–91, 195, 266, 279, 287,
    363n, 370n, 391n
environment, environmental
    protections, 253, 275, 283, 303–4
  climate change, 183–84, 262, 396n
  wetlands, 306
Environmental Protection Agency
    (EPA), 106, 145–46, 251, 253, 288,
    355n, 357n, 396n
Ephesus, 25–27
EpiPen, 283
Epstein, Jeffrey, 106–12, 116–17, 296,
    337n, 338n, 339n, 341n
Erdogan, Recep Tayyip, 276, 281
Espinosa, Paul, 301
Eucharist, 29, 231
Europe, 59–70, 95
European Union, 5, 147

Fang, Lee, 390n
Farmer, Annie, 107
Farmer, Maria, 107–8, 338n
farmers, 141, 146, 148, 185, 217–26,
    247, 304
  African American, 219–20, 222, 222,
    223
  crop lien system and, 218–21, 374n
  Farmers' Alliance, 217, 220–26, 228,
    253, 288–89, 375n
  opium, 218–19
  poultry, 374n
fat, dietary, 183
FBI, 140, 164, 165, 167
Federal Aviation Administration (FAA),
    162, 164, 361n
Federal Deposit Insurance Corporation
    (FDIC), 104, 122, 164, 169, 345n
Federal Election Commission (FEC),
    127, 148, 288
  Citizens United v. Federal Election
    Commission, 179–80, 197
Federal Emergency Management
    Agency (FEMA), 377–78n
federal government positions, hiring for,
    148–49
Federal Grain Inspection Service, 254
Federal Home Loan Bank Board,
    162–63

Federalist Society, 98, 120–21, 180, 254, 336*n*

Federal Reserve, 78, 105, 157–58, 164, 169, 170, 178–79, 302

Federal Sentencing Guidelines, 5, 13

Ferguson, Thomas, 118, 127–28, 255–57, 260, 298–99, 332*n,* 333*n,* 376*n*

fiction, 323*n*

Field, Stephen, 79

financial crisis of 2008, 46, 60–61, 85, 101, 104, 157–58, 167*n,* 170, 266

financial institutions, *see* banking and financial services

Financial Institutions Reform, Recovery, and Enforcement Act, 162

First World Oil War, The (Winegard), 233

Fisk, Jim, 71, 76

Fiske & Hatch, 63

Fitzgerald, John Francis "Honey Fitz," 82–83, 86, *243,* 379*n*

Fitzgeralds and the Kennedys, The (Goodwin), 84

Florence, 97

Flynn, Elizabeth Gurley, 130

Flynn, Michael, 280

Foner, Eric, 262

Forbes, 54, 67, 389*n*

Forbes, Malcolm, 389–90*n*

force, government use of, 129–32

Foremost, 154, 155

Fore River Shipyard, 239, 240

fossil fuels, 98, 114, 184, 185, 253, 254, 283

see also oil and gas industry

Founders' Period, 61–62

Founding Fathers, 32, 127

Fourteenth Amendment, 79, 118

Fox News, 117

France, 65–67, 70

anti-Semitism in, 70

Belle Époque in, 64–68

in World War I, 233, 234–35, *235*

Francisco, Noel, 188

freedom, 49, 74, 75, 158, 177, 224–25, 237, 252, 262, 271, 275, 287, 344*n*

FreedomWorks, 119

Frick, Henry Clay, 213, 239

Fridman, Mikhail, 271

Fritz, Charles, 229–32, 234, 236, 237

From, Al, 259–60, 263

Frontier Services Group, 281

Ganz, Marie, 210

Garfield, Bob, 68

Garfield, James, 62

gay marriage, 121

Gazprom, 155, 276

GDP (gross domestic product), 54, 163, 262, 289–90

Geffen, David, 197

Geithner, Timothy, 165

General Dynamics, 140

General Electric, 122

General Motors, 297, 379*n*

George Mason University, 98, 120

Georgia Pacific Railroad, 131, 353*n*

Gephardt, Dick, 260

Germany, 61–63, 70, 379*n*

in World War I, 233, 234

in World War II, 85, 89–91, 233–34

Ghanem, Nizar, 173

Giancana crime family, 86

Gilded Age, 59–60, 64, 68, 71–81, 82–91, 95, 98, 99, 101–3, 130–32, 141, 147, 178–79, 185, 190, 191, 201, 202, 204–6, 213, 214, 217, 220, 227, 231, 232, 234, 238–40, 242, 248, 251, 252, 255, 265, 268, 273, 277, 279, 292, 366*n,* 379*n*

economic crises caused by, 277

Great Depression and, 233–34, 240

World War I and, 232–33

Gilded Age, The: A Tale of Today (Twain and Warner), 59–61, 64, 134, 169

Gilman, Nils, 274

Gingrich, Newt, 149, 151, 152, 184, 266

Ginsburg, Ruth Bader, 191, 195

Giuffre, Virginia Roberts, 338*n*

Giuliani, Rudolph, 60, 273, 276, 322*n,* 394*n*

Gladwell, Malcolm, 340*n*

Glass-Steagall Act, 163

Glenny, Misha, 270–71, 273

globalization, 266, 275–76

God, and money, 48, 55
Goering, Hermann, 90, 379*n*
gold, 27, 220
  gold standard, 64, 220, 221
  Midas myth and, *see* Midas
  in Temple of Jerusalem, 37–38
Goldberg, Daniel, 121
Goldman, Emma, 209, 212
Goldman Sachs, 101–2, 104, 106, 168,
  169, 261, 264, 334*n*, 386*n*
Goldstein, Robert, 130
Goodwin, Doris Kearns, 84, 87, 238,
  239, 242
Goodwin, Lawrence, 219–20
Gordon, Colin, 248
Gore, Al, 136, 164, 260
Gorsuch, Anne, 106, 253
Gorsuch, Neil, 106, 254
Gould, Jay, 76
Government Accountability Office, 150
Gramm, Phil and Wendy, 279
Grant, Ulysses S., 62, 78, 279
Gray, C. Boyden, 194
Gray, Edwin, 162
Gray, James, 188–89
Great Depression, 63, 85, 233–34, 236,
  240, 242, 277
Great Recession, 69, 158, 166, 168, 169,
  279, 360*n*
Greece, ancient, 24–28, 30–31, 316*n*,
  317*n*
  aristocracy in, 41–42
  gift-giving in, 41, 42, 52, 54
  money and, 30–31, 40–41, 43, 44,
  46, 52
  spits and meat sharing in, 27–28, 30,
  36, 39, 52, 211, 316*n*
  values in, 40, 41–42
Greek mythology:
  Minos in, 319*n*, 394*n*
  see also Hydra; Midas
Green, James, 207
Greenberg, Jonathan, 67–68
Greenspan, Alan, 157, 164–66
Gründerzeit, 61–62
Guatemala, 171–72, 292
Guggenheim Museum, 103
Gun Owners of America, 193

Hammergren, John, 182
Hancock, John, 32
Hanna, Autumn, 142
Harjo, Joy, 292
Harper's Magazine, 185
Hartogensis, Gordon, 153
Harvard Crimson, 108
Harvard University, 83, 87, 108, 109,
  120, 271, 272
Hawthorne, Nathaniel, 42–43, 55, 108
Haymarket Square rally, 131, 208, *208,*
  212, 224
health-care fraud, 164, 165
heart disease, 183
Heartland Institute, 184
Henry, Patrick, 32
Heritage Foundation, 192, 253, 254,
  390*n*
Hermes, 316*n*
Herodotus, 25
heroism, 201
Hersh, Seymour, 86
Hesiod, 316*n*
Hitler, Adolf, 85, 242
Hocking, W. E., 237
Hoffenberg, Steven, 111
Holder, Eric, 167, 363*n*
Holder, Mark, 370*n*
Hollywood, 84
Home Depot, 98
Home Loan Bank Board, 167
Homer, *Iliad,* 41, 46
"Homeric Hymn to Hermes" (Hesiod),
  316*n*
Homestead strike, 131, 239
Honduras, 7, 11, 22–23, *114,* 128, 147,
  148, 149, 194, 368*n*, 390*n*
Hoover Institution, 98
House of Representative, U.S., 143, 149,
  159
  Committee on Banking and Currency,
  84
  elections for, 125–29
  impeachment authority of, 116
  staff for, 149–51
Houston Chronicle, 230
Howard, Roy, 89
Howe, Louis, 89

Humbert, Thérèse, 66, *67,* 68, 73, 160, 191, 277, 391*n*
Hungary, 7
Hunt, Howard "Sonny," 188–89
hunting, hunter-gatherers, 29–30, 122, 175, 215, 293–94, 321*n*
Hurricane Harvey, 230
Hurricane Katrina, 231, 232
Hyde, Lewis, 316*n*
Hydra, 95–96, *96,* 171, 285, *286,* 306
hydras, 96, 98, 99, 98, 99, 102, 115, 121, 123,1 24, 129, 132, 140, 141, 143, 144, 145, 151, 152, 171, 172, 201, 247, 270
see also networks

Icahn, Carl, 280
Iceland, 172, 300
Ickes, Harold, 89
identities, 174–76
   divides among, 175, 205, 222–23
   political, 126, 174–75
Iliad (Homer), 41, 46
immigrants, 205
   Irish, 83
   Jewish, 209–12, *211*
incomes, 47, 239, 248, 251, 255, 267, 268, 279, 303, 323*n,* 380*n,* 382*n*
   CEO compensation, 248, *249,* 380*n*
   federal salaries, 381*n*
   of top 1 percent, 248, *267,* 268, 381*n*
Independent Women's Forum, 98
Indonesia, 281
Industrial Workers of the World, 205
IndyMac, 104, 169
infrastructure, 69, 102, 142, 348*n*
Ingraham Angle, The, 117
initiation rites, 177–78, 180, 211
In re Debs, 79, 88
insider information, 64, 73, 84, 104, 128, 168, 186, 272, 279, 302, 383*n*
Instituto Nacional Agrario (INA), 148
Interior Department, U.S., 142, 143, 144
Internal Revenue Service (IRS), 127, 257, 288, 380*n*
International Coal Group, 168
Interstate Commerce Act, 79, 328*n*

Inuit, 29
investment firms, *see* banking and financial services; private equity investors
Iran, 276, 281
Iran-Contra affair, 278
Iran-Iraq War, 278
Iraq, 133, 135, 281
"iron triangle," 138
ISIS, 133
Israel, 107, 278, 281

Jackson, Michael, 105
James Madison Center for Free Speech, 193
Japan, 105, 234
Jaurès, Jean, 233
Jay Cooke & Co., 63, 72–75, *73,* 78, 102, 220
Jefferson, Thomas, 116
Jerusalem, 38
   Temple of, 34–40, *35,* 55, 214
Jerusalem: Portrait of the City in the Second Temple Period (Levine), 37
Jesus, 23, 34–43, 55, 211–12, 214–15, 319*n,* 340*n*
   money changers and, 34–40, *35,* 55, 214
Jews, 55, 70
   in Nazi Germany, 90
   in New York City, 209–12, *211*
Johnson, Lyndon Baines, 251
Jones Day, 187, 188, 190, 195
Jorgensen, Paul, 127–28
Josephson, Matthew, 78, 81
Judd, Donald, *103*
Junger, Sebastian, 53, 230–31
junk bonds, 59, 61, 65, 66, 102, 252, 277, 325*n*
justice, 115–23, 170, 193, 215, 254, 336*n,* 340*n,* 345*n,* 366*n,* 380*n*
Justice (goddess), 123, *123*
Justice Department, U.S. (DoJ), 12, 15, 116, 162, 167, 170, 190, 192, 254, 265–66, 355*n,* 363*n*

Kabul, 6
Kandahar, 5, 76, 124, 213

Karzai, Hamid, 116, 117, 121, 124–25, 185
Karzai, Qayum, 185
Kathmandu, 46, 117, 342*n*
Kavanaugh, Brett, 105–6, 116, 254, 336*n*
Kelly, Bridget Anne, 271, 314*n*, 371*n*
Kennedy, Anthony, 106, 336*n*
Kennedy, John F., 82, 86, 242–43, *243*, 251
Kennedy, Joseph P., 82–91, *90*, 102, 104, 234, 238–43, *243*, 334*n*, 379*n*
Kennedy, Justin, 106
Kennedy, Patrick (P. J.), 82, 84
Kennedy, Robert F., 243, 289–90
Kennedy, Rose Fitzgerald, 83, 238–39
Kentucky, 153–55, 358*n*
  insurance scam in, 188–91
Kerry, John, 125
Khodorkovsky, Mikhail, 271
Kirkland & Ellis, 105–6, 116, 117, 336*n*
Klein, Naomi, 183–84
kleptocracy, 39, 59, 101, 116, 133, 147, 154, 174–75, 253, 262, 265, 266, 269–70, 273–74, 287, 295, 341*n*
  in developing world, 69, 73, 98, 113–15
  networks in, *see* networks
Knights of Labor, 204–6, 222
Knittel, Deborah, 45
Koch, Charles; Koch network, 98–101, 119, 120, 142, 179–80, 184, 185, 192, 193, 253, *267*, 268, 279, 333*n*, 336*n*, 353*n*, 355*n*, 370*n*, 390*n*
  democracy and, 332*n*
Koch, David, 180, *267*, 268, 353*n*
Kohler, Walter, 193
Kosslyn, Stephen, 108
Kristallnacht, 90
Kushner, Jared, 281–82, 392*n*

labor, 63, 74, 138, 260, 350*n*, 351*n*
  capital and, 75
  forced, 131, 204, 219, 225, 347*n*, 374*n*
  laws, 99, 275, 348*n*
labor movement, organized labor, 201–8, 216, 224, 228, 233, 347*n*, 372*n*, 384*n*
  eight-hour day and, 204, 207, 224, 228
  Knights of Labor in, 204–6, 222

Parsons in, 207–9, *207*, 212, 223, 224
  Reagan and, 252, 255
  Red scares and, 208, *208*, 216
  unions, 79, 130, 205–6, 209, 358*n*
labor strikes, 130, 206, 238
  by air traffic controllers, 255
  by coal miners, 131
  for eight-hour day, 207, 224
  Great Railroad Strike of 1877, *203*
  Pullman, 88, 130, 348*n*
  by steelworkers, 201–2, 206, 239, 378*n*
  Strike Commission and, 130
  by textile workers, 129–30, *129*
lamb, 36–37, 38, 44
Lance, Bert, 278, 391*n*
land, 74, 140–43, 144, 148, 198, 303, 353*n*
Langston, Robin, 236
Larson, Jon, 48, 50
Latin America, 269, 278, 279, 390*n*
Latvia, 272
law, 8, 9, 11, 30–31, 36, 69, 79–86, 105, 115–23, 139, 141, 144–45, 149, 151–52, 158, 164, 180, 188–97, 225, 232, 275, 287, 300
Lawrence, Mass., textile workers' strike, 129–30, *129*
lawsuits, 185, 368*n*
Lebanon, 6, 172–73, 293
  You Stink movement in, 173, 174
Lee, Spike, 299
Lefkowitz, Jay, 106, 336*n*
Leftwich, David, 230, 231
Lehman Brothers, 264
Leonardo da Vinci, 329*n*
Levine, Lee, 37
Liberia, 299
Libre Parole, 70
Libya, 114, 281
Life Is a Miracle (Berry), 321*n*
lightbulbs, 77
Lincoln, Abraham, 75
link analysis, 97–98, 104, *139*, 172
Lipton, David, 272
literature, 323*n*
Litman, Harry, 194
lobbyists, 139–40, 150, 194, 259, 294, 301, 303, 356*n*

Lockheed Martin, 140, 352*n*
London, 32, 61, 89–91, 278, 296
Long-Term Capital Management, 278
Lopez, Barry, 29
Lord, Ellen, 140
Louisiana, 132, 230
Lucas, Lissa, 21
Lute, Douglas, 6
Lydia, 24–26, 41
Lynn, William, 140
Lyon, 234, 237

MacDougall, Ian, 185
Macgill, Martha, 35–36, 39–40
MacLean, Nancy, 98–100
  Democracy in Chains, 98, 120
Macune, Charles, 224
Mafia, 86, 116
Maguire, Joseph, 151
Malaysia, 102, 105, 172
Mallinckrodt, 182
Manafort, Paul, 105, 187, 273, 394*n*
Manchin, Joe, 283, 392*n*
Maraniss, David, 263, 264
Maritime Commission, 89, 241
Marvel Inc., 96
Mason, Lilliana, 126, 173, 174
Massachusetts Institute of Technology, 108
Master, Howard, 13
Mattis, James, 140, 352*n*
Maxwell, Ghislaine, 107
Maxwell, Robert, 107
Mayer, Arno, 233
Mayer, Jane, *Dark Money*, 98, 120, 179
McCain, John, 339*n*
McConnell, Mitch, 128, 152–55, 193, 280–81, *280,* 346*n,* 358*n*
McDonnell, Bob, 3–5
  McDonnell v. United States, 3–5, 7–15, 22, 123, 167, 188, 192–96, 312*n,* 313*n*
McDonnell, Mrs. Bob, 4, 10
McKesson, 182
McKinley, William, 213, 227
McKinsey, 276
McMafia (Glenny), 270–71
McNally, Charles, 188
McNally v. United States, 188–92, 196

meat, 146
  lamb sacrifice, 36–37, 38, 44
  sharing of, 27–30, 39, 52, 122, 175, 211, 215, 231, 316*n,* 317*n*
medical profession, 182, 230, 293
Medicare, 11–12
Medici, Cosimo de', 97
Meelia, Richard, 182
Meese, Edwin, 120, 254
Mellon, Andrew, 71, 88
Menendez, Robert, 11–12, 283
Mercatus Center, 98
Mermeix, 70
Merrill Lynch, 254
Mesopotamia, 27
Metropolitan Museum of Art, 261
Miami Herald, 117
Midas, 24–27, 34, 37, 42–43, 55, 56, 65
  Marygold and, 42–43, 55, 65, 108
  Midas disease, 56, 59, 70, 80, 87–88, 104, 109, 148, 186, 189, 205, 220, 234, 261, 263, 273, 283, 286, 304
Midas Touch: Why Some Entrepreneurs Get Rich—and Why Most Don't (Trump and Kiyosaki), 56
middle class, 173, 235, 255, 256, 274, 382*n*
Midtown Kitchen Collective, 230
migrations, mass, 7, 205, 210, 380*n*
military, U.S., 155
  Army, 88, 131, 132, 134–35, 348*n*
  contracts and expenditures for, 60, 133–39, *137*
  Navy, 60, *137,* 239
  see also defense spending, defense industry
Military Professional Resources Inc., 138
Minos, Minotaur, 319*n,* 394*n*
Mirror Group, 107
Miss Universe, 110, 272
Mitchell, Charles E., 85
Mnuchin, Adriana, 103
Mnuchin, Alan, 102
Mnuchin, Robert, 102–4, *103*
Mnuchin, Steven, 101, 102, 104, 106, 153, 168–69, 335*n*
Mohammed, Abdulkareem, 47, 51
Mohammed bin Salman, 329*n*

Mokhiber, Russell, 265
Moldova, 272, 394*n*
Monaco, 110
money, 21–33, 197, 225, 250, 259, 262,
    317*n*, 321*n*
  ancient Greeks and, 30–31, 40–41, 43,
    44, 46, 52
  coins, 25–27, *26,* 30, 31, 38, 41, 55, 63
  desire for, 45, 50, 54, 80
  God and, 48, 55
  gold standard and, 64, 220, 221
  happiness and, 54
  historical origins of, 25–27, 30
  obsession with, 48
  paper, 32, 61, 64, 220, 225, 228
  paradoxes of, 33, 52, 54
  power and, 314*n*
  as social measuring rod, 51–52, 54
  sources of, vii, 47, 113, 218
  success measured by, 48, 51, 54, 228
  technology and, 275
  and willingness to help others, 52–53
  see also wealth
Money and the Early Greek Mind
    (Seaford), 27, 28
Money in the House (Currinder), 151
money laundering, 103, 168, 272, 276
monopolies, 79, 84
Monsanto, 185
Montalieu, 234, *235*
Morales, Jimmy, 172
*More Bucks Less Bang: How the
    Pentagon Buys Ineffective Weapons*
    (Rasor), 136
Morgan, John Pierpont (J. P.), 63, 69,
    71–72, *72,* 75, 77, 83, 84, 136, 214,
    215
Morgan, Junius, 69
Morocco, 28
mortgage lending, securities, 68, 101,
    104, 105, 128, 157, 164, 165, 168,
    169, 327*n,* 333*n,* 336*n,* 346*n,* 360*n,*
    362*n,* 364*n*
Mortara, Michael, 101
Most, Johann, 209, 213
Mountain States Legal Foundation, 253
movies, 48–50
Mubarak, Hosni, 171

Mukasey, Michael, 167
Mullarkey, Maureen, 104
Mullen, Mike, 6
Müller, Hermann, 234
Murray Energy, 358*n*
Museum of Contemporary Art, Los
    Angeles, 104
Mylan, 283
myth, 22, 48, 56, 74, 105, 143, 177, 211,
    240, 285, 286, 288
  see also Greek mythology; Hydra;
    Midas

Naskapi, 29
National Constitution Center, 9
National Institutes of Health, 151
National Oceanic and Atmospheric
    Administration, 151
National Portrait Gallery, 296
National Public Radio, 7
National Security Council, 149
Native Americans/indigenous peoples,
    74, 128, 140, 148, 172, 176, 292
NATO, 214
natural disasters, 230–32, 377*n*
  values and, 229–32, 236–38, 262
Navy, U.S., 60, *137,* 239
Nazarbayev, Nursultan, 276
Nazism, 90, 233–34
Neidich, Daniel, 104
Nepal, 46–47, 117–18, 342*n*
networks, 14–15, 69, 76–79, 82, 88, 95,
    98–112, 113, 115, 132, 340*n*
  in Afghanistan, 96–97, 100
  Atlas, 390*n*
  colluders and, 187–98
  criminals in, 85–86
  global, 275–77
  Koch, 98–101, 119, 120, 142, 179–80,
    184, 185, 192, 193, 253, *267,* 279,
    333*n,* 336*n,* 353*n,* 355*n,* 390*n*
  link analysis and, 97–98, 104, *139,* 172
  tactics and countermoves by, 171–86
  see also hydras; kleptocracy
New, Elisa, 109
New Deal, 121, 201, 248, 250, 259
*New Democrats and the Return to
    Power, The* (From), 260, 263

New York Academy of Art, 108
New York City, 60, 61, 296
  Jewish immigrants and anarchist
    community in, 209–12, *211*
  sweatshops in, 209, *211*
  Tammany Hall in, 60, 78, 82
New Yorker, 98, 109
New York Sun, 62
New York Times, 46, 62, 102, 103, 107,
    122, 130, 338*n*
Nigeria, vii, 5, 6, 11, 23–24, 47, 48,
    113–14, 118, 133, 165, 169, 282, 286,
    322*n*
  defense spending in, 133–34, 137, 138,
    349*n*
9/11 terrorist attacks, 5, 134, 138, 143,
    157, 164, 165, 214–16, 231, 322*n*
1980s, 247–57, 273, 277–78
1980s–1990s, 258–68
1990s–, 269–84
Nixon, Richard, 115
*No Off Season: The Constant Pursuit of
    More* (Jones), 45
Nord Stream 2, 276
North Dakota, 132, 348*n*
Northern Pacific Railroad, 73, *73*
Norway, 47–48, 149, 378*n*
  dugnad tradition in, 52
nuclear weapons, 136, 274
Nunn, Sam, 260

Obama, Barack, 109, 139–40, 146,
    166–67, 167*n*, 179, 187, 194, 339*n*,
    363*n*
Obasogie, Fisa Nyoni, 47
obfuscation, 180–81, 290
Occupational Safety and Health
    Administration, 251, 254
Office of Technology Assessment, 150
Of Wolves and Men (Lopez), 29
oil and gas industry, 23, 184, 190, 233,
    241
  pipelines, 132, 185, 348*n*
Oliver, Mary, 196
Olney, Richard, 88, 130
Olokun, 23–24
1MDB, 102, 105
OneWest, 104, 169

On the Media, 68, 326*n*, 336*n*, 364*n*,
    365*n*
opioid epidemic, opium, 182–83, 186,
    218–19, 278, 336*n*, 366*n*, 369*n*
Ovid, 24–25
Oxford University, 276
OxyContin, 182–83

Pacific Legal Foundation, 192, 195
Padgett, John, 97
Paine, Thomas, 32
Pakistan, 70
Panama, 149
Panama Canal, 65–66, 70
Panic of 1873, 63–64, 72, *73,* 130, 158,
    220, 277
Paradise Built in Hell, A (Solnit),
    230–31, 230*n*, 237
Paribas, BNP, 69
Paris, 61, 64–66, 229, 233, 273
Parker, Marietta, 164–65, 167
Parson, Albert, 207, 208, *208,* 224
Parsons, Lucy, 207–9, *207,* 212, 223,
    224, 373*n*
Patagonia, 296
Paulson, Henry, 102, 165
Peace Corps, 28
Pelosi, Nancy, 151, 184
Pension Benefit Guaranty Corporation,
    153, 169
pension funds, 153, 169
People's Curriculum, 289–91
performance art, 210, 213, 214, 293
Perry, Rick, 280
Petraeus, David, 7, 177, 365*n*
pharmaceutical companies, 4, 40, 183,
    184, 186, 283, 369*n*
philanthropy, 46, 71, 104, 110, 339*n*
Philip Morris, 119
Philippines, 137
Phoebus cartel, 77
Phrygia, 24–26
Piketty, Thomas, 140, 188
Pink Floyd, 251
pipelines (oil and gas), 132, 185, 348*n*
planned obsolescence, 77
Podesta, John, 339*n*
police, 6, 10

political identities, 126, 174–75
Polk, Sam, 46, 54
Politics (Aristotle), 44
Populists, Populist Party, 213*n*, 222, 226–27
Poseidon, 41, 319*n*
Posse Comitatus Act, 348*n*
Post and Courier (Charleston, S.C.), 69
Postel, Charles, 221
Powell, Lewis, 118–20, 122, 183, 390*n*
  memo to Chamber of Commerce, 119–20, 122, 184, 250, 252–53, 262
presidential election of 2016, 5, 15–16, 128–29, 153
presidents, U.S., 115–16
Prince, Erik, 281
private equity investors, 104, 168, 169, 335*n*
  see also banking and financial services
Progressive Farmer, 218, 221, 223
Project on Government Oversight (POGO), 138, 139, 350*n*
propaganda by the deed, 213–16, 293
Prosperi, Paul, 110
Protestants, 48, 55, 87
protests, public, 6, 63, 78, 118, 130, 132, 172–74, 207–8, 221, 292–93, 348*n*, 365*n*
Pruitt, Scott, 145, 280
psychopath/sociopath, 76, 111, 165, 382*n*
public-private partnerships, 69, 287, 327*n*
Pullman Strike, 88, 130, 348*n*
punishment, 13–14, 30, 143, 162, 167, 175, 193, 195, 286, 287, 293, 301, 316*n*, 317*n*
Purdue Pharma, 183
Puritans, 48, 55
Putin, Vladimir, 110, 154, 155, 187, 194, 272, 275, 335*n*

Qatar, 149

railroads, 69, 74, 79, 84, 86, 88, 141, 190, 224, 225
  Georgia Pacific, 131, 353*n*
  Great Railroad Strike of 1877, *203*

Northern Pacific, 73, *73*
Pullman Strike, 88, 130, 348*n*
Transcontinental, 62
Union Pacific, 62–63, 65, 102, 325*n*, 326*n*
Wabash v. Illinois and, 328*n*
Ranieri, Lewis, 101
Rasor, Dina, 135–38, 140, 350*n*
Ratf**ked: Why Your Vote Doesn't Count (Daley), 125–26
RatPac–Dune Entertainment, 335*n*
Raytheon, 140
Reagan, Ronald, 49, 106, 120, 121, 158, 162, 164, 194, 252–57, 258, 260–63, 266, 272, 275, 360*n*, 383*n*, 384*n*
  tax policies of, 255–57, 259, 260
Reagan Revolution, 252, 265
real estate, 61, 64, 77, 83, 141, 157–58, 168, 306
Reason Institute, 355*n*
Recession, Great, 69, 158, 166, 168, 169, 279, 360*n*
REDMAP, 126–27
Red scares, 208, *208,* 216
Reformation, Protestant, 48
Regan, Donald, 254
Rehm, Diane, 7, 9, 10
Reich, Richard, 370*n*
Reich, Robert, 50
Reid, Herbert, 264, 265
Rembrandt van Rijn, *35,* 48
Republican Party, Republicans, 149, 150, 256–57, 258, 260, 267*n*, 281
  in congressional elections, 125–26
  Populists and, 226, 227
Resolution Trust Corporation, 105
revolving door, 102, 128, 139, 302
reward, 29, 30, 51, 161, 170, 238, 253, 261
Right Turn (Ferguson and Rogers), 257
Rise of the Conservative Legal Movement, The (Teles), 120
Risky Business (Brickman), 49–50, 74, 161, 197, 261
R. J. Reynolds, 119
Robb, Chuck, 260
Robbers Cave experiment (Eagles and Rattlers), 173–74

Robert M. Bass Group, 169
Roberts, John, 14, 15, 122, 194, 344*n*
Rockefeller, John D., 71, 77
Rogers, Joel, 255–57
Roman Empire, 34
Romer, Paul, 161
Roosevelt, Franklin Delano, 88–89, 90, 90, 91, 228, 237, 240–41, 259, 334*n*, 379*n*
  Commonwealth Club address of, 240–41
Rose Law Firm, 264, 278, 390*n*
Rosen, Jeffrey, 9–10
Rosneft, 276
Ross, Wilbur, 67, 105, 168, 185
Rothschild, Lynn Forester de, 339*n*, 365*n*
Rothschild banking house, 70
Rove, Karl, 125
Rubin, Robert, 102, 165, 264, 272, 388*n*
Rusal, 154–56
Russia, 133, 140, 153–56, 168, 233, 269, 275, 276, 278–80, 283, 359*n*
Russian Privatization Center, 272
Rybolovlev, Dmitry, 110

Sachs, Jeffrey, 272
Sackler family, 181–85, 296
Sackler Gallery, 181–82, 181, 184–85
sacrifice, 27, 36–37, 38, 44, 226, 231, 233, 252, 274, 316*n*, 319*n*
Sagebrush Rebellion, 141, 143, 353*n*
Sago Mine, 168
St. Louis Post-Dispatch, 136, 138
St. Marys, W.Va., 21–22, 127, 197
Sanders, Bernie, 15
Sansom, William, 238
Sardis, 25, 26
savings and loan institutions (S&Ls; thrifts), 158–65, 168–70, 191, 254, 277
Scaramucci, Anthony, 365*n*
Schea, Trond Eirik, 47, 52
Schiff, Adam, 312*n*
Schiff, Jacob, 329*n*
Schroeder, Gerhard, 276
Schwab, Charles, 239
Schwarzman, Steven, 61

science, 22, 25, 26, 37, 247, 306
  theories and consensus in, 362*n*
Seaford, Richard, 27, 28, 30
secrecy, 176–80
Securities and Exchange Commission (SEC), 89, 148, 241
Security Assistance Monitor, 350*n*
Senate, U.S., 149, 159, 280
  elections for, 125–29, 225, 228
  filibusters in, 152
  Finance Committee, 101
  Judiciary Committee, 192, 312*n*
  staff for, 149–51
sex trafficking, 110, 111, 338*n*
shaming, 293
Shanahan, Patrick, 140
Shays' Rebellion, 319*n*
Sheridan, Jimmy, 236
Sherman Antitrust Act, 79, 131
Shleifer, Andrei, 272
Shreeve, Kent, 323*n*
silver, 27, 31, 38
  in Temple of Jerusalem, 37
Silver, Sheldon, 13, 312*n*
Singer, Gordon, 100
Singer, Paul, 100
el-Sisi, Abdel Fattah, 118, 137, 171
Skelos, Adam, 312*n*
Skelos, Dean, 312*n*
skewers (spits), 27–28, 30, 36, 211, 316*n*
Skilling, Jeffrey, 190, 195
  Skilling v. United States, 191, 192, 195–96
SLAPP (Strategic Lawsuit Against Public Participation), 368*n*
Slavery by Another Name (Blackmon), 131
slaves, former, 75, 79, 118, 131
Smith, Stephen, 300–301
Smithberger, Mandy, 139
smugglers, 71, 85, 289
socialism, socialists, 15, 75, 206, 250, 274
social shaming, 293
Solnit, Rebecca, 230–31, 230*n*, 232, 234, 237, 377*n*
Solon, 30–31, 321*n*
Somalia, 281
Somerset Importers, 86, 89

Sophocles, 43
Soros, George, 104
South, southern (U.S.), 217, 220, 226, 260, 263, 264
South Korea, 105, 168, 172, 292
Southwest Airlines, 361*n*
sovereignty, 32, 115, 318*n*, 390*n*
Soviet Union, 136, 274, 387*n*
  Cold War with, 250, 274
  collapse of, 140, 154, 266, 269–75
Spanish (Hapsburg) Empire, 31
spits (skewers), 27–28, 30, 36, 211, 316*n*
Stack (Judd), *103*
Stanford, Leland, 79
Stanford University, 98
Starr, Kenneth, 105–6, 117
State Department, U.S., 6, 12, 101, 137
State Policy Network, 98
steel industry, 77, 83, 131, 204
  strikes and, 201–2, 206, 239, 378*n*
Stephens, Jackson, 278
Stevens, John Paul, 190
stock market, 63, 85, 101, 141, 241, 277
  crash of 1929, 85, 277
stocks and bonds, 61, 63, 72–73, 84, 85, 102, 160, 330*n*
  Northern Pacific Railroad, 73, *73*
  see also junk bonds
Stone, Oliver, 50
strikes, *see* labor strikes
Sudan, 7
sugar, 183–85
Summers, Lawrence, 108–9, 272
Superstorm Sandy, 230
Supreme Court, U.S., 5, 15, 106, 118, 127*n*, 195, 197, 259, 292, 299, 300, 344*n*
  Americans for Prosperity Foundation v. Becerra, 365*n*
  "Bridgegate" and, 313*n*
  Citizens United v. Federal Election Commission, 179–80, 299, 365*n*, 370*n*
  contracts and, 121–23
  frieze in courtroom of, *123*
  In re Debs, 79, 88
  McDonnell v. United States, 3–5, 7–15, 22, 123, 167, 188, 192–96, 312*n*, 313*n*

McNally v. United States, 188–92, 196
  Powell on, 118–20, 122
  Skilling v. United States, 191, 192, 195–96
  Wabash v. Illinois, 328*n*
  Whole Woman's Health v. Hellerstedt, 3
symbols, 27–28, 147, 156, 214, 316*n*, 323*n*
Syria, 283

Taiwan, 105
Taliban, 5, 6, 76, 97, 98, 124, 148, 214
Tammany Hall, 60, 78, 82
TARP (Troubled Asset Relief Program), 166, 167*n*
taxes, 103, 197, 259, 294, 303
  progressive income tax, 225, 253
  Reagan's policies on, 255–57, 259, 260
  2017 overhaul of, 150
Taxpayers for Common Sense, 142
Taylor, Stuart, 10
Teachout, Zephyr, 301
Tea Party, 119, 141, 180, 333*n*
Teapot Dome Scandal, 241
Teles, Steven, 120
Temple of Jerusalem, 34–40, *35*, 55, 214
Temps, 64
Terkel, Studs, 236
terrorism, 6, 164, 165, 213–16
  9/11 attacks, 5, 134, 138, 143, 157, 164, 165, 214–16, 231, 322*n*
Teva Pharmaceutical Industries, 185, 336*n*
Texas, 224, 231
textile mills, 204
  workers' strike, 129–30, *129*
Textron, 140
Thailand, 278–79
Theranos, 391*n*
Thieves of State: Why Corruption Threatens Global Security (Chayes), 6, 311*n*, 338*n*, 341*n*, 348*n*, 374*n*
Thomas, Clarence, 332*n*
Thunberg, Greta, 324*n*
Time Warner Center, 61, 324*n*
Tippett, Krista, 323*n*
tobacco, tobacco industry, 4–5, 8, 40, 98, 119, 127, 183, 184, 192

Tohme, Alexandra, 173
tornadoes, 231
Toyota, 122
Transcontinental Railroad, 62
Treasury Department, U.S., 73, 102, 153–54, 166–67, 272, 302, 335*n*
Tribe (Junger), 53, 230–31
Trickster Makes This World: Mischief, Myth and Art (Hyde), 316*n*
Troubled Asset Relief Program (TARP), 166, 167*n*
Trudeau, Mark, 182
Trump, Donald, 73, 105, 106, 109–10, 116, 117, 121, 151, 168–70, 185, 194, 253, 259, 266, 272, 279–83, 371*n*
  business operations of, 275
  Department of Defense and, 140
  drain-the-swamp rhetoric of, 16
  EPA and, 146
  Epstein and, 109–11, 338*n*
  federal hiring and, 148–49
  impeachment trial of, 108, 272, *280,* 282–83, 312*n*, 313*n*, 371*n*
  Midas Touch book coauthored by, 56
  net worth of, 67–68, 326*n*
  in presidential election of 2016, 5, 129
  secrecy of, 178
  tax returns of, 178
Trump, Donald, Jr., 282
Trump, Eric, 282
Trump, Friedrich, 330*n*
Trump, Ivanka, 282, 392*n,* 393*n*
Trump family, 68, 330*n*
Trump Foundation, 111
Trump Organization, 69
Trump Tower, 38
trusts, 77, 79, 131, 251–52
  antitrust laws, 79, 131, 251, 266
Tunisia, 11, 114–15, 274
Turkey, 7, 27
Twain, Mark, 64
  The Gilded Age, 59–61, 64, 134, 169
Tweed, William "Boss," 60, 78, 82
Tyson Foods, 264–65

Ukraine, 6, 37–38, 105, 133, 187, 194, 272–73, 283, 292

Uncivil Agreement: How Politics Became Our Identity (Mason), 126, 173, 174
Union Générale, 64, 69, 70
Union Pacific Railroad, 62–63, 65, 102, 325*n, 326n*
unions, 79, 130, 205–6, 209, 358*n*
  see also labor movement, organized labor; labor strikes
United Arab Emirates (UAE), 278, 281
United Kingdom, 5
United Mineworkers of America, 358*n*
University of Chicago, 71
University of Virginia, 4
U.S. Agency for International Development (USAID), 101, 388*n*
U.S. Steel, 77, 83, 131
Uzbekistan, 6, 131, 274

Valium, 183
value, values, 13–14, 30, 40, 75, 99, 141, 248–50, 305, 321*n*
  ancient Greece and, 40, 41–42
  disasters and, 229–32, 236–38, 262
  money and, 42
Vanderbilt, Cornelius, 76, 78
Varughese, George, 342*n*
Vekselberg, Viktor, 154, 271, 335*n*
Victoria's Secret, 107, 110
Vienna, 61, 69, 158, 324*n, 325n*
Vietnam War, 136, 380*n*
Violence Against Women Act, 153
Vorse, Mary Heaton, 201–2, 204, 295
VTB, 154, 155

Wabash v. Illinois, 328*n*
Wall Street, 50, 51, 54, 63, 78, 84, 85, 87, 89, 148, 165, 167, 167*n,* 168, 170, 216
  bombing of 1920, 214, *215*
  crash of 1929, 85, 277
  Democratic Party and, 258, 259
  Ivy League schools and, 261, 386*n*
  see also banking and financial services
Wall Street (Stone), 48–50, 252
Wall Street Journal, 125
Walmart, 127, 388*n*
Warburg, Paul, 329*n*

Warner, Charles, 59
Washington, George, 32, 140
Washington Post, 111, 184
Watergate scandal, 250–51
water sources, 101, 114–15, 138, 145, 186, 283, 304, 306, 355*n*
Watt, James, 253
wealth, 23, 32, 42, 44–56, 80, 205, 233, 275, 314*n*
  Aristophanes on, 45–46, 321*n*
  Aristotle on, 44–45
  biblical views on, 55
  displays of, 80, 273
  see also money
Wealth (Aristophanes), 45–46, 321*n*
Weatherford, Jack, 31
Wedel, Janine, 270, 277
Weinberg, Sidney, 334*n*
Weinberger, Caspar, *137*
Wells Fargo, 122, 197, 294, 345*n*, 395–96*n*
West Virginia, 267, 300–301
  St. Marys, 21–22, 127, 197
wetlands, 27, 283, 306
Whalen, Richard, 85, 86–87
white-collar crime, 10, 193, 254, 265–66, 287
white elephants, 69
Whitney Museum, 103, 104
Whole Woman's Health v. Hellerstedt, 3
Wiener Bank-Verein, 69
WikiLeaks, 176–77, 339*n*
Williams, Jonnie, 4–5, 8
Wilson, Henry, 62–63
Wilson, Woodrow, 78, 329*n,* 379*n*

Winegard, Timothy, 233
wisdom, 23, 143, 285, 290, 306, 354*n*
wolves, 29, 74
women, 205, 206, 237
Wombwell Insurance Company, 189
Wood, Gordon, 32
work, workplace:
  factory shifts, 267
  standards in, 251, 275
  see also labor movement, organized labor; unions
World War I, 84, 85, 234–36, 238–40, 242
  causes of, 232–33
  France in, 234–35, *235,* 237
World War II, 85, 87, 89–91, 229–30, 233–38, 242–43, 248, 250
  economy following, 248
World Wildlife Fund, 143
Wrangham, Richard, 78, 96, 316*n*
Wright, Rich, 36–37, 40
Wu, Tim, 266

Yale Law School, 105–6, 120, 263, 387*n*
Yanukovych, Viktor, 37–38, 187, 184
Yeltsin, Boris, 271, 272

Zangger, Eberhard, 305–6
Zaslavskiy, Ilya, 269, 271, 273, 274, 276–77
Zeus, 321*n*
Zimmer, Kenyon, 210, 212
Zinke, Ryan, 144, 280
Zola, Émile, 64–65

ILLUSTRATION CREDITS

26 The Trustees of the British Museum

35 Courtesy of The Metropolitan Museum of Art

67 Courtesy of the author

72 Alamy

73 Courtesy of Heritage Auctions, HA.com

90 Courtesy of the John F. Kennedy Presidential Library and Museum, Boston

96 Courtesy of the J. Paul Getty Museum, Malibu

103 Michael Nagel/*The New York Times*/Redux

114 Sarah Chayes; courtesy of Carnegie Endowment for International Peace

123 Collection of the Supreme Court of the United States

129 Courtesy of the Library of Congress

137 Courtesy of the Herb Block Foundation

139 Janine Wedel, Mapping Shadow Influence Project, and Julia Ellegood Pfaff

181 Courtesy of the author

203 Courtesy of the Library of Congress

207 Courtesy of the Newberry Library, Chicago

208 Courtesy of the Chicago History Museum, ICHi-019645

211 Courtesy of the George Eastman Museum

215 Courtesy of the Library of Congress

222 *The Progressive Farmer,* 1891; courtesy of the Library of Congress

235 Courtesy of the author

243 Courtesy of the John F. Kennedy Presidential Library and Museum, Boston

249 (top) Economic Policy Institute

249 (bottom) Federal Reserve Bank of St. Louis

267 (top) Gustavo Berrizbeitia

267 (bottom) The Democracy Lab

280 Alex Roblewski

286 Courtesy of Paris Musées/Petit Palais, Musées des Beaux Arts de la Ville de Paris

381 Gustavo Berrizbeitia

382 Gustavo Berrizbeitia

A NOTE ON THE TYPE

The text of this book was set in Simoncini Garamond, a modern version by Francesco Simoncini of the type attributed to the famous Parisian type cutter Claude Garamond (ca. 1480–1561). Garamond was a pupil of Geoffroy Tory and is believed to have based his letters on the Venetian models, although he introduced a number of important differences, and it is to him we owe the letter that we know as old style. He gave to his letters a certain elegance and a feeling of movement that won for their creator an immediate reputation and the patronage of Francis I of France.

Typeset by North Market Street Graphics,
Lancaster, Pennsylvania

Designed by Betty Lew